Western Europe

PHRASEBOOK & DICTIONARY

Acknowledgments

Associate Publisher Mina Patria
Managing Editor Bruce Evans
Editors Kate Mathews, Mardi O'Connor
Series Designer Mark Adams
Managing Layout Designer Chris Girdler
Layout Designer Carol Jackson
Production Support Larissa Frost

Thanks

Sasha Baskett, Melanie Dankel, Brendan Dempsey, Ben Handicott,
James Hardy, Sandra Helou, Nic Lehman, Annelies Mertens, Wayne
Murphy, Naomi Parker, Trent Paton, Piers Pickard, Mazzy Prinsep,
Branislava Vladisavljevic

Published by Lonely Planet Publications Pty Ltd

ABN 36 005 607 983

5th Edition – February 2013
ISBN 978 1 74179 011 5
Text © Lonely Planet 2013
Cover Image Old Fiat in Centro Storico, Rome, Lazio, Italy
Will Salter/Lonely Planet Images ©
Printed in China 10 9 8 7 6 5 4 3 2 1

Contact lonelyplanet.com/contact

MIX
Paper from
responsible sources
FSC™ C021741

acknowledgments

This book is based on existing editions of Lonely Planet's phrasebooks as well as new content. It was developed with the help of the following people:

- Karin Vidstrup Monk for the Danish chapter
- Annelies Mertens for the Dutch chapter
- Michael Janes for the French chapter
- Gunter Muehl for the German chapter
- Thanasis Spilias for the Greek chapter
- Karina Coates, Pietro Iagnocco and Susie Walker for the Italian chapter
- Anne Stensletten for the Norwegian chapter
- Robert Landon and Anabela de Azevedo Teixeira Sobrinho for the Portuguese chapter
- Marta López for the Spanish chapter
- Emma Koch for the Swedish chapter
- Arzu Kürklü for the Turkish chapter

Thank you to Elmar Duenschede (German), Floriana Badalotti (Italian), Gina Tsarouhas (Greek), Gus Balbontin (Spanish), Jean-Pierre Masclef (French), William Gourlay (Turkish) and Yukiyoshi Kamimura (Portuguese) for additional language expertise.

acknowledgments

contents

Western Europe

0 ————————— 500 km
0 ————————— 300 mi

NORWAY

SWEDE

DENMARK

Skagerrak

Copenhagen ⊛

NORTH
SEA

Ireland

Great
Britain

ATLANTIC
OCEAN

English Channel

NETHERLANDS
Amsterdam ⊛

Hamburg

GERMANY

Berlin ⊛

Düsseldorf
Cologne

Leipzig

Brussels ⊛

BELGIUM

Dresden

LUXEMBOURG

Czech
Republic

Paris ⊛

Stuttgart

Nantes

FRANCE

Munich

Vienna ⊛

LIECHTENSTEIN

AUSTRIA

Bern ⊛

SWITZERLAND

Slovenia

Bay of
Biscay

Bordeaux

Lyon

Turin

Milan

Venice

Croatia

Porto

Bilbao

Toulouse

Marseille

SAN
MARINO

Adriatic

PORTUGAL

Madrid

ANDORRA

Barcelona

MONACO

Florence

ITALY

Lisbon

SPAIN

Valencia

Corsica

Rome ⊛

Seville

Málaga

Murcia

BALEARIC
ISLANDS

Naples

Gibraltar (UK)

Strait of Gibraltar

Sardinia

Tyrrhenian
Sea

Ceuta (Sp)

Palermo

Melilla (Sp.)

M E D I T E R R A N E A N

Sicily

Morocco

Algeria

Isole
Pelagie

Malta

Tunisia

■ Danish
■ Dutch
■ French
■ German

■ Greek
■ Italian
■ Norwegian
■ Portuguese

Scandinavia: same scale as main map

NORWEGIAN
SEA

Estonia

Latvia

Russia

N

BALTIC SEA

See inset

Lithuania

Kaliningrad
(Russia)

Belarus

Poland

Ukraine

Finland

Slovakia

Moldova

NORWAY

SWEDEN

Gulf
of
Bothnia

Hungary

Romania

Oslo ✪

✪
Stockholm

Estonia

Bosnia &
Hercegovina

Serbia

Montenegro

Bulgaria

DENMARK

Skagerrak

BALTIC
SEA

Latvia

FYROM

BLACK SEA

Armenia

Albania

Sea

Istanbul

Ankara
✪

Ionian
Sea

Thessaloniki

Aegean
Sea

TURKEY

GREECE

Izmir

Athens
✪

Syria

Iraq

SEA

Sea of Crete

Nicosia
(Lefkosia)
✪

Crete

CYPRUS

Lebanon

Spanish

Swedish

Turkish

Note: Language areas are approximate only.
For more details see the relevant introduction.

EUROPE

language map

7

western europe – at a glance

One of the most rewarding things about travelling through Western Europe is the rich variety of cuisine, customs, architecture and history. The flipside of course is that you'll encounter a number of very different languages. Most languages spoken in Western Europe, including English, belong to what's known as the Indo-European language family, believed to have originally developed from one language spoken thousands of years ago. Luckily for English speakers, all but one use Roman script.

The Romance languages (French, Italian, Spanish and Portuguese) all developed from Vulgar Latin, which spread through Western Europe during the rule of the Roman Empire. The freedom with which English has borrowed Latin-based vocabulary means you'll quickly recognise many words from these languages. The Germanic languages – Dutch and German – are more closely related to English. The Scandinavian languages (Danish, Norwegian and Swedish) form the northern branch of the Germanic languages tree, having developed from Old Norse, the language of the Vikings. Their big advantage is that, being so closely related, once you've got the hang of one language, the others should seem quite familiar. Greek, the language of the *Iliad* and the *Odyssey*, forms a single branch of the Indo-European language family and uses Greek script. Finally, Turkish is part of the Ural-Altaic language family, which includes languages spoken from the Balkan Peninsula to northeast Asia. Arabic script was replaced by Roman script for Turkish in the early 20th century.

did you know?

- The European Union (EU) was established by the Maastricht Treaty in 1992. It developed from the European Economic Community, founded by the Treaty of Rome in 1957. Since the 2007 enlargement, it has 27 member states and 23 official languages.
- The EU flag is a circle of 12 gold stars on a blue background – the number 12 representing wholeness.
- The EU anthem is the 'Ode to Joy' from Beethoven's Ninth Symphony.
- Europe Day, 9 May, commemorates the 1950 declaration by French Foreign Minister Robert Schuman, which marks the creation of the European Union.
- The euro has been in circulation since E-Day, 1 January 2002. The euro's symbol (€) was inspired by the Greek letter epsilon (ε) – Greece being the cradle of European civilisation and ε being the first letter of the word 'Europe'.
- The Eurovision Song Contest, held each May, has been running since 1956. For the larger part of the competition's history, the performers were only allowed to sing in their country's national language, but that's no longer the case.

Danish

danish alphabet

A a aa	*B b* bey	*C c* sey	*D d* dey	*E e* ey
F f ef	*G g* gey	*H h* haw	*I i* ee	*J j* yawdh
K k kaw	*L l* el	*M m* em	*N n* en	*O o* oh
P p pey	*Q q* koo	*R r* er	*S s* es	*T t* tey
U u oo	*V v* vey	*W w* *do*-belt vey	*X x* eks	*Y y* ew
Z z zet	*Æ æ* e	*Ø ø* eu	*Å å* aw	

■ danish

DANSK

DANISH

introduction

What do the fairy tales of Hans Christian Andersen and the existentialist philosophy of Søren Kierkegaard have in common (apart from pondering the complexities of life and human character)? Danish (*dansk* dansk), of course – the language of the oldest European monarchy. Danish contributed to the English of today as a result of the Viking conquests of the British Isles in the form of numerous personal and place names, as well as many basic words.

As a member of the Scandinavian or North Germanic language family, Danish is closely related to Swedish and Norwegian. It's particularly close to one of the two official written forms of Norwegian, *Bokmål* – Danish was the ruling language in Norway between the 15th and 19th centuries, and was the base of this modern Norwegian literary language. In pronunciation, however, Danish differs considerably from both of its neighbours thanks to its softened consonants and often 'swallowed' sounds. Among the foreign influences on Danish, German is the most notable: a consequence of both warfare and trade through centuries.

Writing in Danish starts with the runic alphabet – used mainly on stone for the common ancestor of all Scandinavian languages as far back as AD 200 – which flourished during the Viking age from the 9th century. The earliest examples of what can be considered Danish text date from that period, when Danish began to take shape as a distinct language. The Roman alphabet in which Danish is written today was first introduced by Christian missionaries. It started replacing the runic alphabet in the 12th century and was modified through a series of spelling reforms.

The current international status of Danish (with about 5.5 million speakers) is the legacy of its historical expansion. It's the official language of Denmark and has co-official status – with Greenlandic and Faroese respectively – in Greenland and the Faroese Islands, which are autonomous Danish territories. Until 1944 it was the official language of Iceland and today is taught in schools there as the first foreign language. Danish is also a minority language in the area of Schleswig-Holstein in northern Germany, where it has some 30,000 speakers. And if all that isn't enough, just think of the whole corpus of words for which English is indebted to its old Viking conquerors – one of those essential words thought to have Danish origin is 'smile', so whenever you're taking photos on your travels, remember to thank the Danes!

pronunciation

vowel sounds

The Danish vowel system has long and short versions of each vowel, and additional 'combined vowels' or diphthongs. Most of the vowels have equivalents in English – but as ever, it's best to listen carefully to native speakers and follow their lead. By using our coloured pronunciation guides, you're sure to be understood.

symbol	english equivalent	danish example	transliteration
a	act	*plads*	plas
aa	father	*trafik*	traa-*feek*
ai	aisle	*jeg*	yai
aw	saw	*håndklæde*	*hawn*-kle-dhe
e	bet	*hotel*	hoh-*tel*
ee	see	*turist*	too-*reest*
eu	nurse	*købe*	*keu*-be
ew	ee pronounced with rounded lips	*cykel*	*sew*-kel
ey	as in 'bet', but longer	*bestille*	bey-*sti*-le
i	hit	*forsinket*	for-*sing*-ket
o	pot	*postkontor*	post-kon-*tohr*
oh	oh	*postkontor*	post-kon-*tohr*
oo	soon	*forbudt*	for-*boot*
ow	how	*afgangshal*	*ow*-gaangs-hal
oy	toy	*toilet*	toy-*let*

word stress

In Danish, stress often falls on the first syllable in a word. Compound words can have more than one syllable stressed. In this chapter, the stressed syllables are in italics.

consonant sounds

Most Danish consonants are also found in English, including the 'soft' sounds (such as dh). However, the consonants in Danish can be 'swallowed' and even omitted completely, creating, in conjunction with vowels, a glottal stop or *stød* steudh. Its sounds rather like the Cockney pronunciation of the 'tt' in 'bottle'.

symbol	english equivalent	danish example	transliteration
b	bed	*bord*	bohr
ch	cheat	*chips*	cheeps
d	dog	*dansk*	dansk
dh	that	*hvid*	veedh
f	fat	*finde*	fi·ne
g	go	*glas*	glas
h	hat	*hente*	hen·te
j	joke	*juice*	joos
k	kit	*koncert*	kon·sert
l	lot	*lang*	laang
m	man	*maskine*	mas·kee·ne
n	not	*nogle*	noh·le
ng	ring	*synge*	sewng·e
p	pet	*penge*	peng·e
r	red (trilled)	*rejse*	rai·se
s	sun	*seng*	seng
sh	shot	*chokolade*	shoh·koh·la·dhe
t	top	*ting*	ting
v	very	*vin*	veen
w	win	*whiskey, peber*	wees·kee, pey·wa
y	yellow	*jeg*	yai

basics

language difficulties

Do you speak English?
Taler De/du engelsk? pol/inf   ta·la dee/doo eng·elsk

Do you understand?
Forstår De/du? pol/inf   for·stawr dee/doo

I (don't) understand.
Jeg forstår (ikke).   yai for·stawr (i·ke)

What does (hyggelig) mean?
Hvad betyder (hyggelig)?   va bi·tew·dha (hew·ge·lee)

How do you ...?	Hvordan ...?	vor·dan ...
pronounce this	udtaler man det	oodh·ta·la man dey
write (hyggelig)	skriver man (hyggelig)	skree·va man (hew·ge·lee)

Could you	Kunne De/	koo·ne dee/
please ...?	du ...? pol/inf	doo ...
repeat that	gentage det	gen·ta dey
speak more slowly	tale langsommere	ta·la laang·so·ma
write it down	skrive det ned	skree·ve dey nidh

essentials

Yes.	Ja.	ya
No.	Nej.	nai
Please.	Vær så venlig.	ver saw ven·lee
Thank you (very much).	(Mange) Tak.	(mang·e) taak
You're welcome.	Selv tak.	sel taak
Excuse me.	Undskyld mig.	awn·skewl mai
Sorry.	Undskyld.	awn·skewl

numbers

0	nul	nawl	16	seksten	sais·ten	
1	en	in	17	sytten	sew·ten	
2	to	toh	18	atten	a·ten	
3	tre	trey	19	nitten	ni·ten	
4	fire	feer	20	tyve	tew·ve	
5	fem	fem	21	enogtyve	eyn·o·tew·ve	
6	seks	seks	22	toogtyve	toh·o·tew·ve	
7	syv	sew	30	tredive	traadh·ve	
8	otte	aw·te	40	fyrre	fewr·re	
9	ni	nee	50	halvtreds	hal·tres	
10	ti	tee	60	tres	tres	
11	elleve	el·ve	70	halvfjerds	hal·fyers	
12	tolv	tol	80	firs	feers	
13	tretten	traa·ten	90	halvfems	hal·fems	
14	fjorten	fyor·ten	100	hundrede	hoon·re·dhe	
15	femten	fem·ten	1000	tusind	too·sen	

time & dates

What time is it?	Hvad er klokken?	va ir klo·ken
It's one o'clock.	Klokken er et.	klo·ken ir it
It's (two) o'clock.	Klokken er (to).	klo·ken ir (toh)
Quarter past (one).	Kvarter over (et).	kvaar·teyr o·va (it)
Half past (one).	Halv (to). (lit: half two)	hal (toh)
Quarter to (eight).	Kvarter i (otte).	kvaar·teyr ee (aw·te)
At what time ...?	Hvad tid ...?	va teedh ...
At ...	Klokken ...	klo·ken ...
am (morning)	om morgenen	om mor·nen
pm (afternoon)	om eftermiddagen	om ef·taa·mi·da·en
pm (evening)	om aftenen	om aaft·nen
Monday	mandag	man·da
Tuesday	tirsdag	teers·da
Wednesday	onsdag	awns·da
Thursday	torsdag	tors·da
Friday	fredag	fre·da
Saturday	lørdag	leur·da
Sunday	søndag	seun·da

January	januar	*ya·*noo·ar
February	februar	*feb·*roo·ar
March	marts	maarts
April	april	a·*preel*
May	maj	mai
June	juni	*yoo·*nee
July	juli	*yoo·*lee
August	august	ow·*gawst*
September	september	sip·*tem·*ba
October	oktober	ohk·*toh·*ba
November	november	noh·*vem·*ba
December	december	dey·*sem·*ba

What date is it today?
Hvilken dato er det i dag?   vil·ken *da·*toh ir dey ee da

It's (15 December).
Det er den (femtende december).   dey ir den (*fem·*te·ne dey·*sem·*ba)

| since (May) | siden (maj) | *see·*dhen (mai) |
| until (June) | indtil (juni) | *in·*til (*yoo·*nee) |

yesterday	i går	ee gawr
last night	i går aftes	ee gawr *aaf·*tes
today	i dag	ee da
tonight	i aften	ee *aaf·*ten
tomorrow	i morgen	ee morn

last/next ...	sidste/næste ...	*sees·*te/*nes·*te ...
week	uge	*oo·*e
month	måned	*maw·*nedh
year	år	awr

yesterday ...	i går ...	ee gawr ...
morning	morges	*mo·*res
afternoon	eftermiddags	*ef·*taa·mi·das
evening	aftes	*aaf·*tes

tomorrow ...	i morgen ...	ee morn ...
morning	tidlig	*teedh·*lee
afternoon	eftermiddag	*ef·*taa·mi·da
evening	aften	*aaf·*ten

weather

What's the weather like?	Hvordan er vejret?	vor·*dan* ir *vey*·ret

It's ...

cloudy	Det er overskyet.	dey ir o·va·skew·et
cold	Det er koldt.	dey ir kolt
hot	Det er varmt.	dey ir vaarmt
raining	Det regner.	dey rain·a
snowing	Det sner.	dey sneyr
sunny	Solen skinner.	soh·len ski·na
warm	Det er varmt.	dey ir vaarmt
windy	Det blæser.	dey ble·sa

spring	forår n	for·awr
summer	sommer	so·ma
autumn	efterår n	ef·taa·awr
winter	vinter	vin·ta

border crossing

I'm here ...	Jeg er ...	yai ir ...
in transit	i transit	ee traan·seet
on business	på forretningsrejse	paw for·rat·nings·rai·se
on holiday	på ferie	paw feyr·ye

I'm here for ...	Jeg er her i ...	yai ir heyr ee ...
(10) days	(ti) dage	(tee) da·e
(three) weeks	(tre) uger	(trey) oo·a
(two) months	(to) måneder	(toh) maw·ne·dha

I'm going to (Valby).
Jeg skal til (Valby).
yai skal til (val·bew)

I'm staying at the (Hotel Europa).
Jeg bor på (Hotel Europa).
yai bohr paw (hoh·tel e·oo·roh·pa)

I have nothing to declare.
Jeg har ingenting at fortolde.
yai haar ing·en·ting at for·to·le

I have something to declare.
Jeg har noget at fortolde.
yai haar naw·et at for·to·le

That's (not) mine.
Det er (ikke) mit.
dey ir (i·ke) meet

transport

tickets & luggage

Where can I buy a ticket?
Hvor kan jeg købe en billet? vor ka yai *keu*-be in bi-*let*

Do I need to book a seat?
Er det nødvendigt at bestille plads? ir dey neudh-*ven*-deet at bey-*sti*-le plas

One ... ticket	*En ... billet*	in ... bee-*let*
(to Odense), please.	*(til Odense), tak.*	(til *oh*-dhen-se) taak
one-way	*enkelt*	*eng*-kelt
return	*retur*	rey-*toor*

I'd like to ... my	*Jeg vil gerne ...*	yai vil *gir*-ne ...
ticket, please.	*min billet, tak.*	meen bee-*let* taak
cancel	*afbestille*	*ow*-bey-sti-le
change	*ændre*	*en*-dre
collect	*hente*	*hen*-te
confirm	*bekræfte*	bey-*kref*-te

I'd like a ... seat,	*Jeg vil gerne have*	yai vil *gir*-ne ha
please.	*en ... plads, tak.*	in ... plas taak
nonsmoking	*ikke-ryger*	*i*-ke-*rew*-a
smoking	*ryger*	*rew*-a

How much is it?
Hvor meget koster det? vor *maa*-yet *kos*-ta dey

Is there air conditioning?
Er der aircondition? ir deyr eyr-kon-*dee*-shen

Is there a toilet?
Er der et toilet? ir deyr it toy-*let*

How long does the trip take?
Hvor længe varer turen? vor *leng*-e *vaa*-ra *too*-ren

Is it a direct route?
Er det en direkte forbindelse? ir deyr in *dee*-rek-te for-*bi*-nel-se

I'd like a luggage locker.
Jeg vil gerne have et yai vil *gir*-ne ha it
bagageskab med lås. ba-*gaa*-she-skaab me laws

My luggage	*Min bagage*	meen ba-*gaa*-she
has been ...	*er blevet ...*	ir *bley*-vet ...
damaged	*beskadiget*	bey-*ska*-dhee-et
lost	*væk*	vek
stolen	*stjålet*	*styaw*-let

getting around

Where does flight (71) arrive/depart?
Hvor ankommer/afgår fly   vor *an*-ko-ma/*ow*-gawr flew
nummer (71)?   *naw*-ma (eyn-o-hal-*fyers*)

Where's (the) ...?	*Hvor er ...?*	vor ir ...
arrivals hall	*ankomsthallen*	*an*-komst-*ha*-len
departures hall	*afgangshallen*	*ow*-gaangs-*ha*-len
duty-free shop	*den toldfri butik*	den *tol*-free boo-*teek*
gate (12)	*gate (tolv)*	gayt (tol)

Is this the ... to	*Er dette ... til*	ir *dey*-te ... til
(Aarhus)?	*(Århus)?*	(*awr*-hoos)
boat	*båden*	*baw*-dhen
bus	*bussen*	*boo*-sen
plane	*flyet*	*flew*-et
train	*toget*	*taw*-et

What time's the ... bus?	*Hvad tid er den ... bus?*	va teedh ir den ... boos
first	*første*	*feurs*-te
last	*sidste*	*sees*-te
next	*næste*	*nes*-te

At what time does (the train) arrive/leave?
Hvornår ankommer/afgår (toget)?   vor-*nawr* an-ko-ma/*ow*-gawr (*taw*-et)

How long will (the train) be delayed?
Hvor meget er (toget) forsinket?   vor *maa*-yet ir (*taw*-et) for-*sing*-ket

What station/stop is this?
Hvad station/stoppested er dette?   va sta-*shohn*/*sto*-pe-stedh ir *dey*-te

What's the next station/stop?
Hvad er næste station/stoppested?   va ir *nes*-te sta-*shohn*/*sto*-pe-stedh

Does it stop at (Østerport)?
Stopper den/det på (Østerport)?   *sto*-pa den/dey paw (*eus*-ta-port)

Please tell me when we get to (Roskilde).
Sig venligst til når vi kommer — see *ven*·leest til nawr vee *ko*·ma
til (Roskilde). — til (*ros*·kee·le)

How long do we stop here?
Hvor længe stopper vi her? — vor *leng*·e *sto*·pa vee heyr

Is this seat available?
Er denne plads fri? — ir *de*·ne plas free

That's my seat.
Det er min plads. — dey ir meen plas

I'd like a taxi ...	*Jeg vil gerne have en taxa ...*	yai vil *gir*·ne ha in *tak*·sa ...
at (9am)	*klokken (ni om morgenen)*	*klo*·ken (nee om *mor*·nen)
now	*nu*	noo
tomorrow	*i morgen*	ee morn

Is this taxi available?
Er denne taxa fri? — ir *de*·ne *tak*·sa free

How much is it to ...?
Hvad koster det til ...? — va *kos*·ta dey til ...

Please put the meter on.
Vær venlig at sætte taxametret. — ver *ven*·lee at *se*·te tak·sa·*mey*·tret

Please take me to (this address).
Vær venlig at køre mig til — ver *ven*·lee at *keu*·re mai til
(denne adresse). — (*de*·ne a·*draa*·se)

Please ...	*Venligst ...*	*ven*·leest ...
slow down	*kør langsommere*	keur *laang*·so·ma
stop here	*stop her*	stop heyr
wait here	*vent her*	vent heyr

car, motorbike & bicycle hire

I'd like to hire a ...	*Jeg vil gerne leje en ...*	yai vil *gir*·ne *lai*·ye in ...
bicycle	*cykel*	*sew*·kel
car	*bil*	beel
motorbike	*motorcykel*	*moh*·tor·sew·kel

with ...	med ...	me ...
a driver	chauffør	shoh-feur
air conditioning	air-conditioning	eyr-kon-dee-shoh-ning
antifreeze	defroster	dey-fros-ta

How much for	Hvor meget koster	vor maa-yet kos-ta
... hire?	det per ...?	dey peyr ...
hourly	time	tee-me
daily	dag	da
weekly	uge	oo-e

air	luft n	lawft
oil	olie	ohl-ye
petrol	benzin n	ben-seen
tyres	dæk n pl	dek

I need a mechanic.
Jeg har brug for en mekaniker.   yai haar broo for in mi-ka-ni-ka

I've run out of petrol.
Jeg er løbet tør for benzin.   yai ir leu-bet teur for ben-seen

I have a flat tyre.
Jeg er punkteret.   yai ir pawng-tey-ret

directions

Where's the ...?	Hvor er ...?	vor ir ...
bank	der en bank	deyr in baank
city centre	bycentrum	bew-sen-trawm
hotel	der et hotel	deyr it hoh-tel
market	der et marked	deyr it maar-kedh
police station	politistationen	poh-lee-tee-sta-shoh-nen
post office	der et postkontor	deyr it post-kon-tohr
public toilet	der et offentligt toilet	deyr it o-fent-leet toy-let
tourist office	turistkontoret	too-reest-kon-toh-ret

Is this the road to (Kronborg Slot)?
Fører denne vej til (Kronborg Slot)?   feu-ra de-ne vai til (krohn-borg slot)

Can you show me (on the map)?
Kan De/du vise mig det   kan dee/doo vee-se mai dey
(på kortet)? pol/inf   (paw kor-tet)

What's the address?
Hvad er adressen?   va ir a-draa-sen

How far (away) is it?
Hvor langt (væk) er det?   vor laangt (vek) ir dey

How do I get there?
Hvordan kommer jeg derhen?   vor·*dan* ko·ma yai deyr·hen

Can I get there by bicycle?
Kan jeg cykle derhen?   kan yai *sewk*·le deyr·hen

Turn . . .	*Drej . . .*	drai . . .
at the corner	*ved hjørnet*	vi *yeur*·nedh
at the traffic lights	*ved trafiklyset*	vi traa·*feek*·lew·set
left/right	*til venstre/højre*	til *vens*·tre/*hoy*·re

It's . . .	*Det er . . .*	dey ir . . .
behind . . .	*bag . . .*	ba . . .
far (away)	*langt (væk)*	laangt (vek)
here	*her*	heyr
in front of . . .	*foran . . .*	fo·ran . . .
left	*til venstre*	til *vens*·tre
near (to . . .)	*nær (ved . . .)*	ner (vi . . .)
next to . . .	*ved siden af . . .*	vi *see*·dhen a . . .
on the corner	*på hjørnet*	paw *yeur*·net
opposite . . .	*på modsate side af . . .*	paw *mohdh*·sa·te *see*·dhe a . . .
right	*til højre*	til *hoy*·re
straight ahead	*lige ud*	*li*·e oodh
there	*der*	deyr

by bicycle	*på cykel*	paw *sew*·kel
by bus	*med bus*	me boos
by taxi	*med taxa*	me *tak*·sa
by train	*med tog*	me taw
on foot	*til fods*	til fohdhs

north	*nord*	nohr
south	*syd*	sewdh
east	*øst*	eust
west	*vest*	vest

Indgang/Udgang	*in*-gaang/*udh*-gaang	**Entrance/Exit**
Åben/Lukket	*aw*-ben/*law*-ket	**Open/Closed**
Ledige værelser	*ley*-dhee-e *verl*-sa	**Rooms Available**
Alt optaget	alt *op*-ta-yet	**No Vacancies**
Information	in-for-ma-*shohn*	**Information**
Politistation	poh-lee-*tee*-sta-shohn	**Police Station**
Forbudt	for-*boot*	**Prohibited**
Toilet	toy-*let*	**Toilets**
Herrer	*hey*-ra	**Men**
Damer	*daa*-ma	**Women**
Varm/Kold	vaarm/kol	**Hot/Cold**

accommodation

finding accommodation

Where's a ...?	*Hvor er der ...?*	vor ir deyr ...
camping ground	*en campingplads*	in *kaam*-ping-plas
guesthouse	*et gæstehus*	it *ges*-te-hoos
hotel	*et hotel*	it hoh-*tel*
youth hostel	*et ungdomsherberg*	it *awng*-doms-heyr-beyrg

Can you recommend somewhere ...?	*Kan De/du anbefale et ... sted?* pol/inf	kan dee/doo *an*-bey-fa-le it ... stedh
cheap	*billigt*	*bee*-leet
good	*godt*	got

Can you recommend somewhere nearby?
Kan De/du anbefale et sted i nærheden? pol/inf
kan dee/doo *an*-bey-fa-le it stedh ee *ner*-hey-dhen

I'd like to book a room, please.
Jeg vil gerne bestille et værelse.
yai vil *gir*-ne bey-*sti*-le it *verl*-se

I have a reservation.
Jeg har en reservation.
yai haar in rey-ser-vaa-*shohn*

My name's ...
Mit navn er ...
meet nown ir ...

Do you have a twin room?
Har I et værelse med to senge? haar ee it *verl*·se me toh *seng*·e

Do you have a ... room?	*Har I et ... værelse?*	haar ee it ... *verl*·se
single	*enkelt*	*eng*·kelt
double	*dobbelt*	*do*·belt

How much is	*Hvor meget koster*	vor *maa*·yet *kos*·ta
it per ...?	*det per ...?*	dey peyr ...
night	*nat*	nat
person	*person*	per·*sohn*

Can I pay ...?	*Kan jeg betale med ...?*	kan yai bey·*taa*·le me ...
by credit card	*kreditkort*	kre·*deet*·kort
with a travellers cheque	*rejsecheck*	*rai*·se·shek

I'd like to stay for (two) nights.
Jeg vil gerne blive (to) nætter. yai vil *gir*·ne *blee*·ve (toh) ne·ta

From (2 July) to (6 July).
Fra (anden juli) til fraa (*a*·nen *yoo*·lee) til
(sjette juli). (*sye*·te *yoo*·lee)

Can I see it?
Må jeg se det? maw yai sey dey

Am I allowed to camp here?
Må jeg campere her? maw yai kaam·*pey*·a heyr

Is there a campsite nearby?
Er der en campingplads ir deyr in *kaam*·ping·plas
i nærheden? ee *ner*·hey·dhen

requests & queries

When's breakfast served?
Hvornår er der morgenmad? vor·*nawr* ir deyr *morn*·madh

Where's breakfast served?
Hvor serveres der morgenmad? vor ser·*vey*·res deyr *morn*·madh

Please wake me at (eight).
Vær så venlig at vække mig ver saw *ven*·lee at *ve*·ke mai
klokken (otte). *klo*·ken (*aw*·te)

Could I have my key, please?
Må jeg få min nøgle, tak? — maw yai faw meen *noy*·le taak

Can I get another (quilt)?
Må jeg få en ekstra dyne? — maw yai faw en *eks*·tra (*dew*·ne)

Is there a/an ...?	Er der ...?	ir deyr ...
elevator	en elevator	in ey·ley·*va*·tor
safe	et pengeskab	it *peng*·e·skaab

The room is too ...	Det her værelse er for ...	dey heyr *verl*·se ir for ...
expensive	dyrt	dewrt
noisy	larmende	*laar*·me·ne
small	lille	*lee*·le

The ... doesn't work.	... virker ikke.	... *veer*·ka *i*·ke
air conditioning	Air-conditioningen	eyr·kon·dee·shoh·ning·en
fan	Viften	*vif*·ten
toilet	Toilettet	toy·*le*·tet

This ... isn't clean.	... er snavset.	... ir *snow*·set
pillow	Denne pude	*de*·ne *poo*·dhe
sheet	Dette lagen	*dey*·te *la*·yen
towel	Dette håndklæde	*dey*·te *hawn*·kle·dhe

checking out

What time is checkout?
Hvad tid er checkout? — va teedh ir chek·*owt*

Can I leave my luggage here?
Kan jeg efterlade min bagage her? — kan yai *ef*·ta·la·dhe meen ba·*gaa*·she heyr

Could I have my ..., please?	Må jeg få ..., tak?	maw yai faw ... taak
deposit	mit depositum	meet dey·*poh*·see·tawm
passport	mit pas	meet pas
valuables	mine værdigenstande	*mee*·ne ver·*dee*·gen·sta·ne

communications & banking

the internet

Where's the local Internet café?
Hvor er den lokale internet café?   vor ir den loh·*ka*·le *in*·ta·net ka·*fey*

How much is it per hour?
Hvad koster det per time?   va *kos*·ta dey peyr *tee*·me

I'd like to ...	Jeg vil gerne ...	yai vil *gir*·ne ...
check my email	checke mine emails	*che*·ke *mee*·ne *ee*·mayls
get Internet access	have internet adgang	ha *in*·ta·net *adh*·gaang
use a printer	benytte en printer	bey·*new*·te in *preen*·ta
use a scanner	benytte en skanner	bey·*new*·te in *ska*·na

mobile/cell phone

I'd like a ...	Jeg vil gerne ...	yai vil *gir*·ne ...
mobile/cell phone for hire	leje en mobil-telefon	*lai*·ye in moh·*beel*·tey·*ley*·fohn
SIM card for your network	have et SIM-kort til jeres netværk	ha it *seem*·kort til *ye*·res *net*·verk

What are the rates?
Hvad er taksterne?   va ir *taaks*·ta·ne

telephone

What's your phone number?
Hvad er Deres/dit
telefonnummer? pol/inf   va ir *de*·res/deet
tey·ley·*fohn*·naw·ma

The number is ...
Nummeret er ...   *naw*·ma·et ir ...

Where's the nearest public phone?
Hvor er den nærmeste
telefonboks?   vor ir den *ner*·mes·te
tey·ley·*fohn*·boks

I'd like to buy a phonecard.
Jeg vil gerne købe et telefonkort.   yai vil *gir*·ne *keu*·be it tey·ley·*fohn*·kort

I want to ...	Jeg vil gerne ...	yai vil *gir*·ne ...
call (Singapore)	ringe til (Singapore)	*ring*·e til (*seeng*·ga·pohr)
make a local call	ringe lokalt	*ring*·e loh·*kalt*
reverse the charges	have at modtageren betaler	ha at *mohdh*·ta·yaan bey·*ta*·la

How much does ... cost?	Hvor meget koster ...?	vo *maa*·yet *kos*·ta ...
a (three)-minute call	det for (tre) minutter	dey for (trey) mee·*noo*·ta
each extra minute	hvert ekstra minut	vert *eks*·traa mee·*noot*

It's ... per minute.	... per minut.	... peyr mee·*noot*
(one) euro	(En) euro	(eyn) *euw*·roh
(three) kroner	(Tre) kroner	(trey) *kroh*·na

post office

I want to send a ...	Jeg vil gerne sende ...	yai vil *gir*·ne *sen*·ne ...
fax	en fax	in faaks
letter	et brev	it brev
parcel	en pakke	in *paa*·ke
postcard	et postkort	it *post*·kort

I want to buy ...	Jeg vil gerne købe ...	yai vil *gir*·ne *keu*·be ...
an envelope	en konvolut	in kon·voh·*loot*
stamps	frimærker	*free*·mer·ka

Please send it (to Australia) by ...	Kan I sende det (til Australien) per ...	kan ee *sen*·ne dey (til ow·*straa*·lee·en) peyr ...
airmail	luftpost	*lawft*·post
express mail	eksprespost	eks·*pres*·post
registered mail	anbefalet post	*an*·bey·fa·let post
surface mail	pakkepost	*paa*·ke·post

Is there any mail for me?	Er der post til mig?	ir deyr post til mai

bank

Where's a/an ...?	*Hvor er der ...?*	vor ir deyr ...
ATM	*en hæveautomat*	in *he*·ve·ow·toh·mat
foreign exchange office	*et vekselkontor*	it *veks*·le·kon·tohr

I'd like to ...	*Jeg vil gerne ...*	yai vil *gir*·ne ...
arrange a transfer	*foretage en overførsel*	*fo*·re·ta in *o*·va·feur·sel
cash a cheque	*veksle en check*	*veks*·le in shek
change money	*veksle nogle penge*	*veks*·le *noh*·le *peng*·e
change travellers cheques	*veksle rejsechecks*	*veks*·le *rai*·se·sheks
get a cash advance	*få et forskud*	faw it *for*·skoodh
withdraw money	*hæve penge*	*he*·ve *peng*·e

What's the ...?	*Hvad ...?*	va ...
charge for that	*koster det*	*kos*·ta dey
exchange rate	*er vekselkursen*	ir *veks*·le·koor·sen

It's ...	*Det ...*	dey ...
(12) euros	*koster (tolv) euroer*	*kos*·ta (tol) *euw*·roh
(50) kroner	*koster (halvtreds) kroner*	*kos*·ta (hal·*tres*) *kroh*·na
free	*er gratis*	ir *graa*·tees

What time does the bank open?
Hvornår åbner banken?   vor·*nawr* awb·na *baang*·ken

Has my money arrived yet?
Er mine penge kommet?   ir *mee*·ne *peng*·e ko·met

sightseeing

getting in

What time does it open/close?
Hvornår åbner/lukker de?   vor·*nawr* awb·na/*law*·ka de

What's the admission charge?
Hvad koster adgang?   va *kos*·ta *adh*·gaang

Is there a discount for students/children?
Er der studenterabat/børnerabat?   ir deyr stoo·*den*·ta·raa·bat/beur·ne·raa·bat

I'd like a …	*Jeg vil gerne have …*	yai vil *gir*·ne ha …
catalogue	*et katalog*	it ka·ta·*loh*
guide	*en rejsehåndbog*	in *rai*·se·*hawn*·borw
local map	*et lokalkort*	it loh·*kal*·kort

I'd like to see …	*Jeg vil gerne se …*	yai vil *gir*·ne sey …
What's that?	*Hvad er det?*	va ir dey
Can I take a photo?	*Må jeg tage et foto?*	maw yai ta it *foh*·toh

tours

When's the	*Hvornår er den*	vor·*nawr* ir den
next …?	*næste …?*	*nes*·te …
boat trip	*bådtur*	*bawdh*·toor
day trip	*dagstur*	*dows*·toor
tour	*ekskursion*	eks·koor·*shohn*

Is … included?	*Er … inkluderet?*	ir … in·kloo·*dey*·ret
accommodation	*ophold*	*op*·hol
the admission charge	*entreen*	ang·*trey*·en
food	*mad*	madh
transport	*transport*	traans·*port*

How long is the tour?
Hvor lang er turen? vor laang ir *too*·ren

What time should we be back?
Hvornår kommer vi tilbage? vor·*nawr* ko·ma vee til·*ba*·ye

sightseeing		
castle	*slot* n	slot
cathedral	*katedral*	ka·te·*draal*
church	*kirke*	*keer*·ke
main square	*storetorv* n	*stoh*·re·torw
monastery	*kloster* n	*klos*·ta
monument	*monument* n	moh·noo·*ment*
museum	*museum* n	moo·*se*·awm
old city	*den gamle bydel*	den *gaam*·le *bew*·deyl
palace	*palads* n	pa·*las*
ruins	*ruiner*	roo·*ee*·na
stadium	*stadion* n	*sta*·dee·on
statue	*statue*	*sta*·too·e

shopping

enquiries

Where's a ...?	*Hvor er der ...?*	vor ir deyr ...
bank	*en bank*	in baank
bookshop	*en boghandel*	in *borw*·ha·nel
camera shop	*en fotohandel*	in *foh*·toh·ha·nel
department store	*et stormagasin*	it *stohr*·maa·ga·seen
grocery store	*en købmand*	in *keub*·man
market	*et marked*	it *maar*·kedh
newsagency	*en kiosk*	in kee·*osk*
supermarket	*et supermarked*	it *soo*·pa·maar·kedh

Where can I buy (a padlock)?
Hvor kan jeg købe (en hængelås)?   vor kan yai *keu*·be (in *heng*·e·laws)

I'm looking for ...
Jeg leder efter ...   yai *li*·dha *ef*·ta ...

Can I have a look?
Må jeg se?   maw yai sey

Do you have any others?
Har I andre?   haar ee *aan*·dre

Does it have a guarantee?
Er der garanti?   ir deyr gaa·raan·*tee*

Can I have it sent abroad?
Kan jeg få det sendt udenlands?   kan yai faw dey sent *oo*·dhen·lans

Can I have my (watch) repaired?
Kan jeg få mit (ur) repareret?   kan yai faw meet (oor) rey·paa·*rey*·ret

It's faulty.
Det er i stykker.   dey ir ee *stew*·ka

I'd like ..., please.	*Jeg vil gerne ..., tak.*	yai vil *gir*·ne ... taak
a bag	*have en pose*	ha in *poh*·se
a refund	*have en refundering*	ha in re·fawn·*dey*·ring
to return this	*returnere dette*	rey·toor·*ney*·re *dey*·te

paying

How much is it?
Hvor meget koster det?
vor *maa*·yet *kos*·ta dey

Can you write down the price?
Kan De/du skrive prisen ned? pol/inf
ka dee/doo *skree*·ve *pree*·sen nidh

That's too expensive.
Det er for dyrt.
dey ir for dewrt

What's your lowest price?
Hvad er jeres laveste pris?
va ir *ye*·res *la*·ve·ste prees

I'll give you (five) euros.
Jeg vil betale (fem) euro.
yai vil bey·*ta*·le (fem) *eu*·roh

I'll give you (20) kroner.
Jeg vil betale (tyve) kroner.
yai vil bey·*ta*·le (*tew*·ve) *kroh*·na

There's a mistake in the bill. (restaurant/shop)
Der er en fejl i regningen/
deyr ir in fail ee *rai*·ning·en/
kvitteringen.
kvee·*tey*·ring·en

Do you accept ...?	*Tager I ...?*	ta ee ...
credit cards	*kreditkort*	kre·*deet*·kort
debit cards	*hævekort*	*he*·ve·kort
travellers cheques	*rejsechecks*	*rai*·se·sheks
I'd like ..., please.	*Jeg vil gerne have ..., tak.*	yai vil *gir*·ne ha ... taak
a receipt	*en kvittering*	in kvee·*tey*·ring
my change	*mine byttepenge*	*mee*·ne *bew*·te·peng·e

clothes & shoes

Can I try it on?
Må jeg prøve?
maw yai *preu*·ve

My size is (40).
Jeg er størrelse (fyrre).
yai ir *steu*·rel·se (*fewr*·re)

It doesn't fit.
Det passer ikke.
dey *pa*·sa *i*·ke

small	*lille*	*lee*·le
medium	*medium*	*mey*·dee·awm
large	*stor*	stohr

books & music

I'd like a . . .	*Jeg vil gerne have en . . .*	yai vil *gir·ne* ha in . . .
newspaper	*avis*	a·*vees*
(in English)	*(på engelsk)*	(paw *eng·*elsk)
pen	*kuglepen*	*koo·*le·pen

Is there an English-language bookshop?
Er der en engelsksproget   ir deyr in eng·elsk·*spraw·*wet
boghandel?   borw·ha·nel

I'm looking for something by (Kim Larsen).
Jeg leder efter noget af   yai *li·*dha *ef·*ta *naw·*et a
(Kim Larsen).   (keem *laar·*sen)

Can I listen to this?
Må jeg lytte til den?   maw yai *lew·*te til den

photography

Could you . . .?	*Kan I . . .?*	kan ee . . .
burn a CD from	*brænde en CD fra*	*bre·*ne in *sey·*dey fraa
my memory card	*mit hukommelseskort*	meet hoo·*ko·*mel·ses·kort
develop this film	*fremkalde denne film*	*frem·*ka·le *de·*ne feelm
load my film	*sætte min film i*	*se·*te meen feelm ee

I need a/an . . . film	*Jeg har brug for . . .*	yai haar broo for . . .
for this camera.	*film til dette kamera.*	feelm til *dey·*te *ka·*me·raa
APS	*APS-*	aa pey es
B&W	*sort-hvid*	*sort·*veedh
colour	*farve*	*faar·*ve
slide	*dias-*	*dee·*as
(200) speed	*(to hundrede) ISO*	(toh *hoon·*re·dhe) *ee·*soh

When will it be ready?
Hvornår er den færdig?   vor·*nawr* ir den *fer·*dee

DANSK – shopping

32

meeting people

greetings, goodbyes & introductions

Hello.	Goddag.	go·da
Hi.	Hej/Dav.	hai/dow
Good night.	Godnat.	go·nat
Goodbye.	Farvel.	faar·vel
Bye.	Hej hej.	hai hai
See you later.	Vi ses.	vee seys
Mr	Hr	heyr
Mrs	Fru	froo
Miss	Frøken	freu·ken

How are you?
   Hvordan går det?   vor·*dan* gawr dey

Good, thanks.
   Godt, tak.   got taak

What's your name?
   Hvad hedder De/du? pol/inf   va *hey*·dha dee/doo

My name is . . .
   Mit navn er . . .   mit nown ir . . .

I'm pleased to meet you.
   Hyggeligt at møde Dem/dig. pol/inf   *hew*·ge·leet at *meu*·dhe dem/dai

This is my . . .	Det er min . . .	dey ir meen . . .
boyfriend	kæreste	ker·ste
brother	bror	brohr
daughter	datter	da·ta
father	far	faar
friend	ven/veninde m/f	ven/ven·i·ne
girlfriend	kæreste	ker·ste
husband	mand	man
mother	mor	mohr
partner (intimate)	kæreste	ker·ste
sister	søster	seus·ta
son	søn	seun
wife	kone	koh·ne

Here's my ...	Her er min ...	heyr ir meen ...
What's your ...?	Hvad er Deres/	va ir de·res/
	din ...? pol/inf	deen ...
address	adresse	a·draa·se
email address	email adresse	ee·mayl a·draa·se
Here's my ...	Her er mit ...	heyr ir meet ...
What's your ...?	Hvad er Deres/	va ir de·res/
	dit ...? pol/inf	deet ...
fax number	fax nummer	faks naw·ma
phone number	telefonnummer	tey·ley·fohn·naw·ma

occupations

What's your occupation?
   Hvad laver De/du? pol/inf   va la·va dee/doo

I'm a/an ...	Jeg er ...	yai ir ...
artist	kunstner	kawnst·na
business person	forretningsdrivende	for·rat·nings·dree·ve·ne
farmer	landmand	lan·man
manual worker	arbejder	aar·bai·da
office worker	kontorarbejder	kon·tohr·aar·bai·da
scientist	forsker	fors·ka
student	studerende	stoo·dey·re·ne
tradesperson	næringsdrivende	ne·rings·dree·ven·e

background

Where are you from?
   Hvor kommer De/du fra? pol/inf   vor ko·ma dee/doo fraa

I'm from ...	Jeg er fra ...	yai ir fraa ...
Australia	Australien	ow·straa·lee·en
Canada	Kanada	ka·na·da
England	England	eng·lan
New Zealand	New Zealand	new see·lan
the USA	USA	oo es a

Are you married?	Er De/du gift?	ir dee/doo geeft
I'm married.	Jeg er gift.	yai ir geeft
I'm single.	Jeg er ugift.	yai ir oo·geeft

age

How old ...?	*Hvor gammel er ...?*	vor *gaa*·mel ir ...
are you	*du*	doo
is your daughter	*din datter*	deen *da*·ta
is your son	*din søn*	deen seun
I'm ... years old.	*Jeg er ... år gammel.*	yai ir ... awr *gaa*·mel
He/She is ... years old.	*Han/Hun er ... år gammel.*	han/hoon ir ... awr *gaa*·mel

feelings

I'm (not) ...	*Jeg er (ikke) ...*	yai ir (*i*·ke) ...
Are you ...?	*Er du ...?*	ir doo ...
happy	*glad*	gladh
hungry	*sulten*	*sool*·ten
sad	*trist*	treest
thirsty	*tørstig*	*teus*·tee
Are you cold?	*Fryser du?*	*frew*·sa doo
I'm (not) cold.	*Jeg fryser (ikke).*	yai *frew*·sa (*i*·ke)
Are you hot?	*Har du det varmt?*	haar doo dey vaarmt
I'm (not) hot.	*Jeg har det (ikke) varmt.*	yai haar dey (*i*·ke) vaarmt

entertainment

going out

Where can I find ...?	*Hvor kan jeg finde ...?*	vor kan yai *fi*·ne ...
clubs	*natklubber*	*nat*·kloo·ba
gay venues	*bøsseklubber*	*beu*·se·kloo·ba
pubs	*pubber*	*paw*·ba
I feel like going to a/the ...	*Jeg har lyst til at tage ...*	yai haar lewst til at ta ...
concert	*til koncert*	til kon·*sert*
movies	*i biografen*	ee bee·oh·*graa*·fen
party	*til fest*	til fest
restaurant	*på restaurant*	paw res·toh·*rang*
theatre	*i teatret*	ee tey·*a*·ta

interests

Do you like ...?	*Kan De/du*	kan dee/doo
	lide ...? pol/inf	lee ...
I (don't) like ...	*Jeg synes (ikke) om ...*	yai sewns (*i*·ke) om ...
art	*kunst*	kawnst
cooking	*madlavning*	madh·low·ning
movies	*film*	feelm
reading	*at læse*	at *le*·se
shopping	*at handle*	at *han*·le
sport	*sport*	sport
travelling	*at rejse*	at *rai*·se
Do you like to ...?	*Kan De/du lide*	kan dee/doo lee
	at ...? pol/inf	at ...
dance	*danse*	*dan*·se
go to concerts	*gå til koncert*	gaw til kon·*sert*
listen to music	*høre musik*	*heu*·re moo·*seek*

food & drink

finding a place to eat

Can you	*Kan De/du*	kan dee/doo
recommend a ...?	*anbefale en ...?* pol/inf	*an*·bey·fa·le in ...
bar	*bar*	baar
café	*café*	ka·*fey*
restaurant	*restaurant*	res·toh·*rang*
I'd like ..., please.	*Jeg vil gerne ..., tak.*	yai vil *gir*·ne ... taak
a table for (four)	*have et bord til (fire)*	ha it bohr til (feer)
the (non)smoking	*sidde i (ikke-)*	*si*·dha ee (*i*·ke·)
section	*rygerafdelingen*	rew·a·ow·*dey*·ling·en

ordering food

breakfast	*morgenmad*	*morn*·madh
lunch	*frokost*	*froh*·kost
dinner	*middag*	*mi*·da
snack n	*mellemmåltid*	*me*·lem·mawl·teedh

What would you recommend?
Hvad kan De/du anbefale? pol/inf   va kan dee/doo *an*·bey·fa·le

I'd like (the) ..., please.	*Jeg vil gerne have ..., tak.*	yai vil *gir*·ne ha ... taak
bill	*regningen*	*rai*·ning·en
drink list	*vinkortet*	*veen*·kor·tet
menu	*menuen*	me·*new*·en
that dish	*den ret*	den ret

drinks

(cup of) coffee ...	*(en kop) kaffe ...*	(in kop) *ka*·fe ...
(cup of) tea ...	*(en kop) te ...*	(in kop) tey ...
with milk	*med mælk*	me melk
without sugar	*uden sukker*	*oo*·dhen *saw*·ka
boiled water	*kogt vand*	kogt van
(orange) juice	*(appelsin)juice*	(aa·pel·*seen*·)joos
mineral water	*mineralvand/danskvand*	mee·ne·*ral*·van/*dansk*·van
soft drink	*sodavand*	*soh*·da·van

in the bar

I'll have (a gin).	*(En gin), tak.*	(in jeen) taak
I'll buy you a drink.	*Jeg giver en drink.*	yai geer in drink
What would you like?	*Hvad vil du have?* inf	va vil doo ha
Cheers!	*Skål!*	skawl
cocktail	*cocktail*	*kok*·tayl
cognac	*konjak*	*kon*·yak
a shot of (whisky)	*et shot (whiskey)*	it shot (*wees*·kee)
snaps	*snaps*	snaaps
a ... of beer	*... øl*	... eul
bottle	*en flaske*	in *flas*·ke
glass	*et glas*	it glas
a bottle of ...	*en flaske ...*	in *flas*·ke ...
a glass of ...	*et glas ...*	it glas ...
red wine	*rødvin*	*reudh*·veen
sparkling wine	*mousserende vin*	moo·*sey*·ra·ne veen
white wine	*hvidvin*	*veedh*·veen

self-catering

What's the local speciality?
Hvad er den lokale specialitet?   va ir den loh·*ka*·le spey·sha·lee·*teyt*

What's that?
Hvad er det?   va ir dey

How much is it?
Hvor meget koster det?   vor *maa*·yet *kos*·ta dey

I'd like ...	*Jeg vil gerne have ...*	yai vil *gir*·ne ha ...
(100) grams	*(hundrede) gram*	(*hoon*·re·dhe) graam
(two) kilos	*(to) kilo*	(toh) *kee*·lo
(three) pieces	*(tre) stykker*	(trey) *stew*·ka
(six) slices	*(seks) skiver*	(seks) *skee*·va

Less.	*Mindre.*	*min*·dra
Enough.	*Nok.*	nok
More.	*Mere.*	*mey*·a

special diets & allergies

Is there a vegetarian restaurant near here?
Er der en vegetarisk   ir deyr in vey·gey·*taa*·reesk
restaurant i nærheden?   res·toh·*rang* ee *ner*·hey·dhen

Do you have vegetarian food?
Har I vegetarmad?   haar ee vey·ge·*taar*·madh

Could you prepare	*Kan I lave et*	kan ee *la*·ve it
a meal without ...?	*måltid uden ...?*	*mawl*·teedh *oo*·dhen ...
butter	*smør*	smeur
eggs	*æg*	eg
meat stock	*kødboullion*	*keudh*·boo·lee·yong

I'm allergic to ...	*Jeg er allergisk over for ...*	yai in a·*ler*·geesk *o*·va for ...
dairy produce	*mælkeprodukter*	*mel*·ke·proh·*dawk*·ta
gluten	*gluten*	*gloo*·ten
MSG	*monosodium*	moh·noh·*soh*·dee·awm
	glutamat	gloo·ta·*mat*
nuts	*nødder*	*neu*·dha
seafood	*skaldyr*	*skaal*·dewr

menu decoder

boller i karry	*bo*-la ee *kaa*-ree	*meatballs in a curry sauce, served with rice or potatoes*
budding	*boo*-dhing	*a kind of pudding flavoured with rum or almonds, served warm*
bøf med løg	beuf me loy	*hamburger served with fried onions, potatoes & brown gravy*
bøftartar	*beuf*-ta-taar	*beef tartar – raw ground beef topped with a raw egg yolk, raw onions & capers*
champignoner	shaam-peen-*yong*-a	*mushrooms*
dyrlægens natmad	*dewr*-le-yens *nat*-madh	*liver pâté on sourdough ryebread, with a slice of salt beef, raw onions & beef jelly*
engelsk bøf	*eng*-elsk beuf	*sirloin steak*
fiskesuppe	*fis*-ke-saw-pe	*fish soup, usually creamy*
flæskesteg	*fles*-ke-stai	*pork roast served with potatoes, brown gravy & pickled cucumbers*
forel	foh-*rel*	*trout*
frikadeller	fri-ka-*de*-la	*pork & veal meatballs*
fromage	froh-*ma*-she	*a kind of mousse flavoured with lemon, served cold*
fyldt hvidkålshoved n	fewlt *veedh*-kawls-hoh-vedh	*ground beef wrapped in cabbage leaves*
gravad laks	*gra*-vadh laks	*gravlax – traditional salt-cured raw salmon with a sweet mustard sauce*
grønsagssuppe	*greun*-sas-saw-pe	*vegetable soup*
gule ærter	*goo*-le *eyr*-ta	*split pea soup, served with pork*
hakkebøf	*haa*-ke-beuf	*hamburger*
havregrød	*how*-re-greudh	*porridge*
hønsekødssuppe	*heun*-se-keudh-saw-pe	*chicken soup*
jordbær med fløde	*yohr*-beyr me *fleu*-dhe	*strawberries with cream*
kartoffel	kaar-*to*-fel	*potato*
kogt torsk	kogt torsk	*poached cod in mustard sauce, served with boiled potatoes*

konditorkager	kon·*dee*·tor·ka·ya	*French pastries*
koteletter	ko·te·*le*·ta	*meat chops*
lammesteg	*laa*·me·stai	*roast lamb*
leverpostej	ley·va·poo·*stai*	*liver pâté*
marineret sild	maa·ree·*ney*·ret seel	*pickled herring, served with raw onions*
medisterpølse	mey·*dees*·ta·*peul*·se	*large fried sausage*
mørbrad	*meur*·braadh	*sirloin*
oksesteg	*ok*·se·stai	*roast beef*
ostemad	aws·te·*madh*	*open cheese sandwich*
pandekager	*pa*·ne·ka·ya	*crepes with jam, sugar or ice cream*
rejemad	*rai*·ye·maadh	*small shrimp served on bread with mayonnaise & lemon slices*
rejer	*rai*·ya	*shrimps*
rødgrød med fløde	reudh·greudh me *fleu*·dhe	*fruit pudding (red currant, raspberry, strawberry) served with cream*
røget ål	*reu*·yet awl	*smoked eel*
røget laks	*reu*·yet laks	*smoked salmon with scrambled eggs*
røget sild	*reu*·yet seel	*smoked herring on rye bread with raw onions, chives & a raw egg yolk*
røræg	*reur*·eg	*scrambled eggs*
spaghetti med kødsovs	spa·*ge*·tee me *keudh*·saws	*spaghetti with ground beef in a tomato sauce*
stegt ål med stuvede kartofler	stegt awl me *stoo*·ve·dhe kaar·*tof*·la	*fried eel with boiled potatoes in a white sauce*
stegt flæsk med persillesovs	stegt flesk me per·*si*·le·saws	*fried pork strips served with potatoes*
stegt sild	stegt seel	*fried herring, rolled in rye flour & served with potatoes & a white parsley sauce*
syltede agurker	*sewl*·te·dhe a·*goor*·ka	*pickled cucumbers*
wienerbrød n	*vee*·na·breudh	*Danish pastry*
æggekage	e·ge·*ka*·ye	*egg dish (made with flour) with bacon*
øllebrød	*eu*·le·breudh	*a smooth beer & bread dish served hot with milk or whipped cream*

emergencies

basics

Help!	*Hjælp!*	yelp
Stop!	*Stop!*	stop
Go away!	*Gå væk!*	gaw vek
Thief!	*Tyv!*	tew
Fire!	*Ildebrand!*	ee·le·braan
Watch out!	*Pas på!*	pas paw

Call ...!	*Ring efter ...!*	ring *ef*·ta ...
a doctor	*en læge*	in *le*·ye
an ambulance	*en ambulance*	in aam·boo·*laang*·se
the police	*politiet*	poh·lee·*tee*·et

It's an emergency!
Det er et nødstilfælde! dey ir it *neudhs*·til·fe·le

Could you help me, please?
Kan De/du hjælpe mig? pol/inf kan dee/doo *yel*·pe mai

I have to use the telephone.
Jeg skal bruge en telefon. yai skal *broo*·e en tey·ley·*fohn*

I'm lost.
Jeg er faret vild. yai ir *faa*·ret veel

Where's the toilet?
Hvor er toilettet? vor ir toy·*le*·tet

police

Where's the police station?
Hvor er politistationen? vor ir poh·lee·*tee*·sta·shoh·nen

I want to report an offence. (minor/serious)
Jeg vil gerne anmelde en yai vil *gir*·ne an·me·le in
lovovertrædelse/forbrydelse. *law*·o·va·tre·dhel·se/for·*breu*·dhel·se

I have insurance.
Jeg har forsikring. yai haar for·*sik*·ring

I've been ...	*Jeg er blevet ...*	yai ir *bley*·vet ...
assaulted	*overfaldet*	*o*·va·fa·let
raped	*voldtaget*	*vol*·ta·yet
robbed	*bestjålet*	bey·*styaw*·let

I've lost my ...	Jeg har mistet ...	yai haar *mis*·tet ...
backpack	min rygsæk	meen *reug*·sek
bags	min bagage	meen ba·*gaa*·she
credit card	mit kreditkort	meet kre·*deet*·kort
handbag	min håndtaske	meen *hawn*·tas·ke
jewellery	mine smykker	*mee*·ne *smew*·ka
money	mine penge	*mee*·ne *peng*·e
passport	mit pas	meet pas
travellers cheques	mine rejsechecks	*mee*·ne *rai*·se·sheks
wallet	min pung	meen pawng

I want to contact my ...	Jeg vil gerne kontakte ...	yai vil *gir*·ne kon·*taak*·te ...
consulate	mit konsulat	meet kon·soo·*lat*
embassy	min ambassade	meen aam·ba·*sa*·dhe

health

medical needs

DANSK – health

Where's the nearest ...?	Hvor er der ...?	vor ir deyr ...
dentist	en tandlæge	in *tan*·le·ye
doctor	en læge	in *le*·ye
hospital	et hospital	it hos·pi·*tal*
(night) pharmacist	et (nat)apotek	it (*nat*·)aa·poh·*tek*

I need a doctor (who speaks English).

Jeg har brug for en læge
(som taler engelsk).

yai haar broo for in *le*·ye
(som *ta*·la *eng*·elsk)

Could I see a female doctor?

Må jeg få en kvindelig læge?

maw yai faw in *kvi*·ne·lee *le*·ye

I've run out of my medication.

Jeg er løbet tør for medicin.

yai ir *leu*·bet teur for mey·dee·*seen*

42

symptoms, conditions & allergies

| I'm sick. | Jeg er syg. | yai ir sew |
| It hurts here. | Det gør ondt her. | dey geur awnt heyr |

I have (a) ...	Jeg har ...	yai haar ...
asthma	astma	ast·ma
bronchitis	bronkitis	brawng·kee·tees
constipation	forstoppelse	for·sto·pel·se
cough	hoste	hoh·ste
diabetes	sukkersyge	saw·ka·sew·ye
diarrhoea	diarré	dee·a·rey
fever	feber	fey·ba
headache	hovedpine	hoh vedh·pee·ne
heart condition	hjerteproblemer	yer·te·proh·bley·ma
nausea	kvalme	kval·me
pain	smerter	smeyr·ta
sore throat	ondt i halsen	awnt ee hal·sen
toothache	tandpine	tan·pee·ne

I'm allergic to ...	Jeg er allergisk over for ...	yai ir a·ler·geesk o·va for ...
antibiotics	antibiotika	an·tee·bee·oh·tee·ka
anti-inflammatories	betændelseshæmmende medicin	bey·te·nel·ses·ha·me·ne mey·dee·seen
aspirin	aspirin	as·pee·reen
bees	bier	bee·a
codeine	kodein	koh·dey·een
penicillin	penicillin	pen·sey·leen

antiseptic	antiseptisk	an·tee·sep·teesk
bandage	forbinding	for·bi·ning
condoms	kondomer	kon·doh·ma
contraceptives	preservativer	pre·seyr·va·tee·va
diarrhoea medicine	diarré medicin	dee·a·rey mey·dee·seen
insect repellent	insektspray	in·sekt·spray
laxatives	afføringsmiddel	ow·feu·rings·mee·dhel
painkillers	smertestillende middel	smer·te·sti·le·ne mee·dhel
rehydration salts	vanddrivende piller	van·dree·ve·ne pi·la
sleeping tablets	sovepiller	so·ve·pi·la

english–danish dictionary

In this dictionary, words are marked as n (noun), a (adjective), v (verb), sg (singular), pl (plural), inf (informal) and pol (polite) where necessary. Note that Danish nouns are either 'common gender' (masculine or feminine forms but never referred to as such) or neuter. Common gender takes the indefinite article en (a) while the neuter forms take the article et (a). Every Danish noun needs to be learned with its indefinite article (en or et). We've only indicated the neuter nouns with ⓝ after the translation. Note also that the ending 't' is added to adjectives for the neuter form (ie when they accompany indefinite singular nouns).

A

accident ulykke oo-lew-ke
accommodation indkvartering in-kvaar-tey-ring
adaptor adapter a-dap-ter
address n adresse a-draa-se
after efter ef-ter
air conditioning aircondition eyr-kon-dee-shen
airplane fly ⓝ flew
airport lufthavn lawft-hawn
alcohol alkohol al-koh-hol
all a alt/alle sg/pl alt/a-le
allergy allergi a-ler-gee
ambulance ambulance am-boo-lang-se
and og o
ankle ankel aang-kel
arm arm aarm
ashtray askebæger ⓝ as-ke-be-ya
ATM hæveautomat he-ve-ow-toh-mat

B

baby baby bey-bee
back (body) ryg reug
backpack rygsæk reug-sek
bad dårlig(t) dawr-lee(t)
bag taske tas-ke
baggage claim bagageudlevering ba-gaa-she-oodh-ley-vey-ring
bank bank baank
bar bar baar
bathroom badeværelse ⓝ ba-dhe-verl-se
battery batteri ⓝ ba-ta-ree
beautiful smuk(t) smawk(t)
bed seng seng
beer øl eul
before før feur
behind bag ba

bicycle cykel sew-kel
big stor(t) stohr(t)
bill regning rai-ning
black sort sohrt
blanket tæppe ⓝ te-pe
blood group blodgruppe blohdh-groo-pe
blue blå blaw
boat båd bawdh
book (make a reservation) v bestille bey-sti-le
bottle flaske flas-ke
bottle opener proptrækker prop-trai-ka
boy dreng draing
brakes (car) bremser brem-sa
breakfast morgenmad morn-madh
broken (faulty) i stykker ee stew-ka
bus bus boos
business forretninger for-rat-ning-a
buy købe keu-be

C

café café ka-fey
camera kamera ⓝ ka-me-raa
camp site campingplads kaam-ping-plas
cancel aflyse ow-lew-se
can opener dåseåbner daw-se-awb-na
car bil beel
cash n kontanter kon-tan-ta
cash (a cheque) v veksle (en check) veks-le (in shek)
cell phone mobiltelefon moh-beel-tey-ley-fohn
centre center ⓝ sen-ta
change (money) v veksle (penge) veks-le (peng-e)
cheap billig(t) bee-lee(t)
check (bill) regning rai-ning
check-in n check-in chek-in
chest bryst ⓝ breust
child barn ⓝ baarn
cigarette cigaret see-ga-ret

city *storby* stohr-bew
clean a *ren(t)* ren(t)
closed *lukket* law-ket
coffee *kaffe* ka-fe
coins *mønter* meun-ta
cold a *kold(t)* kol(t)
collect call *modtageren betaler* mohdh-ta-yaan bey-ta-la
come *komme* ko-me
computer *computer* kom-pyoo-ta
condom ⓝ *kondom* kon-dohm
contact lenses *kontaktlinser* kon-takt-lin-sa
cook v *lave mad* la-ve madh
cost ⓝ *udgift* oodh-geeft
credit card *kreditkort* ⓝ kre-deet-kort
cup *kop* kop
currency exchange *vekslekontor* ⓝ veks-le-kon-tohr
customs (immigration) *told* tol

D

dangerous *farlig(t)* faar-lee(t)
Danish (language) *dansk* dansk
Danish a *dansk* dansk
date (time) *dato* da-toh
day *dag* day
delay ⓝ *forsinkelse* for-sing-kel-se
Denmark *Danmark* dan-mark
dentist *tandlæge* tan-le-ye
depart *afrejse* ow-rai-se
diaper *ble* bley
dictionary *ordbog* ohr-borw
dinner *middag* mi-da
direct *direkte* dee-rek-te
dirty *snavset* snow-set
disabled *handikappet* han-dee-ka-pet
discount ⓝ *rabat* raa-bat
doctor *læge* le-ye
double bed *dobbeltseng* ⓝ do-belt-seng
double room *dobbeltværelse* ⓝ do-belt-verl-se
drink ⓝ *drink* drink
drive v *køre* keu-re
drivers licence *kørekort* ⓝ keu-re-kort
drugs (illicit) *stoffer* sto-fa
dummy (pacifier) *sut* soot

E

ear *øre* ⓝ eu-re
east *øst* eust
eat *spise* spee-se

economy class *økonomiklasse* eu-koh-noh-mee-kla-se
electricity *elektricitet* ey-lek-tree-see-teyt
elevator *elevator* ey-ley-va-tor
email *email* ee-meyl
embassy *ambassade* aam-ba-sa-dhe
emergency *nødstilfælde* ⓝ neudhs-til-fe-le
English (language) *engelsk* eng-elsk
entrance *indgang* in-gaang
evening *aften* aaf-ten
exchange rate *vekslekurs* veks-le-koors
exit ⓝ *udgang* oodh-gaang
expensive *dyr(t)* dewr(t)
express mail *eksprespost* eks-pres-post
eye *øje* ⓝ oy-e

F

far (away) *langt (væk)* laangt (vek)
fast *hurtig(t)* hoor-tee(t)
father *far* faar
film (camera) *film* feelm
finger *finger* fing-aa
first-aid kit *førstehjælp* feur-ste-yelp
first class *første klasse* feur-ste kla-se
fish ⓝ *fisk* fisk
food *mad* madh
foot *fod* fohdh
fork *gaffel* gaa-fel
free (of charge) *gratis* graa-tees
friend *ven/veninde* ⓜ/ⓕ ven/ven-i-ne
fruit *frugt* frawgt
full *fuld(t)* fool(t)
funny *skæg(t)* skeg(t)

G

gift *gave* gaa-ve
girl *pige* pee-ye
glass (drinking) *glas* ⓝ glas
glasses *briller* bre-la
go *gå* gaw
good *god(t)* gohdh/got
green *grøn* greun
guide (person) ⓝ *guide* gaid

H

half ⓝ *halv* hal
hand *hånd* hawn
handbag *håndtaske* hawn-tas-ke

happy *glad* gladh
have *have* ha/*ha*-ve
he *han* han
head *hoved* ⓝ hoh-vedh
heart *hjerte* ⓝ yer-te
heat ⓝ *varme* vaar-me
heavy *tung(t)* tawng(t)
help v *hjælpe* yel-pe
here *her* heyr
high *høj(t)* hoy(t)
highway *motorvej* moh-tor-vai
hike v *vandre* vaan-dre
holidays *ferie* feyr-ye
homosexual a *homoseksuel* hoh-moh-sek-soo-el
hospital *hospital* ⓝ hos-pi-*tal*
hot *varm(t)* vaarm(t)
hotel *hotel* ⓝ hoh-*tel*
hungry *sulten(t)* sool-ten(t)
husband *mand* man

I

I *jeg* yai
identification (card) *ID-kort* ⓝ ee-dey-kort
ill *syg(t)* sew(t)
important *vigtig(t)* vig-tee(t)
included *inklusive* in-kloo-seev
injury *skade* ska-dhe
insurance *forsikring* for-sik-ring
Internet *internet* in-ta-net
interpreter *tolk* tolk

J

jewellery *smykker* smew-ka
job *job* ⓝ job

K

key *nøgle* noy-le
kilogram *kilogram* ⓝ kee-lo-graam
kitchen *køkken* ⓝ keu-ken
knife *kniv* kneev

L

laundry (place) *møntvaskeri* ⓝ meunt-vas-ka-ree
lawyer *advokat* adh-voh-*kaat*
left (direction) *venstre* ven-stre

left-luggage office *rejsegodskontor* ⓝ
  rai-se-gaws-kon-tohr
leg *ben* beyn
lesbian a *lesbisk* les-beesk
less *mindre* min-dra
letter (mail) *brev* ⓝ brev
lift (elevator) *elevator* ey-ley-va-tor
light ⓝ *lys* lews
like v *kunne lide* koo-ne lee-dhe
lock ⓝ *lås* laws
long *lang(t)* laang(t)
lost *mistet* mis-tet
lost-property office *hittegodskontor* ⓝ
  hee-te-gaws-kon-tohr
love v *elske* els-ke
luggage *bagage* ba-*gaa*-she
lunch *frokost* froh-kost

M

mail ⓝ *post* post
man *mand* maan
map *kort* ⓝ kort
market *marked* ⓝ maar-kedh
matches *tændstikker* ten-sti-ka
meat *kød* keudh
medicine *medicin* me-dee-*seen*
menu *menu* me-*new*
message *besked* bey-skeydh
milk *mælk* melk
minute *minut* ⓝ mee-*noot*
mobile phone *mobiltelefon* moh-beel-tey-ley-*fohn*
money *penge* peng-e
month *måned* maw-nedh
morning *morgen* mawr-en
mother *mor* mohr
motorcycle *motorcykel* moh-tor-sew-kel
motorway *motorvej* moh-tor-vai
mouth *mund* mawn
music *musik* moo-*seek*

N

name *navn* ⓝ nown
napkin *serviet* seyr-vee-*yet*
nappy *ble* bley
near *nær(t)* ner(t)
neck *hals* hals
new *ny(t)* new(t)
news *nyheder* new-hey-dha

newspaper *avis* a-*vees*
night *nat* nat
no *nej* nai
noisy *støjende* sto-ye-ne
nonsmoking *ikke-ryger* i-ke-*rew*-a
north *nord* nohr
nose *næse* ne-se
now *nu* noo
number *nummer* naw-ma

O

oil (engine) *olie* ohl-ye
old *gammel* gaa-mel
one-way ticket *enkeltbillet* eng-kelt-bee-let
open a *åben(t)* aw-ben(t)
outside *udenfor* oo-dhen-for

P

package *pakke* paa-ke
paper *papir* (n) pa-*peer*
park (car) v *parkere* paar-key-ra
passport *pas* (n) pas
pay *betale* bey-*taa*-le
pen *pen* pen
petrol *benzin* ben-*seen*
pharmacy *apotek* aa-poh-*tek*
phonecard *telefonkort* (n) tey-ley-*fohn*-kort
photo *fotografi* (n) foh-toh-graa-*fee*
plate *tallerken* ta-*ler*-ken
police *politi* (n) poh-lee-*tee*
postcard *postkort* (n) *post*-kort
post office *postkontor* (n) *post*-kon-tohr
pregnant *gravid* graa-*veedh*
price *pris* prees

Q

quiet *stille* sti-le

R

rain n *regn* rain
razor *barbermaskine* baar-beyr-ma-*skee*-ne
receipt n *kvittering* kvee-*tey*-ring
red *rød* reudh
refund n *refundering* rey-foon-*dey*-ring
registered mail *anbefalet post* an-bey-fa-let post
rent v *leje* lai-ye

repair v *reparere* rey-paa-*rey*-ra
reservation *reservation* rey-sa-vaa-*shohn*
restaurant *restaurant* res-toh-*rang*
return v *returnere* rey-toor-*ney*-ra
return ticket *returbillet* rey-toor-bee-let
right (direction) *højre* hoy-re
road *vej* vai
room *værelse* (n) verl-se

S

safe a *sikker(t)* si-ka(t)
sanitary napkin *bind* (n) bin
seat *siddeplads* si-dhe-plas
send *sende* se-ne
service station *benzinstation* ben-*seen*-sta-shohn
sex *sex* seks
shampoo *shampoo* shaam-poh
share (a dorm) *dele* dey-le
shaving cream *barberskum* baar-*beyr*-skawm
she *hun* hoon
sheet (bed) *lagen* (n) *la*-yen
shirt *skjorte* skyor-te
shoes *sko* skoh
shop n *butik* boo-*teek*
short *kort* kort
shower n *brusebad* (n) *broo*-se-badh
single room *enkeltværelse* (n) eng-kelt-verl-se
skin *hud* hoodh
skirt *nederdel* ney-dha-deyl
sleep v *sove* so-ve
slowly *langsomt* laang-somt
small *lille* lee-le
smoke (cigarettes) v *ryge* rew-ye
soap *sæbe* se-be
some *nogle* noh-le
soon *snart* snart
south *syd* sewdh
souvenir shop *souvenirbutik* soo-ve-*neer*-boo-teek
speak v *tale* ta-le
spoon *ske* skey
stamp *frimærke* (n) *free*-mer-ke
stand-by ticket *stand-by billet* stand-*bai* bee-*let*
station (train) *station* sta-*shohn*
stomach *mave* ma-ve
stop v *stoppe* sto-pe
stop (bus) n *busstoppested* (n) *boos*-sto-pe-stedh
street *gade* ga-dhe
student *studerende* stuo-*dey*-re-ne
sun *sol* sohl

O

english–danish

47

sunscreen *solcreme* sohl-kreym
swim v *svømme* sveu-me

T

tampons *tamponer* taam-pong-a
taxi *taxi* tak-see
teaspoon *teske* tey-skey
teeth *tænder* ten-a
telephone n *telefon* tey-ley-fohn
television *fjernsyn* ⓝ fyern-sewn
temperature (weather) *temperatur* tem-praa-toor
tent *telt* ⓝ telt
that (one) *den/det* ⓝ (der) den/dey (deyr)
they *de* dey
thirsty *tørstig(t)* teurs-tee(t)
this (one) *denne/dette* ⓝ (her) de-ne/dey-te (heyr)
throat *hals* hals
ticket *billet* bee-let
time *tid* tidh
tired *træt* tret
tissues *ansigtsservietter* an-sigts-ser-vee-e-ta
today *i dag* ee da
toilet *toilet* toy-let
tomorrow *i morgen* ee morn
tonight *i aften* ee aaf-ten
toothbrush *tandbørste* taan-beurs-te
toothpaste *tandpasta* taan-paas-taa
torch (flashlight) *lygte* lewg-te
tour n *tur* toor
tourist office *turistkontor* ⓝ too-reest-kon-tohr
towel *håndklæde* ⓝ hawn-kle-dhe
train *tog* ⓝ taw
translate *oversætte* o-va-se-te
travel agency *rejseagent* rai-se-a-gent
travellers cheque *rejsecheck* rai-se-shek
trousers *bukser* bawk-sa
twin beds *to senge* toh seng-e
tyre *dæk* ⓝ dek

U

underwear *undertøj* aw-na-toy
urgent *vigtig(t)* vig-tee(t)

V

vacant *ledig(t)* ⓝ ley-dhee(t)
vacation *ferie* feyr-yē
vegetable n *grønsag* greun-saa
vegetarian a *vegetarisk* vey-gey-taa-reesk
visa *visum* ⓝ vee-sawm

W

waiter *tjener* tye-na
walk v *gå* gaw
wallet *pung* pawng
warm a *varm(t)* vaarm(t)
wash (something) *vaske* vas-ke
watch n *ur* ⓝ oor
water *vand* van
we *vi* vee
weekend *weekend* wee-kend
west *vest* vest
wheelchair *kørestol* keu-re-stohl
when *hvornår* vor-nawr
where *hvor* vor
white *hvid* veedh
who *hvem* vem
why *hvorfor* vor-for
wife *kone* koh-ne
window *vindue* ⓝ vin-doo
wine *vin* veen
with *med* medh
without *uden* oo-dhen
woman *kvinde* kvi-ne
write *skrive* skree-ve

Y

yellow *gul* gool
yes *ja* ya
yesterday *i går* ee gawr
you sg inf *du* doo
you sg pol *De* dee
you pl *I* ee

DICTIONARY

T

Dutch

dutch alphabet

A a aa	*B b* bey	*C c* sey	*D d* dey	*E e* ey
F f ef	*G g* khey	*H h* haa	*I i* ee	*J j* yey
K k kaa	*L l* el	*M m* em	*N n* en	*O o* oh
P p pey	*Q q* kew	*R r* er	*S s* es	*T t* tey
U u ew	*V v* vey	*W w* wey	*X x* iks	*Y y* *eep*-see-lon/ey
Z z zet				

dutch

introduction

If you like to indulge in *booze* or *cookies*, have ever tried to *sketch* a *landscape*, are known to *bluff* or act *aloof*, dream of becoming a *mannequin* or going on a *cruise*, hate your *boss*, believe in *Santa Claus*, or you're simply a *Yankee* from *Brooklyn* or *Harlem*, you should know that all these words and many more came from Dutch (*Nederlands* ney-duhr-lants). Dutch is the third largest member of the Germanic language family, after English and German, and shares common roots with these languages. In grammar, in particular, it's close to German, but Dutch pronunciation presents a challenge for German and English speakers alike, due to some unusual sounds it employs.

Don't be confused when you hear the term Flemish (*Vlaams* vlaams) – from a linguistic point of view, it's really the same language as Dutch, but for historical and cultural reasons this is the name often used to refer to the language spoken in the north of Belgium. There are slight differences between this variety and the Dutch spoken in the Netherlands (they are indicated with ⓝ/ⓑ in this chapter). However, both the Netherlands and Belgium are members of the *Nederlandse Taalunie* (Dutch Language Union), the supreme authority on modern language standards. In both countries Dutch has official status (shared in Belgium with French and German).

The boundaries of various local dialects throughout both the Netherlands and Belgium are historical rather than political. The standard language is based on the northern dialects, mainly as spoken around Amsterdam. One of the major influences on the modern language came from the Bible translation of 1637, known as the *Staten-Bijbel*. Dutch is written with the 26-letter Roman alphabet, just like English.

With over 20 million speakers, Dutch has a strong presence on the world linguistic stage. Its global influence came with the expansion of the Dutch empire during the 16th and 17th centuries. Thanks to the explorers and traders who brought Dutch to many corners of the globe, today it has official status in Aruba, the Dutch Antilles and Suriname. There are still Dutch speakers in Indonesia, although the local varieties that developed in this former colony of the Netherlands are now virtually extinct. In New York (formerly known as New Amsterdam), a simplified form of Dutch was still in use during the 18th century. But the greatest achievement of the Dutch linguistic expansion is its famous offspring – Afrikaans, now considered a separate language and spoken by around six million people in South Africa.

pronunciation

vowel sounds

Dutch is rich in vowels – it's important to distinguish between the long and short versions of each vowel sound. There are also a few combined vowels or 'diphthongs' that can be a bit tricky for English speakers to pronounce (eg the öy sound, which has no equivalent in English). If you listen carefully to native speakers and follow our coloured pronunciation guides, you shouldn't have any problems being understood.

symbol	english equivalent	dutch example	transliteration
a	run	*vak*	vak
aa	father	*vaak*	vaak
aw	saw	*lauw, koud*	law, kawt
e	bet	*bed*	bet
ee	see	*niet*	neet
eu	nurse	*leuk*	leuk
ew	ee pronounced with rounded lips	*u, uur*	ew, ewr
ey	as in 'bet', but longer	*beet, reis, mijn*	beyt, reys, meyn
i	hit	*ik*	ik
o	pot	*bot*	bot
oh	**oh**	*boot*	boht
oo	**zoo**	*boer*	boor
öy	her year (without the 'r')	*buik*	böyk
u	put	*hut*	hut
uh	ago	*het, een*	huht, uhn

word stress

There are no universal rules on stress in Dutch. Just follow our pronunciation guides, in which the stressed syllables are indicated with italics.

consonant sounds

Dutch consonants are pretty straightforward to pronounce, as most are identical to those in English. You might need a little practice with the kh sound, which is guttural and harsher than the English 'h' (it sounds like a hiss produced between the tongue and the back roof of the mouth).

symbol	english equivalent	dutch example	transliteration
b	bed	*bed*	bet
ch	cheat	*kindje*	*kin*·chuh
d	dog	*dag*	dakh
f	fat	*fiets*	feets
g	go	*gate*	geyt
h	hat	*hoed*	hoot
k	kit	*klok*	klok
kh	as the 'ch' in the Scottish *loch*	*goed, schat*	khoot, skhat
l	lot	*lied*	leet
m	man	*man*	man
n	not	*niet*	neet
ng	ring	*haring*	*haa*·ring
p	pet	*pot*	pot
r	red (trilled)	*rechts*	rekhs
s	sun	*slapen*	*slaa*·puhn
sh	shot	*alsjeblieft*	a·*shuh*·*bleeft*
t	top	*tafel*	*taa*·fuhl
v	very	*vlucht*	vlukht
w	win	*water*	*waa*·tuhr
y	yes	*je*	yuh
z	zero	*zomer*	*zoh*·muhr
zh	pleasure	*garage*	kha·*raa*·zhuh

basics

language difficulties

Do you speak English?
Spreekt u Engels? pol
spreykt ew *eng*·uhls

Do you understand?
Begrijpt u? pol
buh·*khreypt* ew

I (don't) understand.
Ik begrijp het (niet).
ik buh·*khreyp* huht (neet)

What does (*verboden*) mean?
Wat betekent (verboden)?
wat buh·*tey*·kuhnt (vuhr·*boh*·duhn)

Could you please speak more slowly?
Kunt u alstublieft wat
kunt ew al·stew·*bleeft* wat
trager spreken? pol
traa·khuhr *sprey*·kuhn

How do you ...?
Hoe ...?
hoo ...
  pronounce this
  spreek je dit uit
  spreyk yuh dit öyt
  write (*dank u wel*)
  schrijf je (dank u wel)
  skhreyf yuh (dangk ew wel)

Could you
Kunt u dat
kunt ew dat
please ...?
alstublieft ...? pol
al·stew·*bleeft* ...
  repeat that
  herhalen
  her·*haa*·luhn
  write it down
  opschrijven
  op·skhrey·vuhn

essentials

Yes.	*Ja.*	yaa
No.	*Nee.*	ney
Please.	*Alstublieft.* pol	al·stew·*bleeft*
	Alsjeblieft. inf	a·shuh·*bleeft*
Thank you	*Dank u (wel).* pol	dangk ew (wel)
(very much).	*Dank je (wel).* inf	dangk yuh (wel)
Thanks.	*Bedankt.*	buh·*dangt*
You're welcome.	*Graag gedaan.*	khraakh khuh·*daan*
Excuse me.	*Pardon.*	par·*don*
Sorry.	*Sorry.*	*so*·ree

numbers

0	*nul*	nul		16	*zestien*	zes·teen	
1	*één*	eyn		17	*zeventien*	zey·vuhn·teen	
2	*twee*	twey		18	*achttien*	akh·teen	
3	*drie*	dree		19	*negentien*	ney·khuhn·teen	
4	*vier*	veer		20	*twintig*	twin·tikh	
5	*vijf*	veyf		21	*eenentwintig*	eyn·en·twin·tikh	
6	*zes*	zes		22	*tweeëntwintig*	twey·en·twin·tikh	
7	*zeven*	zey·vuhn		30	*dertig*	der·tikh	
8	*acht*	akht		40	*veertig*	feyr·tikh	
9	*negen*	ney·khuhn		50	*vijftig*	feyf·tikh	
10	*tien*	teen		60	*zestig*	ses·tikh	
11	*elf*	elf		70	*zeventig*	sey·vuhn·tikh	
12	*twaalf*	twaalf		80	*tachtig*	tukh·tikh	
13	*dertien*	der·teen		90	*negentig*	ney·khuhn·tikh	
14	*veertien*	veyr·teen		100	*honderd*	hon·duhrt	
15	*vijftien*	veyf·teen		1000	*duizend*	döy·zuhnt	

time & dates

What time is it?	*Hoe laat is het?*	hoo laat is huht
It's one o'clock.	*Het is één uur.*	huht is eyn ewr
It's (two) o'clock.	*Het is (twee) uur.*	huht is (twey) ewr
Quarter past (one).	*Kwart over (één).*	kwart oh·vuhr (eyn)
Half past (one).	*Half (twee). (lit: half two)*	half (twey)
Quarter to (eight).	*Kwart voor (acht).*	kwart vohr (akht)
At what time ...?	*Hoe laat ...?*	hoo laat ...
At ...	*Om ...*	om ...
in the morning	*'s morgens/'s ochtends*	smor·khuhns/sokh·tuhns
in the afternoon	*'s middags*	smi·dakhs
in the evening	*'s avonds*	saa·vonts
Monday	*maandag*	maan·dakh
Tuesday	*dinsdag*	dins·dakh
Wednesday	*woensdag*	woons·dakh
Thursday	*donderdag*	don·duhr·dakh
Friday	*vrijdag*	vrey·dakh
Saturday	*zaterdag*	zaa·tuhr·dakh
Sunday	*zondag*	zon·dakh

basics – DUTCH

January	*januari*	ya-new-*waa*-ree
February	*februari*	fey-brew-*waa*-ree
March	*maart*	maart
April	*april*	a-*pril*
May	*mei*	mey
June	*juni*	*yew*-nee
July	*juli*	*yew*-lee
August	*augustus*	aw-*khus*-tus
September	*september*	sep-*tem*-buhr
October	*oktober*	ok-*toh*-buhr
November	*november*	noh-*vem*-buhr
December	*december*	dey-*sem*-buhr

What date is it today?
De hoeveelste is het vandaag?   duh hoo-*veyl*-stuh is huht van-*daakh*

It's (9 January).
Het is (negen januari).   huht is (*ney*-khuhn ya-new-*waa*-ree)

since (May)	*sinds (mei)*	sins (mey)
until (June)	*tot (juni)*	tot (*yew*-nee)

yesterday	*gisteren*	*khis*-tuh-ruhn
today	*vandaag*	van-*daakh*
tonight (before midnight)	*vanavond*	va-*naa*-vont
tonight (after midnight)	*vannacht*	va-*nakht*
tomorrow	*morgen*	*mor*-khuhn

last/next night (before midnight)	*gisteravond/ morgenavond*	*khis*-tuhr-*aa*-vont/ *mor*-khuhn-*aa*-vont
last/next year	*vorig/komend jaar*	*voh*-rikh/*koh*-muhnt yaar

last/next ...	*vorige/komende ...*	*voh*-ri-khuh/*koh*-muhn-duh ...
night (after midnight)	*nacht*	nakht
week	*week*	weyk
month	*maand*	maant

yesterday/tomorrow ...	*gister-/morgen- ...*	*khis*-tuhr-/*mor*-khuhn- ...
morning	*ochtend*	*okh*-tuhnt
afternoon	*middag*	*mi*-dakh
evening	*avond*	*aa*-vont

weather

What's the weather like?
Hoe is het weer?   hoo is huht weyr

It's ...	*Het is ...*	huht is ...
cloudy	*bewolkt*	buh·*wolkt*
cold	*koud*	kawt
foggy	*mistig*	*mis*·tikh
hot	*zeer warm*	zeyr warm
rainy	*regenachtig*	*rey*·khuhn·akh·tikh
sunny	*zonnig*	*zo*·nikh
warm	*warm*	warm

It's ...	*Het ...*	huht ...
freezing	*vriest*	vreest
raining	*regent*	*rey*·khuhnt
snowing	*sneeuwt*	sneywt
windy	*waait*	waayt

spring	*lente*	*len*·tuh
summer	*zomer*	*zoh*·muhr
autumn	*herfst*	herfst
winter	*winter*	*win*·tuhr

border crossing

I'm here ...	*Ik ben hier ...*	ik ben heer ...
in transit	*op doorreis*	op *doh*·reys
on business	*voor zaken*	vohr *zaa*·kuhn
on holiday	*met vakantie*	met va·*kan*·see

I'm here for ...	*Ik ben hier voor ...*	ik ben heer vohr ...
(10) days	*(tien) dagen*	(teen) *daa*·khuhn
(three) weeks	*(drie) weken*	(dree) *wey*·kuhn
(two) months	*(twee) maanden*	(twey) *maan*·duhn

I'm going to (Den Helder).
Ik ben op weg naar (Den Helder).   ik ben op wekh naar (duhn *hel*·duhr)

I'm staying at the (Hotel Industrie).
Ik verblijf in (Hotel Industrie).   ik vuhr·*bleyf* in (hoh·*tel* in·dus·*tree*)

I have nothing to declare.
Ik heb niets aan te geven.   ik hep neets aan tuh *khey*·vuhn

I have something to declare.
Ik heb iets aan te geven.   ik hep eets aan tuh *khey*·vuhn

That's (not) mine.
Dat is (niet) van mij.   dat is (neet) van mey

I didn't know I had to declare it.
Ik wist niet dat ik het   ik wist neet dat ik huht
moest aangeven.   moost *aan*·khey·vuhn

transport

tickets & luggage

Where can I buy a ticket?
Waar kan ik een kaartje/ticket   waar kan ik uhn *kaar*·chuh/ti·*ket*
kopen? ⊗/℗   *koh*·puhn

Do I need to book a seat?
Moet ik een zitplaats reserveren?   moot ik uhn *zit*·plaats rey·zer·*vey*·ruhn

One ... (to Antwerp), please.	Een ... (naar Antwerpen) graag.	uhn ... (naar *ant*·wer·puhn) khraakh
one-way ticket	enkele reis	*eng*·kuh·luh reys
return ticket	retourtje	ruh·*toor*·chuh

I'd like to ... my ticket, please.	Ik wil graag mijn kaartje/ticket ... ⊗/℗	ik wil khraakh meyn *kaar*·chuh/ti·*ket* ...
cancel	annuleren	a·new·*ley*·ruhn
change	wijzigen	*wey*·zi·khuhn
collect	afhalen	*af*·haa·luhn
confirm	bevestigen	buh·*ves*·ti·khuhn

How much is it?
Hoeveel kost het?   hoo·*veyl* kost huht

Is there air conditioning?
Is er airconditioning?   is uhr *eyr*·kon·di·shuh·ning

Is there a toilet?
Is er een toilet?   is uhr uhn twa·*let*

How long does the trip take?
Hoe lang duurt de reis?   hoo lang dewrt duh reys

Is it a direct route?
Is het een rechtstreekse verbinding?   is huht uhn *rekh*·streyk·suh vuhr·*bin*·ding

I'd like a luggage locker.
Ik wil graag een bagagekluis.   ik wil khraakh uhn ba·*khaa*·zhuh·klöys

My luggage has been ...	*Mijn bagage is ...*	meyn ba·*khaa*·zhuh is ...
damaged	*beschadigd*	buh·*skhaa*·dikht
lost	*verloren*	vuhr·*loh*·ruhn
stolen	*gestolen*	khuh·*stoh*·luhn

getting around

Where does flight (KL1082) arrive?
Waar komt vlucht   waar komt vlukht
(KL1082) aan?   (kaa el teen *twey*·en·takh·tikh) aan

Where does flight (KL1083) depart?
Waar vertrekt vlucht   waar vuhr·*trekt* vlukht
(KL1083)?   (kaa el teen *dree*·en·takh·tikh)

Where's (the) ...?	*Waar is ...?*	waar is ...
arrivals hall	*de aankomsthal*	duh *aan*·komst·hal
departures hall	*de vertrekhal*	duh vuhr·*trek*·hal
duty-free shop	*de duty-free*	duh dew·tee·*free*
gate (12)	*gate (twaalf)*	geyt (twaalf)

| **Is this the ... to** | *Is dit ... naar* | is dit ... naar |
(Amsterdam)?	*(Amsterdam)?*	(am·stuhr·*dam*)
boat	*de boot*	duh boht
bus	*de bus*	duh bus
plane	*het vliegtuig*	huht *vleekh*·töykh
train	*de trein*	duh treyn

| **What time's** | *Hoe laat gaat* | hoo laat khaat |
the ... bus?	*de ... bus?*	duh ... bus
first	*eerste*	*eyr*·stuh
last	*laatste*	*laat*·stuh
next	*volgende*	*vol*·khuhn·duh

transport – DUTCH

At what time does (the train) leave?
Hoe laat vertrekt (de trein)?   hoo laat vuhr-*trekt* (duh treyn)

At what time does (the train) arrive?
Hoe laat komt (de trein) aan?   hoo laat komt (duh treyn) aan

How long will it be delayed?
Hoeveel vertraging is er?   hoo-*veyl* vuhr-*traa*-khing is uhr

What station is this?
Welk station is dit?   welk sta-*syon* is dit

What stop is this?
Welke stop is dit?   *wel*-kuh stop is dit

What's the next station?
Welk is het volgende station?   welk is huht *vol*-khuhn-duh sta-*syon*

What's the next stop?
Welk is de volgende stop?   welk is duh *vol*-khuhn-duh stop

Does it stop at (Berchem)?
Stopt het in (Berchem)?   stopt huht in (*ber*-khuhm)

Please tell me when we get to (Dordrecht).
Kunt u me laten weten wanneer   kunt ew muh *laa*-tuhn *wey*-tuhn wa-*neyr*
we in (Dordrecht) aankomen? pol   wuh in (*dor*-drekht) *aan*-koh-muhn

How long do we stop here?
Hoe lang houden we hier halt?   hoo lang *haw*-duhn wuh heer halt

Is this seat available?
Is deze zitplaats vrij?   is *dey*-zuh *zit*-plaats vrey

That's my seat.
Dat is mijn zitplaats.   dat is meyn *zit*-plaats

I'd like a taxi ...	*Ik wil graag een taxi ...*	ik wil khraakh uhn *tak*-see ...
at (9am)	*om (negen uur*	om (*ney*-khuhn ewr
	's morgens)	smor-khuhns)
now	*nu*	new
tomorrow	*voor morgen*	vohr *mor*-khuhn

Is this taxi available?
   Is deze taxi vrij?   is *dey*·zuh *tak*·see vrey

How much is it to ...?
   Hoeveel kost het naar ...?   hoo·*veyl* kost huht naar ...

Please take me to (this address).
   Breng me alstublieft naar   breng muh al·stew·*bleeft* naar
   (dit adres). pol   (dit a·*dres*)

Please slow down.
   Rijd alstublieft wat langzamer. pol   reyt al·stew·*bleeft* wat *lang*·zaa·muhr

Please stop here.
   Stop hier alstublieft. pol   stop heer al·stew·*bleeft*

Please wait here.
   Wacht hier alstublieft. pol   wakht heer al·stew·*bleeft*

car, motorbike & bicycle hire

I'd like to hire a ...	*Ik wil graag een ...*	ik wil khraakh uhn ...
	huren.	*hew*·ruhn
bicycle	*fiets*	feets
car	*auto*	*aw*·toh
motorbike	*motorfiets*	*moh*·tor·feets
with ...	*met ...*	met ...
air conditioning	*airconditioning*	*eyr*·kon·di·shuh·ning
antifreeze	*antivries*	an·tee·*vrees*
snow chains	*sneeuwkettingen*	*sneyw*·ke·ting·uhn
How much for ... hire?	*Hoeveel is het per ...?*	hoo·*veyl* is huht puhr ...
hourly	*uur*	ewr
daily	*dag*	dakh
weekly	*week*	weyk
How much is it per ...?	*Hoeveel is het per ...?*	hoo·*veyl* is huht puhr ...
morning	*ochtend*	*okh*·tuhnt
afternoon	*middag*	*mi*·dakh
air	*lucht*	lukht
oil	*olie*	*oh*·lee
petrol	*benzine*	ben·*zee*·nuh
tyres	*banden*	*ban*·duhn

I need a mechanic.
Ik heb een monteur/mecanicien   ik hep uhn mon-*teur*/mey-ka-nee-*sye*
nodig. ⑬/⑯   noh-dikh

I've run out of petrol.
Ik zit zonder benzine.   ik zit *zon*-duhr ben-*zee*-nuh

I have a flat tyre.
Ik heb een lekke band.   ik hep uhn *le*-kuh bant

directions

Where's the ...?	*Waar is ...?*	waar is ...
bank	*de bank*	duh bangk
city centre	*het stadscentrum*	huht *stat*-sen-truhm
hotel	*het hotel*	huht hoh-*tel*
market	*de markt*	duh mart
police station	*het politiebureau*	huht po-*leet*-see-bew-roh
post office	*het postkantoor*	huht *post*-kan-tohr
public toilet	*het openbaar toilet*	huht *oh*-puhn-baar twa-*let*
tourist office	*de VVV* ⑬	duh vey-vey-*vey*
	het toerismebureau ⑯	huht too-*ris*-muh-bew-roh

Is this the road to (Katwijk)?
Gaat deze weg naar (Katwijk)?   khaat *dey*-zuh wekh naar (*kat*-weyk)

Can you show me (on the map)?
Kunt u het aanwijzen   kunt ew huht *aan*-wey-zuhn
(op de kaart)? pol   (op duh kaart)

What's the address?
Wat is het adres?   wat is huht a-*dres*

How far is it?
Hoe ver is het?   hoo ver is huht

How do I get there?
Hoe kom ik er?   hoo kom ik uhr

Can I get there by (bicycle)?
Kun je er met de (fiets) heen?   kun yuh uhr met duh (feets) heyn

Turn left/right ...	Sla linksaf/rechtsaf ...	slaa *lings*·af/*rekhs*·af ...
at the corner	op de hoek	op duh hook
at the traffic lights	bij de verkeerslichten	bey duh vuhr·*keyrs*·likh·tuhn

It's ...	Het is ...	huht is ...
behind ...	achter ...	*akh*·tuhr ...
far away	ver	ver
here	hier	heer
in front of ...	voor ...	vohr ...
left	links	lingks
near	dichtbij	dikht·*bey*
near to ...	dicht bij ...	dikht bey ...
next to ...	naast ...	naast ...
opposite ...	tegenover ...	tey·khuh·*noh*·vuhr ...
right	rechts	rekhs
straight ahead	rechtdoor	rekh·*dohr*
there	daar	daar

north	noord	nohrt
south	zuid	zöyt
east	oost	ohst
west	west	west

by bicycle	met de fiets	met duh feets
by bus	met de bus	met duh bus
by taxi	met de taxi	met duh *tak*·see
by train	met de trein	met duh treyn
on foot	te voet	tuh voot

signs

Ingang/Uitgang	in·khang/*öyt*·khang	Entrance/Exit
Open/Gesloten	oh·puhn/khuh·*sloh*·tuhn	Open/Closed
Kamers Vrij	kaa·muhrs vrey	Rooms Available
Volzet	vol·*zet*	No Vacancies
Inlichtingen	in·likh·ting·uhn	Information
Politiebureau	po·*leet*·see·bew·roh	Police Station
Verboden	vuhr·*boh*·duhn	Prohibited
Toiletten/WC's	twa·*le*·tuhn/wey·*seys*	Toilets
Heren	hey·ruhn	Men
Dames	daa·muhs	Women
Warm/Koud	warm/kawt	Hot/Cold

accommodation

finding accommodation

Where's a ...?	*Waar vind ik een ...?*	waar vint ik uhn ...
camping ground	*camping*	*kem*·ping
guesthouse	*pension*	pen·*syon*
hotel	*hotel*	hoh·*tel*
youth hostel	*jeugdherberg*	*yeukht*·her·berkh

Can you recommend	*Kunt u iets ...*	kunt ew eets ...
somewhere ...?	*aanbevelen?* pol	*aan*·buh·vey·luhn
cheap	*goedkoops*	khoot·*kohps*
good	*goeds*	khoots
nearby	*dichtbij*	dikht·*bey*

I'd like to book a room, please.
Ik wil graag een kamer reserveren.   ik wil khraakh uhn *kaa*·muhr rey·zer·*vey*·ruhn

I have a reservation.
Ik heb een reservatie.   ik hep uhn rey·zer·*vaa*·see

My name's ...
Mijn naam is ...   meyn naam is ...

Do you have a ... room?	*Heeft u een ...?* pol	heyft ew uhn ...
single	*eenpersoonskamer*	*eyn*·puhr·sohns·kaa·muhr
double	*tweepersoonskamer*	*twey*·puhr·sohns·kaa·muhr
	met een dubbel bed	met uhn *du*·buhl bet
twin	*tweepersoonskamer*	*twey*·puhr·sohns·kaa·muhr
	met twee enkele	met twey *eng*·kuh·luh
	bedden	be·duhn

How much is it per ...?	*Hoeveel is het per ...?*	hoo·*veyl* is huht puhr ...
night	*nacht*	nakht
person	*persoon*	puhr·*sohn*

Can I pay ...?	*Kan ik met ... betalen?*	kan ik met ... buh·*taa*·luhn
by credit card	*mijn kredietkaart*	meyn krey·*deet*·kaart
with a travellers	*een reischeque*	uhn *reys*·shek
cheque		

I'd like to stay for (two) nights.
(Twee) overnachtingen graag.   (twey) oh·vuhr·*nakh*·ting·uhn khraakh

From (2 July) to (6 July).
Van (twee juli) tot (zes juli).   van (twey *yew*·lee) tot (zes *yew*·lee)

Can I see it?
Kan I ee een kijkje nemen?   kan ik uhn *keyk*·yuh *ney*·muhn

Am I allowed to camp here?
Mag ik hier kamperen?   makh ik heer kam·*pey*·ruhn

Is there a camping ground nearby?
Is er een camping in de buurt?   is uhr uhn *kem*·ping in duh bewrt

requests & queries

When's breakfast served?
Hoe laat wordt het ontbijt   hoo laat wort huht ont·*beyt*
geserveerd?   khuh·ser·*veyrt*

Where's breakfast served?
Waar wordt het ontbijt geserveerd?   waar wort huht ont·*beyt* khuh·ser·*veyrt*

Please wake me at (seven).
Maak mij wakker om (zeven) uur   maak mey *wa*·kuhr om (*zey*·vuhn) ewr
alstublieft. pol   al·stew·*bleeft*

Could I have my key, please?
Kan ik mijn sleutel hebben   kan ik meyn *sleu*·tuhl *he*·buhn
alstublieft? pol   al·stew·*bleeft*

Can I get another (blanket)?
Kan ik een nog een (deken)   kan ik nokh uhn (*dey*·kuhn)
hebben alstublieft? pol   *he*·buhn al·stew·*bleeft*

Is there an elevator/a safe?
Heeft u een lift/kluis? pol   heyft ew uhn lift/klüys

The room is too ...	*De kumer is te ...*	duh *kaa*·muhr is tuh ...
expensive	*duur*	dewr
noisy	*lawaaierig*	la·*waa*·yuh·rikh
small	*klein*	kleyn

The ... doesn't work.	*... is stuk.*	... is stuk
air conditioning	*De airconditioning*	duh *eyr*·kon·di·shuh·ning
fan	*De ventilator*	duh ven·tee·*laa*·tor
toilet	*Het toilet*	huht twa·*let*

This ... isn't clean.	*... is niet schoon.*	... is neet skhohn
pillow	*Dit kussen*	dit *ku*·suhn
sheet	*Dit laken*	dit *laa*·kuhn
towel	*Deze handdoek*	*dey*·zuh han·dook

checking out

What time is checkout?
Hoe laat is het uitchecken?   hoo laat is huht *öyt*-che-kuhn

Can I leave my luggage here?
Kan ik mijn bagage hier laten?   kan ik meyn ba-*khaa*-zhuh heer *laa*-tuhn

Could I have my ..., please? pol	Kan ik mijn ... hebben alstublieft?	kan ik meyn ... he-buhn al-stew-bleeft
deposit	borg	borkh
passport	paspoort	pas-pohrt
valuables	waardevolle bezittingen	waar-duh-vo-luh buh-zi-ting-uhn

communications & banking

the internet

Where's the local Internet café?
Waar is het plaatselijke internetcafé?   waar is huht *plaat*-suh-luh-kuh *in*-tuhr-net-ka-fey

How much is it per hour?
Hoeveel is het per uur?   hoo-*veyl* is huht puhr ewr

I'd like to ...	Ik wil graag ...	ik wil khraakh ...
check my email	mijn e-mails checken	meyn *ee*-meyls *che*-kuhn
get Internet access	op het internet gaan	op huht *in*-tuhr-net khaan
use a printer	een printer gebruiken	uhn *prin*-tuhr khuh-*bröy*-kuhn
use a scanner	een scanner gebruiken	uhn *ska*-nuhr khuh-*bröy*-kuhn

mobile/cell phone

I'd like a ...	Ik wil graag een ...	ik wil khraakh uhn ...
mobile/cell phone for hire	mobiele telefoon huren Ⓝ	moh-*bee*-luh tey-ley-*fohn* hew-ruhn
	GSM huren Ⓑ	khey-es-*em* hew-ruhn
SIM card for your network	sim-kaart voor uw netwerk	*sim*-kaart vohr ew *net*-werk

What are the rates?   *Wat zijn de tarieven?*   wat zeyn duh ta-*ree*-vuhn

telephone

What's your phone number?
Wat is uw/jouw   wat is ew/yaw
telefoonnummer? pol/inf   tey·ley·*foh*·nu·muhr

The number is ...
Het nummer is ...   huht *nu*·muhr is ...

Where's the nearest public phone?
Waar is de dichstbijzijnde   waar is duh dikhs·bey·*zeyn*·duh
openbare telefoon?   oh·puhn·*baa*·ruh tey·ley·*fohn*

I'd like to buy a phonecard.
Ik wil graag een telefoonkaart   ik wil khraakh uhn tey·ley·*fohn*·kaart
kopen.   *koh*·puhn

I want to ...	*Ik wil ...*	ik wil ...
call (Ireland)	*(Ierland) bellen*	*(eer·*lant) be·luhn
make a local call	*een lokaal telefoon-*	uhn loh·*kaal* tey·ley·*fohn*·
	gesprek maken	khuh·*sprek maa*·kuhn
reverse the	*dat de ontvanger*	dat duh ont·*vang*·uhr
charges	*betaalt*	buh·*taalt*

How much does	*Hoeveel kost ...?*	hoo·*veyl* kost ...
... cost?		
a (three)-minute	*een gesprek van*	uhn khuh·*sprek* van
call	*(drie) minuten*	(dree) mee·*new*·tuhn
each extra	*het per extra*	huht puhr *eks*·traa
minute	*minuut*	mee·*newt*

(One euro) per minute. *(Één euro) per minuut.* (eyn *ew*·roh) puhr mee·*newt*

post office

I want to send a ...	*Ik wil een ... sturen.*	ik wil uhn ... *stew*·ruhn
fax	*fax*	faks
letter	*brief*	breef
parcel	*pakje*	*pak*·yuh
postcard	*ansichtkaart*	*an*·sikht·kaart

I want to buy a/an ...	*Ik wil een ... kopen.*	ik wil uhn ... *koh*·puhn
envelope	*envelop*	en·vuh·*lop*
stamp	*postzegel*	*post*·zey·khuhl

Please send it (to Australia) by ...	Stuur het alstublieft (naar Australië) per ... pol	stewr huht al-stew-bleeft (naar aw-straa-lee-yuh) puhr ...
airmail	luchtpost	lukht-post
express mail	exprespost	eks-pres-post
registered mail	aangetekende post	aan-khuh-tey-kuhn-duh post
surface mail	gewone post	khuh-woh-nuh post
Is there any mail for me?	Is er post voor mij?	is uhr post vohr mey

bank

Where's a/an ...?	Waar vind ik een ...?	waar vint ik uhn ...
ATM	pin-automaat ⓝ	pin-aw-toh-maat
	geldautomaat ⓑ	khelt-aw-toh-maat
foreign exchange office	wisselkantoor	wi-suhl-kan-tohr

I'd like to ...	Ik wil graag ...	ik wil khraakh ...
Where can I ...?	Waar kan ik ...?	waar kan ik ...
arrange a transfer	geld overmaken	khelt oh-vuhr-maa-kuhn
cash a cheque	een cheque innen	uhn shek i-nuhn
change a travellers cheque	een reischeque innen	uhn reys-shek i-nuhn
change money	geld wisselen	khelt wi-suh-luhn
get a cash advance	een voorschot bekomen	uhn vohr-skhot buh-koh-muhn
withdraw money	geld afhalen	khelt af-haa-luhn

What's the ...?	Wat is de ...?	wat is duh ...
charge for that	kost hiervoor	kost heer-vohr
commission	commissie	ko-mi-see
exchange rate	wisselkoers	wi-suhl-koors

It's ...	Het is ...	huht is ...
(12) euros	(twaalf) euro	(twaalf) ew-roh
free	gratis	khraa-tis

What time does the bank open?
Hoe laat gaat de bank open? hoo laat khaat duh bangk oh-puhn

Has my money arrived yet?
Is mijn geld al aangekomen? is meyn khelt al aan-khuh-koh-muhn

sightseeing

getting in

What time does it open/close?
Hoe laat gaat het open/dicht?   hoo laat khaat huht *oh*-puhn/dikht

What's the admission charge?
Wat is de toegangsprijs?   wat is duh *too*-khangs-preys

Is there a discount for students/children?
Is er korting voor studenten/   is uhr *kor*-ting vohr stew-*den*-tuhn/
kinderen?   *kin*-duh-ruhn

I'd like a ...	*Ik wil graag een ...*	ik wil khraakh uhn ...
catalogue	*cataloog*	ka-ta-*lohkh*
guide	*gids*	khits
map (building)	*plattegrond*	pla-tuh-*khront*
map (town)	*kaart*	kaart

I'd like to see ...   *Ik wil graag ... zien.*   ik wil khraakh ... zeen
What's that?   *Wat is dat?*   wat is dat
Can I take a photo?   *Mag ik een foto nemen?*   makh ik uhn *foh*-toh *ney*-muhn

tours

When's the	*Wanneer is de*	wa-*neyr* is duh
next ...?	*volgende ...?*	*vol*-khuhn-duh ...
day trip	*daguitstap*	dakh-öyt-stap
tour	*rondleiding*	ront-ley-ding

Is ... included?	*Is ... inbegrepen?*	is ... in-buh-*khrey*-puhn
accommodation	*accommodatie*	a-koh-moh-*daa*-see
the admission	*de toegangsprijs*	duh *too*-khangs-preys
charge		
food	*het eten*	huht *ey*-tuhn
transport	*het transport*	huht trans-*port*

How long is the tour?
Hoe lang duurt de rondleiding?   hoo lang dewrt duh ront-*ley*-ding

What time should we be back?
Hoe laat moeten we terug zijn?   hoo laat *moo*-tuhn wuh tuh-*rukh* zeyn

sightseeing

bridge	brug	brukh
castle	kasteel n	kas·teyl
cathedral	kathedraal	ka·tey·draal
church	kerk	kerk
main square	stadsplein n	stats·pleyn
(wind)mill	(wind)molen	(wint·)moh·luhn
monastery	klooster n	kloh·stuhr
monument	monument n	mo·new·ment
museum	museum n	mew·see·yum
old city	oude stad	aw·duh stat
palace	paleis n	pa·leys
ruins	ruines	rwee·nuhs
stadium	stadion n	staa·dyon
statue	standbeeld n	stant·beylt

shopping

enquiries

Where's a ... ?	Waar vind ik een ...?	waar vint ik uhn ...
bank	bank	bangk
bookshop	boekhandel	book·han·duhl
camera shop	fotozaak	foh·toh·zaak
department store	warenhuis ⓝ	waa·ruhn·höys
	grootwarenhuis ⓑ	khroht·waa·ruhn·höys
grocery store	kruidenier	kröy·duh·neer
market	markt	mart
newsagency	krantenzaak	kran·tuhn·zaak
supermarket	supermarkt	sew·puhr·mart

Where can I buy (a padlock)?
Waar kan ik (een hangslot) kopen?   waar kan ik (uhn hang·slot) koh·puhn

I'm looking for ...
Ik ben op zoek naar ...   ik ben op zook naar ...

Can I look at it?
Kan ik het even zien?   kan ik huht ey·vuhn zeen

Do you have any others?
Heeft u nog andere? pol   heyft ew nokh *an*·duh·ruh

Does it have a guarantee?
Komt het met garantie?   komt huht met kha·*ran*·see

Can I have it sent abroad?
Kan ik het naar het buitenland   kan ik huht naar huht *böy*·tuhn·lant
sturen?   *stew*·ruhn

Can I have my ... repaired here?
Kan ik mijn ... hier laten herstellen?   kan ik meyn ... heer *laa*·tuhn her·*ste*·luhn

It's faulty.
Het werkt niet.   huht werkt neet

I'd like ..., please.   *Ik wil graag ...*   ik wil khraakh ...
     a bag   *een draagtasje*   uhn *draakh*·ta·shuh
     a refund   *mijn geld terug*   meyn gelt tuh·*rukh*
     to return this   *dit retourneren*   dit ruh·toor·*ney*·ruhn

paying

How much is it?
Hoeveel kost het?   hoo·*veyl* kost huht

Can you write down the price?
Kunt u de prijs opschrijven? pol   kunt ew duh preys *op*·skhrey·vuhn

That's too expensive.
Dat is te duur.   dat is tuh dewr

What's your lowest price?
Wat is uw beste prijs? pol   wat is ew *bes*·tuh preys

I'll give you (five) euros.
Ik wil er (vijf) euro voor betalen.   ik wil uhr (veyf) *ew*·roh vohr buh·*taa*·luhn

There's a mistake in the bill.
Er zit een fout in de rekening.   uhr zit eyn fawt in duh *rey*·kuh·ning

Do you accept ...?   *Accepteert u ...?* pol   ak·sep·*teyrt* ew ...
     credit cards   *kredietkaarten*   krey·*deet*·kaar·tuhn
     debit cards   *debetkaarten*   *dey*·bet·kaar·tuhn
     travellers cheques   *reischeques*   *reys*·sheks

I'd like ..., please.   *Ik wil graag ...*   ik wil khraakh ...
     a receipt   *een kwitantie*   uhn kwee·*tan*·see
     my change   *mijn wisselgeld*   meyn *wi*·suhl·gelt

clothes & shoes

Can I try it on?	Kan ik het passen?	kan ik huht pa·suhn
My size is (40).	Ik heb maat (veertig).	ik hep maat (feyr·tikh)
It doesn't fit.	Het past niet.	huht past neet
small	small	smal
medium	medium	mey·dyum
large	large	larsh

books & music

I'd like a ...	Ik wil graag een ...	ik wil khraakh uhn ...
newspaper	krant	krant
(in English)	(in het Engels)	(in huht eng·uhls)
pen	balpen	bal·pen

Is there an English-language bookshop?
Is er een Engelstalige boekhandel? is uhr uhn eng·uhls·taa·li·khuh book·han·duhl

I'm looking for something by (Hugo Claus).
Ik ben op zoek naar iets van ik ben op zook naar eets van
(Hugo Claus). (hew·khoh klaws)

Can I listen to this?
Kan ik hier naar dit luisteren? kan ik heer naar dit löy·stuh·ruhn

photography

Could you ...?	Kunt u ...? pol	kunt ew ...
burn a CD from	deze geheugenkaart	dey·zuh khuh·heu·khuhn·kaart
my memory card	op cd zetten	op sey·dey ze·tuhn
develop this film	deze film ontwikkelen	dey·zuh film ont·wi·kuh·luhn
load my film	mijn film laden	meyn film laa·duhn
I need a/an ... film	Ik heb een ... nodig	ik hep uhn ... noh·dikh
for this camera.	voor dit fototoestel.	vohr dit foh·toh·too·stel
APS	APS film	aa·pey·es film
B&W	zwart-wit film	zwart·wit film
colour	kleurenfilm	kleu·ruhn·film
slide	diafilm	dee·ya·film
(200) speed	film van	film van
	(tweehonderd) ASA	(twey·hon·duhrt) aa·sa
When will it be ready?	Wanneer is het klaar?	wa·neyr is huht klaar

meeting people

greetings, goodbyes & introductions

Hello/Hi.	Goedendag/Dag/Hallo.	khoo-duh-dakh/dakh/ha-loh
Good evening.	Goedenavond.	khoo-duh-naa-vont
Good night.	Goedenacht.	khoo-duh-nakht
Goodbye/Bye.	Dag.	dakh
See you later.	Tot ziens.	tot seens
Mr	Meneer	muh-neyr
Mrs	Mevrouw	muh-vraw
Miss	Juffrouw	yu-fraw

How are you?
   Hoe gaat het met u/jou? pol/inf   hoo khaat huht met ew/yaw

Fine. And you?
   Goed. En met u/jou? pol/inf   khoot en met ew/yaw

What's your name?
   Hoe heet u/je? pol/inf   hoo heyt ew/yuh

My name is ...
   Ik heet ...   ik heyt ...

I'm pleased to meet you.
   Aangenaam.   aan-khuh-naam

This is my ...	Dit is mijn ...	dit is meyn ...
boyfriend	vriend	vreent
brother	broer	broor
daughter	dochter	dokh-tuhr
father	vader	vaa-duhr
fiancé(e)	verloofde	vuhr-lohf-duh
friend	vriend/vriendin m/f	vreent/vreen-din
girlfriend	vriendin	vreen-din
husband	man	man
mother	moeder	moo-duhr
partner (intimate)	partner	part-nuhr
sister	zus	zus
son	zoon	zohn
wife	vrouw	vraw

meeting people – DUTCH

Here's my ...	Dit is mijn ...	dit is meyn ...
What's your ...?	Wat is uw/	wat is ew/
	jouw ...? pol/inf	yaw ...
address	adres	a·dres
email address	e-mailadres	ee·meyl·a·dres
fax number	faxnummer	faks·nu·muhr
phone number	telefoonnummer	tey·ley·foh·nu·muhr

occupations

What's your occupation?

Wat is uw/jouw beroep? pol/inf   wat is ew/yaw buh·*roop*

I'm a/an ...	Ik ben ...	ik ben ...
artist	kunstenaar m	kun·stuh·naar
	kunstenares f	kun·stuh·naa·*res*
businessperson	zakenman m	zaa·kuh·man
	zakenvrouw f	zaa·kuh·vraw
farmer	boer/boerin m/f	boor/boo·*rin*
manual worker	arbeider m	ar·bey·duhr
	arbeidster f	ar·beyt·stuhr
scientist	wetenschapper m&f	wey·tuhn·skha·puhr
student	student m&f	stew·*dent*

background

Where are you from?

Waar komt u vandaan? pol   waar komt ew van·*daan*

Waar kom je vandaan? inf   waar kom yuh van·*daan*

I'm from ...	Ik kom uit ...	ik kom öyt ...
Australia	Australië	aw·*straa*·lee·yuh
Canada	Canada	ka·na·da
England	Engeland	eng·uh·lant
New Zealand	Nieuw-Zeeland	neew·*zey*·lant
the USA	de Verenigde Staten	duh vuh·*rey*·nikh·duh *staa*·tuhn

Are you married?	Bent u getrouwd? pol	bent ew khuh·*trawt*
	Ben je getrouwd? inf	ben yuh khuh·*trawt*
I'm married.	Ik ben getrouwd.	ik ben khuh·*trawt*
I'm single.	Ik ben vrijgezel.	ik ben *vrey*·khuh·zel

age

How old ...?	Hou oud ...?	hoo awt ...
are you	ben je inf	ben yuh
is your daughter	is jouw dochter inf	is yaw *dokh*·tuhr
is your son	is jouw zoon inf	is yaw zohn

| I'm ... years old. | Ik ben ... jaar. | ik ben ... yaar |
| He/She is ... years old. | Hij/Zij is ... jaar. | hey/zey is ... yaar |

feelings

I'm (not) ...	Ik ben (niet) ...	ik ben (neet) ...
Are you ...?	Ben jij ...? inf	ben yey ...
happy	blij	bley
sad	droef	droof

I'm (not) ...	Ik heb (geen) ...	ik hep (kheyn) ...
Are you ...?	Heb je ...? inf	hep yey ...
hungry	honger	*hong*·uhr
thirsty	dorst	dorst

I'm (not) ...	Ik heb het (niet) ...	ik hep huht (neet) ...
Are you ...?	Heb jij het ...? inf	hep yey huht ...
cold	koud	kawt
hot	warm	warm

entertainment

going out

Where can I find ...?	Waar vind ik de ...?	waar vint ik duh ...
(night)clubs	(nacht)clubs	(*nakht*·)klups
gay venues	homotenten	*hoh*·moh·ten·tuhn
pubs	kroegen/cafés Ⓝ/Ⓑ	*khroo*·khuhn/ka·*feys*

I feel like going to ...	Ik heb zin om naar ... te gaan.	ik hep zin om naar ... tuh khaan
a/the concert	een/het concert	uhn/huht kon·*sert*
the movies	de bioscoop	duh bee·yos·*kohp*
a/the party	een/het feestje	uhn/huht *fey*·shuh
a restaurant	op restaurant	op res·toh·*rant*
the theatre	het toneel	huht toh·*neyl*

interests

Do you like ...?	*Hou je van ...?* inf	haw yuh van ...
I (don't) like ...	*Ik hou (niet) van ...*	ik haw (neet) van ...
art	*kunst*	kunst
cooking	*koken*	*koh*-kuhn
movies	*films*	films
reading	*lezen*	*ley*-zuhn
shopping	*winkelen*	*wing*-kuh-luhn
sport	*sport*	sport
travelling	*reizen*	*rey*-zuhn

Do you like to dance?
Hou je van dansen? inf   haw yuh van *dan*-suhn

Do you like to listen to music?
Luister je graag naar muziek? inf   *löys*-tuhr yuh khraakh naar mew-*zeek*

food & drink

finding a place to eat

Can you recommend a ...?	*Kunt u een ... aanbevelen?* pol	kunt ew uhn ... *aan*-buh-vey-luhn
bar	*bar*	bar
café	*eethuisje/taverne* ⑩/⑱	*eyt*-höy-shuh/ta-*ver*-nuh
restaurant	*restaurant*	res-toh-*rant*
I'd like ..., please.	*Ik wil graag ...*	ik wil khraakh ...
a table for (four)	*een tafel voor (vier)*	uhn *taa*-fuhl vohr (veer)
the (non)smoking section	*(niet-)roken*	(neet-)roh-kuhn

ordering food

breakfast	*ontbijt* n	ont-*beyt*
lunch	*middageten* n	*mi*-dakh-ey-tuhn
dinner	*avondeten* n	*aa*-vont-ey-tuhn
snack	*snack*	snek/snak ⑩/⑱
today's special	*dagschotel*	*dakh*-shoh-tuhl

What would you recommend?
Wat kunt u aanbevelen? pol   wat kunt ew *aan*-buh-vey-luhn

I'd like (the) ..., please.	..., graag.	... khraakh
bill	De rekening	duh rey-kuh-ning
drink list	De drankkaart	duh drang-kaart
menu	De menu	duh muh-new
that dish	Dat gerecht	dat guh-rekht
wine list	De wijnkaart	duh weyn-kaart

drinks

(cup of) coffee ...	(een tas) koffie ...	(uhn tas) ko-fee ...
(cup of) tea ...	(een tas) thee ...	(uhn tas) tey ...
with milk	met melk	met melk
without sugar	zonder suiker	zon-duhr söy-kuhr
(orange) juice	(sinaasappel)sap	(see-naas-a-puhl-)sap
soft drink	frisdrank	fris-drangk
flat mineral water	spa blauw/plat Ⓝ/Ⓑ	spa blaw/plat
mineral/bottled water	mineraalwater n	mee-ney-raal-waa-tuhr
sparkling mineral water	spa rood/bruis Ⓝ/Ⓑ	spa roht/bröys

in the bar

I'll have ...	Voor mij ...	vohr mey ...
My shout/round.	Mijn rondje.	meyn ron-chuh
What would you like? inf	Wat wil je drinken?	wat wil yuh dring-kuhn
Cheers!	Proost!	prohst
brandy	brandewijn	bran-duh-weyn
gin	jenever	zhuh-ney-vuhr
a shot of (whisky)	een glas (whisky)	uhn khlas (wis-kee)
strong alcoholic drink	borrel	bo-ruhl
beer on tap	bier van 't vat	beer vant vat
bottled beer	bier op fles	beer op fles
a bottle/glass of beer	een flesje/glas bier	uhn fle-shuh/khlas beer
a bottle/glass of ...	een fles/glas ...	uhn fles/khlas ...
red wine	rode wijn	roh-duh weyn
sparkling wine	mousserende wijn Ⓝ	moo-sey-ruhn-duh weyn
	schuimwijn Ⓑ	skhöym-weyn
white wine	witte wijn	wi-tuh weyn

food & drink – DUTCH

self-catering

What's the local speciality?
Wat is het streekgerecht? — wat is huht *streyk*·khuh·rekht

What's that?
Wat is dat? — wat is dat

How much is (a kilo of cheese)?
Hoeveel kost (een kilo kaas)? — hoo·*veyl* kost (uhn *kee*·loh kaas)

I'd like ... *Ik wil graag ...* — ik wil khraakh ...
- (100) grams *(honderd) gram* — (*hon*·duhrt) khram
- (two) kilos *(twee) kilo* — (twey) *kee*·loh
- (three) pieces *(drie) stuks* — (dree) stuks
- (six) slices *(zes) plakken/sneetjes* ⑧/⑧ — (zes) *pla*·kuhn/*sney*·chuhs

Less. *Minder.* — *min*·duhr
Enough. *Dat is genoeg.* — dat is khuh·*nookh*
More. *Meer.* — meyr

special diets & allergies

Is there a vegetarian restaurant near here?
Is er hier een vegetarisch restaurant in de buurt? — is uhr heer uhn vey·khey·*taa*·ris res·toh·*rant* in duh bewrt

Do you have vegetarian food?
Heeft u vegetarische maaltijden? — heyft ew vey·khey·*taa*·ri·suh *maal*·tey·duhn

Could you prepare a meal without ...? *Zou u een maaltijd zonder ... kunnen klaarmaken?* — zaw ew uhn *maal*·teyt *zon*·duhr ... *ku*·nuhn *klaar*·maa·kuhn
- butter *boter* — *boh*·ter
- eggs *eieren* — *ey*·yuh·ruhn
- meat stock *vleesbouillon* — *vleys*·boo·yon

I'm allergic to ... *Ik ben allergisch voor ...* — ik ben a·*ler*·khis vohr ...
- dairy produce *zuivelproducten* — *zöy*·vuhl·pro·duk·tuhn
- gluten *gluten* — *khlew*·tuhn
- MSG *MSG/vetsin* — em·es·*khey*/vet·*seen*
- nuts *noten* — *noh*·tuhn
- seafood *vis, schaal- en schelpdieren* — vis skhaal en *skhelp*·dee·ruhn

menu decoder

aardappels	*aart*-a-puhls	potatoes
appelmoes	*a*-puhl-moos	apple sauce
beignet	bey-*nye*	fritter
beschuit	buh-*shöyt*	typical Dutch light crisp bread (often round)
biefstuk tartaar	*beef*-stuk tar-*taar*	raw minced beef with eggs & spices
bloedworst	*bloot*-worst	black pudding • blood sausage – called **pens** pens or **beuling** beu-ling in Belgium
boterham	*boh*-tuhr-ham	sandwich (of sliced bread)
brood n	broht	bread
croque monsieur	krok muh-*sye*	toasted sandwich with cheese & ham
drop	drop	sweet or salty liquorice
ei/eieren n	ey/*ey*-yuh-ruhn	egg/eggs
flensjes	*flen*-shuhs	small thin pancakes
friet/frieten/frit(es)	freet/*free*-tuhn/frit	chips (also called **patat** pa-*tat*)
gebak n	khuh-*bak*	cakes & pastries
gehakt n	khuh-*hakt*	minced meat
gevogelte n	khuh-*voh*-khuhl-tuh	fowl
groenten	*khroon*-tuhn	vegetables
hagelslag	*haa*-khuhl-slakh	chocolate vermicelli
haring	*haa*-ring	herring
hutsepot	*hut*-suh-pot	stew of potatoes, onions & carrots
jachtschotel	*yakht*-skhoh-tuhl	oven dish with meat & potatoes
kaas	kaas	cheese
karbonade	kar-boh-*naa*-duh	chop – also called **kotelet** ko-tuh-*let*
lekkerbekje n	le-kuhr-bek-yuh	deep-fried fish fillet
muisjes	*möy*-shuhs	sugar-coated aniseed

oliebol	*oh*-lee-bol	*dough fritter*
ontbijtkoek	ont-*beyt*-kook	*gingerbread-style honey cake – called* **peperkoek** *pey-puhr-kook in Belgium*
paddestoelen	*pa*-duh-stoo-luhn	*mushrooms*
poffertjes	*po*-fuhr-chuhs	*small puffed-up pancakes served with butter & icing sugar*
puree	pew-*rey*	*mash*
rolmops	*rol*-mops	*pickled herring with gherkin/onion*
(slag)room	(*slakh*-)rohm	*(whipped) cream*
saucijzebroodje n	saw-*sey*-zuh-broh-chuh	*sausage roll – in Belgium called* **worstebrood** *wor-stuh-broht*
schaal- en schelpdieren	skhaal en *skhelp*-dee-ruhn	*crustaceans & shellfish*
slakken	*sla*-kuhn	*snails – in Belgium called* **escargots** *es-kar-khohs*
spek	spek	*bacon*
stamppot/stoemp	*stam*-pot/stoomp	*mashed potatoes & vegetables*
stoofschotel	*stohf*-skhoh-tuhl	*casserole*
stoofvlees n	*stohf*-vleys	*beef stew traditionally served with fries*
tompoes	tom-*poos*	*custard slice with icing*
uitsmijter	*öyt*-smey-tuhr	*sliced bread with cold meat covered with eggs & served with a garnish*
vlaai	vlaay	*sweet tart/cake/pie*
vlees n	vleys	*meat*
vogelnestje n	*voh*-khuhl-ne-shuh	*'bird's nest' – meat loaf with egg inside*
waterzooi	*waa*-tuhr-zohy	*creamy soup with potatoes, vegetables & chicken or fish*
wild n	wilt	*game*
worst	worst	*sausage*

emergencies

basics

Help!	*Help!*	help
Stop!	*Stop!*	stop
Go away!	*Ga weg!*	khaa wekh
Thief!	*Dief!*	deef
Fire!	*Brand!*	brant
Watch out!	*Pas op!*	pas op
Call ...!	*Bel ...!*	bel ...
a doctor	*een doktor*	uhn *dok*·tuhr
an ambulance	*een ambulance*	uhn am·bew·*lans*
the police	*de politie*	duh poh·*leet*·see

It's an emergency!
Het is een noodgeval. — huht is uhn *noht*·khuh·val

Could you help me, please?
Kunt u mij alstublieft helpen? pol — kunt ew mey al·stew·*bleeft* hel·puhn

I have to use the telephone.
Ik heb een telefoon nodig. — ik hep uhn tey·ley·*fohn* noh·dikh

I'm lost.
Ik ben de weg kwijt. — ik ben duh wekh kweyt

Where are the toilets?
Waar zijn de toiletten? — waar zeyn duh twa·*le*·tuhn

police

Where's the police station?
Waar is het politiebureau? — waar is huht poh·*leet*·see·bew·roh

I want to report an offence. (minor/serious)
Ik wil aangifte doen van — ik wil *aan*·khif·tuh doon van
een overtreding/misdrijf. — uhn oh·vuhr·*trey*·ding/*mis*·dreyf

I have insurance.
Ik heb verzekering. — ik hep vuhr·*zey*·kuh·ring

I've been ...	*Ik ben ...*	ik ben ...
assaulted	*aangevallen*	*aan*·khuh·va·luhn
raped	*verkracht*	vuhr·*khrakht*
robbed	*bestolen*	buh·*stoh*·luhn

I've lost my ...	Ik heb mijn ... verloren.	ik hep meyn ... vuhr·loh·ruhn
My ... was/were stolen.	Mijn ... is/zijn gestolen.	meyn ... is/zeyn khuh·stoh·luhn
backpack	rugzak	rukh·zak
bags	tassen	ta·suhn
credit card	kredietkaart	krey·deet·kaart
handbag	handtas	han·tas
jewellery	juwelen	yew·wey·luhn
money	geld	khelt
passport	paspoort	pas·pohrt
travellers cheques	reischeques	reys·sheks
wallet	portefeuille	por·tuh·föy
I want to contact my ...	Ik wil contact opnemen met mijn ...	ik wil kon·takt op·ney·muhn met meyn ...
consulate	consulaat	kon·sew·laat
embassy	ambassade	am·ba·saa·duh

health

medical needs

Where's the nearest ...?	Waar is de dichtsbijzijnde ...?	waar is duh dikhs·bey·zeyn·duh ...
dentist	tandarts	tan·darts
doctor	dokter	dok·tuhr
(night) pharmacist	(nacht)apotheek	(nakht·)a·poh·teyk

Where's the nearest hospital?

Waar is het dichtsbijzijnde ziekenhuis?

waar is huht dikhs·bey·zeyn·duh zee·kuhn·höys

I need a doctor (who speaks English).

Ik heb een dokter nodig (die Engels spreekt).

ik hep uhn dok·tuhr noh·dikh (dee eng·uhls spreykt)

Could I see a female doctor?

Zou ik een vrouwelijke dokter kunnen zien?

zaw ik uhn vraw·wuh·ley·kuh dok·tuhr ku·nuhn zeen

I've run out of my medication.

Mijn medicijnen zijn op.

meyn mey·dee·sey·nuhn zeyn op

symptoms, conditions & allergies

I'm sick.	Ik ben ziek.	ik ben zeek
It hurts here.	Hier doet het pijn.	heer doot huht peyn
I have nausea.	Ik ben misselijk.	ik ben *mi*·suh·luhk

I have (a) ...	Ik heb ...	ik hep ...
asthma	astma	*ast*·ma
bronchitis	bronchitis	bron·*khee*·tees
constipation	last van constipatie	last van kon·stee·*paa*·see
cough	een hoest	uhn hoost
diabetes	diabetes/	dee·ya·*bey*·tes/
	suikerziekte	*söy*·kuhr·zeek·tuh
diarrhoea	diarree	dee·ya·*rey*
fever	koorts	kohrts
headache	hoofdpijn	*hohft*·peyn
heart condition	een hartkwaal	uhn *hart*·kwaal
pain	pijn	peyn
sore throat	keelpijn	*keyl*·peyn
toothache	kiespijn	*kees*·peyn

I'm allergic to ...	Ik ben allergisch voor ...	ik ben a·*ler*·khis vohr ...
antibiotics	antibiotica	an·tee·bee·*yoh*·tee·ka
anti-inflammatories	ontstekingsremmende medicijnen	ont·*stey*·kings·re·muhn·duh mey·dee·*sey*·nuhn
aspirin	aspirine	as·pee·*ree*·nuh
bees	bijen	*bey*·yuhn
codeine	codeïne	koh·dey·*ee*·nuh
penicillin	penicilline	pey·nee·see·*lee*·nuh

antiseptic n	ontsmettend middel n	ont·*sme*·tuhnt *mi*·duhl
bandage	verband n	vuhr·*bant*
condoms	condooms n pl	kon·*dohms*
contraceptives	anticonceptiemiddelen n pl	an·tee·kon·*sep*·see·mi·duh·luhn
diarrhoea medicine	middel tegen diarree n	*mi*·duhl *tey*·khuhn dee·ya·*rey*
insect repellent	insectverdrijvend middel n	in·sekt·vuhr·drey·vuhnt *mi*·duhl
laxatives	laxeermiddelen n pl	lak·*seyr*·mi·duh·luhn
painkillers	pijnstillers	*peyn*·sti·luhrs
rehydration salts	rehydratatie-oplossing	rey·hee·dra·*ta*·see·op·lo·sing
sleeping tablets	slaappillen	*slaa*·pi·luhn

health – DUTCH

83

english–dutch dictionary

In this dictionary, words are marked as n (noun), a (adjective), v (verb), sg (singular), pl (plural), inf (informal) and pol (polite) where necessary. Note that Dutch nouns are either masculine, feminine or neuter. Masculine and feminine forms (known as 'common gender') take the definite article *de* (the) while neuter forms take the article *het* (the). Every Dutch noun needs to be learned with its definite article (*de* or *het*). Only in archaic forms is the distinction between masculine and feminine still relevant, so we've only indicated the neuter nouns with ⑩ after the translation. We've also used the symbols ⑩/⑧ for some words which are different in the Netherlands and Belgium respectively.

A

accident *ongeval* ⑩ *on*-khuh-val
accommodation *accommodatie* a-koh-moh-*daa*-see
adaptor *adapter* a-*dap*-tuhr
address n *adres* ⑩ a-*dres*
after *na* naa
air-conditioned *met airconditioning*
  met *eyr*-kon-dee-shuh-ning
airplane *vliegtuig* ⑩ *vleekh*-töykh
airport *luchthaven* *lukht*-haa-vuhn
alcohol *alcohol* al-koh-hol
all a *alle* a-luh
allergy *allergie* a-ler-*khee*
ambulance *ambulance* am-bew-*lans*
and *en* en
ankle *enkel* *eng*-kuhl
arm *arm* arm
ashtray *asbak* *as*-bak
ATM *pin-automaat/geldautomaat* ⑩/⑧
  pin-aw-toh-maat/*khelt*-aw-toh-maat

B

baby *baby* *bey*-bee
back (body) *rug* rukh
backpack *rugzak* *rukh*-zak
bad *slecht* slekht
bag *tas* tas
baggage claim *bagage afhalen* ba-*khaa*-zhuh af-*haa*-luhn
bank *bank* bangk
bar *bar* bar
bathroom *badkamer* *bat*-kaa-muhr
battery *batterij* ba-tuh-*rey*
beautiful *mooi* mohy
bed *bed* ⑩ bet
beer *bier* ⑩ beer
before *voor* vohr

behind *achter* akh-tuhr
Belgian a *Belgisch* bel-khis
Belgium *België* *bel*-khee-yuh
bicycle *fiets* feets
big *groot* khroht
bill *rekening* *rey*-kuh-ning
black *zwart* zwart
blanket *deken* *dey*-kuhn
blood group *bloedgroep* *bloot*-khroop
blue *blauw* blaw
boat *boot* boht
book (make a reservation) v *reserveren*
  rey-zer-*vey*-ruhn
bottle *fles* fles
bottle opener *flesopener* *fles*-oh-puh-nuhr
boy *jongen* *yong*-uhn
brakes (car) *remmen* re-muhn
breakfast *ontbijt* ⑩ ont-*beyt*
broken (faulty) *stuk* stuk
bus *bus* bus
business *zaken* *zaa*-kuhn
buy *kopen* *koh*-puhn

C

café *eethuisje* ⑩/*taverne* ⑩/⑧
  eyt-höy-shuh/ta-*ver*-nuh
camera *fototoestel* ⑩ *foh*-toh-too-stel
camping ground *camping* *kem*-ping
camp site *kampeerplaats* kam-*peyr*-plaats
cancel *annuleren* a-new-*ley*-ruhn
can opener *blikopener* *blik*-oh-puh-nuhr
car *auto* *aw*-toh
cash n *baar geld* ⑩ baar khelt
cash (a cheque) v *(een cheque) innen* (uhn shek) *i*-nuhn
cell phone *mobiele telefoon/GSM* ⑩/⑧
  moh-*bee*-luh tey-ley-fohn/khey-es-em
centre n *centrum* ⑩ *sen*-truhm
change (money) v *(geld) wisselen* (khelt) *wi*-suh-luhn

cheap *goedkoop* khoot-*kohp*
check (bill) *rekening* rey-kuh-ning
check-in n *check-in* chek-in
chest *borst* borst
child *kind* ⓝ kint
cigarette *sigaret* see-kha-*ret*
city *stad* stat
clean a *schoon* skhoon
closed *gesloten* khuh-*sloh*-tuhn
coffee *koffie* ko-fee
coins *muntstukken* ⓝ pl *munt*-stu-kuhn
cold a *koud* kawt
collect call *collect call* ko-*lekt* kawl
come *komen* koh-muhn
computer *computer* kom-*pyoo*-tuhr
condom *condoom* ⓝ kon-*dohm*
contact lenses *contactlenzen* kon-*takt*-len-zuhn
cook v *bereiden* be-*rey*-duhn
cost n *kost* kost
credit card *kredietkaart* krey-*deet*-kaart
cup *tas* tas
currency exchange *wisselkantoor* ⓝ *wi*-suhl-kan-tohr
customs (immigration) *douane* doo-*waa*-nuh

D

dangerous *gevaarlijk* khuh-*vaar*-luhk
date (time) *datum* daa-tum
day *dag* dakh
delay n *vertraging* vuhr-*traa*-khing
dentist *tandarts* tan-darts
depart *vertrekken* vuhr-*tre*-kuhn
diaper *luier* *löy*-yuhr
dictionary *woordenboek* ⓝ *wohr*-duhn-book
dinner *avondeten* ⓝ aa-vont-*ey*-tuhn
direct *rechtstreeks* rekh-*streyks*
dirty *vuil* vöyl
disabled *gehandicapt* khuh-*han*-dee-kapt
doctor *dokter* dok-tuhr
double bed *dubbel bed* ⓝ *du*-buhl bet
double room *tweepersoonskamer*
    twey-puhr-sohns-kaa-muhr
drink n *drinken* dring-kuhn
drive v *rijden* *rey*-duhn
drivers licence *rijbewijs* ⓝ *rey*-buh-weys
drugs (illicit) *drugs* drukhs
dummy (pacifier) *fopspeen* *fop*-speyn
Dutch (language) *Nederlands* ⓝ *ney*-duhr-lants
Dutch a *Nederlands* *ney*-duhr-lants

E

ear *oor* n ohr
east *oost* ohst
eat *eten* *ey*-tuhn
economy class *economy klas* ey-ko-no-mee klas
electricity *elektriciteit* ey-lek-tree-see-*teyt*
elevator *lift* lift
email *e-mail* ee-meyl
embassy *ambassade* am-ba-*saa*-duh
emergency *noodgeval* ⓝ *noht*-khuh-val
English (language) *Engels* ⓝ *eng*-uhls
entrance *ingang* *in*-khang
evening *avond* aa-vont
exchange rate *wisselkoers* *wi*-suhl-koors
exit n *uitgang* öyt-khang
expensive *duur* dewr
express mail *exprespost* eks-*pres*-post
eye *oog* ⓝ ohkh

F

far *ver* ver
fast *snel* snel
father *vader* vaa-duhr
film (camera) *film* ⓝ film
finger *vinger* ving-uhr
first-aid kit *verbandkist* vuhr-*bant*-kist
first class *eerste klas* eyr-stuh klas
fish n *vis* vis
Flanders *Vlaanderen* vlaan-duh-ruhn
Flemish (language) *Vlaams* ⓝ vlaams
Flemish a *Vlaams* vlaams
food *eten* ⓝ *ey*-tuhn
foot *voet* voot
fork *vork* vork
free (of charge) *gratis* khraa-tis
French (language) *Frans* ⓝ frans
friend *vriend/vriendin* ⓜ/ⓕ vreend/vreen-*din*
fruit *fruit* ⓝ freyt
full *vol* vol
funny *grappig* khra-pikh

G

German (language) *Duits* ⓝ döyts
gift *cadeau* ⓝ ka-*doh*
girl *meisje* ⓝ *mey*-shuh
glass (drinking) *glas* ⓝ khlas
glasses *bril* bril

go *gaan* khaan
good *goed* khoot
green *groen* khroon
guide n *gids* khits

H

half n *helft* helft
hand *hand* hant
handbag *handtas* han-tas
happy *blij* bley
have *hebben* he-buhn
he *hij* hey
head *hoofd* ⓝ hohft
heart *hart* ⓝ hart
heat n *warmte* warm-tuh
heavy *zwaar* zwaar
help v *helpen* hel-puhn
here *hier* heer
high *hoog* hohkh
highway *snelweg* snel-wekh
hike v *trekken* tre-kuhn
holidays *vakantie* va-kant-see
homosexual n&a *homosexueel* hoh-moh-sek-sew-weyl
hospital *ziekenhuis* ⓝ zee-kuhn-höys
hot *warm* warm
hotel *hotel* ⓝ hoh-tel
(to be) hungry *honger (hebben)* hong-uhr (he-buhn)
husband *man* man

I

I *ik* ik
identification (card) *identiteitsbewijs* ⓝ ee-den-tee-teyts-buh-weys
ill *ziek* zeek
important *belangrijk* buh-lang-reyk
included *inbegrepen* in-buh-khrey-puhn
injury *verwonding* vuhr-won-ding
insurance *verzekering* vuhr-zey-kuh-ring
Internet *internet* ⓝ in-tuhr-net
interpreter *vertaler* vuhr-taa-luhr

J

jewellery *juwelen* ⓝ pl yew-wey-luhn
job *baan/werk* ⓝ/ⓑ baan/werk

K

key *sleutel* sleu-tuhl
kilogram *kilogram* kee-lo(-khram)

kitchen *keuken* keu-kuhn
knife *mes* ⓝ mes

L

laundry (place) *wasserette* wa-suh-ret
lawyer *advokaat* at-voh-kaat
left (direction) *links* lingks
left-luggage office *garderobe/vestiaire* ⓝ/ⓑ khar-duh-roh-buh/ves-tyeyr
leg *been* ⓝ beyn
lesbian a *lesbisch* les-bis
less *minder* min-duhr
letter (mail) *brief* breef
lift (elevator) *lift* lift
light n *licht* ⓝ likht
like v *houden van* haw-duhn van
lock n *slot* ⓝ slot
long *lang* lang
lost *verloren* vuhr-loh-ruhn
lost-property office *verloren voorwerpen* vuhr-loh-ruhn vohr-wer-puhn
love v *houden van* haw-duhn van
luggage *bagage* ba-khaa-zhuh
lunch *middageten* ⓝ mi-dakh-ey-tuhn

M

mail n *post* post
man *man* man
map (building) *plattegrond* pla-tuh-khront
map (town) *kaart* kaart
market *markt* mart
matches *lucifers* lew-see-fers
meat *vlees* ⓝ vleys
medicine *medicijn* ⓝ mey-dee-seyn
menu ⓜ&ⓝ *menu* muh-new
message *bericht* ⓝ buh-rikht
milk *melk* melk
minute *minuut* mee-newt
mobile phone *mobiele telefoon/GSM* ⓝ/ⓑ moh-bee-luh tey-ley-fohn/khey-es-em
money *geld* ⓝ khelt
month *maand* maant
morning *ochtend* okh-tuhnt
mother *moeder* moo-duhr
motorcycle *motorfiets* moh-tor-feets
motorway *snelweg* snel-wekh
mouth *mond* mont
music *muziek* mew-zeek

N

name *naam* naam
napkin *servet* ⓝ ser·vet
nappy *luier* löy·yuhr
near *dicht bij* dikht bey
neck *nek* nek
(the) Netherlands *Nederland* ney·duhr·lant
new *nieuw* neew
news *nieuws* ⓝ neews
newspaper *krant* krant
night *nacht* nakht
no *nee* ney
noisy *lawaaierig* la·waa·yuh·rikh
nonsmoking *niet-roken* neet·roh·kuhn
north *noord* nohrt
nose *neus* neus
now *nu* new
number *nummer* ⓝ nu·muhr

O

oil (engine) *olie* oh·lee
old *oud* awt
one-way ticket *enkele reis* eng·kuh·luh reys
open a *open* oh·puhn
outside *buiten* böy·tuhn

P

package *pakje* ⓝ pak·yuh
paper *papier* ⓝ pa·peer
park (car) v *parkeren* par·key·ruhn
passport *paspoort* ⓝ pas·pohrt
pay *betalen* buh·taa·luhn
pen *balpen* bal·pen
petrol *benzine* ben·zee·nuh
pharmacy *apotheek* a·poh·teyk
phonecard *telefoonkaart* tey·ley·fohn·kaart
photo *foto* foh·toh
plate *bord* ⓝ bort
police *politie* po·leet·see
postcard *ansichtkaart* an·sikht·kaart
post office *postkantoor* ⓝ post·kan·tohr
pregnant *zwanger* zwang·uhr
price *prijs* preys

Q

quiet *stil* stil

R

rain n *regen* rey·khuhn
razor (electrical) *scheerapparaat* ⓝ skheyr·a·pa·raat
razor (manual) *scheermesje* ⓝ skheyr·me·shuh
receipt n *kwitantie* kwee·tan·see
red *rood* roht
refund n *terugbetaling* tuh·rukh·buh·taa·ling
registered mail *aangetekende post*
  aan·khuh·tey·kuhn·duh post
rent v *huren* hew·ruhn
repair v *herstellen* her·ste·luhn
reservation *reservatie* rey·ser·vaa·see
restaurant *restaurant* ⓝ res·toh·rant
return v *terugkomen* tuh·rukh·koh·muhn
return ticket *retourtje* ⓝ ruh·toor·chuh
right (direction) *rechts* rekhs
road *weg* wekh
room *kamer* kaa·muhr

S

safe a *veilig* vey·likh
sanitary napkin *maandverband* ⓝ maant·vuhr·bant
seat *zitplaats* zit·plaats
send *sturen* stew·ruhn
service station *tankstation* ⓝ tank·sta·syon
sex *seks* seks
shampoo *shampoo* sham·poh
share *delen* dey·luhn
shaving cream *scheerschuim* ⓝ skheyr·skhöym
she *zij* zey
sheet (bed) *laken* ⓝ laa·kuhn
shirt *hemd* ⓝ hemt
shoes *schoenen* skhoo·nuhn
shop n *winkel* wing·kuhl
short *kort* kort
shower n *douche* doo·shuh
single room *eenpersoonskamer*
  eyn·puhr·sohns·kaa·muhr
skin *huid* höyt
skirt *rok* rok
sleep v *slapen* slaa·puhn
slowly *traag* traakh
small *klein* kleyn
smoke (cigarettes) v *roken* roh·kuhn
soap *zeep* zeyp
some *enkele* eng·kuh·luh
soon *gauw* khaw
south *zuid* zöyt
souvenir shop *souvenirwinkel* soo·vuh·neer·wing·kuhl

speak *spreken* sprey-kuhn
spoon *lepel* ley-puhl
stamp *postzegel* post-zey-khuhl
stand-by ticket *stand-by ticket* stent-baay ti-ket
station (train) *station* sta-*syon*
stomach *maag* maakh
stop v *stoppen* sto-puhn
stop (bus) n *(bus)stop* (bus-)stop
street *straat* straat
student *student* stew-*dent*
sun *zon* zon
sunscreen *zonnebrandolie* zo-nuh-brant-oh-lee
swim v *zwemmen* zwe-muhn

T

tampons *tampons* tam-pons
taxi *taxi* tak-see
teaspoon *lepeltje* ley-puhl-chuh
teeth *tanden* tan-duhn
telephone n *telefoon* tey-ley-*fohn*
television *televisie* tey-ley-*vee*-zee
temperature (weather) *temperatuur* tem-pey-ra-*tewr*
tent *tent* tent
that (one) *die* & ⨍/*dat* dee/dat
they *zij* zey
(to be) thirsty *dorst (hebben)* dorst (*he*-buhn)
this (one) *deze* & ⨍/*dit* *dey*-zuh/dit
throat *keel* keyl
ticket *kaartje* /*ticket*   *kaar*-chuh/ti-ket
time *tijd* teyt
tired *moe* moo
tissues *tissues* ti-*sews*
today *vandaag* van-*daakh*
toilet *toilet* /WC twa-let/wey-*sey*
tomorrow *morgen* mor-khuhn
tonight (after midnight) *vannacht* va-*nakht*
tonight (before midnight) *vanavond* va-*naa*-vont
toothbrush *tandenborstel* tan-duhn-bors-tuhl
toothpaste *tandpasta* tant-pas-ta
torch (flashlight) *zaklantaarn* zak-lan-taarn
tour n *rondleiding* ront-ley-ding
tourist office *VVV/toerismebureau*
vey-vey-vey/too-ris-muh-bew-roh
towel *handdoek* han-dook
train *trein* treyn
translate *vertalen* vuhr-*taa*-luhn
travel agency *reisbureau* reys-bew-roh
travellers cheque *reischeque* reys-shek
trousers *broek* brook

twin beds *enkele bedden* *eng*-kuh-luh *be*-duhn
tyre *band* bant

U

underwear *ondergoed* *on*-duhr-khoot
urgent *dringend* dring-uhnt

V

vacant *vrij* vrey
vacation *vakantie* va-*kan*-see
vegetable n *groente* khroon-tuh
vegetarian a *vegetarisch* vey-khey-*taa*-ris
visa *visum* *vee*-sum

W

waiter *ober* oh-buhr
walk v *gaan* khaan
wallet *portefeuille* por-tuh-*föy*
warm a *warm* warm
wash (something) *wassen* wa-suhn
watch n *horloge* hor-*loh*-khuh
water *water* *waa*-tuhr
we *wij* wey
weekend *weekeinde* weyk-eyn-duh
west *west* west
wheelchair *rolstoel* rol-stool
when *wanneer* wa-*neyr*
where *waar* waar
white *wit* wit
who *wie* wee
why *waarom* waa-*rom*
wife *vrouw* vraw
window *raam* raam
wine *wijn* weyn
with *met* met
without *zonder* zon-duhr
woman *vrouw* vraw
write *schrijven* skhrey-vuhn

Y

yellow *geel* kheyl
yes *ja* yaa
yesterday *gisteren* khis-tuh-ruhn
you sg inf *je* yuh
you sg pol *u* ew
you pl *jullie* yu-lee

French

french alphabet

A a a	*B b* be	*C c* se	*D d* de	*E e* eu
F f ef	*G g* zhe	*H h* ash	*I i* i	*J j* zhi
K k ka	*L l* el	*M m* em	*N n* en	*O o* o
P p pe	*Q q* kew	*R r* er	*S s* es	*T t* te
U u ew	*V v* ve	*W w* dubl ve	*X x* iks	*Y y* i grek
Z z zed				

FRANÇAIS

french

FRENCH

introduction

What do you think of when the word 'French' comes up? A *bon vivant*, drinking an *apéritif tête-à-tête* with a friend at a *café*, while studying the *à la carte* menu and making some witty *double entendres*? Are you getting *déjà vu* yet? Chances are you already know a few fragments of French (*français* fron·sey) – *bonjour*, *oui*, *au revoir*, *bon voyage* and so on. Even if you missed out on French lessons, though, that first sentence (forgive the stereotyping) is evidence that you probably know quite a few French words without realising it. And thanks to the Norman invasion of England in the 11th century, many common English words have a French origin – some estimate, in fact, that three-fifths of everyday English vocabulary arrived via French.

So, after centuries of contact with English, French offers English speakers a relatively smooth path to communicating in another language. The structure of a French sentence won't come as a surprise and the sounds of the language are generally common to English as well. The few sounds that do differ will be familiar to most through television and film examples of French speakers – the silent 'h' and the throaty 'r', for example. French is a distant cousin of English, but is most closely related to its Romance siblings, Italian and Spanish. These languages developed from the Latin spoken by the Romans during their conquests of the 1st century BC.

Almost 30 countries cite French as an official language (not always the only language, of course), in many cases due to France's colonisation of various countries in Africa, the Pacific and the Caribbean. It's the mother tongue of around 80 million people in places like Belgium, Switzerland, Luxembourg, Monaco, Canada and Senegal as well as France, and another 50 million speak it as a second language. French was the language of international diplomacy until the early 20th century, and is still an official language of a number of international organisations, including the Red Cross, the United Nations and the International Olympic Committee.

As well as the advantage of learning a language that's spoken all around the world, there are more subtle benefits to French. Being told of a wonderful vineyard off the tourist track, for example, or discovering that there's little truth in the cliché that the French are rude. And *regardez* the significant body of literature (the Nobel Prize for Literature has gone to French authors a dozen times), film and music … You'll find the reasons to speak French just keep growing.

pronunciation

vowel sounds

Generally, French vowel sounds are short and don't glide into other vowels. Note that the ey in *café* is close to the English sound, but it's shorter and sharper.

symbol	english equivalent	french example	transliteration
a	**run**	*tasse*	tas
ai	**aisle**	*travail*	tra·vai
air	**fair**	*faire*	fair
e	**bet**	*fesses*	fes
ee	**see**	*lit*	lee
eu	**nurse**	*deux*	deu
ew	ee pronounced with rounded lips	*tu*	tew
ey	as in '**bet**', but longer	*musée*	moo·zey
o	**pot**	*pomme*	pom
oo	**moon**	*chou*	shoo

There are also four nasal vowels in French. They're pronounced as if you're trying to force the sound out of your nose rather than your mouth. In French, nasal vowels cause the following nasal consonant sound to be omitted, but a 'hint' of what the implied consonant is can sometimes be heard. We've used nasal consonant sounds (m, n, ng) with the nasal vowel to help you produce the sound with more confidence. Since the four nasal sounds can be quite close, we've simplified it this way:

symbol	english equivalent	french example	transliteration
om/on/ong	like the 'o' in '**pot**', plus nasal consonant sound	*mouton*	moo·**ton**
um/un/ung	similar to the 'a' in '**bat**', plus nasal consonant sound	*magasin*	ma·ga·**zun**

consonant sounds

symbol	english equivalent	french example	transliteration
b	bed	*billet*	bee-yey
d	dog	*date*	dat
f	fat	*femme*	fam
g	go	*grand*	gron
k	kit	*carte*	kart
l	lot	*livre*	leev-re
m	man	*merci*	mair-see
n	not	*non*	non
ny	canyon	*signe*	see-nye
ng	ring	*cinquante*	sung-kont
p	pet	*parc*	park
r	run (throaty)	*rue*	rew
s	sun	*si*	see
sh	shot	*changer*	shon-zhey
t	top	*tout*	too
v	very	*verre*	vair
w	win	*oui*	wee
y	yes	*payer*	pe-yey
z	zero	*vous avez*	voo-za-vey
zh	pleasure	*je*	zhe

word stress

Syllables in French words are, for the most part, equally stressed. English speakers tend to stress the first syllable, so try adding a light stress on the final syllable to compensate. The rhythm of a French sentence is based on breaking the phrase into meaningful sections, then stressing the final syllable pronounced in each section. The stress at these points is characterised by a slight rise in intonation.

basics

language difficulties

Do you speak English?
Parlez-vous anglais? par·ley·voo ong·gley

Do you understand?
Comprenez-vous? kom·pre·ney·voo

I understand.
Je comprends. zhe kom·pron

I don't understand.
Je ne comprends pas. zhe ne kom·pron pa

What does (beaucoup) mean?
Que veut dire (beaucoup)? ke veu deer (bo·koo)

How do you ...?	*Comment ...?*	ko·mon ...
pronounce this	*le prononcez-vous*	le pro·non·sey voo
write (*bonjour*)	*est-ce qu'on écrit*	es kon ey·kree
	(bonjour)	(bon·zhoor)

Could you	*Pourriez-vous ...,*	poo·ree·yey voo ...
please ...?	*s'il vous plaît?*	seel voo pley
repeat that	*répéter*	rey·pey·tey
speak more slowly	*parler plus lentement*	par·ley plew lon·te·mon
write it down	*l'écrire*	ley·kreer

essentials

Yes.	*Oui.*	wee
No.	*Non.*	non
Please.	*S'il vous plaît.*	seel voo pley
Thank you (very much).	*Merci (beaucoup).*	mair·see (bo·koo)
You're welcome.	*Je vous en prie.*	zhe voo zon·pree
Excuse me.	*Excusez-moi.*	ek·skew·zey·mwa
Sorry.	*Pardon.*	par·don

numbers

0	*zéro*	zey·ro	16	*seize*	sez
1	*un*	un	17	*dix-sept*	dee·set
2	*deux*	deu	18	*dix-huit*	dee·zweet
3	*trois*	trwa	19	*dix-neuf*	deez·neuf
4	*quatre*	ka·tre	20	*vingt*	vung
5	*cinq*	sungk	21	*vingt et un*	vung tey un
6	*six*	sees	22	*vingt-deux*	vung·deu
7	*sept*	set	30	*trente*	tront
8	*huit*	weet	40	*quarante*	ka·ront
9	*neuf*	neuf	50	*cinquante*	sung·kont
10	*dix*	dees	60	*soixante*	swa·sont
11	*onze*	onz	70	*soixante-dix*	swa·son·dees
12	*douze*	dooz	80	*quatre-vingts*	ka·tre·vung
13	*treize*	trez	90	*quatre-vingt-dix*	ka·tre·vung·dees
14	*quatorze*	ka·torz	100	*cent*	son
15	*quinze*	kunz	1000	*mille*	meel

time & dates

What time is it?	*Quelle heure est-il?*	kel eur ey·teel
It's one o'clock.	*Il est une heure.*	ee·ley ewn eu
It's (10) o'clock.	*Il est (dix) heures.*	ee·ley (deez) eu
Quarter past (one).	*Il est (une) heure et quart.*	ee·ley (ewn) eu ey kar
Half past (one).	*Il est (une) heure et demie.*	ee·ley (ewn) eu ey de·mee
Quarter to (one).	*Il est (une) heure*	ee·ley (ewn) eu
	moins le quart.	mwun le kar
At what time ...?	*À quelle heure ...?*	a kel eu ...
At ...	*À ...*	a ...
in the morning	*du matin*	dew ma·tun
in the afternoon	*de l'après-midi*	de la·prey·mee·dee
in the evening	*du soir*	dew swar
Monday	*lundi*	lun·dee
Tuesday	*mardi*	mar·dee
Wednesday	*mercredi*	mair·kre·dee
Thursday	*jeudi*	zheu·dee
Friday	*vendredi*	von·dre·dee
Saturday	*samedi*	sam·dee
Sunday	*dimanche*	dee·monsh

January	*janvier*	zhon·vyey
February	*février*	feyv·ryey
March	*mars*	mars
April	*avril*	a·vreel
May	*mai*	mey
June	*juin*	zhwun
July	*juillet*	zhwee·yey
August	*août*	oot
September	*septembre*	sep·tom·bre
October	*octobre*	ok·to·bre
November	*novembre*	no·vom·bre
December	*décembre*	dey·som·bre

What date is it today?
   C'est quel jour aujourd'hui?   sey kel zhoor o·zhoor·dwee

It's (18 October).
   C'est le (dix-huit octobre).   sey le (dee·zwee tok·to·bre)

since (May)	*depuis (mai)*	de·pwee (mey)
until (June)	*jusqu'à (juin)*	zhoos·ka (zhwun)
today	*aujourd'hui*	o·zhoor·dwee
tonight	*ce soir*	se swar

last ...
night	*hier soir*	ee·yair swar
week	*la semaine dernière*	la se·men dair·nyair
month	*le mois dernier*	le mwa dair·nyey
year	*l'année dernière*	la·ney dair·nyair

next ...
week	*la semaine prochaine*	la se·men pro·shen
month	*le mois prochain*	le mwa pro·shen
year	*l'année prochaine*	la·ney pro·shen

yesterday/tomorrow ...   *hier/demain ...*   ee·yair/de·mun ...
morning	*matin*	ma·tun
afternoon	*après-midi*	a·pre·mee·dee
evening	*soir*	swar

weather

What's the weather like?	*Quel temps fait-il?*	kel tom fey·teel
It's ...		
cloudy	*Le temps est couvert.*	le tom ey koo·vair
cold	*Il fait froid.*	eel fey frwa
hot	*Il fait chaud.*	eel fey sho
raining	*Il pleut.*	eel pleu
snowing	*Il neige.*	eel nezh
sunny	*Il fait beau.*	eel fey bo
warm	*Il fait chaud.*	eel fey sho
windy	*Il fait du vent.*	eel fey dew von
spring	*printemps* m	prun·tom
summer	*été* m	ey·tey
autumn	*automne* m	o·ton
winter	*hiver* m	ee·vair

border crossing

I'm here ...	*Je suis ici ...*	zhe swee zee·see ...
in transit	*de passage*	de pa·sazh
on business	*pour le travail*	poor le tra·vai
on holiday	*pour les vacances*	poor ley va·kons
I'm here for ...	*Je suis ici pour ...*	zhe swee zee·see poor ...
(10) days	*(dix) jours*	(dees) zhoor
(three) weeks	*(trois) semaines*	(trwa) se·men
(two) months	*(deux) mois*	(deu) mwa

I'm going to (Paris).
Je vais à (Paris).   zhe vey a (pa·ree)

I'm staying at the (Hotel Grand).
Je loge à (l'hotel Grand).   zhe lozh a (lo·tel gron)

I have nothing to declare.
Je n'ai rien à déclarer.   zhe ney ryun a dey·kla·rey

I have something to declare.
J'ai quelque chose à déclarer.   zhey kel·ke·shoz a dey·kla·rey

That's not mine.
Ce n'est pas à moi.   se ney pa a mwa

transport

tickets & luggage

Where can I buy a ticket?
Où peut-on acheter un billet?   oo pe·ton ash·tey um bee·yey

Do I need to book a seat?
Est-ce qu'il faut réserver une place?   es·keel fo rey·zer·vey ewn plas

One ... ticket	*Un billet ... (pour*	um bee·yey ... (poor
(to Bordeaux), please.	*Bordeaux), s'il vous plaît.*	bor·do) seel voo pley
one-way	*simple*	sum·ple
return	*aller et retour*	a·ley ey re·toor

I'd like to ... my	*Je voudrais ... mon*	zhe voo·drey ... mom
ticket, please.	*billet, s'il vous plaît.*	bee·yey seel voo pley
cancel	*annuler*	a·new·ley
change	*changer*	shon·zhey
collect	*retirer*	re·tee·rey
confirm	*confirmer*	kon·feer·mey

I'd like a ... seat,	*Je voudrais une place*	zhe voo·drey ewn plas
please.	*..., s'il vous plaît.*	... seel voo pley
(non)smoking	*non-fumeur*	non few·me
smoking	*fumeur*	few·me

How much is it?
C'est combien?   sey kom·byun

Is there air conditioning?
Est-qu'il y a la climatisation?   es·keel ya la klee·ma·tee·za·syon

Is there a toilet?
Est-qu'il y a des toilettes?   es·keel ya dey twa·let

How long does the trip take?
Le trajet dure combien de temps?   le tra·zhey dewr kom·byun de tom

Is it a direct route?
Est-ce que c'est direct?   es·ke sey dee·rekt

I'd like a luggage locker.
Je voudrais une   zhe voo·drey ewn
consigne automatique.   kon·see·nye o·to·ma·teek

My luggage has been ...	Mes bagages ont été ...	mey ba·gazh on tey·tey ...
damaged	endommagés	on·do·ma·zhey
lost	perdus	per·dew
stolen	volés	vo·ley

getting around

Where does flight (008) arrive?
Où atteri le vol (008)?
oo a·te·ree le vol (zey·ro zey·ro weet)

Where does flight (008) depart?
D'où décolle le vol (008)?
doo dey·kol le vol (zey·ro zey·ro weet)

Where's (the) ...?	Où se trouve ...?	oo se troo·ve ...
arrivals hall	le hall d'arrivée	le hol da·ree·vey
departures hall	le hall des departs	le hol dey dey·par
duty-free shop	le magasin duty-free	le ma·ga·zun dyoo·tee free
gate (12)	porte (douze)	port (dooz)

Is this the ... to (Nice)?	Est ce ... pour (Nice)?	es se ... poor (nees)
boat	le bateau	le ba·to
bus	le bus	le bews
plane	l'avion	la·vyon
train	le train	le trun

What time's the ... bus?	Le ... bus passe à quelle heure?	le ... bews pas a kel e
first	premier	pre·myey
last	dernier	dair·nyey
next	prochain	pro·shun

At what time does it arrive/leave?
A quelle heure est ce qu'il arrive/part?
a kel eur es se keel a·ree·ve/par

How long will it be delayed?
De combien de temps est-il retardé?
de kom·byun de tom es·teel re·tar·dey

What station is this?
C'est quelle gare?
sey kel gar

What's the next station?
Quelle est la prochaine gare?
kel ey la pro·shen gar

Does it stop at (Amboise)?
Est-ce qu'il s'arrête à (Amboise)?
es·kil sa·ret a (om·bwaz)

Please tell me when we get to (Nantes).
Pouvez-vous me dire quand nous arrivons à (Nantes)?
poo·vey·voo me deer kon noo za·ree·von a (nont)

How long do we stop here?
Combien de temps on s'arrête ici?
kom·byun de tom on sa·ret ee·see

Is this seat available?
Est-ce que cette place est libre?
es·ke set plas ey lee·bre

That's my seat.
C'est ma place.
sey ma plas

I'd like a taxi ...	*Je voudrais un taxi ...*	zhe voo·drey un tak·see ...
at (9am)	*à (neuf heures du matin)*	a (neu veur dew ma·tun)
now	*maintenant*	mun·te·non
tomorrow	*demain*	de·mun

Is this taxi available?
Vous êtes libre?
voo·zet lee·bre

How much is it to ...?
C'est combien pour aller à ...?
sey kom·byun poor a·ley a ...

Please put the meter on.
Mettez le compteur, s'il vous plaît.
me·tey le kon·teseel voo pley

Please take me to (this address).
Conduisez-moi à (cette adresse), s'il vous plaît.
kon·dwee·zey mwa a (set a·dres) seel voo pley

Please ...	*..., s'il vous plaît.*	... seel voo pley
slow down	*Roulez plus lentement*	roo·ley plew lont·mon
stop here	*Arrêtez-vous ici*	a·rey·tey voo ee·see
wait here	*Attendez ici*	a·ton·dey ee·see

car, motorbike & bicycle hire

I'd like to hire a ...	*Je voudrais louer ...*	zhe voo·drey loo·wey ...
bicycle	*un vélo*	un vey·lo
car	*une voiture*	ewn vwa·tewr
motorbike	*une moto*	ewn mo·to
with ...	*avec ...*	a·vek ...
a driver	*un chauffeur*	un sho·feur
air conditioning	*climatisation*	klee·ma·tee·za·syon

How much for ... hire?	*Quel est le tarif par ...?*	kel ey le ta·reef par ...
hourly	*heure*	eur
daily	*jour*	zhoor
weekly	*semaine*	se·men

air	*air* m	air
oil	*huile* f	weel
petrol	*essence* f	es·sons
tyres	*pneus* f pl	pneu

I need a mechanic.
J'ai besoin d'un mécanicien.   zhey be·zwun dun mey·ka·nee·syun

I've run out of petrol.
Je suis en panne d'essence.   zhe swee zon pan de·sons

I have a flat tyre.
Mon pneu est à plat.   mom pneu ey ta pla

directions

Where's the ...?	*Où est-ce qu'il y a ...?*	oo es·keel ya ...
bank	*la banque*	la bongk
city centre	*le centre-ville*	ler son·tre·veel
hotel	*l'hôtel*	lo·tel
market	*le marché*	le mar·shey
police station	*le commissariat*	le kom·mee·sar·ya
	de police	de po·lees
post office	*le bureau de poste*	le bew·ro de post
public toilet	*des toilettes*	dey twa·let
tourist office	*l'office de tourisme*	lo·fees de too·rees·me

Is this the road to (Toulouse)?
C'est la route pour (Toulouse)?   sey la root poor (too·looz)

Can you show me (on the map)?
Pouvez-vous m'indiquer (sur la carte)?   poo·vey·voo mun·dee·key (sewr la kart)

What's the address?
Quelle est l'adresse?   kel ey la·dres

How far is it?
C'est loin?   sey lwun

How do I get there?
Comment faire pour y aller?   ko·mon fair poor ee a·ley

FRANÇAIS – transport

Turn ...	Tournez ...	toor·ney ...
at the corner	au coin	o kwun
at the traffic lights	aux feux	o feu
left/right	à gauche/droite	a gosh/drwat

It's ...	C'est ...	sey ...
behind ...	derrière ...	dair·yair ...
far away	loin d'ici	lwun dee·see
here	ici	ee·see
in front of ...	devant ...	de·von ...
left	à gauche	a gosh
near (to ...)	près (de ...)	prey (de ...)
next to ...	à côté de ...	a ko·tey de ...
opposite ...	en face de ...	on fas de ...
right	à droite	a drwat
straight ahead	tout droit	too drwa
there	là	la

north	nord m	nor
south	sud m	sewd
east	est m	est
west	ouest m	west

by bus	en bus	om bews
by taxi	en taxi	on tak·see
by train	en train	on trun
on foot	à pied	a pyey

signs

Entrée/Sortie	on·trey/sor·tee	**Entrance/Exit**
Ouvert/Fermé	oo·vair/fair·mey	**Open/Closed**
Chambre Libre	shom·bre lee·bre	**Rooms Available**
Complet	kom·pley	**No Vacancies**
Renseignements	ron·sen·ye·mon	**Information**
Commissariat De Police	ko·mee·sar·ya de po·lees	**Police Station**
Interdit	in·teyr·dee	**Prohibited**
Toilettes	twa·let	**Toilets**
Hommes	om	**Men**
Femmes	fam	**Women**
Chaude/Froide	shod/frwad	**Hot/Cold**

102

accommodation

finding accommodation

Where's a ...?	Où est-ce qu'on peut trouver ...?	oo es·kon peu troo·vey ...
camping ground	un terrain de camping	un tey·run de kom·peeng
guesthouse	une pension	ewn pon·see·on
hotel	un hôtel	un o·tel
youth hostel	une auberge de jeunesse	ewn o·bairzh de zhe·nes

Can you recommend somewhere ...?	Est-ce que vous pouvez recommander un logement ...?	es·ke voo poo·vey re·ko·mon·dey un lozh·mon ...
cheap	pas cher	pa shair
good	de bonne qualité	de bon ka·lee·tey
nearby	près d'ici	prey dee·see

I'd like to book a room, please.
Je voudrais réserver
une chambre, s'il vous plaît.
zhe voo·drey rey·zair·vey
ewn shom·bre seel voo pley

I have a reservation.
J'ai une réservation.
zhey ewn rey·zair·va·syon

My name is ...
Mon nom est ...
mon nom ey ...

Do you have a ... room?	Avez-vous une chambre ...?	a·vey·voo ewn shom·bre ...
single	à un lit	a un lee
double	avec un grand lit	a·vek ung gron lee
twin	avec des lits jumeaux	a·vek dey lee zhew·mo

Can I pay by ...?	Est-ce qu'on peut payer avec ...?	es·kom peu pey·yey a·vek ...
credit card	une carte de crédit	ewn kart de krey·dee
travellers cheque	des chèques de voyage	dey shek de vwa·yazh

How much is it per ...?	Quel est le prix par ...?	kel ey le pree par ...
night	nuit	nwee
person	personne	pair·son

I'd like to stay for (two) nights.
Je voudrais rester pour (deux) nuits. zhe voo·drey res·tey poor (der) nwee

From (July 2) to (July 6).
Du (deux juillet) au (six juillet). dew (de zhwee·yey) o (see zhwee·yey)

Can I see it?
Est-ce que je peux la voir? es·ke zhe peu la vwar

Am I allowed to camp here?
Est-ce que je peux camper ici? es·ke zhe peu kom·pey ee·see

Where's the nearest camp site?
Où est le terrain de camping oo ey ler tey·run de kom·peeng
le plus proche? le plew prosh

requests & queries

When/Where is breakfast served?
Quand/Où le petit kon/oo le pe·tee
déjeuner est-il servi? dey·zhe·ney ey·teel sair·vee

Please wake me at (seven).
Réveillez-moi à (sept) rey·vey·yey·mwa a (set)
heures, s'il vous plaît. eur seel voo pley

Could I have my key, please?
Est-ce que je pourrais avoir es·ke zhe poo·rey a·vwar
la clé, s'il vous plaît? la kley seel voo pley

Can I get another (blanket)?
Est-ce que je peux avoir es·ke zhe pe a·vwar
une autre (couverture)? ewn o·tre (koo·vair·tewr)

Is there a/an ...?	*Avez-vous un ...?*	a·vey·voo un ...
elevator	*ascenseur*	a·son·seur
safe	*coffre-fort*	ko·fre·for

The room is too ...	*C'est trop ...*	sey tro ...
expensive	*cher*	shair
noisy	*bruyant*	brew·yon
small	*petit*	pe·tee

The ... doesn't work.	... ne fonctionne pas.	... ne fong·syon pa
air conditioning	La climatisation	klee·ma·tee·za·syon
fan	Le ventilateur	le von·tee·la·teur
toilet	Les toilettes	le twa·let

This ... isn't clean.	... n'est pas propre.	... ney pa pro·pre
pillow	Cet oreiller	set o·rey·yey
sheet	Ce drap	se drap
towel	Cette serviette	set sair·vee·et

checking out

What time is checkout?
Quand faut-il régler? — kon fo·teel rey·gley

Can I leave my luggage here?
Puis-je laisser mes bagages? — pweezh ley·sey mey ba·gazh

Could I have my ..., please?	Est-ce que je pourrais avoir ..., s'il vous plaît?	es·ke zhe poo·rey a·vwar ... seel voo pley
deposit	ma caution	ma ko·syon
passport	mon passeport	mon pas·por
valuables	mes biens précieux	mey byun prey·syeu

communications & banking

the internet

Where's the local Internet café?
Où est le cybercafé du coin? — oo ey le see·bair·ka·fey dew kwun

How much is it per hour?
C'est combien l'heure? — sey kom·byun leur

I'd like to ...	Je voudrais ...	zhe voo·drey ...
check my email	consulter mon courrier électronique	kon·sewl·tey mong koor·yey ey·lek·tro·neek
get Internet access	me connecter à l'internet	me ko·nek·tey a lun·tair·net
use a printer	utiliser une imprimante	ew·tee·lee·zey ewn um·pree·mont
use a scanner	utiliser un scanner	ew·tee·lee·zey un ska·nair

mobile/cell phone

I'd like a ...	Je voudrais ...	zhe voo·drey ...
mobile/cell phone	louer un	loo·ey um
for hire	portable	por·ta·ble
SIM card for	une carte SIM	ewn kart seem
your network	pour le réseau	poor le rey·zo

What are the rates?	Quels sont les tarifs?	kel son ley ta·reef

telephone

What's your phone number?
Quel est votre numéro de téléphone?   kel ey vo·tre new·mey·ro de tey·ley·fon

The number is ...
Le numéro est ...   le new·mey·ro ey ...

Where's the nearest public phone?
Où est le téléphone   oo ey le tey·ley·fon
public le plus proche?   pewb·leek le plew prosh

I'd like to buy a phone card.
Je voudrais acheter   zhe voo·drey ash·tey
une carte téléphonique.   ewn kart tey·ley·fo·neek

I want to ...	Je veux ...	zhe ve ...
call (Singapore)	téléphoner avec	tey·ley·fo·ney a·vek
	préavis (à Singapour)	prey·a·vee (a sung·ga·poor)
make a local call	faire un appel local	fair un a·pel lo·kal
reverse the charges	téléphoner en PCV	tey·ley·fo·ney om pey·sey·vey

How much does ... cost?	Quel est le prix ...?	kel ey le pree ...
a (three)-minute	d'une communication	dewn ko·mew·nee·ka·syon
call	de (trois) minutes	de (trwa) mee·newt
each extra	de chaque minute	de shak mee·newt
minute	supplémentaire	sew·pley·mon·tair

It's (one euro) per (minute).
(Un euro) pour (une minute).   (un eu·ro) poor (ewn mee·newt)

post office

I want to send a ...	Je voudrais envoyer ...	zhe voo·drey on·vwa·yey ...
fax	un fax	un faks
letter	une lettre	ewn le·tre
parcel	un colis	ung ko·lee
postcard	une carte postale	ewn kart pos·tal
I want to buy a/an ...	Je voudrais acheter ...	zhe voo·drey ash·tey ...
envelope	une enveloppe	ewn on·vlop
stamp	un timbre	un tum·bre
Please send it	Envoyez-le (en Australie)	on·vwa·yey·le (on os·tra·lee)
(to Australia) by ...	..., s'il vous plaît.	... seel voo pley
airmail	par avion	par a·vyon
express mail	en exprès	on neks·pres
registered mail	en recommandé	on re·ko·mon·dey
surface mail	par voie de terre	par vwa de tair

Is there any mail for me?
Y a-t-il du courrier pour moi?   ya·teel dew koor·yey poor mwa

bank

Where's a/an ...?	Où est ...?	oo ey ...
ATM	le guichet automatique	le gee·shey o·to·ma·teek
foreign exchange office	le bureau de change	le bew·ro de shonzh
I'd like to ...	Je voudrais ...	zhe voo·drey ...
arrange a transfer	faire un virement	fair un veer·mon
cash a cheque	encaisser un chèque	ong·key·sey un shek
change a travellers cheque	changer des chèques de voyage	shon·zhey dey shek de vwa·yazh
change money	changer de l'argent	shon·zhey de lar·zhon
get a cash advance	une avance de crédit	ewn a·vons de krey·dee
withdraw money	retirer de l'argent	re·tee·rey de lar·zhon
What's the ...?	Quel est ...?	kel ey ...
charge for that	le tarif	le ta·reef
exchange rate	le taux de change	le to de shonzh

It's ...	C'est ...	sey ...
(12) euros	*(douze) euros*	(dooz) eu·ro
free	*gratuit*	gra·twee

What time does the bank open?
À quelle heure ouvre la banque?　　a kel eur oo·vre la bongk

Has my money arrived yet?
Mon argent est-il arrivé?　　mon ar·zhon ey·teel a·ree·vey

sightseeing

getting in

What time does it ...?	Quelle est l'heure ...?	kel ey leur ...
close	*de fermeture*	de fer·me·tewr
open	*d'ouverture*	doo·vair·tewr

What's the admission charge?
Quel est le prix d'admission?　　kel ey le pree dad·mee·syon

Is there a discount for children/students?
Il y a une réduction pour les　　eel ya ewn rey·dewk·syon poor ley
enfants/étudiants?　　zon·fon/zey·tew·dyon

I'd like a ...	Je voudrais ...	zhe voo·drey ...
catalogue	*un catalogue*	ung ka·ta·log
guide	*un guide*	ung geed
local map	*une carte de la région*	ewn kart de la rey·zhyon

I'd like to see ...	*J'aimerais voir ...*	zhem·rey vwar ...
What's that?	*Qu'est-ce que c'est?*	kes·ke sey
Can I take photos?	*Je peux prendre*	zhe peu pron·dre
	des photos?	dey fo·to

tours

When's the	C'est quand la	sey kon la
next ...?	prochaine ...?	pro·shen ...
day trip	*excursion*	eks·kewr·syon
	d'une journée	dewn zhoor·ney
tour	*excursion*	eks·kewr·syon

Is ... included?	Est-ce que ... est inclus/incluse? m/f	es·ke ... ey tung·klew/tung·klewz
accommodation	le logement m	le lozh·mon
the admission charge	l'admission f	lad·mee·syon
food	la nourriture f	la noo·ree·tewr
transport	le transport m	le trons·por

How long is the tour?
L'excursion dure combien de temps?   leks·kewr·syon dewr kom·byun de tom

What time should we be back?
On doit rentrer pour quelle heure?   on dwa ron·trey poor kel eur

sightseeing

castle	château m	sha·to
cathedral	cathédrale f	ka·tey·dral
church	église f	ey·gleez
main square	place centrale f	plas son·tral
monastery	monastère m	mo·na·stair
monument	monument m	mo·new·mon
museum	musée m	mew·zey
old city	vieille ville f	vyey veel
palace	palais m	pa·ley
ruins	ruines f pl	rween
stadium	stade m	stad
statues	statues f pl	sta·tew

shopping

enquiries

Where's a ...?	Où est ...?	oo es ...
bank	la banque	la bongk
bookshop	la librairie	la lee·brey·ree
camera shop	le magasin photo	le ma·ga·zun fo·to
department store	le grand magasin	le gron ma·ga·zun
grocery store	l'épicerie	ley·pee·sree
market	le marché	le mar·shey
newsagency	le marchand de journaux	le mar·shon de zhoor·no
supermarket	le supermarché	le sew·pair·mar·shey

109

Where can I buy (a padlock)?
Où puis-je acheter (un cadenas)?　　　oo pweezh ash·tey (un kad·na)

I'm looking for ...
Je cherche ...　　　zhe shairsh ...

Can I look at it?
Est-ce que je peux le voir?　　　es·ke zhe peu le vwar

Do you have any others?
Vous en avez d'autres?　　　voo zon a·vey do·tre

Does it have a guarantee?
Est-ce qu'il y a une garantie?　　　es keel ya ewn ga·ron·tee

Can I have it sent overseas?
Pouvez-vous me l'envoyer à l'étranger?　　　poo·vey·voo me lon·vwa·yey a ley·tron·zhey

Can I have my ... repaired?
Puis-je faire réparer ...?　　　pwee·zhe fair rey·pa·rey ...

It's faulty.
C'est défectueux.　　　sey dey·fek·tweu

I'd like ..., please.	*Je voudrais ..., s'il vous plaît.*	zhe voo·drey ... seel voo pley
a bag	*un sac*	un sak
a refund	*un remboursement*	un rom·boors·mon
to return this	*rapporter ceci*	ra·por·tey se·see

paying

How much is it?
C'est combien?　　　sey kom·byun

Can you write down the price?
Pouvez-vous écrire le prix?　　　poo·vey·voo ey·kreer le pree

That's too expensive.
C'est trop cher.　　　sey tro shair

Can you lower the price?
Vous pouvez baisser le prix?　　　voo poo·vey bey·sey le pree

I'll give you (five) euros.
Je vous donnerai (cinq) euros.　　　zhe voo don·rey (sungk) eu·ro

There's a mistake in the bill.
Il y a une erreur dans la note.　　　eel ya ewn ey·reur don la not

Do you accept ...?	Est-ce que je peux payer avec ...?	es·ke zhe pe pey·yey a·vek ...
credit cards	une carte de crédit	ewn kart de krey·dee
debit cards	une carte de débit	ewn kart de dey·bee
travellers cheques	des chèques de voyages	dey shek de vwa·yazh

I'd like ..., please.	Je voudrais ..., s'il vous plaît.	zhe voo·drey ... seel voo pley
a receipt	un reçu	un re·sew
my change	ma monnaie	ma mo·ney

clothes & shoes

Can I try it on?	Puis-je l'essayer?	pwee·zhe ley·sey·yey
My size is (42).	Je fais du (quarante-deux).	zhe fey dew (ka·ront·deu)
It doesn't fit.	Ce n'est pas la bonne taille.	se ney pa la bon tai
small	petit	pe·tee
medium	moyen	mwa·yen
large	grand	gron

books & music

I'd like a ...	Je voudrais ...	zhe voo·drey ...
newspaper	un journal	un zhoor·nal
(in English)	(en anglais)	(on ong·gley)
pen	un stylo	un stee·lo

Is there an English-language bookshop?
Y a-t-il une librairie anglaise?   ya·teel ewn lee·brey·ree ong·gleyz

I'm looking for something by (Camus).
Je cherche quelque chose de (Camus).   zhe shairsh kel·ke shoz de (ka·mew)

Can I listen to this?
Je peux l'écouter ici?   zhe peu ley·koo·tey ee·see

photography

Can you ...?	Pouvez-vous ...?	poo·vey·voo ...
burn a CD from my memory card	copier un CD de ma carte memoire	ko·pyey un se·de de ma kart mey·mwar
develop this film	développer cette pellicule	dey·vlo·pey set pey·lee·kewl
load my film	charger ma pellicule	shar·zhey ma pey·lee·kewl

I need a/an ... film for this camera.	J'ai besoin d'une pellicule ... pour cet appareil.	zhey be·zwun dewn pey·lee·kewl ... poor sey·ta·pa·rey
APS	APS	a·pey·es
B&W	en noir et blanc	on nwar ey·blong
colour	couleur	koo·leur
slide	diapositive	dya·po·zee·teev
(200) speed	rapidité (deux cent)	ra·pee·dee·tey (deu son)

When will it be ready?
Quand est-ce que cela sera prêt?   kon tes·ke se·la se·ra prey

meeting people

greetings, goodbyes & introductions

Hello.	Bonjour.	bon·zhoor
Hi.	Salut.	sa·lew
Good night.	Bonsoir.	bon·swar
Goodbye.	Au revoir.	o re·vwar
See you later.	À bientôt.	a byun·to
Mr	Monsieur	me·syeu
Mrs	Madame	ma·dam
Miss	Mademoiselle	mad·mwa·zel
How are you?	Comment allez-vous?	ko·mon ta·ley·voo
Fine, thanks. And you?	Bien, merci. Et vous?	byun mair·see ey voo
What's your name?	Comment vous appelez-vous?	ko·mon voo za·pley·voo
My name is ...	Je m'appelle ...	zhe ma·pel ...
I'm pleased to meet you.	Enchanté/Enchantée. m/f	on·shon·tey

This is my ...	Voici mon/ma ... m/f	vwa·see mon/ma ...
boyfriend	petit ami	pe·tee ta·mee
brother	frère	frair
daughter	fille	fee·ye
father	père	pair
friend	ami/amie m/f	a·mee
girlfriend	petite amie	pe·teet a·mee
husband	mari	ma·ree
mother	mère	mair
partner (intimate)	partenaire	par·te·nair
sister	sœur	seur
son	fils	fees
wife	femme	fam

Here's my ...	Voici mon ...	vwa·see mon ...
What's your ...?	Quel est votre ...? pol	kel ey vo·tre ...
	Quel est ton ...? inf	kel ey ton ...
address	adresse	a·dress
email address	e-mail	ey·mel
fax number	numéro de fax	new·mey·ro de faks
phone number	numéro de	new·mey·ro de
	téléphone	tey·ley·fon

occupations

What's your occupation?

Vous faites quoi comme métier? pol	voo fet kwa kom mey·tyey
Tu fais quoi comme métier? inf	tew fey kwa kom mey·tyey

I'm a/an ...	Je suis un/une ... m/f	zhe swee zun/zewn ...
artist	artiste m&f	ar·teest
businessperson	homme/femme	om/fem
	d'affaires m/f	da·fair
farmer	agriculteur m	a·gree·kewl·teur
	agricultrice f	a·gree·kewl·trees
manual worker	ouvrier/ouvrière m/f	oo·vree·yey/oo·vree·yair
office worker	employé/employée	om·plwa·yey
	de bureau m/f	de bew·ro
scientist	scientifique m&f	syon·tee·feek
student	étudiant/étudiante m/f	ey·tew·dyon/ey·tew·dyont
tradesperson	ouvrier qualifié m&f	oo·vree·yey ka·lee·fyey

background

Where are you from?	*Vous venez d'où?* pol	voo ve·ney doo
	Tu viens d'où? inf	tew vyun doo
I'm from ...	*Je viens ...*	zhe vyun ...
Australia	*d'Australie*	dos·tra·lee
Canada	*du Canada*	dew ka·na·da
England	*d'Angleterre*	dong·gle·tair
New Zealand	*de la Nouvelle-Zélande*	de la noo·vel·zey·lond
the USA	*des USA*	dey zew·es·a

Are you married?
Est-ce que vous êtes marié(e)? m/f pol		es·ke voo zet mar·yey
Est-ce que tu es marié(e)? m/f inf		es·ke tew ey mar·yey

I'm married.
Je suis marié/mariée. m/f		zhe swee mar·yey

I'm single.
Je suis célibataire. m&f		zhe swee sey·lee·ba·tair

age

How old ...?	*Quel âge ...?*	kel azh ...
are you	*avez-vous* pol	a·vey·voo
	as-tu inf	a·tew
is your daughter	*a votre fille* pol	a vo·tre fee·ye
is your son	*a votre fils* pol	a vo·tre fees
I'm ... years old.	*J'ai ... ans.*	zhey ... on
He/She is ... years old.	*Il/Elle a ... ans.*	eel/el a ... on

feelings

I'm (not) ...	*Je (ne) suis (pas)...*	zhe (ne) swee (pa) ...
Are you ...?	*Êtes-vous ...?* pol	et voo ...
	Es-tu ...? inf	ey·tew ...
happy	*heureux/heureuse* m/f	er·reu/er·reuz
sad	*triste* m&f	treest

I'm ...	J'ai ...	zhey ...
I'm not ...	Je n'ai pas ...	zhe ney pa ...
Are you ...?	Avez-vous ...? pol	a·vey voo ...
	As-tu ...? inf	a·tew ...
cold	froid/froide m/f	frwa/frwad
hot	chaud/chaude m/f	sho/shod
hungry	faim m&f	fum
thirsty	soif m&f	swaf

entertainment

going out

Where can I find ...?	Où sont les ...?	oo son ley ...
clubs	clubs	kleub
gay venues	boîtes gaies	bwat gey
pubs	pubs	peub
I feel like going	Je voudrais	zhe voo·drey
to a/the ...	aller ...	a·ley ...
concert	à un concert	a ung kon·sair
movies	au cinéma	o see·ney·ma
party	à la fête	a la feyt
restaurant	au restaurant	o res·to·ron
theatre	au théâtre	o tey·a·tre

interests

Do you like ...?	Aimes-tu ...? inf	em·tew ...
I like ...	J'aime ...	zhem ...
I don't like ...	Je n'aime pas ...	zhe nem pa ...
art	l'art	lar
cooking	cuisiner	kwee·zee·ney
movies	le cinéma	le see·ney·ma
nightclubs	les boîtes	ley bwat
reading	lire	leer
shopping	faire des courses	fair dey koors
sport	le sport	le spor
travelling	voyager	vwa·ya·zhey

Do you like to ...?	Aimes-tu ...? inf	em·tew ...
dance	danser	don·sey
go to concerts	aller aux concerts	a·ley o kon·sair
listen to music	écouter de	ey·koo·tey de la
	la musique	mew·zeek

food & drink

finding a place to eat

Can you	Est-ce que vous pouvez	es·ke voo poo·vey
recommend a ...?	me conseiller ...?	me kon·sey·yey ...
bar	un bar	um bar
café	un café	ung ka·fey
restaurant	un restaurant	un res·to·ron
I'd like ..., please.	Je voudrais ...,	zhe voo·drey ...
	s'il vous plaît.	seel voo pley
a table for (five)	une table pour	ewn ta·ble poor
	(cinq) personnes	(sungk) pair·son
the (non)smoking	un endroit pour	un on·drwa poor
section	(non-)fumeurs	non·few·me

ordering food

breakfast	petit déjeuner m	pe·tee dey·zhe·ney
lunch	déjeuner m	dey·zhe·ney
dinner	dîner m	dee·ney
snack	casse-croûte m	kas·kroot

What would you recommend?
Qu'est-ce que vous conseillez?   kes·ke voo kon·sey·yey

I'd like (the) ...,	Je voudrais ...,	zhe voo·drey ...
please.	s'il vous plaît.	seel voo pley
bill	l'addition	la·dee·syon
drink list	la carte des boissons	la kart dey bwa·son
menu	la carte	la kart
that dish	ce plat	ser pla
wine list	la carte des vins	la kart dey vun

drinks

(cup of) coffee ...	*(un) café ...*	(ung) ka·fey ...
(cup of) tea ...	*(un) thé ...*	(un) tey ...
with milk	*au lait*	o ley
without sugar	*sans sucre*	son sew·kre
(orange) juice	*jus (d'orange)* m	zhew (do·ronzh)
soft drink	*boisson non-alcoolisée* f	bwa·son non·al·ko·lee·zey
... water	*eau ...*	o ...
hot	*chaude*	shod
sparkling mineral	*minérale gazeuse*	mee·ney·ral ga·zeuz
still mineral	*minérale non-gazeuse*	mee·ney·ral nong·ga·zeuz

in the bar

I'll have ...	*Je prends ...*	zhe pron ...
I'll buy you a drink.	*Je vous offre un verre.*	zhe voo zo·fre un vair
What would you like?	*Qu'est-ce que vous voulez?*	kes·ke voo voo·ley
Cheers!	*Santé!*	son·tey
brandy	*cognac* m	ko·nyak
champagne	*champagne* m	shom·pan·ye
cocktail	*cocktail* m	kok·tel
a shot of (whisky)	*un petit verre de (whisky)*	um pe·tee vair de (wees·kee)
a bottle of ... wine	*une bouteille de vin ...*	ewn boo·tey de vun ...
a glass of ... wine	*un verre de vin ...*	un vair de vun ...
red	*rouge*	roozh
sparkling	*mousseux*	moo·seu
white	*blanc*	blong
a ... of beer	*... de bière*	... de byair
glass	*un verre*	un vair
bottle	*une bouteille*	ewn boo·tey

self-catering

What's the local speciality?
Quelle est la spécialité locale?   kel ey la spey·sya·lee·tey lo·kal

What's that?
Qu'est-ce que c'est, ça?   kes·ke sey sa

How much is (a kilo of cheese)?
C'est combien (le kilo de fromage)?   sey kom·byun (le kee·lo de fro·mazh)

I'd like ...	*Je voudrais ...*	zhe voo·drey ...
(200) grams	*(deux cents) grammes*	(deu son) gram
(two) kilos	*(deux) kilos*	(deu) kee·lo
(three) pieces	*(trois) morceaux*	(trwa) mor·so
(six) slices	*(six) tranches*	(sees) tronsh

Less.	*Moins.*	mwun
Enough.	*Assez.*	a·sey
More.	*Plus.*	plew

special diets & allergies

Is there a vegetarian restaurant near here?
Y a-t-il un restaurant   ya·teel un res·to·ron
végétarien par ici?   vey·zhey·ta·ryun par ee·see

Do you have vegetarian food?
Vous faites les repas végétarien?   voo fet ley re·pa vey·zhey·ta·ryun

Could you prepare	*Pouvez-vous préparer*	poo·vey·voo prey·pa·rey
a meal without ...?	*un repas sans ...?*	un re·pa son ...
butter	*beurre*	beur
eggs	*œufs*	zeu
meat stock	*bouillon gras*	boo·yon gra

I'm allergic to ...	*Je suis allergique ...*	zhe swee za·lair·zheek ...
dairy produce	*aux produits laitiers*	o pro·dwee ley·tyey
gluten	*au gluten*	o glew·ten
MSG	*au glutamate*	o glew·ta·mat
	de sodium	de so·dyom
nuts	*au noix*	no nwa
seafood	*aux fruits de mer*	o frwee de mair

FRANÇAIS – food & drink

118

baba au rhum m	ba·ba o rom	*small sponge cake, often with raisins, soaked in a rum-flavoured syrup*
béarnaise f	bey·ar·neyz	*white sauce of wine or vinegar beaten with egg yolks & flavoured with herbs*
blanquette de veau f	blong·ket de vo	*veal stew in white sauce with cream*
bombe glacée f	bom·be gla·sey	*ice cream with candied fruits, glazed chestnuts & cream*
bouillabaisse f	bwee·ya·bes	*fish soup stewed in a broth with garlic, orange peel, fennel, tomatoes & saffron*
brioche f	bree·yosh	*small roll or cake sometimes flavoured with nuts, currants or candied fruits*
brochette f	bro·shet	*grilled skewer of meat or vegetables*
consommé m	kon·so·mey	*clarified meat or fish-based broth*
contre-filet m	kon·tre·fee·ley	*beef sirloin roast*
coulis m	koo·lee	*fruit or vegetable purée, used as a sauce*
croque-madame m	krok·ma·dam	*grilled or fried ham & cheese sandwich, topped with a fried egg*
croquembouche m	kro·kom·boosh	*cream puffs dipped in caramel*
croque-monsieur m	krok·mes·yeu	*grilled or fried ham & cheese sandwich*
croustade f	kroo·stad	*puff pastry filled with fish, seafood, meat, mushrooms or vegetables*
dijonnaise	dee·zho·nez	*dishes with a mustard-based sauce*
estouffade f	es·too·fad	*meat stewed in wine with carrots & herbs*
friand m	free·yon	*pastry stuffed with minced sausage meat, ham & cheese, or almond cream*
fricandeau m	free·kon·do	*veal fillet simmered in white wine, vegetables herbs & spices • a pork pâté*

fricassée f	free-ka-sey	*lamb, veal or poultry in a thick creamy sauce with mushrooms & onions*
grenadin m	gre-na-dun	*veal (or sometimes poultry) fillet, wrapped in a thin slice of bacon*
michette f	mee-shet	*savoury bread stuffed with cheese, olives, onions & anchovies*
pan-bagnat m	pun ban-ya	*small round bread loaves, filled with onions, vegetables, anchovies & olives*
plateau de fromage m	pla-to de fro-mazh	*cheese board or platter*
pomme duchesse f	pom dew-shes	*fritter of mashed potato, butter & egg yolk*
pot-au-feu m	po-to-fe	*beef, root vegetable & herb stockpot*
potée f	po-tey	*meat & vegetables cooked in a pot*
profiterole m	pro-fee-trol	*small pastry with savoury or sweet fillings*
puits d'amour m	pwee da-moor	*puff pastry filled with custard or jam*
quenelle f	ke-nel	*fish or meat dumpling, often poached*
quiche f	keesh	*tart with meat, fish or vegetable filling*
raclette f	ra-klet	*hot melted cheese, served with potatoes & gherkins*
ragoût m	ra-goo	*stew of meat, fish and/or vegetables*
ratatouille f	ra-ta-too-ye	*vegetable stew*
roulade f	roo-lad	*slice of meat or fish rolled around stuffing*
savarin m	sa-va-run	*sponge cake soaked with a rum syrup & filled with custard, cream & fruits*
savoie f	sav-wa	*light cake made with beaten egg whites*
tartiflette f	tar-tee-flet	*dish of potatoes, cheese & bacon*
velouté m	ver-loo-tey	*rich, creamy soup, usually prepared with vegetables, shellfish or fish purée*
vol-au-vent m	vo-lo-von	*puff pastry filled with a mixture of sauce & meat, seafood or vegetables*

emergencies

basics

Help!	*Au secours!*	o skoor
Stop!	*Arrêtez!*	a·rey·tey
Go away!	*Allez-vous-en!*	a·ley·voo·zon
Thief!	*Au voleur!*	o vo·leur
Fire!	*Au feu!*	o feu
Watch out!	*Faites attention!*	fet a·ton·syon
Call ...!	*Appelez ...!*	a·pley ...
a doctor	*un médecin*	un meyd·sun
an ambulance	*une ambulance*	ewn om·bew·lons
the police	*la police*	la po·lees

It's an emergency!
C'est urgent!
sey tewr·zhon

Could you help me, please?
Est-ce que vous pourriez
m'aider, s'il vous plaît?
es·ke voo poo·ryey
mey·dey seel voo pley

Could I use the telephone?
Est-ce que je pourrais utiliser
le téléphone?
es·ke zhe poo·rey ew·tee·lee·zey
le tey·ley·fon

I'm lost.
Je suis perdu/perdue. m/f
zhe swee pair·dew

Where are the toilets?
Où sont les toilettes?
oo son ley twa·let

police

Where's the police station?
Où est le commissariat de police?
oo ey le ko·mee·sar·ya de po·lees

I want to report an offence.
Je veux signaler un délit.
zhe veu see·nya·ley un dey·lee

I have insurance.
J'ai une assurance.
zhey ewn a·sew·rons

I've been assaulted.
J'ai été attaqué/attaquée. m/f
zhey ey·tey a·ta·key

I've been raped.
J'ai été violé/violée. m/f zhey ey·tey vyo·ley

I've been robbed.
On m'a volé. on ma vo·ley

I've lost my ...	*J'ai perdu ...*	zhey pair·dew ...
My ... was/were stolen.	*On m'a volé ...*	on ma vo·ley ...
backpack	*mon sac à dos*	mon sak a do
bags	*mes valises*	mey va·leez
credit card	*ma carte de crédit*	ma kart de krey·dee
handbag	*mon sac à main*	mon sak a mun
jewellery	*mes bijoux*	mey bee·zhoo
money	*mon argent*	mon ar·zhon
passport	*mon passeport*	mom pas·por
travellers cheques	*mes chèques de voyage*	mey shek de vwa·yazh
wallet	*mon portefeuille*	mom por·te·feu·ye
I want to contact my ...	*Je veux contacter mon ...*	zher veu kon·tak·tey mon ...
consulate	*consulat*	kon·sew·la
embassy	*ambassade*	om·ba·sad

health

medical needs

Where's the nearest ...?	*Où y a t-il ... par ici?*	oo ee a teel ... par ee·see
dentist	*un dentiste*	un don·teest
doctor	*un médecin*	un meyd·sun
hospital	*un hôpital*	u·no·pee·tal
(night) pharmacist	*une pharmacie (de nuit)*	ewn far·ma·see (de nwee)

I need a doctor (who speaks English).
J'ai besoin d'un médecin (qui parle anglais). zhey be·zwun dun meyd·sun (kee parl ong·gley)

Could I see a female doctor?
Est-ce que je peux voir une femme médecin? es·ke zhe peu vwar ewn fam meyd·sun

I've run out of my medication.
Je n'ai plus de médicaments. zhe ney plew de mey·dee·ka·mon

symptoms, conditions & allergies

I'm sick.	Je suis malade.	zhe swee ma·lad
It hurts here.	J'ai une douleur ici.	zhey ewn doo·leur ee·see
I have (a) ...	J'ai ...	zhey ...
asthma	de l'asthme	de las·me
bronchitis	la bronchite	la bron·sheet
constipation	la constiptation	la kon·stee·pa·syon
cough	la toux	la too
diarrhoea	la diarrhée	la dya·rey
fever	la fièvre	la fyev·re
headache	mal à la tête	mal a la tet
heart condition	maladie de cœur	ma·la·dee de keur
nausea	la nausée	la no·zey
pain	une douleur	ewn doo·leur
sore throat	mal à la gorge	mal a la gorzh
toothache	mal aux dents	mal o don
I'm allergic to ...	Je suis allergique ...	zhe swee za·lair·zheek ...
antibiotics	aux antibiotiques	o zon·tee·byo·teek
anti-inflammatories	aux antiinflammatoires	o zun·tee·un·fla·ma·twar
aspirin	à l'aspirine	a las·pee·reen
bees	aux abeilles	o za·bey·ye
codeine	à la codéine	a la ko·dey·een
penicillin	à la pénicilline	a la pey·nee·see·leen
antiseptic	antiseptique m	on·tee·sep·teek
bandage	pansement m	pons·mon
condoms	préservatifs m pl	prey·zair·va·teef
contraceptives	contraceptifs m pl	kon·tre·sep·teef
diarrhoea medicine	médecine pour la diarrhée f	med·seen poor la dya·ey
insect repellent	repulsif anti-insectes m	rey·pewl·seef on·tee·un·sekt
laxatives	laxatifs m pl	lak·sa·teef
painkillers	analgésiques m pl	a·nal·zhey·zeek
rehydration salts	sels de réhydratation m pl	seyl de rey·ee·dra·ta·syon
sleeping tablets	somnifères m pl	som·nee·fair

english–french dictionary

French nouns and adjectives in this dictionary have their gender indicated by ⓜ (masculine) or ⓕ (feminine). If it's a plural noun, you'll also see pl. Words are also marked as n (noun), a (adjective), v (verb), sg (singular), pl (plural), inf (informal) and pol (polite) where necessary.

A

accident *accident* ⓜ ak-see-don
accommodation *logement* ⓜ lozh-mon
adaptor *adaptateur* ⓜ a-dap-ta-teur
address *adresse* ⓕ a-dres
after *après* a-prey
air-conditioned *climatisé* kee-ma-tee-zey
airplane *avion* ⓜ a-vyon
airport *aéroport* ⓜ a-ey-ro-por
alcohol *alcool* ⓜ al-kol
all a *tout/toute* ⓜ/ⓕ too/toot
allergy *allergie* ⓕ a-lair-zhee
ambulance *ambulance* ⓕ om-bew-lons
and *et* ey
ankle *cheville* ⓕ she-vee-ye
arm *bras* ⓜ bra
ashtray *cendrier* ⓜ son-dree-yey
ATM *guichet automatique de banque* ⓜ
  gee-shey o-to-ma-teek de bonk

B

baby *bébé* ⓜ bey-bey
back (body) *dos* ⓜ do
backpack *sac à dos* ⓜ sak a do
bad *mauvais/mauvaise* ⓜ/ⓕ mo-vey/mo-veyz
bag *sac* ⓜ sak
baggage claim *retrait des bagages* ⓜ
  re-trey dey ba-gazh
bank *banque* ⓕ bonk
bar *bar* ⓜ bar
bathroom *salle de bain* ⓕ sal de bun
battery (car) *batterie* ⓕ bat-ree
battery (general) *pile* ⓕ peel
beautiful *beau/belle* ⓜ/ⓕ bo/bel
bed *lit* ⓜ lee
beer *bière* ⓕ byair
before *avant* a-von
behind *derrière* dair-yair
Belgium *Belgique* ⓕ bel-zheek
bicycle *vélo* ⓜ vey-lo

big *grand/grande* ⓜ/ⓕ gron/grond
bill *addition* ⓕ a-dee-syon
black *noir/noire* ⓜ/ⓕ nwar
blanket *couverture* ⓕ koo-vair-tewr
blood group *groupe sanguin* ⓜ groop song-gun
blue *bleu/bleue* ⓜ/ⓕ bler
book (make a reservation) v *réserver* rey-zair-vey
bottle *bouteille* ⓕ boo-tey
bottle opener *ouvre-bouteille* ⓜ oo-vre-boo-tey
boy *garçon* ⓜ gar-son
brakes (car) *freins* ⓜ frun
breakfast *petit déjeuner* ⓜ pe-tee dey-zheu-ney
broken (faulty) *défectueux/défectueuse* ⓜ/ⓕ
  dey-fek-tweu/dey-fek-tweuz
bus *(auto)bus* ⓜ (o-to)bews
business *affaires* ⓕ a-fair
buy *acheter* ash-tey

C

café *café* ⓜ ka-fey
camera *appareil photo* ⓜ a-pa-rey fo-to
camp site *terrain de camping* ⓜ tey-run de kom-peeng
cancel *annuler* a-new-ley
can opener *ouvre-boîte* ⓜ oo-vre-bwat
car *voiture* ⓕ vwa-tewr
cash *argent* ⓜ ar-zhon
cash (a cheque) v *encaisser* ong-key-sey
cell phone *téléphone portable* ⓜ tey-ley-fon por-ta-ble
centre *centre* ⓜ son-tre
change (money) v *échanger* ey-shon-zhey
cheap *bon marché* ⓜ&ⓕ bon mar-shey
check (bill) *addition* ⓕ a-dee-syon
check-in n *enregistrement* ⓜ on-re-zhee-stre-mon
chest *poitrine* ⓕ pwa-treen
child *enfant* ⓜ&ⓕ on-fon
cigarette *cigarette* ⓕ see-ga-ret
city *ville* ⓕ veel
clean a *propre* ⓜ&ⓕ pro-pre
closed *fermé/fermée* ⓜ/ⓕ fair-mey
coffee *café* ⓜ ka-fey
coins *pièces* ⓕ pyes
cold a *froid/froide* ⓜ/ⓕ frwa/frwad

collect call *appel en PCV* ⓜ a-pel on pey-sey-vey
come *venir* ve-neer
computer *ordinateur* ⓜ or-dee-na-teur
condom *préservatif* ⓜ prey-zair-va-teef
contact lenses *verres de contact* ⓜ vair de kon-takt
cook v *cuire* kweer
cost *coût* ⓜ koo
credit card *carte de crédit* ⓕ kart de krey-dee
cup *tasse* ⓕ tas
currency exchange *taux de change* ⓜ to de shonzh
customs (immigration) *douane* ⓕ dwan

D

dangerous *dangereux/dangereuse* ⓜ/ⓕ
    don-zhreu/don-zhreuz
date (time) *date* ⓕ dat
day *date de naissance* ⓕ dat de ney-sons
delay *retard* ⓜ re-tard
dentist *dentiste* ⓕ don-teest
depart *partir* par-teer
diaper *couche* ⓕ koosh
dictionary *dictionnaire* ⓜ deek-syo-nair
dinner *dîner* ⓜ dee-ney
direct *direct/directe* ⓜ/ⓕ dee-rekt
dirty *sale* ⓜ&ⓕ sal
disabled *handicapé/handicapée* ⓜ/ⓕ on-dee-ka-pey
discount *remise* ⓕ re-meez
doctor *médecin* ⓜ meyd-sun
double bed *grand lit* ⓜ gron lee
double room *chambre pour deux personnes* ⓕ
    shom-bre poor de pair-son
drink *boisson* ⓕ bwa-son
drive v *conduire* kon-dweer
drivers licence *permis de conduire* ⓜ
    pair-mee de kon-dweer
drugs (illicit) *drogue* ⓕ drog
dummy (pacifier) *tétine* ⓕ tey-teen

E

ear *oreille* ⓕ o-rey
east *est* ⓜ est
eat *manger* mon-zhey
economy class *classe touriste* ⓕ klas too-reest
electricity *électricité* ⓕ ey-lek-tree-see-tey
elevator *ascenseur* ⓜ a-son-seur
email *e-mail* ⓜ ey-mel
embassy *ambassade* ⓕ om-ba-sad
emergency *cas urgent* ⓜ ka ewr-zhon

English (language) *anglais/anglaise* ⓜ/ⓕ
    ong-gley/ong-gleyz
entrance *entrée* ⓕ on-trey
evening *soir* ⓜ swar
exchange rate *taux de change* ⓜ to de shonzh
exit *sortie* ⓕ sor-tee
expensive *cher/chère* ⓜ/ⓕ shair
express mail *exprès* eks-pres
eye *œil* ⓜ eu-yee

F

far *lointain/lointaine* ⓜ/ⓕ lwun-tun/lwun-ten
fast *rapide* ⓜ&ⓕ ra-peed
father *père* ⓜ pair
film (camera) *pellicule* ⓕ pey-lee-kewl
finger *doigt* ⓜ dwa
first-aid kit *trousse à pharmacie* ⓕ troos a far-ma-see
first class *première classe* ⓕ pre-myair klas
fish *poisson* ⓜ pwa-son
food *nourriture* ⓕ noo-ree-tewr
foot *pied* ⓜ pyey
fork *fourchette* ⓕ foor-shet
France *France* frons
free (of charge) *gratuit/gratuite* ⓜ/ⓕ
    gra-twee/gra-tweet
French (language) *Français* fron-sey
friend *ami/amie* ⓜ/ⓕ a-mee
fruit *fruit* ⓜ frwee
full *plein/pleine* ⓜ/ⓕ plun/plen
funny *drôle* ⓜ&ⓕ drol

G

gift *cadeau* ⓜ ka-do
girl *fille* ⓕ fee-ye
glass (drinking) *verre* ⓜ vair
glasses *lunettes* ⓕ pl lew-net
go *aller* a-ley
good *bon/bonne* ⓜ/ⓕ bon
green *vert/verte* ⓜ/ⓕ vairt
guide n *guide* ⓜ geed

H

half *moitié* ⓕ mwa-tyey
hand *main* ⓕ mun
handbag *sac à main* ⓕ sak a mun
happy *heureux/heureuse* ⓜ/ⓕ eu-reu/eu-reuz
have *avoir* a-vwar

D

he *il* eel
head *tête* ⓕ tet
heart *cœur* ⓜ keur
heat *chaleur* ⓕ sha-leur
heavy *lourd/lourde* ⓜ/ⓕ loor/loord
help v *aider* ey-dey
here *ici* ee-see
high *haut/haute* ⓜ/ⓕ o/ot
highway *autoroute* ⓕ o-to-root
hike v *faire la randonnée* fair la ron-do-ney
holiday *vacances* ⓕ pl va-kons
homosexual n *homosexuel/homosexuelle* ⓜ/ⓕ
   o-mo-sek-swel
hospital *hôpital* ⓜ o-pee-tal
hot *chaud/chaude* ⓜ/ⓕ sho/shod
hotel *hôtel* ⓜ o-tel
(be) hungry *avoir faim* a-vwar fum
husband *mari* ⓜ ma-ree

I

I *je* zhe
identification (card) *carte d'identité* ⓕ
   kart dee-don-tee-tey
ill *malade* ⓜ&ⓕ ma-lad
important *important/importante* ⓜ/ⓕ
   um-por-ton/um-por-tont
included *compris/comprise* ⓜ/ⓕ
   kom-pree/kom-preez
injury *blessure* ⓕ bley-sewr
insurance *assurance* ⓕ a-sew-rons
Internet *Internet* ⓜ un-tair-net
interpreter *interprète* ⓜ&ⓕ un-tair-pret

J

jewellery *bijoux* ⓜ pl bee-zhoo
job *travail* ⓜ tra-vai

K

key *clé* ⓕ kley
kilogram *kilogramme* ⓜ kee-lo-gram
kitchen *cuisine* ⓕ kwee-zeen
knife *couteau* ⓜ koo-to

L

laundry (place) *blanchisserie* ⓕ blon-shees-ree
lawyer *avocat/avocate* ⓜ/ⓕ a-vo-ka/a-vo-kat

left (direction) *à gauche* a gosh
left-luggage office *consigne* ⓕ kon-see-nye
leg *jambe* ⓕ zhomb
lesbian n *lesbienne* ⓕ les-byen
less *moins* mwun
letter (mail) *lettre* ⓕ ley-trer
lift (elevator) *ascenseur* ⓜ a-son-seur
light *lumière* ⓕ lew-myair
like v *aimer* ey-mey
lock *serrure* ⓕ sey-rewr
long *long/longue* ⓜ/ⓕ long(k)
lost *perdu/perdue* ⓜ/ⓕ pair-dew
lost-property office *bureau des objets trouvés* ⓜ
   bew-ro dey zob-zhey troo-vey
love v *aimer* ey-mey
luggage *bagages* ⓜ pl ba-gazh
lunch *déjeuner* ⓜ dey-zheu-ney

M

mail *courrier* ⓜ koo-ryey
man *homme* ⓜ om
map *carte* ⓕ kart
market *marché* ⓜ mar-shey
matches *allumettes* ⓕ pl a-lew-met
meat *viande* ⓕ vyond
medicine *médecine* ⓕ med-seen
menu *carte* kart
message *message* ⓜ mey-sazh
milk *lait* ⓜ ley
minute *minute* ⓕ mee-newt
mobile phone *téléphone portable* ⓜ
   tey-ley-fon por-ta-ble
money *argent* ⓜ ar-zhon
month *mois* ⓜ mwa
morning *matin* ⓜ ma-tun
mother *mère* ⓕ mair
motorcycle *moto* ⓕ mo-to
motorway *autoroute* ⓕ o-to-root
mouth *bouche* ⓕ boosh
music *musique* ⓕ mew-zeek

N

name *nom* ⓜ nom
napkin *serviette* ⓕ sair-vyet
nappy *couche* ⓕ koosh
near *près de* prey de
neck *cou* ⓜ koo
new *nouveau/nouvelle* ⓜ/ⓕ noo-vo/noo-vel

news *les nouvelles* ley noo-vel
newspaper *journal* ⓜ zhoor-nal
night *nuit* ⓕ nwee
no *non* non
noisy *bruyant/bruyante* ⓜ/ⓕ brew-yon/brew-yont
nonsmoking *non-fumeur* non-few-meur
north *nord* ⓜ nor
nose *nez* ⓜ ney
now *maintenant* mun-te-non
number *numéro* ⓜ new-mey-ro

O

oil (engine) *huile* ⓕ weel
old *vieux/vieille* ⓜ/ⓕ vyeu/vyey
one-way ticket *billet simple* ⓜ bee-yey sum-ple
open a *ouvert/ouverte* ⓜ/ⓕ oo-vair/oo-vairt
outside *dehors* de-or

P

package *paquet* ⓜ pa-key
paper *papier* ⓜ pa-pyey
park (car) v *garer (une voiture)* ga-rey (ewn vwa-tewr)
passport *passeport* ⓜ pas-por
pay *payer* pey-yey
pen *stylo* ⓜ stee-lo
petrol *essence* ⓕ ey-sons
pharmacy *pharmacie* ⓕ far-ma-see
phonecard *télécarte* ⓕ tey-ley-kart
photo *photo* ⓕ fo-to
plate *assiette* ⓕ a-syet
police *police* ⓕ po-lees
postcard *carte postale* ⓕ kart pos-tal
post office *bureau de poste* ⓜ bew-ro de post
pregnant *enceinte* on-sunt
price *prix* ⓜ pree

Q

quiet *tranquille* ⓜ & ⓕ trong-keel

R

rain n *pluie* ⓕ plwee
razor *rasoir* ⓜ ra-zwar
receipt *reçu* ⓜ re-sew
red *rouge* roozh
refund *remboursement* ⓜ rom-boor-se-mon
registered mail *en recommandé* on re-ko-mon-dey

rent v *louer* loo-ey
repair v *réparer* rey-pa-rey
reservation *réservation* ⓕ rey-zair-va-syon
restaurant *restaurant* ⓜ res-to-ron
return v *revenir* rev-neer
return ticket *aller retour* ⓜ a-ley re-toor
right (direction) *à droite* a drwat
road *route* ⓕ root
room *chambre* ⓕ shom-bre

S

safe a *sans danger* ⓜ & ⓕ son don-zhey
sanitary napkin *serviette hygiénique* ⓕ
    sair-vyet ee-zhyey-neek
seat *place* ⓕ plas
send *envoyer* on vwa-yey
service station *station-service* ⓕ sta-syon-sair-vees
sex *sexe* ⓜ seks
shampoo *shampooing* ⓜ shom-pwung
share (a dorm) *partager* par-ta-zhey
shaving cream *mousse à raser* ⓕ moos a ra-zey
she *elle* el
sheet (bed) *drap* ⓜ dra
shirt *chemise* ⓕ she-meez
shoes *chaussures* ⓕ pl sho-sewr
shop *magasin* ⓜ ma-ga-zun
short *court/courte* ⓜ/ⓕ koor/koort
shower *douche* ⓕ doosh
single room *chambre pour une personne* ⓕ
    shom-bre poor ewn pair-son
skin *peau* ⓕ po
skirt *jupe* ⓕ zhewp
sleep v *dormir* dor-meer
slowly *lentement* lon-te-mon
small *petit/petite* ⓜ/ⓕ pe-tee/pe-teet
smoke (cigarettes) v *fumer* few-mey
soap *savon* ⓜ sa-von
some *quelques* kel-ke
soon *bientôt* byun-to
south *sud* ⓜ sewd
souvenir shop *magasin de souvenirs* ⓜ
    ma-ga-zun de soov-neer
speak *parler* par-ley
spoon *cuillère* ⓕ kwee-yair
stamp *timbre* ⓜ tum-bre
stand-by ticket *billet stand-by* ⓜ bee-yey stond-bai
station (train) *gare* ⓕ gar
stomach *estomac* ⓜ es-to-ma
stop v *arrêter* a-rey-tey

stop (bus) *arrêt* ⓜ a-rey
street *rue* ⓕ rew
student *étudiant/étudiante* ⓜ/ⓕ
ey-tew-dyon/ey-tew-dyont
sun *soleil* ⓜ so-ley
sunscreen *écran solaire* ⓜ ey-kron so-lair
swim v *nager* na-zhey
Switzerland *Suisse* swees

T

tampons *tampons* ⓜ pl tom-pon
taxi *taxi* ⓜ tak-see
teaspoon *petite cuillère* ⓕ pe-teet kwee-yair
teeth *dents* ⓕ don
telephone n *téléphone* ⓜ tey-ley-fon
television *télé(vision)* ⓕ tey-ley(vee-zyon)
temperature (weather) *température* ⓕ
tom-pey-ra-tewr
tent *tente* ⓕ tont
that (one) *cela* se-la
they *ils/elles* ⓜ/ⓕ eel/el
(be) thirsty *avoir soif* a-vwar swaf
this (one) *ceci* se-see
throat *gorge* ⓕ gorzh
ticket *billet* ⓜ bee-yey
time *temps* ⓜ tom
tired *fatigué/fatiguée* ⓜ/ⓕ fa-tee-gey
tissues *mouchoirs en papier* ⓜ pl
moo-shwar om pa-pyey
today *aujourd'hui* o-zhoor-dwee
toilet *toilettes* ⓕ pl twa-let
tomorrow *demain* de-mun
tonight *ce soir* se swar
toothbrush *brosse à dents* ⓕ bros a don
toothpaste *dentifrice* ⓜ don-tee-frees
torch (flashlight) *lampe de poche* ⓕ lomp de posh
tour *voyage* ⓜ vwa-yazh
tourist office *office de tourisme* ⓜ
o-fees de too-rees-me
towel *serviette* ⓕ sair-vyet
train *train* ⓜ trun
translate *traduire* tra-dweer
travel agency *agence de voyage* ⓕ
a-zhons de vwa-yazh
travellers cheque *chèque de voyage* ⓜ
shek de vwa-yazh
trousers *pantalon* ⓜ pon-ta-lon

twin beds *lits jumeaux* ⓜ pl dey lee zhew-mo
tyre *pneu* ⓜ pneu

U

underwear *sous-vêtements* ⓜ soo-vet-mon
urgent *urgent/urgente* ⓜ/ⓕ ewr-zhon/ewr-zhont

V

vacant *libre* ⓜ&ⓕ lee-bre
vacation *vacances* ⓕ pl va-kons
vegetable n *légume* ⓜ ley-gewm
vegetarian a *végétarien/végétarienne* ⓜ/ⓕ
vey-zhey-ta-ryun/vey-zhey-ta-ryen
visa *visa* ⓜ vee-za

W

waiter *serveur/serveuse* ⓜ/ⓕ sair-veur/sair-veurz
walk v *marcher* mar-shey
wallet *portefeuille* ⓜ por-te-feu-ye
warm a *chaud/chaude* ⓜ/ⓕ sho/shod
wash (something) *laver* la-vey
watch *montre* ⓕ mon-tre
water *eau* ⓕ o
we *nous* noo
weekend *week-end* ⓜ week-end
west *ouest* ⓜ west
wheelchair *fauteuil roulant* ⓜ fo-teu-ye roo-lon
when *quand* kon
where *où* oo
white *blanc/blanche* ⓜ/ⓕ blong/blonsh
who *qui* kee
why *pourquoi* poor-kwa
wife *femme* ⓕ fam
window *fenêtre* ⓕ fe-ney-tre
wine *vin* ⓜ vun
with *avec* a-vek
without *sans* son
woman *femme* ⓕ fam
write *écrire* ey-kreer

Y

yellow *jaune* zhon
yes *oui* wee
yesterday *hier* ee-yair
you sg inf *tu* tew
you sg pol *vous* voo
you pl *vous* voo

German

german alphabet

A a a	B b be	C c tse	D d de	E e e
F f ef	G g ge	H h ha	I i i	J j yot
K k ka	L l el	M m em	N n en	O o o
P p pe	Q q ku	R r er	S s es	T t te
U u u	V v fau	W w ve	X x iks	Y y ewp-si-lon
Z z tset				

german

introduction

Romantic, flowing, literary . . . not usually how German (*Deutsch* doytsh) is described, but maybe it's time to reconsider. After all, this is the language that's played a major role in the history of Europe and remains one of the most widely spoken languages on the continent. It's taught throughout the world and chances are you're already familiar with a number of German words that have entered English – *kindergarten*, *kitsch* and *hamburger*, for example, are all of German origin.

German is spoken by around 100 million people, and is the official language of Germany, Austria and Liechtenstein, as well as one of the official languages of Belgium, Switzerland and Luxembourg. German didn't spread across the rest of the world with the same force as English, Spanish or French. Germany only became a unified nation in 1871 and never established itself as a colonial power. After the reunification of East and West Germany, however, German has become more important in global politics and economics. Its role in science has long been recognised and German literature lays claim to some of the most famous written works ever printed. Just think of the enormous influence of Goethe, Nietzsche, Freud and Einstein.

German is usually divided into two forms – Low German (*Plattdeutsch* plat-doytsh) and High German (*Hochdeutsch* hokh-doytsh). Low German is an umbrella term used for the dialects spoken in Northern Germany. High German is considered the standard form and is understood throughout German-speaking communities, from the Swiss Alps to the cosy cafés of Vienna; it's also the form used in this phrasebook.

Both German and English belong to the West Germanic language family, along with a number of other languages including Dutch and Yiddish. The primary reason why German and English have grown apart is that the Normans, on invading England in 1066, brought with them a large number of non-Germanic words. As well as the recognisable words, the grammar of German will also make sense to an English speaker. Even with a slight grasp of German grammar, you'll still manage to get your point across. On the other hand, German tends to join words together (while English uses a number of separate words) to express a single notion. You shouldn't be intimidated by this though – after a while you'll be able to tell parts of words and recognising 'the Football World Cup qualifying match' hidden within *Fussballweltmeisterschaftsqualifikationsspiel* won't be a problem at all!

pronunciation

vowel sounds

German vowels can be short or long, which influences the meaning of words. They're pronounced crisply and distinctly, so *Tee* (tea) is tey, not *tey*·ee.

symbol	english equivalent	german example	transliteration
a	run	*hat*	hat
aa	father	*habe*	*haa*·be
ai	aisle	*mein*	main
air	fair	*Bär*	bair
aw	saw	*Boot*	bawt
e	bet	*Männer*	*me*·ner
ee	see	*fliegen*	*flee*·gen
eu	nurse	*schön*	sheun
ew	ee pronounced with rounded lips	*zurück*	tsu·*rewk*
ey	as in 'bet', but longer	*leben*	*ley*·ben
i	hit	*mit*	mit
o	pot	*Koffer*	*ko*·fer
oo	zoo	*Schuhe*	*shoo*·e
ow	now	*Haus*	hows
oy	toy	*Leute, Häuser*	*loy*·te, *hoy*·zer
u	put	*unter*	*un*·ter

word stress

Almost all German words are pronounced with stress on the first syllable. While this is a handy rule of thumb, you can always rely on the coloured pronunciation guides, which show the stressed syllables in italics.

consonant sounds

All German consonant sounds exist in English except for the kh and r sounds. The kh sound is generally pronounced at the back of the throat, like the 'ch' in 'Bach' or the Scottish 'loch'. The r sound is pronounced at the back of the throat, almost like saying g, but with some friction, a bit like gargling.

symbol	english equivalent	german example	transliteration
b	bed	*Bett*	bet
ch	cheat	*Tschüss*	chews
d	dog	*dein*	dain
f	fat	*vier*	feer
g	go	*gehen*	*gey*·en
h	hat	*helfen*	*hel*·fen
k	kit	*kein*	kain
kh	loch	*ich*	ikh
l	lot	*laut*	lowt
m	man	*Mann*	man
n	not	*nein*	nain
ng	ring	*singen*	*zing*·en
p	pet	*Preis*	prais
r	run (throaty)	*Reise*	*rai*·ze
s	sun	*heiß*	hais
sh	shot	*schön*	sheun
t	top	*Tag*	taak
ts	hits	*Zeit*	tsait
v	very	*wohnen*	*vaw*·nen
y	yes	*ja*	yaa
z	zero	*sitzen*	*zi*·tsen
zh	pleasure	*Garage*	ga·*raa*·zhe

basics

language difficulties

Do you speak English?
Sprechen Sie Englisch? — shpre·khen zee eng·lish

Do you understand?
Verstehen Sie? — fer·shtey·en zee

I (don't) understand.
Ich verstehe (nicht). — ikh fer·shtey·e (nikht)

What does (Kugel) mean?
Was bedeutet (Kugel)? — vas be·doy·tet (koo·gel)

How do you ...?	Wie ...?	vee ...
pronounce this	spricht man dieses Wort aus	shprikht man dee·zes vort ows
write (Schweiz)	schreibt man (Schweiz)	shraipt man (shvaits)

Could you please ...?	Könnten Sie ...?	keun·ten zee ...
repeat that	das bitte wiederholen	das bi·te vee·der·haw·len
speak more slowly	bitte langsamer sprechen	bi·te lang·za·mer shpre·khen
write it down	das bitte aufschreiben	das bi·te owf·shrai·ben

essentials

Yes.	Ja.	yaa
No.	Nein.	nain
Please.	Bitte.	bi·te
Thank you.	Danke.	dang·ke
Thank you very much.	Vielen Dank.	fee·len dangk
You're welcome.	Bitte.	bi·te
Excuse me.	Entschuldigung.	ent·shul·di·gung
Sorry.	Entschuldigung.	ent·shul·di·gung

numbers

0	null	nul		16	sechzehn	zeks·tseyn	
1	eins	ains		17	siebzehn	zeep·tseyn	
2	zwei	tsvai		18	achtzehn	akht·tseyn	
3	drei	drai		19	neunzehn	noyn·tseyn	
4	vier	feer		20	zwanzig	tsvan·tsikh	
5	fünf	fewnf		21	einundzwanzig	ain·unt·tsvan·tsikh	
6	sechs	zeks		22	zweiundzwanzig	tsvai·unt·tsvan·tsikh	
7	sieben	zee·ben		30	dreißig	drai·tsikh	
8	acht	akht		40	vierzig	feer·tsikh	
9	neun	noyn		50	fünfzig	fewnf·tsikh	
10	zehn	tseyn		60	sechzig	zekh·tsikh	
11	elf	elf		70	siebzig	zeep·tsikh	
12	zwölf	zveulf		80	achtzig	akht·tsikh	
13	dreizehn	drai·tseyn		90	neunzig	noyn·tsikh	
14	vierzehn	feer·tseyn		100	hundert	hun·dert	
15	fünfzehn	fewnf·tseyn		1000	tausend	tow·sent	

time & dates

What time is it?	Wie spät ist es?	vee shpeyt ist es
It's one o'clock.	Es ist ein Uhr.	es ist ain oor
It's (10) o'clock.	Es ist (zehn) Uhr.	es ist (tseyn) oor
Quarter past (one).	Viertel nach (eins).	fir·tel naakh (ains)
Half past (one).	Halb (zwei). (lit: half two)	halp (tsvai)
Quarter to (one).	Viertel vor (eins).	fir·tel fawr (ains)
At what time ...?	Um wie viel Uhr ...?	um vee feel oor ...
At ...	Um ...	um ...
am	vormittags	fawr·mi·taaks
pm (midday–6pm)	nachmittags	naakh·mi·taaks
pm (6pm–midnight)	abends	aa·bents
Monday	Montag	mawn·taak
Tuesday	Dienstag	deens·taak
Wednesday	Mittwoch	mit·vokh
Thursday	Donnerstag	do·ners·taak
Friday	Freitag	frai·taak
Saturday	Samstag	zams·taak
Sunday	Sonntag	zon·taak

January	Januar	yan·u·aar
February	Februar	fey·bru·aar
March	März	merts
April	April	a·pril
May	Mai	mai
June	Juni	yoo·ni
July	Juli	yoo·li
August	August	ow·gust
September	September	zep·tem·ber
October	Oktober	ok·taw·ber
November	November	no·vem·ber
December	Dezember	de·tsem·ber

What date is it today?
  Der Wievielte ist heute?   dair vee·feel·te ist hoy·te

It's (18 October).
  Heute ist (der achtzehnte Oktober).   hoy·te ist dair (akh·tseyn·te ok·taw·ber)

| since (May) | seit (Mai) | zait (mai) |
| until (June) | bis (Juni) | bis (yoo·ni) |

yesterday	gestern	ges·tern
today	heute	hoy·te
tonight	heute Abend	hoy·te aa·bent
tomorrow	morgen	mor·gen

last ...		
night	vergangene Nacht	fer·gang·e·ne nakht
week	letzte Woche	lets·te vo·khe
month	letzten Monat	lets·ten maw·nat
year	letztes Jahr	lets·tes yaar

next ...		
week	nächste Woche	neykhs·te vo·khe
month	nächsten Monat	neykhs·ten maw·nat
year	nächstes Jahr	neykhs·tes yaar

yesterday/	gestern/	ges·tern/
tomorrow ...	morgen ...	mor·gen ...
morning	Morgen	mor·gen
afternoon	Nachmittag	naakh·mi·taak
evening	Abend	aa·bent

weather

What's the weather like?	*Wie ist das Wetter?*	vee ist das *ve*·ter

It's ...

cloudy	*Es ist wolkig.*	es ist *vol*·kikh
cold	*Es ist kalt.*	es ist kalt
hot	*Es ist heiß.*	es ist hais
raining	*Es regnet.*	es *reyg*·net
snowing	*Es schneit.*	es shnait
sunny	*Es ist sonnig.*	es ist *zo*·nikh
warm	*Es ist warm.*	es ist varm
windy	*Es ist windig.*	es ist *vin*·dikh

spring	*Frühling* m	*frew*·ling
summer	*Sommer* m	*zo*·mer
autumn	*Herbst* m	herpst
winter	*Winter* m	*vin*·ter

border crossing

I'm here ...	*Ich bin hier ...*	ikh bin heer ...
in transit	*auf der Durchreise*	owf dair *durkh*·rai·ze
on business	*auf Geschäftsreise*	owf ge·*shefts*·rai·ze
on holiday	*im Urlaub*	im *oor*·lowp

I'm here for ...	*Ich bin hier für ...*	ikh bin heer fewr ...
(10) days	*(zehn) Tage*	(tseyn) *taa*·ge
(three) weeks	*(drei) Wochen*	(drai) *vo*·khen
(two) months	*(zwei) Monate*	(tsvai) *maw*·na·te

I'm going to (Salzburg).
Ich gehe nach (Salzburg).   ikh *gey*·e nakh *zalts*·boorg

I'm staying at the (Hotel Park).
Ich wohne im (Hotel Park).   ikh *vaw*·ne im (ho·*tel* park)

I have nothing to declare.
Ich habe nichts zu verzollen.   ikh *haa*·be nikhts tsoo fer·*tso*·len

I have something to declare.
Ich habe etwas zu verzollen.   ikh *haa*·be *et*·vas tsoo fer·*tso*·len

That's (not) mine.
Das ist (nicht) meins.   das ist (nikht) mains

transport

tickets & luggage

Where can I buy a ticket?
Wo kann ich eine Fahrkarte kaufen?   vaw kan ikh *ai*·ne *faar*·kar·te *kow*·fen

Do I need to book a seat?
Muss ich einen Platz   mus ikh *ai*·nen plats
reservieren lassen?   re·zer·*vee*·ren *la*·sen

One ...ticket to	Einen ... nach	ai·nen ... naakh
(Berlin), please.	(Berlin), bitte.	(ber·*leen*) bi·te
one-way	einfache Fahrkarte	ain·fa·khe faar·kar·te
return	Rückfahrkarte	rewk·faar·kar·te

I'd like to ...	Ich möchte meine	ikh meukh·te mai·ne
my ticket, please.	Fahrkarte bitte ...	faar·kar·te bi·te ...
cancel	zurückgeben	tsu·rewk·gey·ben
change	ändern lassen	en·dern la·sen
collect	abholen	ab·ho·len
confirm	bestätigen lassen	be·shtey·ti·gen la·sen

I'd like a ...	Ich hätte gern	ikh he·te gern
seat, please.	einen ...	ai·nen ...
nonsmoking	Nichtraucherplatz	nikht·row·kher·plats
smoking	Raucherplatz	row·kher·plats

How much is it?
Was kostet das?   vas *kos*·tet das

Is there air conditioning?
Gibt es eine Klimaanlage?   gipt es *ai*·ne *klee*·ma·an·*laa*·ge

Is there a toilet?
Gibt es eine Toilette?   gipt es *ai*·ne to·a·*le*·te

How long does the trip take?
Wie lange dauert die Fahrt?   vee *lang*·e *dow*·ert dee faart

Is it a direct route?
Ist es eine direkte Verbindung?   ist es *ai*·ne di·*rek*·te fer·*bin*·dung

I'd like a luggage locker.
Ich hätte gern ein Gepäckschließfach.   ikh *he*·te gern ain ge·*pek*·shlees·fakh

My luggage has been ...	Mein Gepäck ist ...	main ge·pek ist ...
damaged	beschädigt	be·shey·dikht
lost	verloren gegangen	fer·law·ren ge·gang·en
stolen	gestohlen worden	ge·shtaw·len vor·den

getting around

Where does flight (D4) arrive?
Wo ist die Ankunft des Fluges (D4)?   vaw ist dee an·kunft des floo·ges (de feer)

Where does flight (D4) depart?
Wo ist die der Abflug des Fluges (D4)?   vaw ist dair ab·flug des floo·ges (de feer)

Where's the ...?	Wo ist ...?	vaw ist ...
arrivalls hall	Ankunftshalle	an·kunfts·ha·le
departures hall	Abflughalle	ab·flug·ha·le

Is this the ...	Fährt ...	fairt ...
to (Hamburg)?	nach (Hamburg)?	nakh (ham·burg)
boat	das Boot	das bawt
bus	der Bus	dair bus
plane	das Flugzeug	das flook·tsoyk
train	der Zug	dair tsook

What time's	Wann fährt der	van fairt dair
the ... bus?	... Bus?	... bus
first	erste	ers·te
last	letzte	lets·te
next	nächste	neykhs·te

At what time does it leave?
Wann fährt es ab?   van fairt es ap

At what time does it arrive?
Wann kommt es an?   van komt es an

How long will it be delayed?
Wie viel Verspätung wird es haben?   vee feel fer·shpey·tung virt es haa·ben

What station/stop is this?
Welcher Bahnhof/Halt ist das?   vel·kher baan·hawf/halt ist das

What's the next station/stop?
Welches ist der nächste   vel·khes ist dair neykhs·te
Bahnhof/Halt?   baan·hawf/halt

Does it stop at (Freiburg)?
Hält es in (Freiburg)?   helt *es* in (*frai*·boorg)

Please tell me when we get to (Kiel).
Könnten Sie mir bitte sagen,   *keun*·ten zee meer *bi*·te *zaa*·gen
wann wir in (Kiel) ankommen?   van veer in (keel) *an*·ko·men

How long do we stop here?
Wie lange halten wir hier?   vee *lan*·ge *hal*·ten veer heer

Is this seat available?
Ist dieser Platz frei?   ist *dee*·zer plats frai

That's my seat.
Dieses ist mein Platz.   *dee*·zes ist main plats

I'd like a taxi ...   *Ich hätte gern*   ikh *he*·te gern
     ein Taxi für ...   ain *tak*·si fewr ...
  at (9am)   *(neun Uhr vormittags)*   (noyn oor *fawr*·mi·taaks)
  now   *sofort*   zo·*fort*
  tomorrow   *morgen*   *mor*·gen

Is this taxi available?
Ist dieses Taxi frei?   ist *dee*·zes *tak*·si frai

How much is it to ...?
Was kostet es bis ...?   vas *kos*·tet es bis ...

Please put the meter on.
Schalten Sie bitte den Taxameter ein.   *shal*·ten zee *bi*·te deyn tak·sa·*mey*·ter ain

Please take me to (this address).
Bitte bringen Sie mich zu   *bi*·te *bring*·en zee mikh tsoo
(dieser Adresse).   (*dee*·zer a·*dre*·se)

Please ...   *Bitte ...*   *bi*·te ...
  slow down   *fahren Sie langsamer*   *faa*·ren zee *lang*·za·mer
  stop here   *halten Sie hier*   *hal*·ten zee heer
  wait here   *warten Sie hier*   *var*·ten zee heer

car, motorbike & bicycle hire

I'd like to hire a …	Ich möchte … mieten.	ikh meukh·te … mee·ten
bicycle	ein Fahrrad	ain faar·raat
car	ein Auto	ain ow·to
motorbike	ein Motorrad	ain maw·tor·raat

with …	mit …	mit …
a driver	Fahrer	faa·rer
air conditioning	Klimaanlage	klee·ma·an·laa·ge

How much for … hire?	Wie viel kostet es pro …?	vee feel kos·tet es praw …
hourly	Stunde	shtun·de
daily	Tag	taak
weekly	Woche	vo·khe

air	Luft f	luft
oil	Öl n	eul
petrol	Benzin n	ben·tseen
tyres	Reifen m pl	rai·fen

I need a mechanic.
Ich brauche einen Mechaniker. — ikh brow·khe ai·nen me·khaa·ni·ker

I've run out of petrol.
Ich habe kein Benzin mehr. — ikh haa·be kain ben·tseen mair

I have a flat tyre.
Ich habe eine Reifenpanne. — ikh haa·be ai·ne rai·fen·pa·ne

directions

Where's the …?	Wo ist …?	vaw ist …
bank	die Bank	dee bangk
city centre	die Innenstadt	i·nen·shtat
hotel	das Hotel	das ho·tel
market	der Markt	dair markt
police station	das Polizeirevier	das po·li·tsai·re·veer
post office	das Postamt	das post·amt
public toilet	die öffentliche Toilette	dee eu·fent·li·khe to·a·le·te
tourist office	das Fremdenverkehrsbüro	das frem·den·fer·kairs·bew·raw

Is this the road to (Frankfurt)?
Führt diese Straße
nach (Frankfurt)?

fewrt dee·ze shtraa·se
naakh (frank·foort)

Can you show me (on the map)?
Können Sie es mir
(auf der Karte) zeigen?

keu·nen zee es meer
(owf dair kar·te) tsai·gen

What's the address?
Wie ist die Adresse?

vee ist dee a·dre·se

How far is it?
Wie weit ist es?

vee vait ist es

How do I get there?
Wie kann ich da hinkommen?

vee kan ikh daa hin·ko·men

Turn ...	Biegen Sie ... ab.	bee·gen zee ... ap
at the corner	an der Ecke	an dair e·ke
at the traffic lights	bei der Ampel	bai dair am·pel
left/right	links/rechts	lingks/rekhts

It's ...	Es ist ...	es ist ...
behind ...	hinter ...	hin·ter ...
far away	weit weg	vait vek
here	hier	heer
in front of ...	vor ...	fawr ...
left	links	lingks
near (to ...)	nahe (zu ...)	naa·e (zoo ...)
next to ...	neben ...	ney·ben ...
on the corner	an der Ecke	an dair e·ke
opposite ...	gegenüber ...	gey·gen·ew·ber ...
right	rechts	rekhts
straight ahead	geradeaus	ge·raa·de·ows
there	dort	dort

north	Norden m	nor·den
south	Süden m	zew·den
east	Osten m	os·ten
west	Westen m	ves·ten

by bus	mit dem Bus	mit deym bus
by taxi	mit dem Taxi	mit deym tak·si
by train	mit dem Zug	mit deym tsook
on foot	zu Fuß	tsoo foos

Eingang/Ausgang	*ain*-gang/*ows*-gang	**Entrance/Exit**
Offen/Geschlossen	*o*-fen/ge-*shlo*-sen	**Open/Closed**
Zimmer Frei	*tsi*-mer frai	**Rooms Available**
Ausgebucht	*ows*-ge-bukht	**No Vacancies**
Auskunft	*ows*-kunft	**Information**
Polizeirevier	po-li-*tsai*-re-veer	**Police Station**
Verboten	fer-*baw*-ten	**Prohibited**
Toiletten/WC	to-a-*le*-ten/vee-*tsee*	**Toilets**
Herren	*hair*-en	**Men**
Damen	*daa*-men	**Women**
Heiß/Kalt	hais/kalt	**Hot/Cold**

accommodation

finding accommodation

Where's a/an ...?	*Wo ist ...?*	vaw ist ...
camping ground	*ein Campingplatz*	ain *kem*-ping-plats
guesthouse	*eine Pension*	*ai*-ne paang-*zyawn*
hotel	*ein Hotel*	ain ho-*tel*
inn	*ein Gasthof*	ain *gast*-hawf
youth hostel	*eine Jugendherberge*	*ai*-ne *yoo*-gent-her-ber-ge
Can you recommend	*Können Sie etwas*	*keu*-nen zee *et*-vas
somewhere ...?	*... empfehlen?*	... emp-*fey*-len
cheap	*Billiges*	*bi*-li-ges
good	*Gutes*	*goo*-tes
luxurious	*Luxuriöses*	luk-su-ri-*eu*-ses
nearby	*in der Nähe*	in dair *ney*-e

I'd like to book a room, please.
Ich möchte bitte ein　　　　　　　ikh *meukh*-te *bi*-te ain
Zimmer reservieren.　　　　　　　*tsi*-mer re-zer-*vee*-ren

I have a reservation.
Ich habe eine Reservierung.　　　ikh *haa*-be *ai*-ne re-zer-*vee*-rung

My name's ...
Mein Name ist ...　　　　　　　　main *naa*-me ist ...

Do you have a . . . room?	Haben Sie ein . . . ?	haa·ben zee ain . . .
single	Einzelzimmer	ain·tsel·tsi·mer
double	Doppelzimmer mit einem Doppelbett	do·pel·tsi·mer mit ai·nem do·pel·bet
twin	Doppelzimmer mit zwei Einzelbetten	do·pel·tsi·mer mit tsvai ain·tsel·be·ten

Can I pay by . . . ?	Nehmen Sie . . . ?	ney·men zee . . .
credit card	Kreditkarten	kre·deet·kar·ten
travellers cheque	Reiseschecks	rai·ze·sheks

How much is it per . . . ?	Wie viel kostet es pro . . . ?	vee feel kos·tet es praw . . .
night	Nacht	nakht
person	Person	per·zawn

I'd like to stay for (two) nights.
Ich möchte für (zwei)
Nächte bleiben.
ikh meukh·te fewr (tsvai)
nekh·te blai·ben

From (July 2) to (July 6).
Vom (zweiten Juli) bis zum
(sechsten Juli).
vom (tsvai·ten yoo·li) bis tsum
(zeks·ten yoo·li)

Can I see it?
Kann ich es sehen?
kan ikh es zey·en

Am I allowed to camp here?
Kann ich hier zelten?
kan ikh heer tsel·ten

Is there a camp site nearby?
Gibt es in der Nähe einen Zeltplatz?
gipt es in dair ney·e ai·nen tselt·plats

requests & queries

When/Where is breakfast served?
Wann/Wo gibt es Frühstück?
van/vaw gipt es frew·shtewk

Please wake me at (seven).
Bitte wecken Sie mich
um (sieben) Uhr.
bi·te ve·ken zee mikh
um (zee·ben) oor

Could I have my key, please?
Könnte ich bitte meinen Schlüssel
haben?
keun·te ikh bi·te mai·nen shlew·sel
haa·ben

Can I get another (blanket)?
Kann ich noch (eine Decke) bekommen?
kan ikh nokh (ai·ne de·ke) be·ko·men

Is there a/an ...?	Haben Sie ...?	*haa·*ben zee ...
elevator	einen Aufzug	*ai·*nen *owf·*tsook
safe	einen Safe	*ai·*nen sayf

The room is too ...	Es ist zu ...	es ist tsoo ...
expensive	teuer	*toy·*er
noisy	laut	lowt
small	klein	klain

The ... doesn't work.	... funktioniert nicht.	... fungk·tsyo·*neert* nikht
air conditioning	Die Klimaanlage	dee *klee·*ma·an·laa·ge
fan	Der Ventilator	dair ven·ti·*laa·*tor
toilet	Die Toilette	dee to·a·*le·*te

This ... isn't clean.	Dieses ... ist nicht sauber.	*dee·*zes ... ist nikht *zow·*ber
pillow	Kopfkissen	*kopf·*ki·sen
sheet	Bettlaken	*bet·*laa·ken
towel	Handtuch	*hant·*tookh

checking out

What time is checkout?
Wann muss ich auschecken? van mus ikh *ows·*che·ken

Can I leave my luggage here?
Kann ich meine Taschen hier lassen? kan ikh *mai·*ne *ta·*shen heer *la·*sen

Could I have my ..., please?	Könnte ich bitte ... haben?	*keun·*te ikh *bi·*te ... *haa·*ben
deposit	meine Anzahlung	*mai·*ne *an·*tsaa·lung
passport	meinen Pass	*mai·*nen pas
valuables	meine Wertsachen	*mai·*ne *vert·*za·khen

communications & banking

the internet

Where's the local Internet café?
Wo ist hier ein Internet-Café? vaw ist heer ain *in·*ter·net·ka·fey

How much is it per hour?
Was kostet es pro Stunde? vas *kos·*tet es praw *shtun·*de

I'd like to ...	Ich möchte ...	ikh *meukh*·te ...
check my email	meine E-Mails checken	*mai*·ne *ee*·mayls *che*·ken
get Internet access	Internetzugang haben	*in*·ter·net·tsoo·gang *haa*·ben
use a printer	einen Drucker benutzen	*ai*·nen *dru*·ker be·*nu*·tsen
use a scanner	einen Scanner benutzen	*ai*·nen *ske*·ner be·*nu*·tsen

mobile/cell phone

I'd like a ...	Ich hätte gern ...	ikh *he*·te gern ...
mobile/cell phone for hire	ein Miethandy	ain *meet*·hen·di
SIM card for your network	eine SIM-Karte für Ihr Netz	*ai*·ne *zim*·kar·te fewr eer nets

What are the rates?
Wie hoch sind die Gebühren? — vee hawkh zint dee ge·*bew*·ren

telephone

What's your phone number?
Wie ist Ihre Telefonnummer? — vee ist *ee*·re te·le·*fawn*·nu·mer

The number is ...
Die Nummer ist ... — dee *nu*·mer ist ...

Where's the nearest public phone?
Wo ist das nächste öffentliche Telefon? — vaw ist das *neykhs*·te *eu*·fent·li·khe te·le·*fawn*

I'd like to buy a phonecard.
Ich möchte eine Telefonkarte kaufen. — ikh *meukh*·te *ai*·ne te·le·*fawn*·kar·te *kow*·fen

I want to ...	Ich möchte ...	ikh *meukh*·te ...
call (Singapore)	(nach Singapur) telefonieren	(naakh *zing*·a·poor) te·le·fo·*nee*·ren
make a local call	ein Ortsgespräch machen	ain *awrts*·ge·shpreykh *ma*·khen
reverse the charges	ein R-Gespräch führen	ain *air*·ge·shpreykh *few*·ren

How much does ... cost?	*Wie viel kostet ...?*	vee feel *kos*·tet ...
a (three)-minute	*ein (drei)-minutiges*	ain (*drai*)·mi·noo·ti·ges
call	*Gespräch*	ge·*shpreykh*
each extra	*jede zusätzliche*	*yey*·de tsoo·*zayts*·li·khe
minute	*Minute*	mi·*noo*·te

It's (one euro) per (minute).
(Ein Euro) für (eine Minute). (ain *oy*·ro) fewr (*ai*·ne mi·*noo*·te)

post office

I want to send a ...	*Ich möchte ... senden.*	ikh *meukh*·te ... *zen*·den
fax	*ein Fax*	ain faks
letter	*einen Brief*	*ai*·nen breef
parcel	*ein Paket*	ain pa·*keyt*
postcard	*eine Postkarte*	*ai*·ne *post*·kar·te

I want to buy a/an ...	*Ich möchte ... kaufen.*	ikh *meukh*·te ... *kow*·fen
envelope	*einen Umschlag*	*ai*·nen *um*·shlaak
stamp	*eine Briefmarke*	*ai*·ne *breef*·mar·ke

Please send it	*Bitte schicken Sie das*	*bi*·te *shi*·ken zee das
(to Australia) by ...	*(nach Australien) per ...*	(nakh ows·*traa*·li·en) per ...
airmail	*Luftpost*	*luft*·post
express mail	*Expresspost*	eks·*pres*·post
registered mail	*Einschreiben*	*ain*·shrai·ben
surface mail	*Landbeförderung*	*lant*·be·feur·de·rung

| Is there any mail for me? | *Ist Post für mich da?* | ist post fewr mikh da |

bank

Where's a/an ...?	*Wo ist ...?*	vaw ist ...
ATM	*der Geldautomat*	dair *gelt*·ow·to·maat
foreign exchange office	*die Geldwechselstube*	dee *gelt*·vek·sel·shtoo·be

I'd like to ...	Ich möchte ...	ikh *meukh*·te ...
Where can I ...?	Wo kann ich ...?	vaw kan ikh ...
arrange a transfer	einen Transfer tätigen	*ai*·nen trans·*fer tey*·ti·gen
cash a cheque	einen Scheck einlösen	*ai*·nen shek *ain*·leu·zen
change a travellers cheque	einen Reisecheck einlösen	*ai*·nen *rai*·ze·shek *ain*·leu·zen
change money	Geld umtauschen	gelt *um*·tow·shen
get a cash advance	eine Barauszahlung	*ai*·ne *baar*·ows·tsaa·lung
withdraw money	Geld abheben	gelt *ap*·hey·ben

What's the ...?	Wie ...?	vee ...
charge for that	hoch sind die Gebühren dafür	hawkh zint dee ge·*bew*·ren da·*fewr*
exchange rate	ist der Wechselkurs	ist dair *vek*·sel·kurs

It's ...	Das ...	das ...
(12) euros	kostet (zwölf) euro	*kos*·tet (zveulf) *oy*·ro
free	ist umsonst	ist um·*zonst*

What time does the bank open?
Wann macht die Bank auf? van makht dee bangk owf

Has my money arrived yet?
Ist mein Geld schon angekommen? ist main gelt shawn *an*·ge·ko·men

sightseeing

getting in

What time does it open/close?
Wann macht es auf/zu? van makht es owf/tsoo

What's the admission charge?
Was kostet der Eintritt? vas *kos*·tet dair *ain*·trit

Is there a discount for children/students?
Gibt es eine Ermäßigung für Kinder/Studenten? gipt es *ai*·ne er·*mey*·si·gung fewr *kin*·der/shtu·*den*·ten

I'd like a ...	Ich hätte gern ...	ikh *he*·te gern ...
catalogue	einen Katalog	*ai*-nen ka·ta·*lawg*
guide	einen Reiseführer	*ai*-nen *rai*·ze·few·rer
local map	eine Karte von hier	*ai*-ne *kar*·te fon heer

I'd like to see ...	Ich möchte ... sehen.	ikh *meukh*·te ... *zey*·en
What's that?	Was ist das?	vas ist das
Can I take a photo?	Kann ich fotografieren?	kan ikh fo·to·gra·*fee*·ren

tours

When's the	Wann ist der/die	van ist dair/dee
next ...?	nächste ...? m/f	*neykhs*·te ...
day trip	Tagesausflug m	*taa*·ges·ows·flook
tour	Tour f	toor

Is ... included?	Ist ... inbegriffen?	ist ... *in*·be·gri·fen
accommodation	die Unterkunft	dee *un*·ter·kunft
the admission charge	der Eintritt	dair *ain*·trit
food	das Essen	das *e*·sen
transport	die Beförderung	dee be·*feur*·de·rung

How long is the tour?
Wie lange dauert die Führung?   vee *lang*·e *dow*·ert dee *few*·rung

What time should we be back?
Wann sollen wir zurück sein?   van *zo*·len veer tsu·*rewk* zain

sightseeing		
castle	Burg f	burk
cathedral	Dom m	dawm
church	Kirche f	*kir*·khe
main square	Hauptplatz m	*howpt*·plats
monastery	Kloster n	*klaws*·ter
monument	Denkmal n	*dengk*·maal
museum	Museum n	mu·*zey*·um
old city	Altstadt f	*alt*·stat
palace	Schloss n	shlos
ruins	Ruinen f pl	ru·*ee*·nen
stadium	Stadion n	*shtaa*·di·on
statues	Statuen f pl	*shtaa*·tu·e

shopping

enquiries

Where's a ...?	*Wo ist ...?*	vaw ist ...
bank	*die Bank*	dee bangk
bookshop	*die Buchhandlung*	dee *bookh*-hand-lung
camera shop	*das Fotogeschäft*	das fo-to-ge-*sheft*
department store	*das Warenhaus*	das *vaa*-ren-hows
grocery store	*der Lebensmittelladen*	dair *ley*-bens-mi-tel-laa-den
market	*der Markt*	dair markt
newsagency	*der Zeitungshändler*	dair *tsai*-tungks-hen-dler
supermarket	*der Supermarkt*	dair *zoo*-per-markt

Where can I buy (a padlock)?
Wo kann ich (ein Vorhängeschloss) kaufen?
vaw kan ikh (ain *fawr*-heng-e-shlos) *kow*-fen

I'm looking for ...
Ich suche nach ...
ikh *zoo*-khe nakh ...

Can I look at it?
Können Sie es mir zeigen?
keu-nen zee es meer *tsai*-gen

Do you have any others?
Haben Sie noch andere?
haa-ben zee nokh *an*-de-re

Does it have a guarantee?
Gibt es darauf Garantie?
gipt es da-*rowf* ga-ran-*tee*

Can I have it sent overseas?
Kann ich es ins Ausland verschicken lassen?
kan ikh es ins *ows*-lant fer-*shi*-ken *la*-sen

Can I have my ... repaired?
Kann ich mein ... reparieren lassen?
kan ikh main ... re-pa-*ree*-ren *la*-sen

It's faulty.
Es ist fehlerhaft.
es ist *fey*-ler-haft

I'd like ..., please.	Ich möchte bitte ...	ikh meukh-te bi-te ...
a bag	eine Tüte	ai-ne tew-te
a refund	mein Geld	main gelt
	zurückhaben	tsu-rewk-haa-ben
to return this	dieses zurückgeben	dee-zes tsu-rewk-gey-ben

paying

How much is it?
Wie viel kostet das? — vee feel kos-tet das

Can you write down the price?
Können Sie den Preis aufschreiben? — keu-nen zee deyn prais owf-shrai-ben

That's too expensive.
Das ist zu teuer. — das ist tsoo toy-er

Can you lower the price?
Können Sie mit dem Preis — keu-nen zee mit dem prais
heruntergehen? — he-run-ter-gey-en

I'll give you (five) euros.
Ich gebe Ihnen (fünf) euro. — ikh gey-be ee-nen (fewnf) oy-ro

There's a mistake in the bill.
Da ist ein Fehler in der Rechnung. — daa ist ain fey-ler in dair rekh-nung

Do you accept ...?	Nehmen Sie ...?	ney-men zee ...
credit cards	Kreditkarten	kre-deet-kar-ten
debit cards	Debitkarten	dey-bit-kar-ten
travellers cheques	Reiseschecks	rai-ze-sheks

I'd like ..., please.	Ich möchte bitte ...	ikh meukh-te bi-te ...
a receipt	eine Quittung	ai-ne kvi-tung
my change	mein Wechselgeld	main vek-sel-gelt

clothes & shoes

Can I try it on?	Kann ich es anprobieren?	kan ikh es an-pro-bee-ren
My size is (40).	Ich habe Größe (vierzig).	ikh haa-be greu-se (feer-tsikh)
It doesn't fit.	Es passt nicht.	es past nikht
small	klein	klaln
medium	mittelgroß	mi-tel-graws
large	groß	graws

I'd like a ...	*Ich hätte gern ...*	ikh *he*·te gern ...
newspaper	*eine Zeitung*	*ai*·ne *tsai*·tung
(in English)	*(auf Englisch)*	(owf *eng*·lish)
pen	*einen Kugelschreiber*	*ai*·nen *koo*·gel·shrai·ber

Is there an English-language bookshop?
Gibt es einen Buchladen   gipt es *ai*·nen *bookh*·laa·den
für englische Bücher?   fewr *eng*·li·she *bew*·kher

I'm looking for something by (Herman Hesse).
Ich suche nach etwas von   ikh *zoo*·khe nakh *et*·vas fon
(Herman Hesse).   (*her*·man *he*·se)

Can I listen to this?
Kann ich mir das anhören?   kan ikh meer das *an*·heu·ren

Can you ...?	*Können Sie ...?*	*keu*·nen zee ...
burn a CD from	*eine CD von meiner*	*ai*·ne tse de von *mai*·ner
my memory card	*Speicherkarte brennen*	*shpai*·kher·*kar*·te *bre*·nen
develop this film	*diesen Film entwickeln*	*dee*·zen film ent·*vi*·keln
load my film	*mir den Film einlegen*	meer deyn film *ain*·ley·gen

I need a ... film	*Ich brauche einen*	ikh *brow*·khe *ai*·nen
for this camera.	*... für diese Kamera.*	... fewr *dee*·ze *ka*·me·ra
APS	*APS-Film*	aa·pey·*es*·film
B&W	*Schwarzweißfilm*	shvarts·*vais*·film
colour	*Farbfilm*	*farp*·film
slide	*Diafilm*	*dee*·a·film
(200) speed	*(zweihundert)-*	(*tsvai*·hun·dert)·
	ASA-Film	*aa*·za·film

When will it be ready?   *Wann ist er fertig?*   van ist air *fer*·tikh

meeting people

greetings, goodbyes & introductions

Hello. (Austria)	*Servus.*	*zer*·vus
Hello. (Germany)	*Guten Tag.*	*goo*·ten taak
Hello. (Switzerland)	*Grüezi.*	*grew*·e·tsi
Hi.	*Hallo.*	*ha*·lo
Good night.	*Gute Nacht.*	*goo*·te nakht
Goodbye.	*Auf Wiedersehen.*	owf *vee*·der·zey·en
Bye.	*Tschüss/Tschau.*	chews/chow
See you later.	*Bis später.*	bis *shpey*·ter

Mr	*Herr*	her
Mrs	*Frau*	frow
Miss	*Fräulein*	*froy*·lain

How are you?	*Wie geht es Ihnen?*	vee geyt es *ee*·nen
Fine. And you?	*Danke, gut. Und Ihnen?*	*dang*·ke goot unt *ee*·nen
What's your name?	*Wie ist Ihr Name?*	vee ist eer *naa*·me
My name is ...	*Mein Name ist ...*	main *naa*·me ist ...
I'm pleased to meet you.	*Angenehm.*	*an*·ge·neym

This is my ...	*Das ist mein/meine ...* m/f	das ist main/*mai*·ne ...
brother	*Bruder*	*broo*·der
daughter	*Tochter*	*tokh*·ter
father	*Vater*	*faa*·ter
friend	*Freund/Freundin* m/f	froynt/*froyn*·din
husband	*Mann*	man
mother	*Mutter*	*mu*·ter
partner (intimate)	*Partner/Partnerin* m/f	*part*·ner/*part*·ne·rin
sister	*Schwester*	*shves*·ter
son	*Sohn*	zawn
wife	*Frau*	frow

Here's my ...	*Hier ist meine ...*	heer ist *mai*·ne ...
What's your...?	*Wie ist Ihre ...?*	vee ist *ee*·re ...
address	*Adresse*	a·*dre*·se
email address	*E-mail-Adresse*	*ee*·mayl·a·dre·se
fax number	*Faxnummer*	*faks*·nu·mer
phone number	*Telefonnummer*	te·le·*fawn*·nu·mer

occupations

What's your occupation?	Als was arbeiten Sie? pol	als vas *ar*·bai·ten zee
	Als was arbeitest du? inf	als vas *ar*·bai·test doo
I'm a/an ...	Ich bin ein/eine ... m/f	ikh bin ain/*ai*·ne ...
artist	Künstler/Künstlerin m/f	*kewnst*·ler/*kewnst*·le·rin
business person	Geschäftsmann m	ge·*shefts*·man
	Geschäftsfrau f	ge·*shefts*·frow
farmer	Bauer/Bäuerin m/f	*bow*·er/*boy*·e·rin
manual worker	Arbeiter/Arbeiterin m/f	*ar*·bai·ter/*ar*·bai·te·rin
office worker	Büroangestellte m&f	bew·*raw*·an·ge·shtel·te
scientist	Wissenschaftler m	*vi*·sen·shaft·ler
	Wissenschaftlerin f	*vi*·sen·shaft·le·rin
student	Student/Studentin m/f	shtu·*dent*/shtu·*den*·tin

background

Where are you from?	Woher kommen Sie? pol	*vaw*·hair *ko*·men zee
	Woher kommst du? inf	*vaw*·hair komst doo
I'm from ...	Ich komme aus ...	ikh *ko*·me ows ...
Australia	Australien	ows·*traa*·li·en
Canada	Kanada	*ka*·na·daa
England	England	*eng*·lant
New Zealand	Neuseeland	noy·*zey*·lant
the USA	den USA	deyn oo·es·*aa*
Are you married?	Sind Sie verheiratet? pol	zint zee fer·*hai*·ra·tet
	Bist du verheiratet? inf	bist doo fer·*hai*·ra·tet
I'm married.	Ich bin verheiratet.	ikh bin fer·*hai*·ra·tet
I'm single.	Ich bin ledig.	ikh bin *ley*·dikh

age

How old ...?	Wie alt ...?	vee alt ...
are you	sind Sie pol	zint zee
	bist du inf	bist doo
is your daughter	ist Ihre Tochter pol	ist *ee*·re *tokh*·ter
is your son	ist Ihr Sohn pol	ist eer zawn
I'm ... years old.	Ich bin ... Jahre alt.	ikh bin ... *yaa*·re alt
He/She is ... years old.	Er/Sie ist ... Jahre alt.	air/zee ist ... *yaa*·re alt

feelings

I'm (not) ...	Ich bin (nicht) ...	ikh bin (nikht) ...
Are you ...?	Sind Sie ...? pol	zint zee ...
	Bist du ...? inf	bist doo ...
happy	glücklich	glewk·likh
sad	traurig	trow·rikh
I'm (not) ...	Ich habe (kein) ...	ikh haa·be (kain) ...
Are you ...?	Haben Sie ...? pol	haa·ben zee ...
	Hast du ...? inf	hast doo ...
hungry	Hunger	hung·er
thirsty	Durst	durst
I'm (not) ...	Mir ist (nicht) ...	meer ist (nikht) ...
Are you ...?	Ist Ihnen/dir ...? pol/inf	ist ee·nen/deer ...
cold	kalt	kalt
hot	heiß	hais

entertainment

going out

Where can I find ...?	Wo sind die ...?	vaw zint dee ...
clubs	Klubs	klups
gay venues	Schwulen- und	shvoo·len unt
	Lesbenkneipen	les·ben·knai·pen
pubs	Kneipen	knai·pen
I feel like going	Ich hätte Lust,	ikh he·te lust
to a/the ...	... zu gehen.	... tsoo gey·en
concert	zum Konzert	tsoom kon·tsert
movies	ins Kino	ins kee·no
party	zu eine Party	tsoo ai·ne par·ti
restaurant	in ein Restaurant	in ain res·to·rang
theatre	ins Theater	ins te·aa·ter

interests

Do you like ...?	*Magst du ...?* inf	maakst doo ...
I (don't) like ...	*Ich mag (keine/*	ikh maak (kai·ne/
	keinen) ... m/f	kai·nen) ...
art	*Kunst* f	kunst
sport	*Sport* m	shport
I (don't) like ...	*Ich ... (nicht) gern.*	ikh ... (nikht) gern
cooking	*koche*	ko·khe
reading	*lese*	ley·ze
travelling	*reise*	rai·ze

Do you like to dance?
Tanzt du gern? inf   tantst doo gern

Do you like music?
Hörst du gern Musik? inf   heurst doo gern mu·zeek

food & drink

finding a place to eat

Can you	*Können Sie ...*	keu·nen zee ...
recommend a ...?	*empfehlen?*	emp·fey·len
bar	*eine Kneipe*	ai·ne knai·pe
café	*ein Café*	ain ka·fey
restaurant	*ein Restaurant*	ain res·to·rang
I'd like ..., please.	*Ich hätte gern ..., bitte.*	ikh he·te gern ... bi·te
a table for (five)	*einen Tisch für*	ai·nen tish fewr
	(fünf) Personen	(fewnf) per·zaw·nen
the (non)smoking	*einen (Nicht-)*	ai·nen (nikht·)
section	*rauchertisch*	row·kher·tish

ordering food

breakfast	*Frühstück* n	frew·shtewk
lunch	*Mittagessen* n	mi·taak·e·sen
dinner	*Abendessen* n	aa·bent·e·sen
snack	*Snack* m	snek

What would you recommend?

    Was empfehlen Sie?   vas emp·*fey*·len zee

I'd like (the) …, please.	*Bitte bringen Sie …*	*bi*·te *bring*·en zee …
bill	*die Rechnung*	dee *rekh*·nung
drink list	*die Getränkekarte*	dee ge·*treng*·ke·kar·te
menu	*die Speisekarte*	dee *shpai*·ze·kar·te
that dish	*dieses Gericht*	*dee*·zes ge·*rikht*

drinks

(cup of) coffee …	*(eine Tasse) Kaffee …*	(*ai*·ne *ta*·se) ka·fey …
(cup of) tea …	*(eine Tasse) Tee …*	(*ai*·ne *ta*·se) tey …
with milk	*mit Milch*	mit milkh
without sugar	*ohne Zucker*	*aw*·ne *tsu*·ker
(orange) juice	*(Orangen)Saft* m	(o·*rang*·zhen·)zaft
mineral water	*Mineralwasser* n	mi·ne·*raal*·va·ser
soft drink	*Softdrink* m	*soft*·dringk
(boiled) water	*(heißes) Wasser* n	(*hai*·ses) *va*·ser

in the bar

I'll have …	*Ich hätte gern …*	ikh *he*·te gern …
I'll buy you a drink.	*Ich gebe dir einen aus.* inf	ikh *gey*·be der *ai*·nen ows
What would you like?	*Was möchtest du?* inf	vas *meukh*·test doo
Cheers!	*Prost!*	prawst
brandy	*Weinbrand* m	*vain*·brant
cognac	*Kognak* m	*ko*·nyak
cocktail	*Cocktail* m	*kok*·tayl
a shot of (whisky)	*einen (Whisky)*	*ai*·nen (*vis*·ki)
a bottle of …	*eine Flasche …*	*ai*·ne *fla*·she …
a glass of …	*ein Glas …*	ain glaas …
red wine	*Rotwein*	*rawt*·vain
sparkling wine	*Sekt*	zekt
white wine	*Weißwein*	*vais*·vain
a … of beer	*… eine Flasche*	… beer
bottle	*eine Flasche*	*ai*·ne *fla*·she
glass	*ein Glas*	ain glaas

self-catering

What's the local speciality?
Was ist eine örtliche Spezialität?   vas ist *ai*·ne *eurt*·li·khe shpe·tsya·li·*teyt*

What's that?
Was ist das?   vas ist das

How much is (a kilo of cheese)?
Was kostet (ein Kilo Käse)?   vas *kos*·tet (ain *kee*·lo *key*·ze)

I'd like ...	Ich möchte ...	ikh *meukh*·te ...
(100) grams	(hundert) Gramm	(hun·dert) gram
(two) kilos	(zwei) Kilo	(tsvai) *kee*·lo
(three) pieces	(drei) Stück	(drai) shtewk
(six) slices	(sechs) Scheiben	(zeks) *shai*·ben

Less.	Weniger.	*vey*·ni·ger
Enough.	Genug.	ge·*nook*
More.	Mehr.	mair

special diets & allergies

Is there a vegetarian restaurant near here?
Gibt es ein vegetarisches   gipt es ain vege·*tar*·ish·shes
Restaurant hier in der Nähe?   res·to·*rang* heer in dair *ney*·e

Do you have vegetarian food?
Haben Sie vegetarisches Essen?   *haa*·ben zee ve·ge·*taa*·ri·shes *e*·sen

Could you prepare	Können Sie ein Gericht	*keu*·nen zee ain ge·*rikht*
a meal without ...?	ohne ... zubereiten?	*aw*·ne ... *tsoo*·be·rai·ten
butter	Butter	*bu*·ter
eggs	Eiern	*ai*·ern
meat stock	Fleischbrühe	*flaish*·brew·e

I'm allergic to ...	Ich bin allergisch	ikh bin a·*lair*·gish
	gegen ...	*gey*·gen ...
dairy produce	Milchprodukte	*milkh*·pro·duk·te
gluten	Gluten	*gloo*·ten
MSG	Natrium-glutamat	*naa*·tri·um·glu·ta·maat
nuts	Nüsse	*new*·se
seafood	Meeresfrüchte	*mair*·res·frewkh·te

menu decoder

Bayrisch Kraut n	*bai*-rish krowt	*shredded cabbage cooked with sliced apples, wine & sugar*
Berliner m	ber-*lee*-ner	*jam doughnut*
Cervelatwurst f	ser-ve-*laat*-vurst	*spicy pork & beef sausage*
Erdäpfelgulasch n	*ert*-ep-fel-goo-lash	*spicy sausage & potato stew*
gekochter Schinken m	ge-*kokh*-ter *shing*-ken	*cooked ham*
Graupensuppe f	*grow*-pen-zu-pe	*barley soup*
Greyerzer m	*grai*-er-tser	*a smooth, rich cheese*
Grießklößchensuppe f	grees-kleus-khen-zu-pe	*soup with semolina dumplings*
Gröstl n	greustl	*grated fried potatoes with meat*
Grünkohl mit Pinkel m	*grewn*-kawl mit *ping*-kel	*cabbage with sausages*
Holsteiner Schnitzel n	*hol*-shtai-ner *shni*-tsel	*veal schnitzel with fried egg & seafood*
Husarenfleisch n	hu-*zaa*-ren-flaish	*braised beef, veal & pork fillets with sweet peppers, onions & sour cream*
Hutzelbrot n	*hu*-tsel-brawt	*bread made of prunes & other dried fruit*
Kaiserschmarren m	*kai*-zer-shmar-ren	*pancakes with raisins, fruit compote or chocolate sauce*
Kaisersemmeln f pl	*kai*-zer-ze-meln	*Austrian bread rolls*
Katenwurst f	*kaa*-ten-vurst	*country-style smoked sausage*
Königinsuppe f	*keu*-ni-gin-zu-pe	*creamy chicken soup*
Königstorte f	*keu*-niks-tor-te	*rum-flavoured fruit cake*
Krautsalat m	*krowt*-za-laat	*coleslaw*
Leipziger Allerlei n	*laip*-tsi-ger *a*-ler-lai	*mixed vegetable stew*
Linzer Torte f	*lin*-tser tor-te	*latticed tart with jam topping*

Nudelauflauf m	*noo-del-owf-lowf*	pasta casserole
Obatzter m	*aw-bats-ter*	Bavarian soft cheese mousse
Ochsenschwanzsuppe f	*ok-sen-shvants-zu-pe*	oxtail soup
Palatschinken m	*pa-lat-shing-ken*	pancakes filled with jam or cheese
Rollmops m	*rol-mops*	pickled herring fillet rolled around chopped onions or gherkins
Sauerbraten m	*zow-er-braa-ten*	marinated roasted beef served with a sour cream sauce
Sauerkraut n	*zow-er-krowt*	pickled cabbage
Schafskäse m	*shaafs-key-ze*	sheep's milk feta
Schmorbraten m	*shmawr-braa-ten*	beef pot roast
Schnitzel n	*shni-tsel*	pork, veal or chicken breast rolled in breadcrumbs & fried
Strammer Max m	*shtra-mer maks*	ham, sausage or pork sandwich, served with fried eggs & onions
Streichkäse m	*shtraikh-key-ze*	any kind of soft cheese spread
Streuselkuchen m	*shtroy-zel-koo-khen*	coffee cake topped with cinnamon
Strudel m	*shtroo-del*	loaf-shaped pastry with a sweet or savoury filling
Tascherl n	*ta-sherl*	pastry with meat, cheese or jam
Voressen n	*fawr-e-sen*	meat stew
Weinkraut n	*vain-krowt*	white cabbage, braised with apples & simmered in wine
Wiener Schnitzel n	*vee-ner shni-tsel*	crumbed veal schnitzel
Wiener Würstchen n	*vee-ner vewrst-khen*	frankfurter (sausage)
Zwetschgendatschi m	*tsvetsh-gen-dat-shi*	damson plum tart
Zwiebelsuppe f	*tsvee-bel-zu-pe*	onion soup
Zwiebelwurst f	*tsvee-bel-vurst*	liver & onion sausage

emergencies

basics

Help!	*Hilfe!*	*hil*·fe
Stop!	*Halt!*	halt
Go away!	*Gehen Sie weg!*	*gey*·en zee vek
Thief!	*Dieb!*	deeb
Fire!	*Feuer!*	*foy*·er
Watch out!	*Vorsicht!*	for·*zikht*
Call ...!	*Rufen Sie ...!*	*roo*·fen zee ...
a doctor	*einen Arzt*	*ai*·nen artst
an ambulance	*einen Krankenwagen*	*ai*·nen *krang*·ken·vaa·gen
the police	*die Polizei*	dee po·li·*tsai*

It's an emergency!
Es ist ein Notfall! es ist ain *nawt*·fal

Could you help me, please?
Könnten Sie mir bitte helfen? *keun*·ten zee meer *bi*·te *hel*·fen

I have to use the telephone.
Ich muss das Telefon benutzen. ikh mus das te·le·*fawn* be·*nu*·tsen

I'm lost.
Ich habe mich verirrt. ikh *haa*·be mikh fer·*irt*

Where are the toilets?
Wo ist die Toilette? vo ist dee to·a·*le*·te

police

Where's the police station?
Wo ist das Polizeirevier? vaw ist das po·li·*tsai*·re·veer

I want to report an offence.
Ich möchte eine Straftat melden. ikh *meukh*·te *ai*·ne *shtraaf*·taat *mel*·den

I have insurance.
Ich bin versichert. ikh bin fer·*zi*·khert

I've been ...	*Ich bin ... worden.*	ikh bin ... *vor*·den
assaulted	*angegriffen*	*an*·ge gri·fen
raped	*vergewaltigt*	fer·ge·*val*·tikht
robbed	*bestohlen*	be·*shtaw*·len

I've lost my...	Ich habe ... verloren.	ikh *haa*·be ... fer·*law*·ren
My ... was/	Man hat mir ...	man hat meer ...
were stolen.	gestohlen.	ge·*shtaw*·len
backpack	meinen Rucksack	*mai*·nen *ruk*·zak
bags	meine Reisetaschen	*mai*·ne *rai*·ze·ta·shen
credit card	meine Kreditkarte	*mai*·ne kre·*deet*·karte
handbag	meine Handtasche	*mai*·ne *hant*·ta·she
jewellery	meinen Schmuck	*mai*·nen shmuk
money	mein Geld	main gelt
passport	meinen Pass	*mai*·nen pas
travellers cheques	meine Reiseschecks	*mai*·ne *rai*·ze·sheks
wallet	meine Brieftasche	*mai*·ne *breef*·ta·she

I want to contact	Ich mochte mich mit	ikh *meukh*·te mikh mit
my ...	... in Verbindung setzen.	... in fer·*bin*·dung ze·tsen
consulate	meinem Konsulat	*mai*·nem kon·zu·*laat*
embassy	meiner Botschaft	*mai*·ner *bawt*·shaft

health

medical needs

Where's the	Wo ist der/die/das	vaw ist dair/dee/das
nearest ...?	nächste ...? m/f/n	*neykhs*·te ...
dentist	Zahnarzt m	*tsaan*·artst
doctor	Arzt m	artst
hospital	Krankenhaus n	*krang*·ken·hows
(night) pharmacist	(Nacht)Apotheke f	(nakht·)a·po·*tey*·ke

I need a doctor (who speaks English).
Ich brauche einen Arzt — ikh *brow*·khe *ai*·nen artst
(der Englisch spricht). — (dair *eng*·lish shprikht)

Could I see a female doctor?
Könnte ich von einer — *keun*·te ikh fon *ai*·ner
Ärztin behandelt werden? — *erts*·tin be·*han*·delt *ver*·den

I've run out of my medication.
Ich habe keine — ikh *haa*·be *kai*·ne
Medikamente mehr. — me·di·ka·*men*·te mair

symptoms, conditions & allergies

| I'm sick. | Ich bin krank. | ikh bin krangk |
| It hurts here. | Es tut hier weh. | es toot heer *vey* |

I have (a) ...	Ich habe ...	ikh *haa*·be ...
asthma	Asthma	*ast*·ma
bronchitis	Bronchitis	bron·*khee*·tis
constipation	Verstopfung	fer·*shtop*·fung
cough	Husten	*hoos*·ten
diarrhoea	Durchfall	*durkh*·fal
fever	Fieber	*fee*·ber
headache	Kopfschmerzen	*kopf*·shmer·tsen
heart condition	Herzbeschwerden	*herts*·be·shver·den
nausea	Übelkeit	*ew*·bel·kait
pain	Schmerzen	*shmer*·tsen
sore throat	Halsschmerzen	*hals*·shmer·tsen
toothache	Zahnschmerzen	*tsaan*·shmer·tsen

I'm allergic to ...	Ich bin allergisch gegen ...	ikh bin a·*lair*·gish *gey*·gen ...
antibiotics	Antibiotika	an·ti·bi·*aw*·ti·ka
anti-inflammatories	entzündungs-hemmende Mittel	en·*tsewn*·dungks·he·men·de *mi*·tel
aspirin	Aspirin	as·pi·*reen*
bees	Bienen	*bee*·nen
codeine	Kodein	ko·de·*een*
penicillin	Penizillin	pe·ni·tsi·*leen*

antiseptic	Antiseptikum n	an·ti·*zep*·ti·kum
bandage	Verband m	fer·*bant*
condoms	Kondom n	kon·*dawm*
contraceptives	Verhütungsmittel n	fer·*hew*·tungks·mi·tel
diarrhoea medicine	Mittel gegen Durchfall n	*mi*·tel *gey*·gen *durkh*·fal
insect repellent	Insektenschutzmittel n	in·*zek*·ten·shuts·mi·tel
laxatives	Abführmittel n	*ap*·fewr·mi·tel
painkillers	Schmerzmittel n	*shmerts*·mi·tel
rehydration salts	Kochsalzlösung n	kokh·zalts·*leu*·zung
sleeping tablets	Schlaftabletten f pl	*shlaaf*·ta·ble·ten

english–german dictionary

German nouns in this dictionary have their gender indicated by ⓜ (masculine), ⓕ (feminine) or ⓝ (neuter). If it's a plural noun, you'll also see pl. Words are also marked as n (noun), a (adjective), v (verb), sg (singular), pl (plural), inf (informal) and pol (polite) where necessary.

A

accident *Unfall* ⓜ un-fal
accommodation *Unterkunft* ⓕ un-ter-kunft
adaptor *Adapter* ⓜ a-dap-ter
address *Adresse* ⓕ a-dre-se
after *nach* naakh
air-conditioned *mit Klimaanlage* ⓕ
   mit klee-ma-an-laa-ge
airplane *Flugzeug* ⓝ flook-tsoyk
airport *Flughafen* ⓜ flook-haa-fen
alcohol *Alkohol* ⓜ al-ko-hawl
all a *alle* a-le
allergy *Allergie* ⓕ a-lair-gee
ambulance *Krankenwagen* ⓜ krang-ken-vaa-gen
and *und* unt
ankle *Knöchel* ⓜ kneu-khel
arm *Arm* ⓜ arm
ashtray *Aschenbecher* ⓜ a-shen-be-kher
ATM *Geldautomat* ⓜ gelt-ow-to-maat
Austria *Österreich* ⓝ eus-ter-raikh

B

baby *Baby* ⓝ bay-bi
back (body) *Rücken* ⓜ rew-ken
backpack *Rucksack* ⓜ ruk-zak
bad *schlecht* shlekht
bag *Tasche* ⓕ ta-she
baggage claim *Gepäckausgabe* ⓕ ge-pek-ows-gaa-be
bank *Bank* ⓕ bangk
bar *Lokal* ⓝ lo-kaal
bathroom *Badezimmer* ⓝ baa-de-tsi-mer
battery *Batterie* ⓕ ba-te-ree
beautiful *schön* sheun
bed *Bett* ⓝ bet
beer *Bier* ⓝ beer
before *vor* fawr
behind *hinter* hin-ter
Belgium ⓝ *Belgien* bel-gi-en

bicycle *Fahrrad* ⓝ faar-raat
big *groß* graws
bill *Rechnung* ⓕ rekh-nung
black *schwarz* shvarts
blanket *Decke* ⓕ de-ke
blood group *Blutgruppe* ⓕ bloot-gru-pe
blue *blau* blow
book (make a reservation) v *buchen* boo-khen
bottle *Flasche* ⓕ fla-she
bottle opener *Flaschenöffner* ⓜ fla-shen-euf-ner
boy *Junge* ⓜ yung-e
brakes (car) *Bremsen* pl brem-zen
breakfast *Frühstück* ⓝ frew-shtewk
broken (faulty) *kaputt* ka-put
bus *Bus* ⓜ bus
business *Geschäft* ⓝ ge-sheft
buy *kaufen* kow-fen

C

café *Café* ⓝ ka-fey
camera *Kamera* ⓕ ka-me-ra
camp site *Zeltplatz* ⓜ tselt-plats
cancel *stornieren* shtor-nee-ren
can opener *Dosenöffner* ⓜ daw-zen-euf-ner
car *Auto* ⓝ ow-to
cash *Bargeld* ⓝ baar-gelt
cash (a cheque) v *(einen Scheck) einlösen*
   (ai-nen shek) ain-leu-zen
cell phone *Handy* ⓝ hen-di
centre *Zentrum* ⓝ tsen-trum
change (money) v *wechseln* vek-seln
cheap *billig* bi-likh
check (bill) *Rechnung* ⓕ rekh-nung
check-in *Abfertigungsschalter* ⓜ
   ap-fer-ti-gungks-shal-ter
chest *Brustkorb* ⓜ brust-korp
child *Kind* ⓝ kint
cigarette *Zigarette* ⓕ tsi-ga-re-te
city *Stadt* ⓕ shtat
clean a *sauber* zow-ber

closed *geschlossen* ge-*shlo*-sen
coffee *Kaffee* Ⓜ ka-fey
coins *Münzen* Ⓕ pl mewn-tsen
cold a *kalt* kalt
collect call *R-Gespräch* Ⓝ air-ge-shpreykh
come *kommen* ko-men
computer *Computer* Ⓜ kom-*pyoo*-ter
condom *Kondom* Ⓝ kon-*dawm*
contact lenses *Kontaktlinsen* Ⓕ pl kon-*takt*-lin-zen
cook v *kochen* ko-khen
cost *Preis* Ⓜ prais
credit card *Kreditkarte* Ⓕ kre-*deet*-kar-te
cup *Tasse* Ⓕ ta-se
currency exchange *Geldwechsel* Ⓜ gelt-*vek*-sel
customs (immigration) *Zoll* Ⓜ tsol

D

dangerous *gefährlich* ge-*fair*-likh
date (time) *Datum* Ⓝ *daa*-tum
day *Tag* Ⓜ taak
delay n *Verspätung* Ⓕ fer-*shpey*-tung
dentist *Zahnarzt/Zahnärztin* Ⓜ/Ⓕ
  tsaan-artst/*tsaan*-erts-tin
depart *abfahren* ap-faa-ren
diaper *Windel* Ⓕ vin-del
dictionary *Wörterbuch* Ⓝ veur-ter-bookh
dinner *Abendessen* Ⓝ *aa*-bent-e-sen
direct *direkt* di-rekt
dirty *schmutzig* shmu-tsikh
disabled *behindert* be-*hin*-dert
discount n *Rabatt* Ⓜ ra-bat
doctor *Arzt/Ärztin* Ⓜ/Ⓕ artst/erts-tin
double bed *Doppelbett* Ⓝ do-pel-bet
double room *Doppelzimmer mit einem Doppelbett* Ⓝ
  do-pel-tsi-mer mit ai-nem do-pel-bet
drink *Getränk* Ⓝ ge-trengk
drive v *fahren* faa-ren
drivers licence *Führerschein* Ⓜ few-rer-shain
drugs (illicit) *Droge* Ⓕ draw-ge
dummy (pacifier) *Schnuller* Ⓜ shnu-ler

E

ear *Ohr* Ⓝ awr
east *Osten* Ⓜ os-ten
eat *essen* e-sen
economy class *Touristenklasse* Ⓕ tu-ris-ten-kla-se
electricity *Elektrizität* Ⓕ e-lek-tri-tsi-teyt
elevator *Lift* Ⓜ lift

email *E-Mail* e-mayl
embassy *Botschaft* Ⓕ *bawt*-shaft
emergency *Notfall* Ⓜ nawt-fal
English (language) *Englisch* Ⓝ eng-lish
entrance *Eingang* Ⓜ ain-gang
evening *Abend* Ⓜ aa-bent
exchange rate *Wechselkurs* Ⓜ vek-sel-kurs
exit *Ausgang* Ⓜ ows-gang
expensive *teuer* toy-er
express mail *Expresspost* Ⓕ eks-*pres*-post
eye *Auge* Ⓝ ow-ge

F

far *weit* vait
fast *schnell* shnel
father *Vater* Ⓜ faa-ter
film (camera) *Film* Ⓜ film
finger *Finger* Ⓜ fing-er
first-aid kit *Verbandskasten* Ⓜ fer-*bants*-kas-ten
first class *erste Klasse* Ⓕ ers-te kla-se
fish *Fisch* Ⓜ fish
food *Essen* Ⓝ e-sen
foot *Fuß* Ⓜ foos
fork *Gabel* Ⓕ *gaa*-bel
free (of charge) *gratis* graa-tis
friend *Freund/Freundin* Ⓜ/Ⓕ froynt/froyn-din
fruit *Frucht* Ⓕ frukht
full *voll* fol
funny *lustig* lus-tikh

G

German (language) *Deutsch* Ⓝ doytsh
Germany *Deutschland* Ⓝ doytsh-lant
gift *Geschenk* Ⓝ ge-shengk
girl *Mädchen* Ⓝ *meyt*-khen
glass (drinking) *Glas* Ⓝ glaas
glasses *Brille* Ⓕ bri-le
go *gehen* gey-en
good *gut* goot
green *grün* grewn
guide *Führer* Ⓜ few-rer

H

half *Hälfte* Ⓕ helf-te
hand *Hand* Ⓕ hant
handbag *Handtasche* Ⓕ hant-ta-she
happy *glücklich* glewk-likh

have *haben* haa-ben
he *er* air
head *Kopf* ⓜ kopf
heart *Herz* ⓝ herts
heat n *Hitze* ⓕ hi-tse
heavy *schwer* shvair
help v *helfen* hel-fen
here *hier* heer
high *hoch* hawkh
highway *Autobahn* ⓕ ow-to-baan
hike v *wandern* van-dern
holiday *Urlaub* ⓜ oor-lowp
homosexual *homosexuell* haw-mo-zek-su-el
hospital *Krankenhaus* ⓝ krang-ken-hows
hot *heiß* hais
hotel *Hotel* ⓝ ho-tel
hungry *hungrig* hung-rikh
husband *Ehemann* ⓜ ey-e-man

I

I *ich* ikh
identification (card) *Personalausweis* ⓜ
  per-zo-naal-ows-vais
ill *krank* krangk
important *wichtig* vikh-tikh
included *inbegriffen* in-be-gri-fen
injury *Verletzung* ⓕ fer-le-tsung
insurance *Versicherung* ⓕ fer-zi-khe-rung
Internet *Internet* ⓝ in-ter-net
interpreter *Dolmetscher/Dolmetscherin* ⓜ/ⓕ
  dol-met-sher/dol-met-she-rin

J

jewellery *Schmuck* ⓜ shmuk
job *Arbeitsstelle* ⓕ ar-baits-shte-le

K

key *Schlüssel* ⓜ shlew-sel
kilogram *Kilogramm* ⓝ kee-lo-gram
kitchen *Küche* ⓕ kew-khe
knife *Messer* ⓝ me-ser

L

laundry (place) *Waschküche* ⓕ vash-kew-khe
lawyer *Rechtsanwalt/Rechtsanwältin* ⓜ/ⓕ
  rekhts-an-valt/rekhts-an-vel-tin

left (direction) *links* lingks
left-luggage office *Gepäckaufbewahrung* ⓕ
  ge-pek-owf-be-vaa-rung
leg *Bein* ⓝ bain
lesbian *Lesbierin* ⓕ les-bi-e-rin
less *weniger* vey-ni-ger
letter (mail) *Brief* ⓜ breef
lift (elevator) *Lift* ⓜ lift
light *Licht* ⓝ likht
like v *mögen* meu-gen
lock *Schloss* ⓝ shlos
long *lang* lang
lost *verloren* fer-law-ren
lost-property office *Fundbüro* ⓝ funt-bew-raw
love v *lieben* lee-ben
luggage *Gepäck* ⓝ ge-pek
lunch *Mittagessen* ⓝ mi-taak-e-sen

M

mail *Post* ⓕ post
man *Mann* ⓜ man
map *Karte* ⓕ kar-te
market *Markt* ⓜ markt
matches *Streichhölzer* ⓝ pl shtraikh-heul-tser
meat *Fleisch* ⓝ flaish
medicine *Medizin* ⓕ me-di-tseen
menu *Speisekarte* ⓕ shpai-ze-kar-te
message *Mitteilung* ⓕ mi-tai-lung
milk *Milch* ⓕ milkh
minute *Minute* ⓕ mi-noo-te
mobile phone *Handy* ⓝ hen-di
money *Geld* ⓝ gelt
month *Monat* ⓜ maw-nat
morning *Morgen* ⓜ mor-gen
mother *Mutter* ⓕ mu-ter
motorcycle *Motorrad* ⓝ maw-tor-raat
motorway *Autobahn* ⓕ ow-to-baan
mouth *Mund* ⓜ munt
music *Musik* ⓕ mu-zeek

N

name *Name* ⓜ naa-me
napkin *Serviette* ⓕ zer-vye-te
nappy *Windel* ⓕ vin-del
near *nahe* naa-e
neck *Hals* ⓜ hals
new *neu* noy
news *Nachrichten* ⓕ pl naakh-rikh-ten

newspaper *Zeitung* ⓕ *tsai*-tung
night *Nacht* ⓕ nakht
no *nein* nain
noisy *laut* lowt
nonsmoking *Nichtraucher* nikht-row-kher
north *Norden* ⓜ nor-den
nose *Nase* ⓕ *naa*-ze
now *jetzt* yetst
number *Zahl* ⓕ tsaal

O

oil (engine) *Öl* ⓝ eul
old *alt* alt
one-way ticket *einfache Fahrkarte* ⓕ
  ain-fa-khe *faar*-kar-te
open a *offen* o-fen
outside *draußen* drow-sen

P

package *Paket* ⓝ pa-*keyt*
paper *Papier* ⓝ pa-*peer*
park (car) v *parken* par-ken
passport *(Reise)Pass* ⓜ (*rai*-ze-)pas
pay *bezahlen* be-*tsaa*-len
pen *Kugelschreiber* ⓜ *koo*-gel-shrai-ber
petrol *Benzin* ⓝ ben-*tseen*
pharmacy *Apotheke* ⓕ a-po-*tey*-ke
phonecard *Telefonkarte* ⓕ te-le-*fawn*-kar-te
photo *Foto* ⓝ *faw*-to
plate *Teller* ⓜ *te*-ler
police *Polizei* ⓕ po-li-*tsai*
postcard *Postkarte* ⓕ *post*-kar-te
post office *Postamt* ⓝ *post*-amt
pregnant *schwanger* *shvang*-er
price *Preis* ⓜ prais

Q

quiet *ruhig* *roo*-ikh

R

rain n *Regen* ⓜ *rey*-gen
razor *Rasierer* ⓜ ra-*zee*-rer
receipt *Quittung* ⓕ *kvi*-tung
red *rot* rawt
refund *Rückzahlung* ⓕ *rewk*-tsaa-lung
registered mail *Einschreiben* ⓝ *ain*-shrai-ben

rent v *mieten* *mee*-ten
repair v *reparieren* re-pa-*ree*-ren
reservation *Reservierung* ⓕ re-zer-*vee*-rung
restaurant *Restaurant* ⓝ res-to-*raang*
return v *zurückkommen* tsu-*rewk*-ko-men
return ticket *Rückfahrkarte* ⓕ *rewk*-faar-kar-te
right (direction) *rechts* rekhts
road *Straße* ⓕ *shtraa*-se
room *Zimmer* ⓝ *tsi*-mer

S

safe a *sicher* *zi*-kher
sanitary napkin *Damenbinden* ⓕ pl *daa*-men-bin-den
seat *Platz* ⓜ plats
send *senden* *zen*-den
service station *Tankstelle* ⓕ tangk-shte-le
sex *Sex* ⓜ seks
shampoo *Shampoo* ⓝ sham-poo
share (a dorm) *teilen (mit)* *tai*-len (mit)
shaving cream *Rasiercreme* ⓕ ra-*zeer*-kreym
she *sie* zee
sheet (bed) *Bettlaken* ⓝ *bet*-laa-ken
shirt *Hemd* ⓝ hemt
shoes *Schuhe* ⓝ pl *shoo*-e
shop n *Geschäft* ⓝ ge-*sheft*
short *kurz* kurts
shower *Dusche* ⓕ *doo*-she
single room *Einzelzimmer* ⓝ *ain*-tsel-tsi-mer
skin *Haut* ⓕ howt
skirt *Rock* ⓜ rok
sleep v *schlafen* *shlaa*-fen
slowly *langsam* *lang*-zaam
small *klein* klain
smoke (cigarettes) v *rauchen* *row*-khen
soap *Seife* ⓕ *zai*-fe
some *einige* *ai*-ni-ge
soon *bald* balt
south *Süden* ⓜ *zew*-den
souvenir shop *Souvenirladen* ⓜ zu-ve-*neer*-laa-den
speak *sprechen* *shpre*-khen
spoon *Löffel* ⓜ *leu*-fel
stamp *Briefmarke* ⓕ *breef*-mar-ke
stand-by ticket *Standby-Ticket* ⓝ stend-*bai*-ti-ket
station (train) *Bahnhof* ⓜ *baan*-hawf
stomach *Magen* ⓜ *maa*-gen
stop v *anhalten* *an*-hal-ten
stop (bus) *Bushaltestelle* ⓕ *bus*-hal-te-shte-le
street *Straße* ⓕ *shtraa*-se

student *Student/Studentin* ⓜ/ⓕ
shtu-*dent*/shtu-*den*-tin
sun *Sonne* ⓕ *zo*-ne
sunscreen *Sonnencreme* ⓕ *zo*-nen-kreym
swim v *schwimmen* *shvi*-men
Switzerland *Schweiz* ⓕ shvaits

T

tampons *Tampons* ⓜ pl *tam*-pons
taxi *Taxi* ⓝ *tak*-si
teaspoon *Teelöffel* ⓜ *tey*-leu-fel
teeth *Zähne* ⓜ pl *tsey*-ne
telephone *Telefon* ⓝ te-le-*fawn*
television *Fernseher* ⓜ *fern*-zey-er
temperature (weather) *Temperatur* ⓕ tem-pe-ra-*toor*
tent *Zelt* ⓝ tselt
that (one) *jene* *yey*-ne
they *sie* zee
thirsty *durstig* *durs*-tikh
this (one) *diese* *dee*-ze
throat *Kehle* ⓕ *key*-le
ticket (transport) *Fahrkarte* ⓕ *faar*-kar-te
ticket (sightseeing) *Eintrittskarte* ⓕ *ain*-trits-kar-te
time *Zeit* ⓕ tsait
tired *müde* *mew*-de
tissues *Papiertaschentücher* ⓝ pl
pa-*peer*-ta-shen-tew-kher
today *heute* *hoy*-te
toilet *Toilette* ⓕ to-a-*le*-te
tomorrow *morgen* *mor*-gen
tonight *heute Abend* *hoy*-te *aa*-bent
toothbrush *Zahnbürste* ⓕ *tsaan*-bewrs-te
toothpaste *Zahnpasta* ⓕ *tsaan*-pas-ta
torch (flashlight) *Taschenlampe* ⓕ *ta*-shen-lam-pe
tour *Tour* ⓕ toor
tourist office *Fremdenverkehrsbüro* ⓝ
frem-den-fer-kairs-bew-raw
towel *Handtuch* ⓝ *hant*-tookh
train *Zug* ⓜ tsook
translate *übersetzen* ew-ber-*ze*-tsen
travel agency *Reisebüro* ⓝ *rai*-ze-bew-raw
travellers cheque *Reisescheck* ⓜ *rai*-ze-shek
trousers *Hose* ⓕ *haw*-ze
twin beds *zwei Einzelbetten* ⓝ pl tsvai *ain*-tsel-be-ten
tyre *Reifen* ⓜ *rai*-fen

U

underwear *Unterwäsche* ⓕ *un*-ter-ve-she
urgent *dringend* *dring*-ent

V

vacant *frei* frai
vacation *Ferien* pl *fair*-i-en
vegetable *Gemüse* ⓝ ge-*mew*-ze
vegetarian a *vegetarisch* ve-ge-*taa*-rish
visa *Visum* ⓝ *vee*-zum

W

waiter *Kellner/Kellnerin* ⓜ/ⓕ *kel*-ner/*kel*-ne-rin
walk v *gehen* *gey*-en
wallet *Brieftasche* ⓕ *breef*-ta-she
warm a *warm* varm
wash (something) *waschen* *va*-shen
watch *Uhr* ⓕ oor
water *Wasser* ⓝ *va*-ser
we *wir* veer
weekend *Wochenende* ⓝ *vo*-khen-en-de
west *Westen* ⓜ *ves*-ten
wheelchair *Rollstuhl* ⓜ *rol*-shtool
when *wann* van
where *wo* vaw
white *weiß* vais
who *wer* vair
why *warum* va-*rum*
wife *Ehefrau* ⓕ *ey*-e-frow
window *Fenster* ⓝ *fens*-ter
wine *Wein* ⓜ vain
with *mit* mit
without *ohne* *aw*-ne
woman *Frau* ⓕ frow
write *schreiben* *shrai*-ben

Y

yellow *gelb* gelp
yes *ja* yaa
yesterday *gestern* *ges*-tern
you sg inf *du* doo
you sg pol *Sie* zee
you pl *Sie* zee

DICTIONARY

168

Greek

greek alphabet

Α α *al*·pha	Β β *vi*·ta	Γ γ *gha*·ma	Δ δ *dhel*·ta	Ε ε *ep*·si·lon
Ζ ζ *zi*·ta	Η η *i*·ta	Θ θ *thi*·ta	Ι ι *yio*·ta	Κ κ *ka*·pa
Λ λ *lam*·dha	Μ μ mi	Ν ν ni	Ξ ξ ksi	Ο ο *o*·mi·kron
Π π pi	Ρ ρ ro	Σ σ/ς* *sigh*·ma	Τ τ taf	Υ υ *ip*·si·lon
Φ φ fi	Χ χ hi	Ψ ψ psi	Ω ω o·*me*·gha	

* The letter Σ has two forms for the lower case – σ and ς. The second one is used at the end of words.

greek

ΕΛΛΗΝΙΚΑ

introduction

Aristotle, Plato, Homer, Sappho and Herodotus can't all be wrong in their choice of language – if you've ever come across arcane concepts such as 'democracy', exotic disciplines like 'trigonometry' or a little-known neurosis termed 'the Oedipus complex', then you'll have some inkling of the widespread influence of Greek (Ελληνικά e·li·ni·ka). With just a little Modern Greek under your belt, you'll have a richer understanding of this language's impact on contemporary Western culture.

Modern Greek is a separate branch of the Indo-European language family, with Ancient Greek its only (extinct) relative. The first records of written Ancient Greek date from the 14th to the 12th centuries BC. By the 9th century BC, the Greeks had adapted the Phoenician alphabet to include vowels – the first alphabet to do so – and the script in use today came to its final form some time in the 5th century BC. The Greek script was the foundation for both the Cyrillic and the Latin alphabet.

Although written Greek has been remarkably stable over the millennia, the spoken language has evolved considerably. In the 5th century, the dialect spoken around Athens (known as 'Attic') became the dominant speech as a result of the city-state's cultural and political prestige. Attic gained even greater influence as the medium of administration for the vast empire of Alexander the Great, and remained the official language of the Eastern Roman Empire and the Orthodox Church after the demise of the Hellenistic world. Once the Ottoman Turks took Constantinople in 1453, the Attic dialect lost its official function. In the meantime, the common language, known as Koine (Κοινή ki·ni), continued to evolve, absorbing vocabulary from Turkish, Italian, Albanian and other Balkan languages.

When an independent Greece returned to the world stage in 1832, it needed to choose a national language. Purists advocated a slightly modernised version of Attic known as Καθαρεύουσα ka·tha·re·vu·sa (from the Greek word for 'clean'), which no longer resembled the spoken language. However, Koine had strong support as it was spoken and understood by the majority of Greeks, and in the end it gained official recognition, although it was banned during the military dictatorship (1967–74).

Today, Greek is the official language of Greece and a co-official language of Cyprus, and has over 13 million speakers worldwide. Start your Greek adventure with this chapter – and if you're having one of those days when you're dying to say 'It's all Greek to me!', remember that in your shoes, a Greek speaker would say: Αυτά για μένα είναι Κινέζικα af·ta yia me·na i·ne ki·ne·zi·ka (This is Chinese to me)!

pronunciation

vowel sounds

Greek vowels are pronounced separately even when they're written in sequence, eg ζώο zo·o (animal). You'll see though, in the table below, that some letter combinations correspond to a single sound – ουρά (queue) is pronounced u·ra. When a word ending in a vowel is followed by another word that starts with the same or a similar vowel sound, one vowel is usually omitted and the two words are pronounced as if they were one – Σε ευχαριστώ se ef·kha·ris·to becomes Σ' ευχαριστώ sef·kha·ris·to (Thank you). Note that the apostrophe (') is used in written Greek to show that two words are joined together.

symbol	english equivalent	greek example	transliteration
a	father	αλλά	a·la
e	bet	πλένομαι	ple·no·me
i	hit	πίσω, πόλη, υποφέρω, είδος, οικογένεια, υιός	pi·so, po·li, i·po·fe·ro, i·dhos, i·ko·ye·ni·a, i·os
ia	nostalgia	ζητιάνος	zi·tia·nos
io	ratio	πιο	pio
o	pot	πόνος, πίσω	po·nos, pi·so
u	put	ουρά	u·ra

word stress

Stress can fall on any of the last three syllables. In our pronunciation guides, the stressed syllable is always in italics, but in written Greek, the stressed syllable is always indicated by an accent over the vowel, eg καλά ka·la (good). If a vowel is represented by two letters, it's written on the second letter, eg ζητιάνος zi·tia·nos (beggar). If the accent is marked on the first of these two letters, they should be read separately, eg Μάιος ma·i·os (May). Where two vowels occur together but are not stressed, a diaeresis (¨) is used to indicate that they should be pronounced separately, eg λαϊκός la·i·kos (popular).

consonant sounds

Most Greek consonant sounds are also found in English – only the guttural gh and kh might need a bit of practice. Double consonants are only pronounced once – άλλος *a*-los (other). However, you'll notice that sometimes two Greek letters in combination form one single consonant sound – the combination of the letters μ and π makes the sound b, and the combination of the letters ν and τ makes the sound d.

symbol	english equivalent	greek example	transliteration
b	bed	μπαρ	bar
d	dog	ντομάτα	do·*ma*·ta
dh	that	δεν	dhen
dz	adds	τζάμι	dza-*mi*
f	fat	φως, αυτή	fos, af-*ti*
g	go	γκαρσόν	gar·*son*
gh	guttural sound, between 'goat' and 'loch'	γάτα	*gha*·ta
h	hat	χέρι	*he*·ri
k	kit	καλά	ka·*la*
kh	loch (guttural sound)	χαλί	kha·*li*
l	let	λάδι	*la*·dhi
m	man	μαζί	ma·*zi*
n	not	ναός	na·*os*
ng	ring	ελέγχω	e·*leng*·kho
p	pet	πάνω	*pa*·no
r	red (trilled)	ράβω	*ra*·vo
s	sun	στυλό	sti·*lo*
t	top	τι	ti
th	thin	θέα	*the*·a
ts	hats	τσέπη	*tse*·pi
v	very	βίζα, αύριο	*vi*·za, *av*·ri·o
y	yes	γέρος	*ye*·ros
z	zero	ζέστη	*ze*·sti

basics

language difficulties

Do you speak English?
Μιλάς Αγγλικά;   mi·*las* ang·gli·*ka*

Do you understand?
Καταλαβαίνεις;   ka·ta·la·*ve*·nis

I understand.
Καταλαβαίνω.   ka·ta·la·*ve*·no

I don't understand.
Δεν καταλαβαίνω.   dhen ka·ta·la·*ve*·no

What does (μώλος) mean?
Τι σημαίνει (μώλος);   ti si·*me*·ni (*mo*·los)

How do you ...?   Πως ...;   pos ...
  pronounce this   προφέρεις αυτό   pro·*fe*·ris af·*to*
  write (Madhuri)   γράφουν (Μαδουρή)   *ghra*·foun (ma·dhu·*ri*)

Could you   Θα μπορούσες   tha bo·*ru*·ses
please ...?   παρακαλώ να ...;   pa·ra·ka·*lo* na ...
  repeat that   το επαναλάβεις   to e·pa·na·*la*·vis
  speak more slowly μιλάς πιο σιγά   mi·*las* pio si·*gha*
  write it down   το γράψεις   to *ghrap*·sis

numbers

0	μυδέν	mi·dhen		15	δεκαπέντε	dhe·ka·pe·de
1	ένας/μία/ένα m/f/n	e·nas/mi·a/e·na		16	δεκαέξι	dhe·ka·ek·si
2	δύο	dhi·o		17	δεκαεφτά	dhe·ka·ef·ta
3	τρεις m&f	tris		18	δεκαοχτώ	dhe·ka·okh·to
	τρία n	tri·a		19	δεκαεννέα	dhe·ka·e·ne·a
4	τέσσερις m&f	te·se·ris		20	είκοσι	i·ko·si
	τέσσερα n	te·se·ra		21	είκοσι	i·ko·si
5	πέντε	pe·de			ένας/μία/	e·nas/mi·a/
6	έξι	ek·si			ένα m/f/n	e·na
7	εφτά	ef·ta		22	είκοσι δύο	i·ko·si dhi·o
8	οχτώ	okh·to		30	τριάντα	tri·a·da
9	εννέα	e·ne·a		40	σαράντα	sa·ra·da
10	δέκα	dhe·ka		50	πενήντα	pe·ni·da
11	έντεκα	e·de·ka		60	εξήντα	ek·si·da
12	δώδεκα	dho·dhe·ka		70	εβδομήντα	ev·dho·mi·da
13	δεκατρείς m&f	dhe·ka·tris		80	ογδόντα	ogh·dho·da
	δεκατρία n	dhe·ka·tri·a		90	ενενήντα	e·ne·ni·da
14	δεκατέσσερις m&f	dhe·ka·te·se·ris		100	εκατό	e·ka·to
	δεκατέσσερα n	dhe·ka·te·se·ra		1000	χίλια	hi·lia

time & dates

What time is it?	Τι ώρα είναι;	ti o·ra i·ne
It's one o'clock.	Είναι (μία) η ώρα.	i·ne (mi·a) i o·ra
It's (10) o'clock.	Είναι (δέκα) η ώρα.	i·ne (dhe·ka) i o·ra
Quarter past (10).	(Δέκα) και τέταρτο.	(dhe·ka) ke te·tar·to
Half past (10).	(Δέκα) και μισή.	(dhe·ka) ke mi·si
Quarter to (10).	(Δέκα) παρά τέταρτο.	(dhe·ka) pa·ra te·tar·to
At what time ...?	Τι ώρα ...;	ti o·ra ...
At ...	Στις ...	stis ...
Monday	Δευτέρα	dhef·te·ra
Tuesday	Τρίτη	tri·ti
Wednesday	Τετάρτη	te·tar·ti
Thursday	Πέμπτη	pem·ti
Friday	Παρασκευή	pa·ra·ske·vi
Saturday	Σάββατο	sa·va·to
Sunday	Κυριακή	ki·ria·ki

January	Ιανουάριος	i·a·nu·*a*·ri·os
February	Φεβρουάριος	fev·ru·*a*·ri·os
March	Μάρτιος	*mar*·ti·os
April	Απρίλιος	a·*pri*·li·os
May	Μάιος	*ma*·i·os
June	Ιούνιος	i·*u*·ni·os
July	Ιούλιος	i·*u*·li·os
August	Αύγουστος	*av*·ghu·stos
September	Σεπτέμβριος	sep·*tem*·vri·os
October	Οκτώβριος	ok·*tov*·ri·os
November	Νοέμβριος	no·*em*·vri·os
December	Δεκέμβριος	dhe·*kem*·vri·os

What date is it today?

Τι ημερομηνία είναι σήμερα;   ti i·me·ro·mi·*ni*·a *i*·ne *si*·me·ra

It's (18 October).

Είναι (δεκαοχτώ Οκτωβρίου).   *i*·ne (dhe·ka·okh·*to* ok·tov·*ri*·u)

| since (May) | από (το Μάιο) | a·*po* (to *ma*·i·o) |
| until (June) | μέχρι (τον Ιούνιο) | *meh*·ri (ton i·*u*·ni·o) |

yesterday	χτες	khtes
today	σήμερα	*si*·me·ra
tonight	απόψε	a·*pop*·se
tomorrow	αύριο	*av*·ri·o

last ...

night	την περασμένη νύχτα	tin pe·raz·*me*·ni *nikh*·ta
week	την περασμένη εβδομάδα	tin pe·raz·*me*·ni ev·dho·*ma*·dha
month	τον περασμένο μήνα	ton pe·raz·*me*·no *mi*·na
year	τον περασμένο χρόνο	ton pe·raz·*me*·no *khro*·no

next ...

week	την επόμενη εβδομάδα	tin e·*po*·me·ni ev·dho·*ma*·dha
month	τον επόμενο μήνα	ton e·*po*·me·no *mi*·na
year	τον επόμενο χρόνο	ton e·*po*·me·no *khro*·no

yesterday/	χτες/	khtes/
tomorrow ...	αύριο το ...	*av*·ri·o to ...
morning	πρωί	pro·*i*
afternoon	απόγευμα	a·*po*·yev·ma
evening	βράδι	*vra*·dhi

weather

What's the weather like?	Πως είναι ο καιρός;	pos i·ne o ke·ros

It's ...		
cloudy	Είναι συννεφιά.	i·ne si·ne·fia
cold	Κάνει κρύο.	ka·ni kri·o
hot	Κάνει πολλή ζέστη.	ka·ni po·li ze·sti
raining	Βρέχει.	vre·hi
snowing	Χιονίζει.	hio·ni·zi
sunny	Είναι λιακάδα.	i·ne lia·ka·dha
warm	Κάνει ζέστη.	ka·ni ze·sti
windy	Φυσάει.	fi·sa·i

spring	άνοιξη f	a·nik·si
summer	καλοκαίρι n	ka·lo·ke·ri
autumn	φθινόπωρο n	fthi·no·po·ro
winter	χειμώνας m	hi·mo·nas

border crossing

I'm here ...	Είμαι εδώ...	i·me e·dho...
in transit	τράνζιτ	tran·zit
on business	για δουλειά	yia dhu·lia
on holiday	σε διακοπές	se dhia·ko·pes

I'm here for (three) ...	Είμαι εδώ για (τρεις) ...	i·me e·dho yia (tris) ...
days	μέρες	me·res
weeks	εβδομάδες	ev·dho·ma·dhes
months	μήνες	mi·nes

I'm going to (Limassol).
Πηγαίνω στη (Λεμεσό).   pi·ye·no sti (le·me·so)

I'm staying at the (Xenia).
Μένω στο (Ξενία).   me·no sto (kse·ni·a)

I have nothing to declare.
Δεν έχω τίποτε να δηλώσω.   dhen e·kho ti·po·te na dhi·lo·so

I have something to declare.
Έχω κάτι να δηλώσω.   e·kho ka·ti na dhi·lo·so

That's (not) mine.
Αυτό (δεν) είναι δικό μου.   af·to (dhen) i·ne dhi·ko mu

transport

tickets & luggage

Where can I buy a ticket?	Που αγοράζω εισιτήριο;	pu a·gho·ra·zo i·si·ti·ri·o
Do I need to book a seat?	Χρειάζεται να κλείσω θέση;	khri·a·ze·te na kli·so the·si
One ... ticket	Ενα εισιτήριο ...	e·na i·si·ti·ri·o ...
to (Patras), please.	για την (Πάτρα), παρακαλώ.	yia tin (pa·tra) pa·ra·ka·lo
one-way	απλό	a·plo
return	με επιστροφή	me e·pi·stro·fi
I'd like to ... my	Θα ήθελα να ... το	tha i·the·la na ... to
ticket, please.	εισιτήριό μου, παρακαλώ.	i·si·ti·ri·o mu pa·ra·ka·lo
cancel	ακυρώσω	a·ki·ro·so
change	αλλάξω	a·lak·so
confirm	επικυρώσω	e·pi·ki·ro·so
I'd like a ... seat.	Θα ήθελα μια θέση ...	tha i·the·la mia the·si ...
nonsmoking	στους μη καπνίζοντες	stus mi kap·ni·zo·des
smoking	στους καπνίζοντες	stus kap·ni·zo·des

How much is it?
Πόσο κάνει;   *po·so ka·ni*

Is there air conditioning?
Υπάρχει έρκοντίσιον;   i·*par*·hi e·kon·*di*·si·on

Is there a toilet?
Υπάρχει τουαλέτα;   i·*par*·hi tu·a·*le*·ta

How long does the trip take?
Πόσο διαρκεί το ταξίδι;   *po*·so dhi·ar·*ki* to tak·*si*·dhi

Is it a direct route?
Πηγαίνει κατ'ευθείαν;   pi·*ye*·ni ka·tef·*thi*·an

Where can I find a luggage locker?
Που μπορώ να βρω τη φύλαξη   pu bo·*ro* na vro ti *fi*·lak·si
αντικειμένων;   a·di·ki·*me*·non

My luggage has	Οι αποσκευές	i a·pos·ke·ves
been ...	μου έχουν ...	mu e·khun ...
damaged	πάθει ζημιά	pa·thi zi·mia
lost	χαθεί	kha·thi
stolen	κλαπεί	kla·pi

getting around

Where does flight (10) arrive/depart?
Που προσγειώνεται/		pu pros·yi·o·ne·te/
απογειώνεται η πτήση (δέκα);		a·po·yi·o·ne·te i pti·si (dhe·ka)

Where's (the) ...? Που είναι ...; pu i·ne ...
arrivals hall	η αίθουσα των αφίξεων	i e·thu·sa tona·fik·se·on
departures hall	η αίθουσα των	i e·thu·sa ton
	ανα χωρήσεων	a·na kho·ri·se·on
duty-free shop	τα αφορολόγητα	ta a·fo·ro·lo·yi·ta
gate (nine)	η θύρα (εννέα)	i thi·ra (e·ne·a)

Is this the ... Είναι αυτό το ... i·ne af·to to ...
to (Athens)?	για την (Αθήνα);	yia tin (a·thi·na)
boat	πλοίο	pli·o
bus	λεωφορείο	le·o·fo·ri·o
ferry	φέρυ	fe·ri
plane	αεροπλάνο	a·e·ro·pla·no
train	τρένο	tre·no

What time's the Πότε είναι το ... po·te i·ne to ...
... (bus)? (λεωφορείο); (le·o·fo·ri·o)
first	πρώτο	pro·to
last	τελευταίο	te·lef·te·o
next	επόμενο	e·po·me·no

At what time does it arrive/depart?
Τι ώρα φτάνει/φεύγει; ti o·ra fta·ni/fev·yi

What time does it get to (Thessaloniki)?
Τι ώρα φτάνει στη (Θεσσαλονίκη); ti o·ra fta·ni sti (the·sa·lo·ni·ki)

How long will it be delayed?
Πόση ώρα θα καθυστερήσει; po·si o·ra tha ka·thi·ste·ri·si

What station is this?
Ποιος σταθμός είναι αυτός; pios stath·mos i·ne af·tos

What stop is this?
Ποια στάση είναι αυτή; pia sta·si i·ne af·ti

What's the next station?
Ποιος είναι ο επόμενος σταθμός; pios i·ne o e·po·me·nos stath·mos

What's the next stop?
Ποια είναι η επόμενη στάση; pia i·ne i e·po·me·ni sta·si

transport – GREEK

179

Does it stop at (Iraklio)?
Σταματάει στο (Ηράκλειο);
sta·ma·*ta*·i sto (i·*ra*·kli·o)

Please tell me when we get to (Thessaloniki).
Παρακαλώ πέστε μου όταν
φτάσουμε στη (Θεσσαλονίκη).
pa·ra·ka·*lo* pe·ste mu *o*·tan
fta·su·me sti (the·sa·lo·*ni*·ki)

How long do we stop here?
Πόση ώρα θα σταματήσουμε εδώ;
po·si *o*·ra tha sta·ma·*ti*·su·me e·*dho*

Is this seat available?
Είναι αυτή η θέση ελεύθερη;
i·ne af·*ti* i *the*·si e·*lef*·the·ri

That's my seat.
Αυτή η θέση είναι δική μου.
af·*ti* i *the*·si *i*·ne dhi·*ki* mu

I'd like a taxi ... | θα ήθελα ένα ταξί ... | tha *i*·the·la *e*·na tak·*si* ...
at (9am) | στις (εννέα | stis (e·*ne*·a
 | πριν το μεσημέρι) | prin to me·si·*me*·ri)
now | τώρα | *to*·ra
tomorrow | αύριο | *av*·ri·o

Is this taxi available?
Είναι αυτό το ταξί ελεύθερο;
i·ne af·*to* to tak·*si* e·*lef*·the·ro

How much is it to ...?
Πόσο κάνει για ...;
po·so *ka*·ni yia ...

Please put the meter on.
Παρακαλώ βάλε το ταξίμετρο.
pa·ra·ka·*lo va*·le to tak·*si*·me·tro

Please take me to (this address).
Παρακαλώ πάρε με σε
(αυτή τη διεύθυνση).
pa·ra·ka·*lo pa*·re me se
(af·*ti* ti dhi·*ef*·thin·si)

Please ... | Παρακαλώ ... | pa·ra·ka·*lo* ...
slow down | πήγαινε πιο σιγά | *pi*·ye·ne pio si·*gha*
stop here | σταμάτα εδώ | sta·*ma*·ta e·*dho*
wait here | περίμενε εδώ | pe·*ri*·me·ne e·*dho*

car, motorbike & bicycle hire

I'd like to | θα ήθελα να | tha *i*·the·la na
hire a ... | ενοικιάσω ένα ... | e·ni·ki·*a*·so *e*·na ...
bicycle | ποδήλατο | po·*dhi*·la·to
car | αυτοκίνητο | af·to·*ki*·ni·to
motorbike | μοτοσικλέτα | mo·to·si·*kle*·ta

with ...	με ...	me ...
a driver	οδηγό	o·dhi·*gho*
air conditioning	έρκοντίσιον	e·kon·*di*·si·on

How much for ... hire?	Πόσο νοικάζεται την ...;	*pu*·so ni·*kia*·ze·te tin ...
hourly	ώρα	*o*·ra
daily	ημέρα	i·*me*·ra
weekly	εβδομάδα	ev·dho·*ma*·dha

air	αέρας m	a·*e*·ras
oil	λάδι αυτοκινήτου n	*la*·dhi af·to·ki·*ni*·tu
petrol	βενζίνα f	ven·*zi*·na
tyres	λάστιχα n	*la*·sti·kha

I need a mechanic.	Χρειάζομαι μηχανικό.	khri·*a*·zo·me mi·kha·ni·*ko*
I've run out of petrol.	Μου τελείωσε η βενζίνα.	mu te·*li*·o·se i ven·*zi*·na
I have a flat tyre.	Μ'έπιασε λάστιχο.	me·pia·se *la*·sti·kho

directions

Where's the ...?	Που είναι ...?	pu *i*·ne ...
bank	η τράπεζα	i *tra*·pe·za
city centre	το κέντρο της πόλης	to *ke*·dro tis *po*·lis
hotel	το ξενοδοχείο	to kse·no·dho·*hi*·o
market	η αγορά	i a·gho·*ra*
police station	ο αστυνομικός	o a·sti·no·mi·*kos*
	σταθμός	stath·*mos*
post office	το ταχυδρομείο	to ta·hi·dhro·*mi*·o
public toilet	τα δημόσια	ta dhi·*mo*·si·a
	αποχωρητήρια	a·po·kho·ri·*ti*·ria
tourist office	το τουριστικό γραφείο	to tu·ri·sti·*ko* ghra·*fi*·o

Is this the road to (Lamia)?
Είναι αυτός ο δρόμος για (τη Λαμία);   *i*·ne af·*tos* o *dhro*·mos yia (ti la·*mi*·a)

Can you show me (on the map)?
Μπορείς να μου δείξεις (στο χάρτη);   bo·*ris* na mu *dhik*·sis (sto *khar*·ti)

What's the address?
Ποια είναι η διεύθυνση;   pia *i*·ne i dhi·*ef*·thin·si

How far is it?
Πόσο μακριά είναι;   *po*·so ma·kri·*a i*·ne

How do I get there?
Πως πηγαίνω εκεί;   pos pi·*ye*·no e·*ki*

Turn ...	Στρίψε ...	*strip·se* ...
at the corner	στη γωνία	sti gho·*ni*·a
at the traffic lights	στα φανάρια	sta fa·*na*·ria
left/right	αριστερά/δεξιά	a·ris·te·*ra*/dhek·si·*a*

It's ...	Είναι ...	*i*·ne ...
behind ...	πίσω ...	*pi*·so ...
far away	μακριά	ma·kri·*a*
here	εδώ	e·*dho*
in front of ...	μπροστά από ...	bros·*ta* a·po ...
near ...	κοντά ...	ko·*da* ...
next to ...	δίπλα από ...	*dhip*·la a·po ...
on the corner	στη γωνία	sti gho·*ni*·a
opposite ...	απέναντι ...	a·*pe*·na·di ...
straight ahead	κατ'ευθείαν	ka·tef·*thi*·an
there	εκεί	e·*ki*

by bus	με λεωφορείο	me le·o·fo·*ri*·o
by boat	με πλοίο	me *pli*·o
by taxi	με ταξί	me tak·*si*
by train	με τρένο	me *tre*·no
on foot	με πόδια	me *po*·dhia

north	βόρια	*vo*·ri·a
south	νότια	*no*·ti·a
east	ανατολικά	a·na·to·li·*ka*
west	δυτικά	dhi·ti·*ka*

signs

Είσοδος/Έξοδος	*i*·so·dhos/*ek*·so·dhos	**Entrance/Exit**
Ανοικτός/Κλειστός	a·nik·*tos*/kli·*stos*	**Open/Closed**
Ελεύθερα Δωμάτια	e·*lef*·the·ra dho·*ma*·ti·a	**Rooms Available**
Πλήρες	*pli*·res	**No Vacancies**
Πληροφορίες	pli·ro·fo·*ri*·es	**Information**
Αστυνομικός Σταθμός	a·sti·no·mi·*kos* stath·*mos*	**Police Station**
Απαγορεύεται	a·pa·gho·*re*·ve·te	**Prohibited**
Τουαλέτες	tu·a·*le*·tes	**Toilets**
Ανδρών	an·*dhron*	**Men**
Γυναικών	yi·ne·*kon*	**Women**
Ζεστό/Κρύο	zes·*to*/*khri*·o	**Hot/Cold**

accommodation

finding accommodation

Where's a ...?	Που είναι ...;	pu *i*·ne ...
camping ground	χώρος για κάμπινγκ	*kho*·ros yia *kam*·ping
guesthouse	ξενώνας	kse·*no*·nas
hotel	ξενοδοχείο	kse·no·dho·*hi*·o
youth hostel	γιουθ χόστελ	yiuth *kho*·stel

Can you recommend	Μπορείτε να συστήσετε	bo·*ri*·te na si·*sti*·se·te
somewhere ...?	κάπου ...;	*ka*·pu ...
cheap	φτηνό	fti·*no*
good	καλό	ka·*lo*
nearby	κοντινό	ko·di·*no*

I'd like to book a room, please.
Θα ήθελα να κλείσω ένα
δωμάτιο, παρακαλώ.
tha *i*·the·la na *kli*·so *e*·na
dho·*ma*·ti·o pa·ra·ka·*lo*

I have a reservation.
Εχω κάνει κάποια κράτηση.
e·kho *ka*·ni *ka*·pia *kra*·ti·si

My name's ...
Με λένε ...
me *le*·ne ...

Do you have a ... room?	Εχετε ένα ... δωμάτιο;	*e*·he·te *e*·na ... dho·*ma*·ti·o
single	μονό	mo·*no*
double	διπλό	dhi·*plo*
twin	δίκλινο	*dhi*·kli·no

How much is it per ...?	Πόσο είναι για κάθε ...;	*po*·so *i*·ne yia *ka*·the ...
night	νύχτα	*nikh*·ta
person	άτομο	*a*·to·mo

Can I pay ...?	Μπορώ να πληρώσω με ...;	bo·*ro* na pli·*ro*·so me ...
by credit card	πιστωτική κάρτα	pi·stu·ti·*kl kar*·ta
with a travellers	ταξιδιωτική	tak·si·dhio·ti·*ki*
cheque	επιταγή	e·pi·ta·*yi*

accommodation – GREEK

183

For (three) nights/weeks.
Για (τρεις) νύχτες/εβδομάδες.   yia (tris) *nikh*·tes/ev·dho·*ma*·dhes

From (2 July) to (6 July).
Από (τις δύο Ιουλίου)   a·*po* (tis *dhi*·o i·u·*li*·u)
μέχρι (τις έξι Ιουλίου).   *me*·khri (tis *ek*·si i·u·*li*·u)

Can I see it?
Μπορώ να το δω;   bo·*ro* na to dho

Am I allowed to camp here?
Μπορώ να κατασκηνώσω εδώ;   bo·*ro* na ka·ta·ski·*no*·so e·*dho*

Where can I find a camp site?
Που μπορώ να βρω το   pu bo·*ro* na vro to
χώρο του κάμπινγκ;   *kho*·ro tu *kam*·ping

requests & queries

When/Where is breakfast served?
Πότε/Που σερβίρεται το πρόγευμα;   *po*·te/pu ser·*vi*·re·te to *pro*·yev·ma

Please wake me at (seven).
Παρακαλώ ξύπνησέ με στις (εφτά).   pa·ra·ka·*lo* ksip·ni·*se* me stis (ef·*ta*)

Could I have my key, please?
Μπορώ να έχω το κλειδί μου   bo·*ro* na *e*·kho to kli·*dhi* mu
παρακαλώ;   pa·ra·ka·*lo*

Can I get another (blanket)?
Μπορώ να έχω και άλλη (κουβέρτα);   bo·*ro* na *e*·kho ke *a*·li (ku·*ver*·ta)

This (towel) isn't clean.
Αυτή (η πετσέτα) δεν είναι καθαρό.   af·*ti* (i pet·*se*·ta) dhen *i*·ne ka·tha·*ri*

Is there a/an ...?	Έχετε ...;	*e*·he·te ...
elevator	ασανσέρ	a·san·*ser*
safe	χρηματοκιβώτιο	khri·ma·to·ki·*vo*·ti·o

The room is too ...	Είναι πάρα πολύ ...	*i*·ne *pa*·ra po·*li* ...
expensive	ακριβό	a·kri·*vo*
noisy	θορυβώδες	tho·ri·*vo*·dhes
small	μικρό	mi·*kro*

The ... doesn't work.	... δεν λειτουργεί.	... dhen li·tur·*ghi*
air conditioning	Το έρκοντίσιον	to er·kon·*di*·si·on
fan	Ο ανεμιστήρας	o a·ne·mi·*sti*·ras
toilet	Η τουαλέτα	i tu·a·*le*·ta

checking out

What time is checkout?

Τι ώρα είναι η αναχώρηση; ti *o*·ra *i*·ne i a·na·*kho*·ri·si

Can I leave my luggage here?

Μπορώ να αφήσω τις βαλίτσες μου εδώ; bo·*ro* na a·*fi*·so tis va·*lit*·ses mu e·*dho*

Could I have my ..., please?	Μπορώ να έχω ... μου παρακλώ;	bo·*ro* na *e*·kho ... mu pa·ra·ka·*lo*
deposit	την προκαταβολή	tin pro·ka·ta·vo·*li*
passport	το διαβατήριο	to dhia·va·*ti*·rio
valuables	τα κοσμήματά	ta koz·*mi*·ma·*ta*

communications & banking

the internet

Where's the local Internet cafe?

Που είναι το τοπικό pu *i*·ne to to·pi·*ko*
καφενείο με διαδίκτυο; ka·fe·*ni*·o me dhi·a·*dhik*·ti·o

How much is it per hour?

Πόσο κοστίζει κάθε ώρα; *po*·so ko·*sti*·zi *ka*·the *o*·ra

I'd like to ...	Θα ήθελα να ...	tha *i*·the·la na ...
check my email	ελέγξω την ηλεκτρονική αλληλογραφία μου	e·*leng*·so tin i·lek·tro·ni·*ki* a·li·lo·ghra·*fi*·a mu
get Internet access	έχω πρόσβαση στο διαδίκτυο	*e*·kho *pros*·va·si sto dhi·a·*dhik*·ti·o
use a printer	χρησιμοποιήσω έναν εκτυπωτή	khri·si·mo·pi·*i*·so *e*·nan ek·ti·po·*ti*
use a scanner	χρησιμοποιήσω ένα σκάνερ	khri·si·mo·pi·*i*·so *e*·na *ska*·ner

mobile/cell phone

I'd like a ...	Θα ήθελα ...	tha i·the·la ...
mobile/cell phone for hire	να νοικιάσω ένα κινητό τηλέφωνο	na ni·kia·so e·na ki·ni·to ti·le·fo·no
SIM card for	μια κάρτα SIM	mia kar·ta sim
your network	για το δίκτυό σας	yia to dhik·tio sas

What are the rates?	Ποιες είναι οι τιμές;	pies i·ne i ti·mes

telephone

What's your phone number?
Τι αριθμό τηλεφώνου έχεις;   ti a·rith·mo ti·le·fo·nu e·his

The number is ...
Ο αριθμός είναι ...   o a·rith·mos i·ne ...

Where's the nearest public phone?
Που είναι το πιο κοντινό   pu i·ne to pio ko·di·no
δημόσιο τηλέφωνο;   dhi·mo·si·o ti·le·fo·no

I'd like to buy a phonecard.
Θέλω να αγοράσω μια   the·lo na a·gho·ra·so mia
τηλεφωνική κάρτα.   ti·le·fo·ni·ki kar·ta

I want to ...	Θέλω να ...	the·lo na ...
call (Singapore)	τηλεφωνήσω (στη Σιγγαπούρη)	ti·le·fo·ni·so (sti sing·ga·pu·ri)
make a local call	κάνω ένα τοπικό τηλέφωνο	ka·no e·na to·pi·ko ti·le·fo·no
reverse the charges	αντιστρέψω τα έξοδα	a·di·strep·so ta ek·so·dha

How much does ... cost?	Πόσο κοστίζει ...;	po·so ko·sti·zi ...
a (three)- minute call	ένα τηλεφώνημα (τριών) λεπτών	e·na ti·le·fo·ni·ma (tri·on) lep·ton
each extra minute	κάθε έξτρα λεπτό	ka·the eks·tra lep·to

It's (40c) per (30) seconds.
(Σαράντα λεπτα) για (τριάντα)   (sa·ra·da lep·ta) yia (tri·a·da)
δευτερόλεπτα.   dhef·te·ro·lep·ta

post office

I want to send a ...	Θέλω να στείλω ...	the·lo na sti·lo ...
fax	ένα φαξ	e·na faks
letter	ένα γράμμα	e·na ghra·ma
parcel	ένα δέμα	e·na dhe·ma
postcard	μια κάρτα	mia kar·ta
I want to buy a/an ...	Θέλω να αγοράσω ένα ...	the·lo na a·gho·ra·so e·na ...
envelope	φάκελο	fa·ke·lo
stamp	γραμματόσημο	ghra·ma·to·si·mo
Please send it (to Australia) by ...	Παρακαλώ στείλτε το ... (στην Αυστραλία).	pa·ra·ka·lo stil·te to ... (stin af·stra·li·a)
airmail	αεροπορικώς	a·e·ro·po·ri·kos
express mail	εξπρές	eks·pres
registered mail	συστημένο	si·sti·me·no
surface mail	δια ξηράς	dhia ksi·ras

Is there any mail for me?
Υπάρχουν γράμματα για μένα;   i·par·khun ghra·ma·ta yia me·na

bank

Where's a/an ...?	Που είναι ...;	pu i·ne ...
ATM	μια αυτόματη μηχανή χρημάτων	mia af·to·ma·ti mi·kha·ni khri·ma·ton
foreign exchange office	ένα γραφείο αλλαγής χρημάτων	e·na ghra·fi·o a·la·yis khri·ma·ton
I'd like to ...	Θα ήθελα να ...	tha i·the·la na ...
Where can I ...?	Που μπορώ να ...;	pu bo·ro na ...
arrange a transfer	τακτοποιήσω μια μεταβίβαση	tak·to·pi·i·so mia me·ta·vi·va·si
cash a cheque	εξαργυρώσω μια επιταγή	ek·sar·yi·ro·so mia e·pi·ta·yi
change a travellers cheque	αλλάξω μια ταξιδιωτική επιταγή	a·lak·so mia tak·si·dhio·ti·ki e·pi·ta·yi
change money	αλλάξω χρήματα	a·lak·so khri·ma·ta
get a cash advance	κάνω μια ανάληψη σε μετρητά	ka·no mia a·na·lip·si se me·tri·ta
withdraw money	αποσύρω χρήματα	a·po·si·ro khri·ma·ta

What's the ...?	Ποια είναι ... ;	pia *i*·ne ...
charge for that	η χρέωση για αυτό	i *khre*·o·si yia af·*to*
exchange rate	η τιμή συναλλάγματος	i ti·*mi* si·na·*lagh*·ma·tos

| It's (12) ... | Κάνει (δώδεκα) ... | *ka*·ni (*dho*·dhe·ka) ... |
| euros | ευρώ | ev·*ro* |

It's free.
Είναι δωρεάν.   *i*·ne dho·re·*an*

What time does the bank open?
Τι ώρα ανοίγει η τράπεζα;   ti *o*·ra a·*ni*·yi i *tra*·pe·za

Has my money arrived yet?
Έχουν φτάσει τα χρήματά μου;   *e*·khun *fta*·si ta *khri*·ma·*ta* mu

sightseeing

getting in

What time does it open/close?
Τι ώρα ανοίγει/κλείνει;   ti *o*·ra a·*ni*·yi/*kli*·ni

What's the admission charge?
Πόσο κοστίζει η είσοδος;   *po*·so ko·*sti*·zi i *i*·so·dhos

Is there a discount for students/children?
Υπάρχει έκπτωση για   i·*par*·hi *ek*·pto·si yia
σπουδαστές/παιδιά;   spu·dha·*stes*/pe·*dhia*

I'd like a ...	Θα ήθελα ...	tha *i*·the·la ...
catalogue	ένα κατάλογο	*e*·na ka·*ta*·lo·gho
guide	έναν οδηγό	*e*·nan o·dhi·*gho*
local map	ένα τοπικό χάρτη	*e*·na to·pi·*ko khar*·ti

I'd like to see ...	Θα ήθελα να δω ...	tha *i*·the·la na dho ...
What's that?	Τι είναι εκείνο;	ti *i*·ne e·*ki*·no
Can I take a photo?	Μπορώ να πάρω μια	bo·*ro* na *pa*·ro mia
	φωτογραφία;	fo·to·ghra·*fi*·a

tours

When's the next tour?

Πότε είναι η επόμενη περιήγηση;   *po*·te *i*·ne i e·*po*·me·ni pe·ri·*i*·yi·si

When's the next ...?   Πότε είναι το επόμενο ...;   *po*·te *i*·ne to e·*po*·me·no ...
- boat trip   ταξίδι με τη βάρκα   tak·*si*·dhi me ti *var*·ka
- day trip   ημερήσιο ταξίδι   i·me·*ri*·si·o tak·*si*·dhi

Is ... included?   Συμπεριλαμβάνεται ...;   si·be·ri·lam·*va*·ne·te ...
- accommodation   κατάλυμα   ka·*ta*·li·ma
- the admission charge   τιμή εισόδου   ti·*mi* i·*so*·dhu
- food   φαγητό   fa·yi·*to*
- transport   μεταφορά   me·ta·fo·*ra*

How long is the tour?

Πόση ώρα διαρκεί η περιήγηση;   *po*·si *o*·ra dhi·ar·*ki* i pe·ri·*i*·yi·si

What time should we be back?

Τι ώρα πρέπει να επιστρέψουμε;   ti *o*·ra *pre*·pi na e·pi·*strep*·su·me

sightseeing

amphitheatre	αμφιθέατρο n	am·fi·*the*·a·tro
castle	κάστρο n	*ka*·stro
cathedral	μητρόπολη f	mi·*tro*·po·li
church	εκκλησία f	e·kli·*si*·a
fresco	φρέσκο n	*fres*·ko
labyrinth	λαβύρινθος m	la·*vi*·rin·thos
main square	κεντρική πλατεία f	ken·dhri·*ki* pla·*ti*·a
monastery	μοναστήρι n	mo·na·*sti*·ri
monument	μνημείο n	mni·*mi*·o
mosaic	μωσαϊκό n	mo·sa·i·*ko*
museum	μουσείο n	mu·*si*·o
old city	αρχαία πόλι	ar·*khe*·a *po*·li
palace	παλάτι n	pa·*la*·ti
ruins	ερρίπια n pl	e·*ri*·pi·a
sculpture	γλυπτική f	ghlip·ti·*ki*
stadium	στάδιο n	*sta*·dhi·o
statue	άγαλμα n	*a*·ghal·ma
temple	ναός m	na·*os*

shopping

enquiries

Where's a ...?	Που είναι ...;	pu i·ne ...
bank	μια τράπεζα	mia tra·pe·za
bookshop	ένα βιβλιοπωλείο	e·na viv·li·o·po·li·o
camera shop	ένα κατάστημα φωτογραφικών ειδών	e·na ka·ta·sti·ma fo·to·ghra·fi·kon i·dhon
department store	ένα κατάστημα	e·na ka·ta·sti·ma
grocery store	ένα οπωροπωλείο	e·na o·po·ro·po·li·o
kiosk	ένα περίπτερο	e·na pe·rip·te·ro
market	μια αγορά	mia a·gho·ra
newsagency	το εφημεριδοπωλείο	to e·fi·me·ri·dho·po·li·o
supermarket	ένα σούπερμάρκετ	e·na su·per·mar·ket

Where can I buy (a padlock)?
Που μπορώ να αγοράσω
(μια κλειδαριά);
pu bo·ro na a·gho·ra·so
(mia kli·dha·ria)

I'd like to buy ...
Θα ήθελα να αγοράσω ...
tha i·the·la na a·gho·ra·so ...

Can I look at it?
Μπορώ να το κοιτάξω;
bo·ro na to ki·tak·so

Do you have any others?
Έχετε άλλα;
e·he·te a·la

Does it have a guarantee?
Έχει εγγύηση;
e·hi e·gi·i·si

Can I have it sent overseas?
Μπορείς να το στείλεις
στο εξωτερικό;
bo·ris na to sti·lis
sto ek·so·te·ri·ko

Can I have ... repaired?
Μπορώ να επισκευάσω εδώ ...;
bo·ro na e·pi·ske·va·so e·dho ...

Can I have a bag, please?
Μπορώ να έχω μια τσάντα, παρακαλώ;
bo·ro na e·kho mia tsa·da pa·ra·ka·lo

It's faulty.
Είναι ελαττωματικό.
i·ne e·la·to·ma·ti·ko

I'd like ..., please.	Θα ήθελα ..., παρακαλώ.	tha i·the·la ... pa·ra·ka·lo
a refund	επιστροφή χρημάτων	e·pi·stro·fi khri·ma·ton
to return this	να επιστρέψω αυτό	na e·pi·strep·so af·to

paying

How much is it?
Πόσο κάνει;   *po·so ka·ni*

Can you write down the price?
Μπορείς να γράψεις την τιμή;   *bo·ris na ghrap·sis tin ti·mi*

That's too expensive.
Είναι πάρα πολύ ακριβό.   *i·ne pa·ra po·li a·kri·vo*

Can you lower the price?
Μπορείς να κατεβάσεις την τιμή;   *bo·ris na ka·te·va·sis tin ti·mi*

I'll give you (five) euros.
Θα σου δώσω (πέντε) ευρώ.   *tha su dho·so (pe·de) ev·ro*

There's a mistake in the bill.
Υπάρχει κάποιο λάθος   *i·par·hi ka·pio la·thos*
στο λογαριασμό.   *sto lo·gha·riaz·mo*

Do you accept ...?	Δέχεστε ...;	*dhe·he·ste ...*
credit cards	πιστωτικές κάρτες	*pi·sto·ti·kes kar·tes*
debit cards	χρεωτικές κάρτες	*khre·o·ti·kes kar·tes*
travellers cheques	ταξιδιωτικές	*tak·si·dhio·ti·kes*
	επιταγές	*e·pi·ta·yes*

I'd like my change, please.
Θα ήθελα τα ρέστα μου, παρακαλώ.   *tha i·the·la ta re·sta mu pa·ra·ka·lo*

Can I have a receipt, please?
Μπορώ να έχω μια   *bo·ro na e·kho mia*
απόδειξη, παρακαλώ;   *a·po·dhik·si pa·ra·ka·lo*

clothes & shoes

Can I try it on?	Μπορώ να το προβάρω;	*bo·ro na to pro·va·ro*
My size is (40).	Το νούμερό μου είναι	*to nu·me·ro mu i·ne*
	(σαράντα).	*(sa·ra·da)*
It doesn't fit.	Δε μου κάνει.	*dhe mu ka·ni*
small	μικρό	*mi·kro*
medium	μεσαίο	*me·se·o*
large	μεγάλο	*me·gha·lo*

books & music

I'd like a ...	Θα ήθελα ...	tha i·the·la ...
newspaper	μια εφημερίδα	mia e·fi·me·ri·dha
(in English)	(στα Αγγλικά)	(sta ang·gli·ka)
pen	ένα στυλό	e·na sti·lo

Is there an English-language bookshop?
Υπάρχει ένα βιβλιοπωλείο   i·par·hi e·na viv·li·o·po·li·o
Αγγλικής γλώσσας;   ang·gli·kis ghlo·sas

I'm looking for something by (Anna Vissi).
Ψάχνω για κάτι (της Άννας Βίσση).   psakh·no yia ka·ti (tis a·nas vi·si)

Can I listen to this?
Μπορώ να το ακούσω;   bo·ro na to a·ku·so

photography

Can you ...?	Μπορείς να ...;	bo·ris na ...
develop this	εμφανίσεις αυτό	em·fa·ni·sis af·to
film	το φιλμ	to film
load my film	βάλεις το φιλμ	va·lis to film
	στη μηχανή μου	sti mi·kha·ni mu
transfer photos	μεταφέρεις	me·ta·fe·ris
from my	φωτογραφίες από	fo·to·ghra·fi·es a·po
camera to CD	την φωτογραφική	ti fo·to·ghra·fi·ki
	μου μηχανή στο CD	mu mi·kha·ni sto si·di

I need a/an ... film	Χρειάζομαι φιλμ ...	khri·a·zo·me film ...
for this camera.	για αυτή τη μηχανή.	yia af·ti ti mi·kha·ni
APS	APS	e·i·pi·es
B&W	μαυρόασπρο	mav·ro·a·spro
colour	έγχρωμο	eng·khro·mo
slide	σλάιντ	sla·id
(200) speed	ταχύτητα (διακοσίων)	ta·hi·ti·ta (dhia·ko·si·on)

When will it be ready?	Πότε θα είναι έτοιμο;	po·te tha i·ne e·ti·mo

meeting people

greetings, goodbyes & introductions

Hello/Hi.	Γεια σου.	yia su
Good night.	Καληνύχτα.	ka·li·*nikh*·ta
Goodbye/Bye.	Αντίο.	a·*di*·o
Mr	Κύριε	*ki*·ri·e
Mrs	Κυρία	ki·*ri*·a
Miss	Δις	dhes·pi·*nis*
How are you?	Τι κάνεις;	ti *ka*·nis
Fine. And you?	Καλά. Εσύ;	ka·*la* e·*si*
What's your name?	Πως σε λένε;	pos se *le*·ne
My name is ...	Με λένε ...	me *le*·ne ...
I'm pleased to meet you.	Χαίρω πολύ.	*he*·ro po·*li*

This is my ...	Από εδώ ... μου.	a·*po* e·*dho* ... mu
boyfriend	ο φίλος	o *fi*·los
brother	ο αδερφός	o a·dher·*fos*
daughter	η κόρη	i *ko*·ri
father	ο πατέρας	o pa·*te*·ras
friend	ο φίλος/η φίλη m/f	o *fi*·los/i *fi*·li
girlfriend	η φιλενάδα	i fi·le·*na*·dha
husband	ο σύζυγός	o *si*·zi·ghos
mother	η μητέρα	i mi·*te*·ra
partner (intimate)	ο/η σύντροφός m/f	o/i si·dro·*fos*
sister	η αδερφή	i a·dher·*fi*
son	ο γιος	o yios
wife	η σύζυγός	i *si*·zi·ghos

Here's my ...	Εδώ είναι ... μου.	e·*dho* *i*·ne ... mu
What's your ...?	Ποιο είναι ... σου;	pio *i*·ne ... su
email address	το ιμέιλ	to i·*me*·il
fax number	το φαξ	to faks
phone number	το τηλέφωνό	to ti·*le*·fo·no

Here's my address.

Εδώ είναι η διεύθυνσή μου.   e·*dho* *i*·ne i dhi·*ef*·thin·*si* mu

What's your address?

Ποια είναι η δική σου διεύθυνση;   pia *i*·ne i dhi·*ki* su dhi·*ef*·thin·si

occupations

What's your occupation?	Τι δουλειά κάνεις;	ti dhu·*lia* ka·nis
I'm a/an ...	Είμαι/Δουλεύω ...	*i*·me/dhou·*lev*·o ...
businessperson	επιχειρηματίας m&f	e·pi·hi·ri·ma·*ti*·as
farmer	γεωργός m&f	ye·or·*ghos*
manual worker	εργάτης/εργάτρια m/f	er·*gha*·tis/er·*gha*·tri·a
office worker	σε γραφείο	se ghra·*phi*·o
scientist	επιστήμονας m&f	e·pi·*sti*·mo·nas
tradesperson	έμπορος m&f	*e*·bo·ros

background

Where are you from?	Από που είσαι;	a·*po* pu *i*·se
I'm from ...	Είμαι από ...	*i*·me a·*po* ...
Australia	την Αυστραλία	tin af·stra·*li*·a
Canada	τον Καναδά	ton ka·na·*dha*
England	την Αγγλία	tin ang·*gli*·a
New Zealand	την Νέα Ζηλανδία	tin *ne*·a zi·lan·*dhi*·a
the USA	την Αμερική	tin A·me·ri·*ki*
Are you married?	Είσαι παντρεμένος/	*i*·se pa·dre·*me*·nos/
	παντρεμένη; m/f	pa·dre·*me*·ni
I'm married.	Είμαι παντρεμένος/	*i*·me pa·dre·*me*·nos/
	παντρεμένη. m/f	pa·dre·*me*·ni
I'm single.	Είμαι ανύπαντρος/	*i*·me a·*ni*·pa·dros/
	ανύπαντρη. m/f	a·*ni*·pa·dri

age

How old ...?	Πόσο χρονών ...;	*po*·so khro·*non* ...
are you	είσαι	*i*·se
is your daughter	είναι η κόρη σου	*i*·ne i *ko*·ri su
is your son	είναι ο γιος σου	*i*·ne o yios su
I'm ... years old.	Είμαι ... χρονών.	*i*·me ... khro·*non*
He/She is ... years old.	Αυτός/αυτή είναι ...	af·*tos*/af·*ti i*·ne ...
	χρονών.	khro·*non*

feelings

I'm (not) ...	(Δεν) Είμαι ...	(dhen) *i*·me ...
Are you ...?	Είσαι ...;	*i*·se ...
happy	ευτυχισμένος m	ef·ti·hiz·*me*·nos
	ευτυχισμένη f	ef·ti·hiz·*me*·ni
hot	ζεστός/ζεστή m/f	ze·*stos*/ze·*sti*
hungry	πεινασμένος m	pi·naz·*me*·nos
	πεινασμένη f	pi·naz·*me*·ni
sad	στενοχωρημένος m	ste·no·kho·ri·*me*·nos
	στενοχωρημένη f	ste·no·kho·ri·*me*·ni
thirsty	διψασμένος m	dhip·saz·*me*·nos
	διψασμένη f	dhip·saz·*me*·ni

entertainment

going out

Where can I find ...?	Που μπορώ να βρω ...;	pu bo·*ro* na vro ...
clubs	κλαμπ	klab
gay venues	Χώρους συνάντησης	*kho*·rus si·*na*·di·sis
	για γκέη	yia *ge*·i
pubs	μπυραρίες	bi·ra·*ri*·es
I feel like going to a/the ...	Εχω όρεξη να πάω σε ...	*e*·kho *o*·rek·si na *pa*·o se ...
concert	κονσέρτο	kon·*ser*·to
the movies	φιλμ	film
party	πάρτυ	*par*·ti
restaurant	εστιατόριο	e·sti·a·*to*·ri·o
theatre	θέατρο	*the*·a·tro

interests

Do you like ...?	Σου αρέσει ...;	su a·*re*·si ...
I (don't) like ...	(Δεν) μου αρέσει ...	(dhen) mu a·*re*·si ...
cooking	η μαγειρική	i ma·yi·ri·*ki*
reading	το διάβασμα	to *dhia*·vaz·ma

Do you like ...?	Σου αρέσουν ...;	su a·re·sun ...
I (don't) like ...	(Δεν) μου αρέσουν τα ...	(dhen) mu a·re·sun ta ...
art	καλλιτεχνικά	ka·li·tekh·ni·ka
movies	φιλμ	film
nightclubs	νάιτ κλαμπ	na·it klab
sport	σπορ	spor

Do you like to ...?	Σου αρέσει να ...;	sou a·re·si na ...
dance	χορεύεις	kho·re·vis
go to concerts	πηγαίνεις σε κονσέρτα	pi·ye·nis se kon·ser·ta
listen to music	ακούς μουσική	a·kus mu·si·ki

food & drink

finding a place to eat

Can you recommend a ...?	Μπορείς να συστήσεις ...;	bo·ris na si·sti·sis ...
bar	ένα μπαρ	e·na bar
café	μία καφετέρια	mi·a ka·fe·te·ria
restaurant	ένα εστιατόριο	e·sti·a·to·ri·o

I'd like ..., please.	Θα ήθελα ..., παρακαλώ.	tha i·thela ... pa·ra·ka·lo
a table for (five)	ένα τραπέζι για (πέντε)	e·na tra·pe·zi yia (pe·de)
the (non)smoking section	στους (μη) καπνίζοντες	stus (mi) kap·ni·zo·des

ordering food

breakfast	πρόγευμα n	pro·yev·ma
lunch	γεύμα n	yev·ma
dinner	δείπνο n	dhip·no
snack	μεζεδάκι n	me·ze·dha·ki

What would you recommend?
Τι θα συνιστούσες;   ti tha si·ni·stu·ses

I'd like (a/the) ..., please.	Θα ήθελα ..., παρακαλώ.	tha *i*·the·la ... pa·ra·ka·*lo*
bill	το λογαριασμό	to lo·gha·riaz·*mo*
drink list	τον κατάλογο με τα ποτά	ton ka·*ta*·lo·gho me ta po·*ta*
menu	το μενού	to me·*nu*
that dish	εκείνο το φαγητό	e·*ki*·no to fa·yi·*to*

drinks

(cup of) coffee ...	(ένα φλυτζάνι) καφέ ...	(e·na fli·*dza*·ni) ka·*fe* ...
(cup of) tea ...	(ένα φλυτζάνι) τσάι ...	(e·na fli·*dza*·ni) tsa·i ...
with milk	με γάλα	me *gha*·la
without sugar	χωρίς ζάχαρη	kho·*ris za*·kha·ri

| (orange) juice | χυμός (πορτοκάλι) m | hi·*mos* (por·to·*ka*·li) |
| soft drink | αναψυκτικό n | a·nap·sik·ti·*ko* |

... water	... νερό	... ne·*ro*
hot	ζεστό	ze·*sto*
(sparkling) mineral	(γαζόζα) μεταλλικό	(gha·*zo*·za) me·ta·li·*ko*

in the bar

I'll have ...	θα πάρω ...	tha *pa*·ro ...
I'll buy you a drink.	θα σε κεράσω εγώ.	tha se ke·*ra*·so e·*gho*
What would you like?	Τι θα ήθελες;	ti tha *i*·the·les
Cheers!	Εις υγείαν!	is i·*yi*·an

brandy	μπράντι n	*bran*·di
champagne	σαμπάνια f	sam·*pa*·nia
a glass/bottle of beer	ένα ποτήρι/μπουκάλι μπύρα	e·na po·*ti*·ri/bu·*ka*·li *bi*·ra
ouzo	ούζο n	*u*·zo
a shot of (whisky)	ένα (ουίσκι)	e·na (u·*i*·ski)

a glass/bottle of ... wine	ένα ποτήρι/μπουκάλι ... κρασί	e·na po·*ti*·ri/bu·*ka*·li ... kra·*si*
red	κόκκινο	*ko*·ki·no
sparkling	σαμπάνια	sam·*pa*·nia
white	άσπρο	*a*·spro

self-catering

What's the local speciality?
Ποιες είναι οι τοπικές λιχουδιές;

pies *i·*ne i to·pi·*kes* li·khu·*dhies*

What's that?
Τι είναι εκείνο;

ti *i·*ne e·*ki·*no

How much is (a kilo of cheese)?
Πόσο κάνει (ένα κιλό τυρί);

*po·*so *ka·*ni (*e·*na ki·*lo* ti·*ri*)

I'd like ...	Θα ήθελα ...	tha *i·*the·la ...
(100) grams	(εκατό) γραμμάρια	(e·ka·*to*) ghra·*ma·*ria
(two) kilos	(δύο) κιλά	(*dhi·*o) ki·*la*
(three) pieces	(τρία) κομμάτια	(*tri·*a) ko·*ma·*tia
(six) slices	(έξι) φέτες	(*ek·*si) *fe·*tes

Less.	Πιο λίγο.	pio *li·*gho
Enough.	Αρκετά.	ar·ke·*ta*
More.	Πιο πολύ.	pio po·*li*

special diets & allergies

Is there a vegetarian restaurant near here?
Υπάρχει ένα εστιατόριο χορτοφάγων
εδώ κοντά;

i·*par·*hi *e·*na e·sti·a·*to·*ri·o hor·to·*fa·*ghon
e·*dho* ko·*da*

Do you have vegetarian food?
Έχετε φαγητό για χορτοφάγους;

*e·*he·te fa·yi·*to* yia khor·to·*fa·*ghus

I don't eat ...	Δεν τρώγω ...	dhen *tro·*gho ...
butter	βούτυρο	*vu·*ti·ro
eggs	αβγά	av·*gha*
meat stock	ζουμί από κρέας	zu·*mi* a·*po* kre·as

I'm allergic to ...	Είμαι αλλεργικός/ αλλεργική ... m/f	*i·*me a·ler·yi·*kos* a·ler·yi·*ki* ...
dairy produce	στα γαλακτικά	sta gha·lak·ti·*ka*
gluten	στη γλουτένη	sti ghlu·*te·*ni
MSG	στο MSG	sto em es dzi
nuts	στους ξηρούς καρπούς	stus ksi·*rus* kar·*pus*
seafood	στα θαλασσινά	sta tha·la·si·*na*

menu decoder

αρνί κοκκινιστό n	ar-*ni* ko-ki-ni-*sto*	lamb braised in white wine
αστακός m	a-sta-*kos*	lobster, boiled or chargrilled
γιαουρτογλού f	yia-ur-to-*ghlu*	grilled meat & yogurt pie
γιουβέτσι n	yiu-*vet*-si	casserole of meat & seafood with tomatoes & pasta
δάχτυλα n pl	*dhakh*-ti-la	deep-fried, nut-filled pastries
ελιές τσακιστές f pl	e-*lies* tsa-ki-*stes*	marinated green olives
ελιές τουρσί f pl	e-*lies* tur-*si*	pickled olives
ιμάμ-μπαϊλντί n	i-*mam*-ba-il-*di*	stuffed eggplant
καβούρι βραστό n	ka-*vu*-ri vra-*sto*	boiled crab with dressing
κακαβιά f	ka-ka-*via*	saltwater fish soup
καλαμάρι Λεβριανά n	ka-la-*ma*-ri lev-ria-*na*	squid stewed in wine
καλαμάρι τηγανητό n	ka-la-*ma*-ri ti-gha-ni-*to*	battered & fried squid rings
καρυδόπιτα f	ka-ri-*dho*-pi-ta	rich moist walnut cake
καταΐφι n	ka-ta-*i*-fi	syrupy nut-filled rolls
κεφτέδες m pl	kef-*te*-dhes	lamb, pork or veal rissoles
κοντοσούβλι n	kon-do-*suv*-li	spit-roast pieces of lamb or pork
κοφίσι n	ko-*fi*-si	fish pie
κρεατόπιτα f	kre-a-*to*-pi-ta	lamb or veal pie
λάχανα με λαρδί n pl	*la*-kha-na me lar-*dhi*	greens & bacon casserole
μηλοπιτάκια n pl	mi-lo-pi-*ta*-kia	apple & walnut pies
μπακλαβάς m pl	ba-kla-*vas*	nut-filled pastry in honey syrup
μπάμιες γιαχνί f pl	*ba*-mies yia-*khni*	braised okra
μπιζελόσουπα f	bi-ze-*lo*-su-pa	fragrant pea soup with dill
μπουρδέτο n	bur-*dhe*-to	salt cod stew

μπριάμι n	bri-*a*-mi	mixed vegetables casserole
μπριζόλες f pl	bri-*zo*-les	chops • steak
μύδια κρασάτα n pl	*mi*-dhia kra-*sa*-ta	poached mussels in wine sauce
ντολμάδες m pl	dol-*ma*-dhes	stuffed vine or cabbage leaves
ντοματόσουπα f	do-ma-*to*-su-pa	tomato soup with pasta
παλικάρια n pl	pa-li-*ka*-ri-a	boiled legumes & grains
ρέγγα f	*reng*-ga	smoked herrings, plain or grilled
ριζάδα f	ri-*za*-dha	thick soup with rice & shellfish
σαλιγκάρια n pl	sa-ling-*ga*-ri-a	snails cooked in the shell
σουβλάκι n	suv-*la*-ki	seasoned or marinated meat or fish, skewered & chargrilled
σπανακόπιτα f	spa-na-*ko*-pi-ta	spinach pie
συκόψωμο n	si-*kop*-so-mo	heavy aromatic fig cake
ταβάς m	ta-*vas*	seasoned beef or lamb casserole
τζατζίκι n	dza-*dzi*-ki	cucumber, yogurt & garlic salad
τυρόπιτα f	ti-*ro*-pi-ta	cheese pie
φακές σούπα f pl	fa-*kes* su-pa	lentil soup
φασολάδα f	fa-so-*la*-dha	thick fragrant bean soup
χαλβάς m	khal-*vas*	sweet of sesame seeds & honey, with pistachio or almonds
χαμψοπίλαφο n	kham-pso-*pi*-la-fo	onion & anchovy pilau
χόρτα τσιγάρι n pl	*khor*-ta tsi-*gha*-ri	lightly fried wild greens
χορτόπιτα f	khor-*to*-pi-ta	pie with seasonal greens
χορτοσαλάτα f	khor-to-sa-*la*-ta	warm salad of greens & dressing
χταπόδι βραστό n	khta-*po*-dhi vra-*sto*	boiled octopus
χωριάτικη σαλάτα f	kho-ri-*a*-ti-ki sa-*la*-ta	salad of tomatoes, cucumber, olives & feta

emergencies

basics

Help!	Βοήθεια!	vo·i·thia
Stop!	Σταμάτα!	sta·ma·ta
Go away!	Φύγε!	fi·ye
Thief!	Κλέφτης!	klef·tis
Fire!	Φωτιά!	fo·tia
Watch out!	Πρόσεχε!	pro·se·he

Call ...!	Κάλεσε ...!	ka·le·se ...
an ambulance	το ασθενοφόρο	to as·the·no·fo·ro
the doctor	ένα γιατρό	e·na yia·tro
the police	την αστυνομία	tin a·sti·no·mi·a

It's an emergency.
Είναι μια έκτακτη ανάγκη.   i·ne mia ek·tak·ti a·na·gi

Could you help me, please?
Μπορείς να βοηθήσεις, παρακαλώ;   bo·ris na vo·i·thi·sis pa·ra·ka·lo

Can I make a phone call?
Μπορώ να κάνω ένα τηλεφώνημα;   bo·ro na ka·no e·na ti·le·fo·ni·ma

I'm lost.
Εχω χαθεί.   e·kho kha·thi

Where are the toilets?
Που είναι η τουαλέτα;   pu i·ne i tu·a·le·ta

police

Where's the police station?
Που είναι ο αστυνομικός σταθμός;   pu i·ne o a·sti·no·mi·kos stath·mos

I want to report an offence.
Θέλω να αναφέρω μια παρανομία.   the·lo na a·na·fe·ro mia pa·ra·no·mi·a

I have insurance.
Εχω ασφάλεια.   e·kho as·fa·li·a

I've been ...	Με έχουν ...	me e·khun ...
assaulted	κακοποιήσει	ka·ko·pi·i·si
raped	βιάσει	vi·a·si
robbed	ληστέψει	li·step·si

I've lost my ...	Έχασα ... μου.	e·kha·sa ... mu
My ... was/were stolen.	Έκλεψαν ... μου.	e·klep·san ... mu
backpack	το σακίδιό	to sa·ki·dhio
bags	τις βαλίτσες	tis va·lits·es
credit card	την πιστωτική	tin pi·sto·ti·ki
	κάρτα	kar·ta
handbag	την τσάντα	tin tsa·da
jewellery	τα κοσμήματά	ta koz·mi·ma·ta
money	τα χρήματά	ta khri·ma·ta
passport	το διαβατήριό	to dhia·va·ti·rio
travellers	τις ταξιδιωτικές	tis tak·si·dhio·ti·kes
cheques	επιταγές	e·pi·ta·yes
wallet	το πορτοφόλι	to por·to·fo·li
I want to contact	Θέλω να έρθω σε	the·lo na er·tho se
my ...	επαφή με ... μου.	e·pa·fi me ... mu
consulate	τηνπρεσβεία	tin prez·vi·a
embassy	το προξενείο	to pro·ksee·ni·o

health

medical needs

Where's the	Που είναι ο πιο	pu i·ne o pio
nearest ...?	κοντινός ...;	ko·di·nos ...
dentist	οδοντίατρος	o·dho·di·a·tros
doctor	γιατρός	yia·tros

Where's the	Που είναι το πιο	pu i·ne to pio
nearest ...?	κοντινό...;	ko·di·no ...
hospital	νοσοκομείο	no·so·ko·mi·o
(night) pharmacy	(νυχτερινό) φαρμακείο	(nikh·te·ri·no) far·ma·ki·o

I need a doctor (who speaks English).

Χρειάζομαι ένα γιατρό   khri·a·zo·me e·na yia·tro
(που να μιλάει αγγλικά).   (pu na mi·la·i ang·gli·ka)

Could I see a female doctor?

Μπορώ να δω μια γυναίκα γιατρό;   bo·ro na dho mia yi·ne·ka yia·tro

I've run out of my medication.

Μου έχουν τελειώσει τα φάρμακά μου.   mu e·khun te·li·o·si ta far·ma·ka mu

symptoms, conditions & allergies

I'm sick.	Είμαι άρρωστος/άρρωστη m/f	i-me a-ro-stos/a-ro-sti
It hurts here.	Πονάει εδώ.	po-na-i e-dho
I have (a/an) ...	Εχω ...	e-kho ...
asthma	άσθμα n	as-thma
bronchitis	βροχίτιδα f	vro-hi-ti-dha
constipation	δυσκοιλιότητα f	dhis-ki-li-o-ti-ta
cough	βήχα m	vi-kha
diarrhoea	διάρροια f	dhi-a-ri-a
fever	πυρετό m	pi-re-to
headache	πονοκέφαλο m	po-no-ke-fa-lo
heart condition	καρδιακή κατάσταση f	kar-dhi-a-ki ka-ta-sta-si
nausea	ναυτία f	naf-ti-a
pain	πόνο m	po-no
sore throat	πονόλαιμο m	po-no-le-mo
toothache	πονόδοντο	po-no-dho-do
I'm allergic to ...	Είμαι αλλεργικός/ αλλεργική ... m/f	i-me a-ler-yi-kos a-ler-yi-ki ...
antibiotics	στα αντιβιωτικά	sta a-di-vi-o-ti-ka
anti-inflammatories	στα αντιφλεγμονώδη	sta a-di-flegh-mo-no-dhi
aspirin	στην ασπιρίνη	stin as-pi-ri-ni
bees	στις μέλισσες	stis me-li-ses
codeine	στην κωδεΐνη	stin ko-dhe-i-ni
penicillin	στην πενικιλλίνη	stin pe-ni-ki-li-ni
antiseptic	αντισηπτικό n	a-di-sip-ti-ko
bandage	επίδεσμος m	e-pi-dhez-mos
condoms	προφυλακτικά n	pro-fi-lak-ti-ka
contraceptives	αντισυλληπτικά n pl	a-di-si-lip-ti-ka
diarrhoea medicine	φάρμακο διάροιας	far-ma-ko dhiar-ghias
insect repellent	εντομοαπωθητικό n	e-do-mo-a-po-thi-ti-ko
laxatives	καθαρτικό n	ka-thar-ti-ko
painkillers	παυσίπονα	paf-si-po-na
rehydration salts	ενυδρωτικά άλατα n pl	en-i-dhro-ti-ka a-la-ta
sleeping tablets	υπνωτικά χάπια n pl	ip-no-ti-ka kha-pia

english–greek dictionary

Greek nouns in this dictionary have their gender indicated by Ⓜ (masculine), Ⓕ (feminine) or Ⓝ (neuter). If it's a plural noun you'll also see pl. Adjectives are given in the masculine form only. Words are also marked as n (noun), a (adjective), v (verb), sg (singular), pl (plural), inf (informal) and pol (polite) where necessary.

A

accident ατύχημα Ⓝ a-*ti*-hi-ma
accommodation κατάλυμα Ⓝ ka-*ta*-li-ma
adaptor μετασχηματιστής Ⓜ me-ta-shi-ma-ti-*stis*
address διεύθυνση Ⓕ dhi-*ef*-thin-si
aeroplane αεροπλάνο Ⓝ a-e-ro-*pla*-no
after μετά me-*ta*
air-conditioned με έρκοντίσιον me er-kon-*di*-si-on
airport αεροδρόμιο Ⓝ a-e-ro-*dhro*-mi-o
alcohol αλκοόλ Ⓝ al-ko-*ol*
all όλοι *o*-li
allergy αλλεργία Ⓕ a-ler-*yi*-a
ambulance νοσοκομειακό Ⓝ no-so-ko-mi-a-*ko*
and και ke
ankle αστράγαλος Ⓜ a-*stra*-gha-los
arm χέρι Ⓝ *he*-ri
ashtray σταχτοθήκη Ⓕ stakh-to-*thi*-ki
ATM αυτόματη μηχανή χρημάτων Ⓕ
    af-*to*-ma-ti mi-kha-*ni* khri-*ma*-ton

B

baby μωρό Ⓝ mo-*ro*
back (body) πλάτη Ⓕ *pla*-ti
backpack σακίδιο Ⓝ sa-*ki*-dhi-o
bad κακός ka-*kos*
bag σάκος Ⓜ *sa*-kos
baggage claim παραλαβή αποσκευών Ⓕ
    pa-ra-la-*vi* a-po-ske-*von*
bank τράπεζα Ⓕ *tra*-pe-za
bar μπαρ Ⓝ bar
bathroom μπάνιο Ⓝ *ba*-nio
battery μπαταρία Ⓕ ba-ta-*ri*-a
beautiful όμορφος o-*mor*-fos
bed κρεβάτι Ⓝ kre-*va*-ti
beer μπύρα Ⓕ *bi*-ra
before πριν prin
behind πίσω *pi*-so
bicycle ποδήλατο Ⓝ po-*dhi*-la-to
big μεγάλος me-*gha*-los

bill λογαριασμός Ⓜ lo-gha-riaz-*mos*
black a μαύρος *mav*-ros
blanket κουβέρτα Ⓕ ku-*ver*-ta
blood group ομάδα αίματος Ⓕ o-*ma*-dha e-ma-tos
blue a μπλε ble
boat βάρκα Ⓕ *var*-ka
book (make a reservation) v κλείσω θέση *kli*-so *the*-si
bottle μπουκάλι Ⓝ bu-*ka*-li
bottle opener ανοιχτήρι Ⓝ a-nikh-*ti*-ri
boy αγόρι Ⓝ a-*gho*-ri
brakes (car) φρένα Ⓝ pl *fre*-na
breakfast πρωινό Ⓝ pro-i-no
broken (faulty) ελαττωματικός e-la-to-ma-ti-*kos*
bus λεωφορείο Ⓝ le-o-fo-*ri*-o
business επιχείρηση Ⓕ e-pi-*hi*-ri-si
buy αγοράζω a-gho-*ra*-zo

C

café καφετέρια Ⓝ ka-fe-*te*-ria
camera φωτογραφική μηχανή Ⓕ
    fo-to-ghra-fi-*ki* mi-kha-*ni*
camp site χώρος για κάμπινγκ Ⓜ *kho*-ros yia *kam*-ping
cancel ακυρώνω a-ki-ro-no
can opener ανοιχτήρι Ⓝ a-nikh-*ti*-ri
car αυτοκίνητο Ⓝ af-to-*ki*-ni-to
cash μετρητά Ⓝ pl me-tri-*ta*
cash (a cheque) v εξαργυρώνω ek-sar-yi-ro-no
cell phone κινητό Ⓝ ki-ni-*to*
centre κέντρο Ⓝ *ke*-dro
change (money) v αλλάζω a-*la*-zo
cheap φτηνός fti-*nos*
check (bill) λογαριασμός Ⓜ lo-gha-riaz-*mos*
check-in ρεσεψιόν Ⓕ re-sep-*sion*
chest στήθος Ⓝ *sti*-thos
child παιδί Ⓝ pe-*dhi*
cigarette τσιγάρο Ⓝ tsi-*gha*-ro
city πόλη Ⓕ *po*-li
clean a καθαρός ka-tha-*ros*
closed κλεισμένος kliz-*me*-nos
coffee καφές Ⓜ ka-*fes*
coins κέρματα Ⓝ pl *ker*-ma-ta
cold a κρυωμένος kri-o-*me*-nos

collect call κλήση με αντιστροφή της επιβάρυνσης ⓕ
   kli-si me a-dis-tro-*fi* tis e-pi-*va*-rin-sis
come έρχομαι er-kho-me
computer κομπιούτερ ⓝ kom-*piu*-ter
condom προφυλακτικό ⓝ pro-fi-lak-ti-*ko*
contact lenses φακοί επαφής ⓜ pl fa-*ki* e-pa-*fis*
cook ∨ μαγειρεύω ma-yi-*re*-vo
cost τιμή ⓕ ti-*mi*
credit card πιστωτική κάρτα ⓕ pi-sto-ti-*ki kar*-ta
cup φλιτζάνι ⓝ fli-*dza*-ni
currency exchange τιμή συναλλάγματος ⓕ
   ti-*mi* si-na-*lagh*-ma-tos
customs (immigration) τελωνείο ⓝ te-lo-*ni*-o
Cypriot (nationality) Κύπριος/Κύπρια ⓜ/ⓕ
   ki-pri-os/*ki*-pri-a
Cypriot ⓐ κυπριακός/κυπριακή ⓜ/ⓕ
   ki-pri-a-*kos*/ki-pri-a-*ki*
Cyprus Κύπρος ⓕ *ki*-pros

D

dangerous επικίνδυνος e-*pi*-*kin*-dhi-nos
date (time) ημερομηνία ⓕ i-me-ro-mi-*ni*-a
day ημέρα ⓕ i-*me*-ra
delay καθυστέρηση ⓕ ka-thi-*ste*-ri-si
dentist οδοντίατρος ⓜ&ⓕ o-dho-*di*-a-tros
depart αναχωρώ a-na-kho-*ro*
diaper πάνα ⓕ *pa*-na
dictionary λεξικό ⓝ lek-si-*ko*
dinner δείπνο ⓝ *dhip*-no
direct άμεσος a-*me*-sos
dirty βρώμικος *vro*-mi-kos
disabled ανάπηρος a-*na*-pi-ros
discount έκπτωση ⓕ *ek*-pto-si
doctor γιατρός ⓜ&ⓕ yia-*tros*
double bed διπλό κρεβάτι ⓝ dhi-*plo* kre-*va*-ti
double room διπλό δωμάτιο ⓝ dhi-*plo* dho-*ma*-ti-o
drink ποτό ⓝ po-*to*
drive ∨ οδηγώ o-dhi-*gho*
drivers licence άδεια οδήγησης ⓕ *a*-dhi-a o-*dhi*-yi-sis
drugs (illicit) ναρκωτικό ⓝ nar-ko-ti-*ko*
dummy (pacifier) πιπίλα ⓕ pi-*pi*-la

E

ear αφτί ⓝ af-*ti*
east ανατολή ⓕ a-na-to-*li*
eat τρώγω *tro*-gho
economy class τουριστική θέση ⓕ tu ri-sti-*ki ihe*-si
electricity ηλεκτρισμός ⓜ i-lek-triz-*mos*

elevator ασανσέρ ⓝ a-san-*ser*
email ημέιλ ⓝ i-*me*-il
embassy πρεσβεία ⓕ pre-*zvi*-a
emergency έκτακτη ανάγκη ⓕ *ek*-tak-ti a-*na*-gi
English (language) Αγγλικά ⓝ ang-gli-*ka*
entrance είσοδος ⓕ *i*-so-dhos
evening βράδι ⓝ *vra*-dhi
exchange rate τιμή συναλλάγματος ⓕ
   ti-*mi* si-na-*lagh*-ma-tos
exit έξοδος ⓕ *ek*-so-dhos
expensive ακριβός a-kri-*vos*
express mail επείγον ταχυδρομείο ⓝ
   e-*pi*-ghon ta-hi-dhro-*mi*-o
eye μάτι ⓝ *ma*-ti

F

far μακριά ma-kri-*a*
fast γρήγορος *ghri*-gho-ros
father πατέρας ⓜ pa-*te*-ras
film (camera) φιλμ ⓝ film
finger δάκτυλο ⓝ *dhak*-ti-lo
first-aid kit κυτίο πρώτων βοηθειών ⓝ
   ki-*ti*-o pro-ton vo-i-thi-on
first class πρώτη τάξη ⓕ *pro*-ti *tak*-si
fish ψάρι ⓝ *psa*-ri
food φαγητό ⓝ fa-yi-*to*
foot πόδι ⓝ *po*-dhi
fork πιρούνι ⓝ pi-*ru*-ni
free (of charge) δωρεάν dho-re-*an*
friend φίλος/φίλη ⓜ/ⓕ *fi*-los/*fi*-li
fruit φρούτα ⓝ pl *fru*-ta
full γεμάτο ye-*ma*-to
funny αστείος a-*sti*-os

G

gift δώρο ⓝ *dho*-ro
girl κορίτσι ⓝ ko-*rit*-si
glass (drinking) ποτήρι ⓝ po-*ti*-ri
glasses γιαλιά ⓝ yia-*lia*
go πηγαίνω pi-*ye*-no
good καλός ka-*los*
Greece Ελλάδα ⓕ e-*la*-dha
Greek (language) Ελληνικά ⓝ e-li-ni-*ka*
Greek (nationality) Έλληνες ⓜ pl *e*-li-nes
green πράσινος *pra*-si-nos
guide οδηγός ⓜ&ⓕ o-dhi-*ghos*

H

half μισό ⓝ mi-*so*
hand χέρι ⓝ *he*-ri
handbag τσάντα ⓕ *tsa*-da
happy ευτυχισμένος ef-ti-hiz-*me*-nos
have έχω *e*-kho
he αυτός ⓜ af-*tos*
head κεφάλι ⓝ ke-*fa*-li
heart καρδιά ⓕ kar-*dhia*
heat ζέστη ⓕ *ze*-sti
heavy βαρύς va-*ris*
help v βοηθώ vo-i-*tho*
here εδώ e-*dho*
high ψηλός psi-*los*
highway δημόσιος δρόμος ⓜ dhi-*mo*-si-os *dhro*-mos
hike v πεζοπορώ pe-zo-po-*ro*
holiday διακοπές ⓕ dhia-ko-*pes*
homosexual ομοφυλόφιλος ⓜ o-mo-fi-*lo*-fi-los
hospital νοσοκομείο ⓝ no-so-ko-*mi*-o
hot ζεστός ze-*stos*
hotel ξενοδοχείο ⓝ kse-no-dho-*hi*-o
hungry πεινασμένος pi-naz-*me*-nos
husband σύζυγος ⓜ *si*-zi-ghos

I

I εγώ e-*gho*
identification (card) ταυτότητα ⓕ taf-*to*-ti-ta
ill άρρωστος *a*-ro-stos
important σπουδαίος spu-*dhe*-os
included συμπεριλαμβανομένου si-be-ri-lam-va-no-*me*-nu
injury πληγή ⓕ pli-*yi*
insurance ασφάλεια ⓕ as-*fa*-li-a
Internet διαδίκτυο ⓝ dhi-a-*dhik*-ti-o
interpreter διερμηνέας ⓜ&ⓕ dhi-er-mi-*ne*-as

J

jewellery κοσμήματα ⓝ pl koz-*mi*-ma-ta
job δουλειά ⓕ dhu-*lia*

K

key κλειδί ⓝ kli-*dhi*
kilogram χιλιόγραμμο ⓝ hi-*lio*-gra-mo
kitchen κουζίνα ⓕ ku-*zi*-na
knife μαχαίρι ⓝ ma-*he*-ri

L

laundry (place) πλυντήριο ⓝ pli-*di*-ri-o
lawyer δικηγόρος ⓜ&ⓕ dhi-ki-gho-ros
left (direction) αριστερός ⓜ a-ri-ste-*ros*
left-luggage office γραφείο φύλαξη αποσκευών ⓝ gra-*fi*-o *fi*-lak-si a-po-ske-*von*
leg πόδι ⓝ *po*-dhi
lesbian λεσβία ⓕ les-*vi*-a
less λιγότερο li-*gho*-te-ro
letter (mail) γράμμα ⓝ *ghra*-ma
lift (elevator) ασανσέρ ⓝ a-san-*ser*
light φως ⓝ fos
like v μου αρέσει mu a-*re*-si
lock κλειδαριά ⓕ kli-dha-*ria*
long μακρύς ma-*kris*
lost χαμένος kha-*me*-nos
lost-property office γραφείο απωλεσθέντων αντικειμένων ⓝ gra-*fi*-o a-po-les-*the*-don a-di-ki-*me*-non
love v αγαπώ a-gha-*po*
luggage αποσκευές ⓕ pl a-po-ske-*ves*
lunch μεσημεριανό φαγητό ⓝ me-si-me-ria-*no* fa-yi-*to*

M

mail (letters) αλληλογραφία ⓕ a-li-lo-ghra-*fi*-a
mail (postal system) ταχυδρομείο ⓝ ta-hi-dhro-*mi*-o
man άντρας ⓜ *a*-dras
map χάρτης ⓜ *khar*-tis
market αγορά ⓕ a-gho-*ra*
matches σπίρτα ⓝ pl *spir*-ta
meat κρέας ⓝ *kre*-as
medicine φάρμακο ⓝ *far*-ma-ko
menu μενού ⓝ me-*nu*
message μήνυμα ⓝ *mi*-ni-ma
milk γάλα ⓝ *gha*-la
minute λεπτό ⓝ lep-*to*
mobile phone κινητό ⓝ ki-ni-*to*
money χρήματα ⓝ *khri*-ma-ta
month μήνας ⓜ *mi*-nas
morning πρωί ⓝ pro-*i*
mother μητέρα ⓕ mi-*te*-ra
motorcycle μοτοσυκλέτα ⓕ mo-to-si-*kle*-ta
motorway αυτοκινητόδρομος ⓜ af-to-ki-ni-*to*-dhro-mos
mouth στόμα ⓝ *sto*-ma
music μουσική ⓕ mu-si-*ki*

N

name όνομα ⓝ *o*-no-ma
napkin πετσετάκι ⓝ pet-se-*ta*-ki
nappy πάνα ⓕ *pa*-na

near κοντά ko-*da*
neck λαιμός ⓜ le-*mos*
new νέος *ne*-os
news νέα ⓝ *ne*-a
newspaper εφημερίδα ⓕ e-fi-me-*ri*-dha
night νύχτα ⓕ *nikh*-ta
no όχι o-hi
noisy a θορυβώδης tho-ri-*vo*-dhis
nonsmoking μη καπνίζοντες mi kap-*ni*-zo-des
north βοράς ⓜ vo-*ras*
nose μύτη ⓕ *mi*-ti
now τώρα *to*-ra
number αριθμός ⓜ a-rith-*mos*

O

oil (engine) λάδι αυτοκινήτου ⓝ *la*-dhi af-to-ki-*ni*-tu
old παλιός pa-*lios*
one-way ticket απλό εισιτήριο ⓝ a-*plo* i-si-*ti*-ri-o
open a ανοιχτός a-nikh-*tos*
outside έξω ek-*so*

P

package πακέτο ⓝ pa-*ke*-to
paper χαρτί ⓝ khar-*ti*
park (car) v παρκάρω par-*ka*-ro
passport διαβατήριο ⓝ dhia-va-*ti*-ri-o
pay v πληρώνω pli-*ro*-no
pen στυλό ⓝ sti-*lo*
petrol πετρέλαιο ⓝ pe-*tre*-le-o
pharmacy φαρμακείο ⓝ far-ma-*ki*-o
phonecard τηλεκάρτα ⓕ ti-le-*kar*-ta
photo φωτογραφία ⓕ fo-to-gra-*fi*-a
plate πιάτο ⓝ *pia*-to
police αστυνομία ⓕ a-sti-no-*mi*-a
postcard κάρτα ⓕ *kar*-ta
post office ταχυδρομείο ⓝ ta-hi-dhro-*mi*-o
pregnant έγκυος e-gi-os
price τιμή ⓕ ti-*mi*

Q

quiet ήσυχος *i*-si-khos

R

rain βροχή vro-*hi*
razor ξυριστική μηχανή ⓕ ksi-ri-sti-*ki* mi-kha-*ni*
receipt απόδειξη ⓕ a-*po*-dhik-si

red κόκκινο *ko*-ki-no
refund n επιστροφή χρημάτων ⓕ
  e-pi-stro-*fi* khri-*ma*-ton
registered mail συστημένο sis-ti-*me*-no
rent v ενοικιάζω e-ni-ki-*a*-zo
repair v επισκευάζω e-pi-ske-*va*-zo
reservation κράτηση ⓕ *kra*-ti-si
restaurant εστιατόριο ⓝ e-sti-a-*to*-ri-o
return v επιστρέφω e-pi-*stre*-fo
return ticket εισιτήριο μετ' επιστροφής ⓝ
  i-si-*ti*-ri-o me-te-pis-tro-*fis*
right (direction) δεξιός dhek-si-*os*
road δρόμος ⓜ *dhro*-mos
room δωμάτιο ⓝ dho-*ma*-ti-o

S

safe a ασφαλής as-fa-*lis*
sanitary napkin πετσετάκι υγείας ⓝ pet-se-*ta*-ki i-*yi*-as
seat θέση ⓕ *the*-si
send στέλνω *stel*-no
service station βενζινάδικο ⓝ ven-zi-*na*-dhi-ko
sex σεξ ⓝ seks
shampoo σαμπουάν ⓝ sam-pu-*an*
share (a dorm) μοιράζομαι mi-*ra*-zo-me
shaving cream κρέμα ξυρίσματος ⓕ
  kre-ma ksi-*riz*-ma-tos
she αυτή af-*ti*
sheet (bed) σεντόνι ⓝ se-*do*-ni
shirt πουκάμισο ⓝ pu-*ka*-mi-so
shoes παπούτσια ⓝ pl pa-*put*-si-a
shop μαγαζί ⓝ ma-gha-*zi*
short κοντός ko-*dos*
shower ντους ⓝ duz
single room μονό δωμάτιο ⓝ mo-*no* dho-*ma*-tio
skin δέρμα ⓝ *dher*-ma
skirt φούστα ⓕ *fu*-sta
sleep v κοιμάμαι ki-*ma*-me
slowly αργά ar-*gha*
small μικρός mi-*kros*
smoke (cigarettes) v καπνίζω kap-*ni*-zo
soap σαπούνι ⓝ sa-*pu*-ni
some μερικοί me-ri-*ki*
soon σύντομα *si*-do-ma
south νότος ⓜ *no*-tos
souvenir shop κατάστημα για σουβενίρ ⓝ
  ka-*ta*-sti-ma yia su-ve-*nir*
speak μιλάω mi-*la*-o
spoon κουτάλι ⓝ ku-*ta*-li
stamp γραμματόσημο ⓝ ghra-ma-*to*-si-mo

stand-by ticket εισιτήριο σταντ μπάι ⓝ
   i·si·*ti*·ri·o stand *ba*·i
station (train) σταθμός ⓜ stath·*mos*
stomach στομάχι ⓝ sto·*ma*·hi
stop v σταματάω sta·ma·*ta*·o
stop (bus) στάση ⓕ *sta*·si
street οδός ⓕ o·*dhos*
student σπουδαστής/σπουδάστρια ⓜ/ⓕ
   spu·dha·*stis*/spu·*dha*·stri·a
sun ήλιος ⓜ *i*·li·os
sunscreen αντιηλιακό ⓝ a·di·i·li·a·*ko*
swim v κολυμπώ ko·li·*bo*

T

tampon ταμπόν ⓝ ta·*bon*
taxi ταξί ⓝ tak·*si*
teaspoon κουτάλι τσαγιού ⓝ ku·*ta*·li tsa·*yiu*
teeth δόντια ⓝ *dho*·dia
telephone τηλέφωνο ⓝ ti·*le*·fo·no
television τηλεόραση ⓕ ti·le·o·ra·si
temperature (weather) θερμοκρασία ⓕ
   ther·mo·kra·*si*·a
tent τέντα ⓕ *te*·da
that (one) εκείνο e·*ki*·no
they αυτοί af·*ti*
thirsty διψασμένος dhip·saz·*me*·nos
this (one) αυτός ⓜ af·*tos*
throat λαιμός ⓜ le·*mos*
ticket εισιτήριο ⓝ i·si·*ti*·ri·o
time ώρα ⓕ *o*·ra
tired κουρασμένος ku·raz·*me*·nos
tissues χαρτομάντηλα ⓝ pl khar·to·*ma*·di·la
today σήμερα *si*·me·ra
toilet τουαλέτα ⓕ tu·a·*le*·ta
tomorrow αύριο *av*·ri·o
tonight απόψε a·*pop*·se
toothbrush οδοντόβουρτσα ⓕ o·dho·*do*·vur·tsa
toothpaste οδοντόπαστα ⓕ o·dho·*do*·pa·sta
torch (flashlight) φακός ⓜ fa·*kos*
tour περιήγηση ⓕ pe·ri·*i*·yi·si
tourist office τουριστικό γραφείο ⓝ
   tu·ri·sti·*ko* ghra·*fi*·o
towel πετσέτα ⓕ pet·*se*·ta
train τρένο ⓝ *tre*·no
translate v μεταφράζω me·ta·*fra*·zo
travel agency ταξιδιωτικό γραφείο ⓝ
   tak·si·dhi·o·ti·*ko* ghra·*fi*·o
travellers cheque ταξιδιωτική επιταγή ⓕ
   tak·si·dhi·o·ti·*ki* e·pi·ta·*yi*

trousers παντελόνι ⓝ pa·de·*lo*·ni
twin beds δίκλινο δωμάτιο ⓝ *dhi*·kli·no dho·*ma*·ti·o
tyre λάστιχο ⓝ *la*·sti·kho

U

underwear εσώρουχα ⓝ pl e·*so*·ru·kha
urgent επείγον e·*pi*·ghon

V

vacant ελεύθερος e·*lef*·the·ros
vacation διακοπές ⓕ dhia·ko·*pes*
vegetable λαχανικά ⓝ pl la·kha·ni·*ka*
vegetarian n χορτοφάγος ⓜ&ⓕ khor·to·*fa*·ghos
visa βίζα ⓕ *vi*·za

W

waiter γκαρσόν ⓝ gar·*son*
walk v περπατάω per·pa·*ta*·o
wallet πορτοφόλι ⓝ por·to·*fo*·li
warm a ζεστός ze·*stos*
wash (something) v πλένω *ple*·no
watch ρολόι ⓝ ro·*lo*·i
water νερό ⓝ ne·*ro*
we εμείς e·*mis*
weekend Σαββατοκύριακο ⓝ sa·va·to·*ki*·ria·ko
west δύση ⓕ *dhi*·si
wheelchair αναπηρική καρέκλα ⓕ
   a·na·pi·ri·*ki* ka·*re*·kla
when όταν o·tan
where πού pu
white άσπρος *as*·pros
who ποιος pios
why γιατί yia·*ti*
wife σύζυγος ⓕ *si*·zi·ghos
window παράθυρο ⓝ pa·*ra*·thi·ro
wine κρασί ⓝ kra·*si*
with με me
without χωρίς kho·*ris*
woman γυναίκα ⓕ yi·*ne*·ka
write v γράφω *ghra*·fo

Y

yellow a κίτρινος *ki*·tri·nos
yes ναι ne
yesterday χτες khtes
you sg inf εσύ e·*si*
you sg pol & pl εσείς e·*sis*

Italian

italian alphabet

A a	B b	C c	D d	E e
a	bee	chee	dee	e
F f	G g	H h	I i	L l
e·fe	jee	a·ka	ee	e·le
M m	N n	O o	P p	Q q
e·me	e·ne	o	pee	koo
R r	S s	T t	U u	V v
e·re	e·se	tee	oo	voo
Z z				
tse·ta				

■ italian

introduction

All you need for *la dolce vita* is to be able to tell your *Moschino* from your *macchiato* and your *Fellini* from your *fettuccine*. Happily, you'll find Italian (*italiano* ee·ta·*lya*·no) an easy language to start speaking as well as a beautiful one to listen to. When even a simple sentence sounds like an aria it can be difficult to resist striking up a conversation – and thanks to widespread migration and the huge popularity of Italian culture and cuisine, you're probably familiar with words like *ciao, pasta* and *bella* already.

There are also many similarities between Italian and English which smooth the way for language learners. Italian is a Romance language – a descendent of Latin, the language of the Romans (as are French, Spanish, Portuguese and Romanian), and English has been heavily influenced by Latin, particularly via contact with French.

Up until the 19th century, Italy was a collection of autonomous states, rather than a nation-state. As a result, Italian has many regional dialects, including Sardinian and Sicilian. Some dialects are so different from standard Italian as to be considered distinct languages in their own right. It wasn't until the 19th century that the Tuscan dialect – the language of Dante, Boccaccio and Petrarch – became the standard language of the nation, and the official language of schools, media and administration. 'Standard Italian' is the variety that will take you from the top of the boot to the very toe – all the language in this phrasebook is in standard Italian.

The majority of the approximately 65 million people who speak Italian live, of course, in Italy. However, the language also has official status in San Marino, Vatican City, parts of Switzerland, Slovenia and the Istrian peninsula of Croatia. Italian was the official language of Malta during the period of the Knights of St John (1530–1798) and afterwards shared that status with English during the British rule. Only in 1934 was Italian withdrawn and substituted with the native Maltese language. Today, Maltese people are generally fluent in Italian. It might surprise you to learn that Italian is also spoken in the African nation of Eritrea, which was a colony of Italy from 1880 until 1941. Most Eritreans nowadays speak Italian only as a second language. Italian is widely used in Albania, Monaco and France, and spoken by large communities of immigrants worldwide. This chapter is designed to help you on your adventures in the Italian-speaking world – so, as the Italians would say, *In bocca al lupo!* een bo·ka·*loo*·po (lit: in the mouth of the wolf) – good luck!

pronunciation

vowel sounds

Italian vowel sounds are generally shorter than those in English. They also tend not to run together to form vowel sound combinations (diphthongs), though it can often sound as if they do to English speakers.

symbol	english equivalent	italian example	transliteration
a	father	*pane*	*pa*·ne
ai	aisle	*mai*	mai
ay	say	*vorrei*	vo·*ray*
e	bet	*letto*	*le*·to
ee	see	*vino*	*vee*·no
o	pot	*molo*	*mo*·lo
oo	zoo	*frutta*	*froo*·ta
oy	toy	*poi*	poy
ow	how	*ciao, autobus*	chow, *ow*·to·boos

word stress

In Italian, you generally emphasise the second-last syllable of a word. When a written word has an accent marked on a vowel, though, the stress is on that syllable. The stressed syllable is always italicised in our pronunciation guides. The characteristic sing-song quality of an Italian sentence is created by pronouncing the syllables evenly and rhythmically, then swinging down on the last word.

consonant sounds

In addition to the sounds described on the next page, Italian consonants can also have a stronger, more emphatic pronunciation. The actual sounds are basically the same, though meaning can be altered between a normal consonant sound and this double consonant sound. The phonetic guides in this book don't distinguish between the two forms. Refer to the written Italian beside each phonetic guide as the cue –

if the word is written with a double consonant, use the stronger form. Even if you never distinguish them, you'll always be understood in context. Here are some examples where this 'double consonant' effect can make a difference:

sonno	*son·no*	**sleep**	*sono*	*so·no*	**I am**
pappa	*pap·pa*	**baby food**	*papa*	*pa·pa*	**pope**

symbol	english equivalent	italian example	transliteration
b	bed	*bello*	*be·lo*
ch	cheat	*centro*	*chen·tro*
d	dog	*denaro*	*de·na·ro*
dz	adds	*mezzo, zaino*	*me·dzo, dzai·no*
f	fat	*fare*	*fa·re*
g	go	*gomma*	*go·ma*
j	joke	*cugino*	*ku·jee·no*
k	kit	*cambio, quanto*	*kam·byo, kwan·to*
l	lot	*linea*	*lee·ne·a*
ly	million	*figlia*	*fee·lya*
m	man	*madre*	*ma·dre*
n	not	*numero*	*noo·me·ro*
ny	canyon	*bagno*	*ba·nyo*
p	pet	*pronto*	*pron·to*
r	red (stronger and rolled)	*ristorante*	*ree·sto·ran·te*
s	sun	*sera*	*se·ra*
sh	shot	*sciare*	*shya·re*
t	top	*teatro*	*te·a·tro*
ts	hits	*grazie, sicurezza*	*gra·tsye, see·koo·re·tsa*
v	very	*viaggio*	*vya·jo*
w	win	*uomo*	*wo·mo*
y	yes	*italiano*	*ee·ta·lya·no*
z	zero	*casa*	*ka·za*

basics

language difficulties

Do you speak English?
Parla inglese? — *par*·la een·*gle*·ze

Do you understand?
Capisce? — ka·*pee*·she

I (don't) understand.
(Non) capisco. — (non) ka·*pee*·sko

What does (*giorno*) mean?
Che cosa vuol dire (giorno)? — ke *ko*·za vwol *dee*·re (*jor*·no)

How do you ...?	*Come si ...?*	*ko*·me see ...
pronounce this	*pronuncia questo*	pro·*noon*·cha *kwe*·sto
write (*arrivederci*)	*scrive (arrivederci)*	*skree*·ve (a·ree·ve·*der*·chee)

Could you please ...?	*Può ... per favore?*	pwo ... per fa·*vo*·re
repeat that	*ripeterlo*	ree·*pe*·ter·lo
speak more	*parlare più*	par·*la*·re pyoo
slowly	*lentamente*	len·ta·*men*·te
write it down	*scriverlo*	*skree*·ver·lo

essentials

Yes.	*Sì.*	see
No.	*No.*	no
Please.	*Per favore.*	per fa·*vo*·re
Thank you (very much).	*Grazie (mille).*	*gra*·tsye (*mee*·le)
You're welcome.	*Prego.*	*pre*·go
Excuse me.	*Mi scusi.* pol	mee *skoo*·zee
	Scusami. inf	*skoo*·za·mee
Sorry.	*Mi dispiace.*	mee dees·*pya*·che

numbers

0	zero	dze·ro	16	sedici	se·dee·chee
1	uno	oo·no	17	diciassette	dee·cha·se·te
2	due	doo·e	18	diciotto	dee·cho·to
3	tre	tre	19	diciannove	dee·cha·no·ve
4	quattro	kwa·tro	20	venti	ven·tee
5	cinque	cheen·kwe	21	ventuno	ven·too·no
6	sei	say	22	ventidue	ven·tee·doo·e
7	sette	se·te	30	trenta	tren·ta
8	otto	o·to	40	quaranta	kwa·ran·ta
9	nove	no·ve	50	cinquanta	cheen·kwan·ta
10	dieci	dye·chee	60	sessanta	se·san·ta
11	undici	oon·dee·chee	70	settanta	se·tan·ta
12	dodici	do·dee·chee	80	ottanta	o·tan·ta
13	tredici	tre·dee·chee	90	novanta	no·van·ta
14	quattordici	kwa·tor·dee·chee	100	cento	chen·to
15	quindici	kween·dee·chee	1000	mille	mee·le

time & dates

What time is it?	Che ora è?	ke o·ra e
It's one o'clock.	È l'una.	e loo·na
It's (two) o'clock.	Sono le (due).	so·no le (doo·e)
Quarter past (one).	(L'una) e un quarto.	(loo·na) e oon kwar·to
Half past (one).	(L'una) e mezza.	(loo·na) e me·dza
Quarter to (eight).	(Le otto) meno un quarto.	(le o·to) me·no oon kwar·to
At what time ...?	A che ora ...?	a ke o·ra ...
At ...	Alle ...	a·le ...
am	di mattina	dee ma·tee·na
pm	di pomeriggio	dee po·me·ree·jo
Monday	lunedì	loo·ne·dee
Tuesday	martedì	mar·te·dee
Wednesday	mercoledì	mer·ko·le·dee
Thursday	giovedì	jo·ve·dee
Friday	venerdì	ve·ner·dee
Saturday	sabato	sa·ba·to
Sunday	domenica	do·me·nee·ka

January	gennaio	je·na·yo
February	febbraio	fe·bra·yo
March	marzo	mar·tso
April	aprile	a·pree·le
May	maggio	ma·jo
June	giugno	joo·nyo
July	luglio	loo·lyo
August	agosto	a·gos·to
September	settembre	se·tem·bre
October	ottobre	o·to·bre
November	novembre	no·vem·bre
December	dicembre	dee·chem·bre

What date is it today?
Che giorno è oggi?   ke *jor*·no e *o*·jee

It's (15 December).
È (il quindici) dicembre.   e (eel *kween*·dee·chee) dee·*chem*·bre

| since (May) | da (maggio) | da (ma·jo) |
| until (June) | fino a (giugno) | fee·no a (joo·nyo) |

yesterday	ieri	ye·ree
today	oggi	o·jee
tonight	stasera	sta·se·ra
tomorrow	domani	do·ma·nee

last ...
night	ieri notte	ye·ree no·te
week	la settimana scorsa	la se·tee·ma·na skor·sa
month	il mese scorso	eel me·ze skor·so
year	l'anno scorso	la·no skor·so

next ...
week	la settimana prossima	la se·tee·ma·na pro·see·ma
month	il mese prossimo	eel me·ze pro·see·mo
year	l'anno prossimo	la·no pro·see·mo

yesterday/tomorrow ...   *ieri/domani ...*   ye·ree/do·ma·nee ...
morning	mattina	ma·tee·na
afternoon	pomeriggio	po·me·ree·jo
evening	sera	se·ra

weather

What's the weather like?	*Che tempo fa?*	ke *tem*·po fa

It's ...

cloudy	*È nuvoloso.*	e noo·vo·*lo*·zo
cold	*Fa freddo.*	fa *fre*·do
hot	*Fa caldo.*	fa *kal*·do
raining	*Piove.*	*pyo*·ve
snowing	*Nevica.*	ne·*vee*·ka
sunny	*È soleggiato.*	e so·le·*ja*·to
warm	*Fa bel tempo.*	fa bel *tem*·po
windy	*Tira vento.*	*tee*·ra *ven*·to

spring	*primavera* f	pree·ma·*ve*·ra
summer	*estate* f	es·*ta*·te
autumn	*autunno* m	ow·*too*·no
winter	*inverno* m	een·*ver*·no

border crossing

I'm here ...	*Sono qui ...*	*so*·no kwee ...
in transit	*in transito*	een *tran*·see·to
on business	*per affari*	per a·*fa*·ree
on holiday	*in vacanza*	een va·*kan*·tsa

I'm here for ...	*Sono qui per ...*	*so*·no kwee per ...
(10) days	*(dieci) giorni*	*(dye*·chee) *jor*·nee
(three) weeks	*(tre) settimane*	(tre) se·tee·*ma*·ne
(two) months	*(due) mesi*	*(doo*·e) me·zee

I'm going to (Perugia).
Vado a (Perugia). va·do a (pe·*roo*·ja)

I'm staying at the (Minerva Hotel).
Alloggio al (Minerva). a·*lo*·jo al (mee·*ner*·va)

I have nothing to declare.
Non ho niente da dichiarare. non o *nyen*·te da dee·kya·*ra*·re

I have something to declare.
Ho delle cose da dichiarare. o de·le *ko*·ze da dee·kya·*ra*·re

That's (not) mine.
(Non) è mio/mia. m/f (non) e *mee*·o/*mee*·a

transport

tickets & luggage

Where can I buy a ticket?
Dove posso comprare un biglietto?   do·ve po·so kom·pra·re oon bee·lye·to

Do I need to book a seat?
Bisogna prenotare un posto?   bee·zo·nya pre·no·ta·re oon pos·to

One ... ticket	*Un biglietto ... (per*	oon bee·lye·to ... (per
(to Rome), please.	*Roma), per favore.*	ro·ma) per fa·vo·re
one-way	*di sola andata*	dee so·la an·da·ta
return	*di andata e ritorno*	dee an·da·ta e ree·tor·no

I'd like to ... my	*Vorrei ... il mio*	vo·ray ... eel mee·o
ticket, please.	*biglietto, per favore.*	bee·lye·to per fa·vo·re
cancel	*cancellare*	kan·che·la·re
change	*cambiare*	kam·bya·re
collect	*ritirare*	ree·tee·ra·re
confirm	*confermare*	kon·fer·ma·re

I'd like a ... seat,	*Vorrei un posto ...,*	vo·ray oon pos·to ...
please.	*per favore.*	per fa·vo·re
nonsmoking	*per non fumatori*	per non foo·ma·to·ree
smoking	*per fumatori*	per foo·ma·to·ree

How much is it?
Quant'è?   kwan·te

Is there air conditioning?
C'è l'aria condizionata?   che la·rya kon·dee·tsyo·na·ta

Is there a toilet?
C'è un gabinetto?   che oon ga·bee·ne·to

How long does the trip take?
Quanto ci vuole?   kwan·to chee vwo·le

Is it a direct route?
È un itinerario diretto?   e oo·nee·tee·ne·ra·ryo dee·re·to

I'd like a luggage locker.
Vorrei un armadietto per   vo·ray oon ar·ma·dye·to per
il bagaglio.   eel ba·ga·lyo

My luggage	Il mio bagaglio	eel *mee*·o ba·*ga*·lyo
has been ...	è stato ...	e *sta*·to ...
damaged	danneggiato	da·ne·*ja*·to
lost	perso	*per*·so
stolen	rubato	roo·*ba*·to

getting around

Where does flight (004) arrive?
Dove arriva il volo (004)? — *do*·ve a·*ree*·va eel *vo*·lo (*dze*·ro *dze*·ro kwa·tro)

Where does flight (004) depart?
Da dove parte il volo (004)? — da *do*·ve *par*·te eel *vo*·lo (*dze*·ro *dze*·ro kwa·tro)

Where's the ...?	Dove sono ...?	*do*·ve *so*·no ...
arrivalls hall	gli arrivi	lyee a·*ree*·vee
departures hall	le partenze	le par·*ten*·dze

Is this the ...	È questo/questa ...	e *kwes*·to/*kwes*·ta ...
to (Venice)?	per (Venezia)? m/f	per (ve·*ne*·tsya)
boat	la nave f	la *na*·ve
bus	l'autobus m	*low*·to·boos
plane	l'aereo m	la·e·re·o
train	il treno m	eel *tre*·no

What time's	A che ora passa	a ke *o*·ra *pa*·sa
the ... bus?	... autobus?	... *ow*·to·boos
first	il primo	eel *pree*·mo
last	l'ultimo	*lool*·tee·mo
next	il prossimo	eel *pro*·see·mo

At what time does it arrive/leave?
A che ora arriva/parte? — a ke *o*·ra a·*ree*·va/*par*·te

How long will it be delayed?
Di quanto ritarderà? — dee *kwan*·to ree·tar·de·*ra*

What station/stop is this?
Che stazione/fermata è questa? — ke sta·*tsyo*·ne/fer·*ma*·ta e *kwe*·sta

What's the next station/stop?
Qual'è la prossima stazione/fermata? — kwa·*le* la *pro*·see·ma sta·*tsyo*·ne/fer·*ma*·ta

Does it stop at (Milan)?
Si ferma a (Milano)? — see *fer*·ma a (mee·*la*·no)

Please tell me when we get to (Taranto).
Mi dica per favore quando — mee dee·ka per fa·vo·re kwan·do
arriviamo a (Taranto). — a·ree·vya·mo a (ta·ran·to)

How long do we stop here?
Per quanto tempo ci fermiamo qui? — per kwan·to tem·po chee fer·mya·mo kwee

Is this seat available?
È libero questo posto? — e lee·be·ro kwe·sto pos·to

That's my seat.
Quel posto è mio. — kwel pos·to e mee·o

I'd like a taxi ...	*Vorrei un tassì ...*	vo·ray oon ta·see ...
at (9am)	*alle (nove*	a·le (no·ve
	di mattina)	dee ma·tee·na)
now	*adesso*	a·de·so
tomorrow	*domani*	do·ma·nee

Is this taxi available?
È libero questo tassì? — e lee·be·ro kwe·sto ta·see

How much is it to ...?
Quant'è per ...? — kwan·te per ...

Please put the meter on.
Usi il tassametro, per favore. — oo·zee eel ta·sa·me·tro per fa·vo·re

Please take me to (this address).
Mi porti a (questo indirizzo), — mee por·tee a (kwe·sto een·dee·ree·tso)
per piacere. — per pya·che·re

Please ...	*..., per favore.*	... per fa·vo·re
slow down	*Rallenti*	ra·len·tee
stop here	*Si fermi qui*	see fer·mee kwee
wait here	*Mi aspetti qui*	mee as·pe·tee kwee

car, motorbike & bicycle hire

I'd like to hire a/an ...	*Vorrei noleggiare ...*	vo·ray no·le·ja·re ...
bicycle	*una bicicletta*	oo·na bee·chee·kle·ta
car	*una macchina*	oo·na ma·kee·na
motorbike	*una moto*	oo·na mo·to
with ...	*con ...*	kon ...
a driver	*un'autista*	oo·now·tee·sta
air conditioning	*aria condizionata*	a·rya kon·dee·tsyo·na·ta

ITALIANO – transport

220

How much for ... hire?	*Quanto costa ...?*	kwan·to *kos*·ta ...
hourly	*all'ora*	a·*lo*·ra
daily	*al giorno*	al *jor*·no
weekly	*alla settimana*	a·la se·tee·*ma*·na

air	*aria* f	*a*·rya
oil	*olio* m	*o*·lyo
petrol	*benzina* f	ben·*dzee*·na
tyres	*gomme* f pl	*go*·me

I need a mechanic.
Ho bisogno di un meccanico.   o bee·*zo*·nyo dee oon me·*ka*·nee·ko

I've run out of petrol.
Ho esaurito la benzina.   o e·zow·*ree*·to la ben·*dzee*·na

I have a flat tyre.
Ho una gomma bucata.   o *oo*·na *go*·ma boo·*ka*·ta

directions

Where's the ...?	*Dov'è ...?*	do·*ve* ...
bank	*la banca*	la *ban*·ka
city centre	*il centro città*	eel *chen*·tro chee·*ta*
hotel	*l'albergo*	lal·*ber*·go
market	*il mercato*	eel mer·*ka*·to
police station	*il posto di polizia*	eel *pos*·to dee po·lee·*tsee*·a
post office	*l'ufficio postale*	loo·*fee*·cho pos·*ta*·le
public toilet	*il gabinetto*	eel ga·bee·*ne*·to
	pubblico	*poo*·blee·ko
tourist office	*l'ufficio del turismo*	loo·*fee*·cho del too·*reez*·mo

Is this the road to (Milan)?
Questa strada porta a (Milano)?   *kwe*·sta *stra*·da *por*·ta a (mee·*la*·no)

Can you show me (on the map)?
Può mostrarmi (sulla pianta)?   pwo mos·*trar*·mee (*soo*·la *pyan*·ta)

What's the address?
Qual'è l'indirizzo?   kwa·*le* leen·dee·*ree*·tso

How far is it?
Quant'è distante?   kwan·*te* dees·*tan*·te

How do I get there?
Come ci si arriva?   *ko*·me chee see a·*ree*·va

ITALIANO – transport

Turn …	Giri …	jee·ree …
at the corner	all'angolo	a·lan·go·lo
at the traffic lights	al semaforo	al se·ma·fo·ro
left/right	a sinistra/destra	a see·nee·stra/de·stra

It's …	È …	e …
behind …	dietro …	dye·tro …
far away	lontano	lon·ta·no
here	qui	kwee
in front of …	davanti a …	da·van·tee a …
left	a sinistra	a see·nee·stra
near (to …)	vicino (a …)	vee·chee·no (a …)
next to …	accanto a …	a·kan·to a …
on the corner	all'angolo	a lan·go·lo
opposite …	di fronte a …	dee fron·te a …
right	a destra	a de·stra
straight ahead	sempre diritto	sem·pre dee·ree·to
there	là	la

by bus	con l'autobus	kon low·to·boos
by taxi	con il tassì	ko·neel ta·see
by train	con il treno	ko·neel tre·no
on foot	a piedi	a pye·dee

north	nord m	nord
south	sud m	sood
east	est m	est
west	ovest m	o·vest

signs

Entrata/Uscita	en·tra·ta/oo·shee·ta	Entrance/Exit
Aperto/Chiuso	a·per·to/kyoo·zo	Open/Closed
Camere Libere	ka·me·re lee·be·re	Rooms Available
Completo	kom·ple·to	No Vacancies
Informazioni	een·for·ma·tsyo·nee	Information
Posto di Polizia	pos·to dee po·lee·tsee·a	Police Station
Proibito	pro·ee·bee·to	Prohibited
Gabinetti	ga·bee·ne·tee	Toilets
Uomini	wo·mee·nee	Men
Donne	do·ne	Women
Caldo/Freddo	kal·do/fre·do	Hot/Cold

222

accommodation

finding accommodation

Where's a/an ...?	Dov'è ...?	do·ve ...
camping ground	un campeggio	oon kam·pe·jo
guesthouse	una pensione	oo·na pen·syo·ne
inn	una locanda	oo·na lo·kan·da
hotel	un albergo	oo·nal·ber·go
youth hostel	un ostello della gioventù	oo·nos·te·lo de·la jo·ven·too

Can you recommend somewhere ...?	Può consigliare qualche posto ...?	pwo kon·see·lya·re kwal·ke pos·to ...
cheap	economico	e·ko·no·mee·ko
good	buono	bwo·no
nearby	vicino	vee·chee·no

I'd like to book a room, please.
Vorrei prenotare una camera, per favore.
vo·ray pre·no·ta·re oo·na ka·me·ra per fa·vo·re

I have a reservation.
Ho una prenotazione.
o oo·na pre·no·ta·tsyo·ne

My name's ...
Mi chiamo ...
mee kya·mo ...

Do you have a ... room?	Avete una camera ...?	a·ve·te oo·na ka·me·ra ...
single	singola	seen·go·la
double	doppia con letto matrimoniale	do·pya kon le·to ma·tree·mo·nya·le
twin	doppia a due letti	do·pya a doo·e le·tee

How much is it per ...?	Quanto costa per ...?	kwan·to kos·ta per ...
night	una notte	oo·na no·te
person	persona	per·so·na

Can I pay by ...?	Posso pagare con ...?	po·so pa·ga·re kon ...
credit card	la carta di credito	la kar·ta dee kre·dee·to
travellers cheque	un assegno di viaggio	oo·na·se·nyo dee vee·a·jo

I'd like to stay for (two) nights.
Vorrei rimanere (due) notti.   vo·*ray* ree·ma·*ne*·re (*doo*·e) *no*·tee

From (July 2) to (July 6).
Dal (due luglio) al (sei luglio).   dal (*doo*·e *loo*·lyo) al (say *loo*·lyo)

Can I see it?
Posso vederla?   *po*·so ve·*der*·la

Am I allowed to camp here?
Si può campeggiare qui?   see pwo kam·pe·*ja*·re kwee

Is there a camp site nearby?
C'è un campeggio qui vicino?   che oon kam·*pe*·jo kwee vee·*chee*·no

requests & queries

When's breakfast served?
A che ora è la prima colazione?   a ke *o*·ra e la *pree*·ma ko·la·*tsyo*·ne

Where's breakfast served?
Dove si prende la prima colazione?   *do*·ve see *pren*·de la *pree*·ma ko·la·*tsyo*·ne

Please wake me at (seven).
Mi svegli alle (sette), per favore.   mee *sve*·lyee *a*·le (*se*·te) per fa·*vo*·re

Could I have my key, please?
Posso avere la chiave, per favore?   *po*·so a·*ve*·re la *kya*·ve per fa·*vo*·re

Can I get another (blanket)?
Può darmi un altra (coperta)?   pwo *dar*·mee oo·*nal*·tra (ko·*per*·ta)

This (sheet) isn't clean.
Questo (lenzuolo) non è pulito.   *kwe*·sto (len·*tzwo*·lo) non e poo·*lee*·to

Is there a/an ...?	C'è ...?	che ...
elevator	*un ascensore*	oo·na·shen·*so*·re
safe	*una cassaforte*	oo·na ka·sa·*for*·te

The room is too ...	La camera è troppo ...	la *ka*·me·ra e *tro*·po ...
expensive	*cara*	*ka*·ra
noisy	*rumorosa*	roo·mo·*ro*·za
small	*piccola*	*pee*·ko·la

The ... doesn't work.	... non funziona.	... non foon·*tsyo*·na
air conditioning	*L'aria condizionata*	*la*·rya kon·dee·*tsyo·na*·ta
fan	*Il ventilatore*	eel ven·tee·la·*to*·re
toilet	*Il gabinetto*	eel ga·bee·*ne*·to

checking out

What time is checkout?
A che ora si deve lasciar   a ke o·*ra* see *de*·ve la·*shar*
libera la camera?   *lee*·be·ra la *ka*·me·ra

Can I leave my luggage here?
Posso lasciare ili mio bagaglio qui?   *po*·so la·*sha*·re eel *mee*·o ba·*ga*·lyo kwee

Could I have my ..., please?	*Posso avere ...,* *per favore?*	*po*·so a·*ve*·re ... per fa·*vo*·re
deposit	*la caparra*	la ka·*pa*·ra
passport	*il mio passaporto*	eel *mee*·o pa·sa·*por*·to
valuables	*i miei oggetti* *di valore*	ee myay o·*je*·tee dee va·*lo*·re

communications & banking

the internet

Where's the local Internet café?
Dove si trova l'Internet point?   *do*·ve see *tro*·va *leen*·ter·net poynt

How much is it per hour?
Quanto costa all'ora?   *kwan*·to *kos*·ta a·*lo*·ra

I'd like to ...	*Vorrei ...*	vo·*ray* ...
check my email	*controllare le mie email*	kon·tro·*la*·re le *mee*·e e·mayl
get Internet access	*usare Internet*	oo·*za*·re *een*·ter·net
use a printer	*usare una stampante*	oo·*za*·re *oo*·na stam·*pan*·te
use a scanner	*scandire*	skan·*dee*·re

mobile/cell phone

I'd like a ...	*Vorrei ...*	vo·*ray* ...
mobile/cell phone for hire	*un cellulare da noleggiare*	oon che·loo·*la*·re da no·le·*ja*·re
SIM card for your network	*un SIM card per la rete telefonica*	oon seem kard per la *re*·te te·le·*fo*·nec ka

What are the rates?   *Quill sono le tariffe?*   *kwa*·lee *so*·no le ta·*ree*·fe

telephone

What's your phone number?
Qual'è il Suo/tuo numero
di telefono? pol/inf
kwa·*le* eel *soo*·o/*too*·o *noo*·me·ro
dee te·*le*·fo·no

The number is ...
Il numero è ...
eel *noo*·me·ro e ...

Where's the nearest public phone?
Dov'è il telefono pubblico
più vicino?
do·*ve* eel te·*le*·fo·no *poo*·blee·ko
pyoo vee·*chee*·no

I'd like to buy a phonecard.
Vorrei comprare una
scheda telefonica.
vo·*ray* kom·*pra*·re *oo*·na
ske·da te·le·*fo*·nee·ka

I want to ...	Vorrei ...	vo·*ray* ...
call (Singapore)	*fare una chiamata* *a (Singapore)*	*fa*·re *oo*·na kya·*ma*·ta a (seen·ga·*po*·re)
make a local call	*fare una chiamata* *locale*	*fa*·re *oo*·na kya·*ma*·ta lo·*ka*·le
reverse the charges	*fare una chiamata a* *carico del destinatario*	*fa*·re *oo*·na kya·*ma*·ta a *ka*·ree·ko del des·tee·na·*ta*·ryo

How much does ... cost?	Quanto costa ...?	kwan·to kos·ta ...
a (three)-minute call	*una telefonata* *di (tre) minuti*	*oo*·na te·le·fo·*na*·ta dee (tre) mee·*noo*·tee
each extra minute	*ogni minuto in più*	*o*·nyee mee·*noo*·to een pyoo

It's (one euro) per (minute).
(Un euro) per (un minuto).
(oon e·*oo*·ro) per (oon mee·*noo*·to)

post office

I want to send a ...	Vorrei mandare ...	vo·*ray* man·*da*·re ...
fax	*un fax*	oon faks
letter	*una lettera*	*oo*·na *le*·te·ra
parcel	*un pacchetto*	oon pa·*ke*·to
postcard	*una cartolina*	*oo*·na kar·to·*lee*·na

I want to buy ...	Vorrei comprare ...	vo·*ray* kom·*pra*·re ...
an envelope	*una busta*	*oo*·na *boo*·sta
stamps	*dei francobolli*	day fran·ko·*bo*·lee

ITALIANO – communications & banking

Please send it (to Australia) by ...	*Lo mandi ... (in Australia), per favore.*	lo man·dee ... (een ow·stra·lya) per fa·vo·re
airmail	*via aerea*	vee·a a·e·re·a
express mail	*posta prioritaria*	pos·ta pryo·ree·ta·rya
registered mail	*posta raccomandata*	pos·ta ra·ko·man·da·ta
surface mail	*posta ordinaria*	pos·ta or·dee·na·rya
Is there any mail for me?	*C'è posta per me?*	che pos·ta per me

bank

Where's a/an ...?	*Dov'è ... più vicino?*	do·ve ... pyoo vee·chee·no
ATM	*il Bancomat*	eel ban·ko·mat
foreign exchange office	*il cambio*	eel kam·byo

I'd like to ...	*Vorrei ...*	vo·ray ...
Where can I ...?	*Dove posso ...?*	do·ve po·so ...
arrange a transfer	*trasferire soldi*	tras·fe·ree·re sol·dee
cash a cheque	*riscuotere un assegno*	ree·skwo·te·re oo·na·se·nyo
change a travellers cheque	*cambiare un assegno di viaggio*	kam·bya·re oo·na·se·nyo dee vee·a·jo
change money	*cambiare denaro*	kam·bya·re de·na·ro
get a cash advance	*prelevare con carta di credito*	pre·le·va·re kon kar·ta dee kre·dee·to
withdraw money	*fare un prelievo*	fa·re oon pre·lye·vo

What's the ...?	*Quant'è ...?*	kwan·te ...
commission	*la commissione*	la ko·mee·syo·ne
exchange rate	*il cambio*	eel kam·byo

It's ...	*È ...*	e ...
(12) euros	*(dodici) euro*	(do·dee·chee) e·oo·ro
free	*gratuito*	gra·too·ee·to

What's the charge for that?
Quanto costa? — kwan·to kos·ta

What time does the bank open?
A che ora apre la banca? — a ke o·ra a·pre la ban·ka

Has my money arrived yet?
È arrivato il mio denaro? — e a·ree·va·to eel mee·o de·na·ro

sightseeing

getting in

What time does it open/close?
A che ora apre/chiude?
a ke o·ra a·pre/kyoo·de

What's the admission charge?
Quant'è il prezzo d'ingresso?
kwan·te eel pre·tso deen·gre·so

Is there a discount for children/students?
C'è uno sconto per
bambini/studenti?
che oo·no skon·to per
bam·bee·nee/stoo·den·tee

I'd like a ...	*Vorrei ...*	vo·ray ...
catalogue	*un catalogo*	oon ka·ta·lo·go
guide	*una guida*	oo·na gwee·da
local map	*una cartina*	oo·na kar·tee·na
	della zona	de·la dzo·na

I'd like to see ... *Vorrei vedere ...* vo·ray ve·de·re ...
What's that? *Cos'è?* ko·ze
Can I take a photo? *Posso fare una foto?* po·so fa·re oo·na fo·to

tours

When's the	*A che ora parte la*	a ke o·ra par·te la
next ...?	*prossima ...?*	pro·see·ma ...
day trip	*escursione*	es·koor·syo·ne
	in giornata	een jor·na·ta
tour	*gita turistica*	jee·ta too·ree·stee·ka

Is ... included?	*È incluso ...?*	e een·kloo·zo ...
accommodation	*l'alloggio*	la·lo·jo
the admission charge	*il prezzo d'ingresso*	eel pre·tso deen·gre·so
food	*il vitto*	eel vee·to
transport	*il trasporto*	eel tras·por·to

How long is the tour?
Quanto dura la gita?
kwan·to doo·ra la jee·ta

What time should we be back?
A che ora dovremmo ritornare?
a ke o·ra dov·re·mo ree·tor·na·re

sightseeing

castle	*castello* m	kas·*te*·lo
cathedral	*duomo* m	*dwo*·mo
church	*chiesa* f	*kye*·za
main square	*piazza principale* f	*pya*·tsa preen·chee·*pa*·le
monastery	*monastero* m	mo·nas·*te*·ro
monument	*monumento* m	mo·noo·*men*·to
museum	*museo* m	moo·*ze*·o
old city	*centro storico* m	*chen*·tro *sto*·ree·ko
palace	*palazzo* m	pa·*la*·tso
ruins	*rovine* f pl	ro·*vee*·ne
stadium	*stadio* m	*sta*·dyo
statues	*statue* f pl	*sta*·too·e

shopping

enquiries

Where's a ... ?	*Dov'è ... ?*	do·*ve* ...
bank	*la banca*	la *ban*·ka
bookshop	*la libreria*	la lee·bre·*ree*·a
camera shop	*il fotografo*	eel fo·*to*·gra·fo
department store	*il grande magazzino*	eel *gran*·de ma·ga·*dzee*·no
grocery store	*la drogheria*	la dro·ge·*ree*·a
market	*il mercato*	eel mer·*ka*·to
newsagency	*l'edicola*	le·*dee*·ko·la
supermarket	*il supermercato*	eel soo·per·mer·*ka*·to

Where can I buy (a padlock)?
Dove posso comprare (un lucchetto)?   do·ve *po*·so kom·*pra*·re (oon loo·*ke*·tn)

I'm looking for ...
Sto cercando ...   sto cher·*kan*·do ...

Can I look at it?
Posso dare un'occhiata?   po·so *da*·re oo·no·*kya*·ta

Do you have any others?
Ne avete altri?   ne a·*ve*·te *al*·tree

Does it have a guarantee?
Ha la garanzia?   a la ga·ran·*tsee*·a

Can I have it sent overseas?
Può spedirlo all'estero?   pwo spe·*deer*·lo a·*les*·te·ro

Can I have my ... repaired?
Posso far aggiustare ... qui?   po·so far a·joo·*sta*·re ... kwee

It's faulty.
È difettoso.   e dee·fe·*to*·zo

I'd like (a) ..., please.	Vorrei ..., per favore.	vo·*ray* ... per fa·*vo*·re
bag	un sacchetto	oon sa·*ke*·to
refund	un rimborso	oon reem·*bor*·so
to return this	restituire questo	res·tee·*twee*·re *kwe*·sto

paying

How much is it?
Quant'è?   kwan·*te*

Can you write down the price?
Può scrivere il prezzo?   pwo *skree*·ve·re eel *pre*·tso

That's too expensive.
È troppo caro.   e *tro*·po *ka*·ro

Can you lower the price?
Può farmi lo sconto?   pwo *far*·mee lo *skon*·to

I'll give you (five) euros.
Le offro (cinque) euro.   le *o*·fro (*cheen*·kwe) e·*oo*·ro

There's a mistake in the bill.
C'è un errore nel conto.   che oon e·*ro*·re nel *kon*·to

Do you accept ...?	Accettate ...?	a·che·*ta*·te ...
credit cards	la carta di credito	la *kar*·ta dee *kre*·dee·to
debit cards	la carta di debito	la *kar*·ta dee *de*·bee·to
travellers cheques	gli assegni di viaggio	lyee a·*se*·nyee dee vee·*a*·jo

I'd like ..., please.	Vorrei ..., per favore.	vo·ray ... per fa·vo·re
a receipt	una ricevuta	oo·na ree·che·voo·ta
my change	il mio resto	eel mee·o res·to

clothes & shoes

Can I try it on?	Potrei provarmelo?	po·tray pro·var·me·lo
My size is (40).	Sono una taglia (quaranta).	so·no oo·na ta·lya (kwa·ran·ta)
It doesn't fit.	Non va bene.	non va be·ne
small	piccola	pee·ko·la
medium	media	me·dya
large	forte	for·te

books & music

I'd like a ...	Vorrei ...	vo·ray ...
newspaper	un giornale	oon jor·na·le
(in English)	(in inglese)	(een een·gle·ze)
pen	una penna	oo·na pe·na

Is there an English-language bookshop?
C'è una libreria specializzata — che oo·na lee·bre·ree·a spe·cha·lee·dza·ta
in lingua inglese? — een leen·gwa een·gle·ze

I'm looking for something by (Alberto Moravia).
Sto cercando qualcosa di — sto cher·kan·do kwal·ko·za dee
(Alberto Moravia). — (al·ber·to mo·ra·vee·a)

Can I listen to this?
Potrei ascoltarlo? — po·tray as·kol·tar·lo

photography

Can you ...?	Potrebbe ...?	po·tre·be ...
burn a CD from	masterizzare un	mas·te·ree·tsa·re oon
my memory card	CD dalla mia	chee dee da·la mee·a
	memory card	me·mo·ree kard
develop this	sviluppare	svee·loo·pa·re
film	questo rullino	kwe·sto roo·lee·no
load my film	inserire il	een·se·ree·re eel
	mio rullino	mee·o roo·lee·no

I need a/an ... film for this camera.	*Vorrei un rullino ... per questa macchina fotografica.*	vo·*ray* oon roo·*lee*·no ... per *kwe*·sta ma·*kee*·na fo·to·*gra*·fee·ka
APS	*da APS*	da a·pee·e·se
B&W	*in bianco e nero*	een *byan*·ko e *ne*·ro
colour	*a colori*	a *ko*·lo·ree
slide	*per diapositive*	per dee·a·po·zee·*tee*·ve
(200) speed	*da (duecento) ASA*	da (*doo*·e *chen*·to) *a*·za
When will it be ready?	*Quando sarà pronto?*	*kwan*·do sa·*ra* pron·to

meeting people

greetings, goodbyes & introductions

Hello.	*Buongiorno.*	bwon·*jor*·no
Hi.	*Ciao.*	chow
Good night.	*Buonanotte.*	bwo·na·*no*·te
Goodbye.	*Arrivederci.*	a·ree·ve·*der*·chee
Bye.	*Ciao.*	chow
See you later.	*A più tardi.*	a pyoo *tar*·dee
Mr	*Signore*	see·*nyo*·re
Mrs	*Signora*	see·*nyo*·ra
Miss	*Signorina*	see·nyo·*ree*·na
How are you?	*Come sta?* pol	*ko*·me sta
	Come stai? inf	*ko*·me stai
Fine. And you?	*Bene. E Lei?* pol	*be*·ne e lay
	Bene. E tu? inf	*be*·ne e too
What's your name?	*Come si chiama?* pol	*ko*·me see *kya*·ma
	Come ti chiami? inf	*ko*·me tee *kya*·mee
My name is ...	*Mi chiamo ...*	mee *kya*·mo ...
I'm pleased to meet you.	*Piacere.*	pya·*che*·re

This is my ...	Le/Ti presento ... pol/inf	le/tee pre·*zen*·to ...
boyfriend	mio ragazzo	mee·o ra·*ga*·tso
brother	mio fratello	mee·o fra·*te*·lo
daughter	mia figlia	mee·a *fee*·lya
father	mio padre	mee·o *pa*·dre
friend	il mio amico m	eel *mee*·o a·*mee*·ko
	la mia amica f	la mee·a a·*mee*·ka
girlfriend	mia ragazza	mee·a ra·*ga*·tsa
husband	mio marito	mee·o ma·*ree*·to
mother	mia madre	mee·a *ma*·dre
partner (intimate)	il mio compagno m	eel *mee*·o kom·*pa*·nyo
	la mia compagna f	la mee·a kom·*pa*·nya
sister	mia sorella	mee·a so·*re*·la
son	mio figlio	mee·o *fee*·lyo
wife	mia moglie	mee·a *mo*·lye
Here's my ...	Ecco il mio ...	e·ko eel mee·o ...
What's your ...?	Qual'è il	kwa·*le* eel
	Suo/tuo ...? pol/inf	soo·o/too·o ...
address	indirizzo	een·dee·*ree*·tso
email address	indirizzo di email	een·dee·*ree*·tso dee e·mayl
fax number	numero di fax	*noo*·me·ro dee faks
phone number	numero di telefono	*noo*·me·ro dee te·*le*·fo·no

occupations

What's your occupation?	Che lavoro fa/fai? pol/inf	ke la·*vo*·ro fa/fai
I'm a/an ...	Sono ...	so·no ...
artist	artista m&f	ar·*tees*·ta
business person	uomo/donna	*wo*·mo/*do*·na
	d'affari m/f	da·*fa*·ree
farmer	agricoltore m	a·gree·kol·*to*·re
	agricoltrice f	a·gree·kol·*tree*·che
manual worker	manovale m&f	ma·no·*va*·le
office worker	impiegato/a m/f	eem·pye·*ga*·to/a
scientist	scienziato/a m/f	shen·tsee·*a*·to/a
student	studente m	stoo·*den*·te
	studentessa f	stoo·den·*te*·sa
tradesperson	operaio/a m/f	o·pe·*ra*·yo/a

background

Where are you from?	*Da dove viene/vieni?* pol/inf	da *do*·ve vye·ne/vye·nee
I'm from ...	*Vengo ...*	*ven*·go ...
Australia	*dall'Australia*	dal·ow·*stra*·lya
Canada	*dal Canada*	dal *ka*·na·da
England	*dall'Inghilterra*	da·leen·geel·*te*·ra
New Zealand	*dalla Nuova Zelanda*	*da*·la nwo·va ze·*lan*·da
the USA	*dagli Stati Uniti*	*da*·lyee sta·tee oo·nee·tee
Are you married?	*È sposato/a?* m/f pol	e spo·*za*·to/a
	Sei sposato/a? m/f inf	say spo·*za*·to/a
I'm married.	*Sono sposato/a.* m/f	so·no spo·*za*·to/a
I'm single.	*Sono celibe/nubile.* m/f	*che*·lee·be/*noo*·bee·le

age

How old ...?	*Quanti anni ...?*	kwan·tee *a*·nee ...
are you	*ha/hai* pol/inf	a/ai
is your daughter	*ha Sua/tua*	a soo·a/*too*·a
	figlia pol/inf	*fee*·lya
is your son	*ha Suo/tuo*	a soo·o/*too*·o
	figlio pol/inf	*fee*·lyo
I'm ... years old.	*Ho ... anni.*	o ... *a*·nee
He/She is ... years old.	*Ha ... anni.*	a ... *a*·nee

feelings

I'm (not) ...	*(Non) Ho ...*	(non) o ...
Are you ...?	*Ha/Hai ...?* pol/inf	a/ai ...
cold	*freddo*	*fre*·do
hot	*caldo*	*kal*·do
hungry	*fame*	*fa*·me
thirsty	*sete*	*se*·te
I'm (not) ...	*(Non) Sono ...*	(non) *so*·no ...
Are you ...?	*È/Sei ...?* pol/inf	e/say ...
happy	*felice*	fe·*lee*·che
sad	*triste*	*tree*·ste

entertainment

going out

Where can I find ...?	*Dove sono ...?*	*do-ve so-no ...*
clubs	*dei clubs*	day kloob
gay venues	*dei locali gay*	day lo-ka-lee ge
pubs	*dei pub*	day pab
I feel like going to a/the ...	*Ho voglia d'andare ...*	o vo-lya dan-da-re ...
concert	*a un concerto*	a oon kon-cher-to
movies	*al cinema*	al chee-nee-ma
party	*a una festa*	a oo-na fes-ta
restaurant	*in un ristorante*	een oon rees-to-ran-te
theatre	*a teatro*	a te-a-tro

interests

Do you like ...?	*Ti piace/ piacciono ...?* sg/pl	tee pya-che/ pya-cho-no ...
I (don't) like ...	*(Non) Mi piace/ piacciono ...* sg/pl	(non) mee pya-che/ pya-cho-no ...
art	*l'arte* sg	lar-te
cooking	*cucinare* sg	koo-chee-na-re
movies	*i film* pl	ee feelm
nightclubs	*le discoteche* pl	le dees-ko-te-ke
reading	*leggere* sg	le-je-re
shopping	*lo shopping* sg	lo sho-ping
sport	*lo sport* sg	lo sport
travelling	*viaggiare* sg	vee-a-ja-re
Do you like to ...?	*Ti piace ...?*	tee pya-che ...
dance	*ballare*	ba-la-re
go to concerts	*andare ai concerti*	an-da-re ai kon-cher-tee
listen to music	*ascoltare la musica*	as-kol-ta-re la moo-zee-ka

food & drink

finding a place to eat

Can you recommend a ...?	Potrebbe consigliare un ...?	po·tre·be kon·see·lya·re oon ...
bar	locale	lo·ka·le
café	bar	bar
restaurant	ristorante	rees·to·ran·te
I'd like ..., please.	Vorrei ..., per favore.	vo·ray ... per fa·vo·re
a table for (four)	un tavolo per (quattro)	oon ta·vo·lo per (kwa·tro)
the (non)smoking section	(non) fumatori	(non) foo·ma·to·ree

ordering food

breakfast	prima colazione f	pree·ma ko·la·tsyo·ne
lunch	pranzo m	pran·dzo
dinner	cena f	che·na
snack	spuntino m	spoon·tee·no

What would you recommend?
Cosa mi consiglia?   ko·za mee kon·see·lya

I'd like (the) ..., please.	Vorrei ..., per favore.	vo·ray ... per fa·vo·re
bill	il conto	eel kon·to
drink list	la lista delle bevande	la lee·sta de·le be·van·de
menu	il menù	eel me·noo
that dish	questo piatto	kwe·sto pya·to

drinks

(cup of) coffee ...	(un) caffè ...	(oon) ka-fe ...
(cup of) tea ...	(un) tè ...	(oon) te ...
with milk	con latte	kon la-te
without sugar	senza zucchero	sen-tsa tsoo-ke-ro
orange juice (bottled)	succo d'arancia m	soo-ko da-ran-cha
orange juice (fresh)	spremuta d'arancia f	spre-moo-ta da-ran-cha
soft drink	bibita f	bee-bee-ta
... water	acqua ...	a-kwa ...
boiled	bollita	bo-lee-ta
mineral	minerale	mee-ne-ra-le
sparkling mineral	frizzante	free-tsan-te
still mineral	naturale	na-too-ra-le

in the bar

I'll have ...	Prendo ...	pren-do ...
I'll buy you a drink.	Ti offro da bere. inf	tee of-ro da be-re
What would you like?	Cosa prendi?	ko-za pren-dee
Cheers!	Salute!	sa-loo-te
brandy	cognac m	ko-nyak
champagne	champagne m	sham-pa-nye
cocktail	cocktail m	kok-tayl
a shot of (whisky)	un sorso di (whisky)	oon sor-so dee (wee-skee)
a ... of beer	... di birra	... dee bee-ra
bottle	una bottiglia	oo-na bo-tee-lya
glass	un bicchiere	oon bee-kye-re
a bottle of ...	una bottiglia di	oo-na bo-tee-lya dee
wine	vino ...	vee-no ...
a glass of ...	un bicchiere di	oon bee-kye-re dee
wine	vino ...	vee-no ...
red	rosso	ro-so
sparkling	spumante	spoo-man-te
white	bianco	byan-ko

self-catering

What's the local speciality?
    Qual'è la specialità   kwa·*le* la spe·cha·lee·*ta*
    di questa regione?   dee *kwe*·sta re·*jo*·ne

What's that?
    Cos'è?   ko·*ze*

How much is (a kilo of cheese)?
    Quanto costa (un chilo   *kwan*·to *kos*·ta (oon *kee*·lo
    di formaggio)?   dee for·*ma*·jo)

I'd like ...	*Vorrei ...*	vo·*ray* ...
100 grams	*un etto*	oo·*ne*·to
(two) kilos	*(due) chili*	(*doo*·e) *kee*·lee
(three) pieces	*(tre) pezzi*	(tre) *pe*·tsee
(six) slices	*(sei) fette*	(say) *fe*·te
Less.	*Meno.*	*me*·no
Enough.	*Basta.*	*bas*·ta
More.	*Più.*	pyoo

special diets & allergies

Is there a vegetarian restaurant near here?
    C'è un ristorante vegetariano   che oon rees·to·*ran*·te ve·je·ta·*rya*·no
    qui vicino?   kwee vee·*chee*·no

Do you have vegetarian food?
    Avete piatti vegetariani?   a·*ve*·te *pya*·tee ve·je·ta·*rya*·nee

Could you prepare	*Potreste preparare*	po·*tres*·te pre·pa·*ra*·re
a meal without ...?	*un pasto senza ...?*	oon *pas*·to *sen*·tsa ...
butter	*burro*	*boo*·ro
eggs	*uova*	*wo*·va
meat stock	*brodo di carne*	*bro*·do dee *kar*·ne

I'm allergic to ...	*Sono allergico/a ...* m/f	*so*·no a·*ler*·jee·ko/a ...
dairy produce	*ai latticini*	ai la·tee·*chee*·nee
gluten	*al glutine*	al *gloo*·tee·ne
MSG	*al glutammato*	al glu·ta·*ma*·to
	monosodico	mo·no·*so*·dee·ko
nuts	*alle noci*	*a*·le *no*·chee
seafood	*ai frutti di mare*	ai *froo*·tee dee *ma*·re

menu decoder

acciughe f pl	a-*choo*-ge	*anchovies*
arancini m pl	a-ran-*chee*-nee	*rice balls stuffed with a meat mixture*
babà m	ba-*ba*	*dessert containing sultanas*
baccalà m	ba-ka-*la*	*dried salted cod*
bagna cauda f	*ban*-ya cow-da	*anchovy, olive oil & garlic dip*
brioche m	bree-*osh*	*breakfast pastry*
bruschetta f	broos-*ke*-ta	*toasted bread with olive oil & toppings*
budino m	bon-*dee*-no	*milk based pudding*
cacciucco m	ka-*choo*-ko	*seafood stew with wine, garlic & herbs*
cannelloni m pl	ka-ne-*lo*-nee	*pasta stuffed with spinach, minced roast veal, ham, eggs, parmesan & spices*
caponata f	ka-po-*na*-ta	*eggplant with a tomato sauce*
ciabatta f	cha-*ba*-ta	*crisp, flat & long bread*
conchiglie f pl	kon-*kee*-lye	*pasta shells*
costine f pl	kos-*tee*-ne	*ribs*
cozze f pl	*ko*-tse	*mussels*
crostata f	kro-*sta*-ta	*fruit tart*
crostini m pl	kro-*stee*-nee	*bread toasted with savoury toppings*
farinata f	fa-ree-*na*-ta	*thin, flat bread made from chickpea flour*
fettuccine f pl	fe-too-*chee*-ne	*long ribbon-shaped pasta*
focaccia f	fo-*ka*-cha	*flat bread filled or topped with cheese, ham, vegetables & other ingredients*
frittata f	free-*ta*-ta	*thick omelette slice, served hot or cold*
funghi m pl	*foon*-gee	*mushrooms*
gamberoni m pl	gam-be-*ro* nee	*prawns*
gelato m	je-*la*-to	*ice cream*

gnocchi m pl	*nyo*-kee	small (usually potato) dumplings
grappa f	*gra*-pa	distilled grape must
involtini m pl	een-vol-*tee*-nee	stuffed rolls of meat or fish
linguine f pl	leen-*gwee*-ne	long thin ribbons of pasta
lumache f pl	loo-*ma*-ke	snails
maccheroni m pl	ma-ke-*ro*-nee	refers to any tube pasta
mascarpone m	mas-kar-*po*-ne	very soft & creamy cheese
minestrone m	mee-ne-*stro*-ne	traditional vegetable soup
ostriche f pl	*os*-tree-ke	oysters
pancetta f	pan-*che*-ta	salt-cured bacon
panzanella f	pan-tsa-*ne*-la	tomato, onion, garlic, olive oil, bread & basil salad
penne f pl	*pe*-ne	short & tubular pasta
pesto m	*pes*-to	paste of garlic, basil, pine nuts & parmesan
polpette m	pol-*pe*-te	meatballs
prosciutto m	pro-*shoo*-to	any type of thinly sliced ham
quattro formaggi	*kwa*-tro for-*ma*-jee	pasta sauce with four different cheeses
quattro stagioni	*kwa*-tro sta-*jo*-nee	pizza with different toppings on each quarter
ragù m	ra-*goo*	meat sauce (sometimes vegetarian)
ravioli m pl	ra-vee-o-*lee*	pasta squares usually stuffed with meat, parmesan cheese & breadcrumbs
rigatoni m pl	ree-ga-*to*-nee	short, fat tubes of pasta
risotto m	ree-*zo*-to	rice dish cooked in broth
spaghetti m pl	spa-*ge*-tee	ubiquitous long thin strands of pasta
tagliatelle f	ta-lya-*te*-le	long, ribbon-shaped pasta
tiramisù m	tee-ra-mee-*soo*	layered sponge cake soaked in coffee
tortellini m pl	tor-te-*lee*-nee	pasta filled with meat, parmesan & egg
vongole f pl	*von*-go-le	clams

emergencies

basics

Help!	*Aiuto!*	ai·*yoo*·to
Stop!	*Fermi!*	*fer*·mee
Go away!	*Vai via!*	vai *vee*·a
Thief!	*Ladro!*	*la*·dro
Fire!	*Al fuoco!*	al *fwo*·ko
Watch out!	*Attenzione!*	a·ten·*tsyo*·ne

Call ...!	*Chiami ...!*	*kya*·mee ...
a doctor	*un medico*	oon *me*·dee·ko
an ambulance	*un'ambulanza*	o·nam·boo·*lan*·tsa
the police	*la polizia*	la po·lee·*tsee*·a

It's an emergency!
È un'emergenza!   e oo·ne·mer·*jen*·tsa

Could you help me, please?
Mi può aiutare, per favore?   mee pwo ai·yoo·*ta*·re per fa·*vo*·re

I have to use the telephone.
Devo fare una telefonata.   *de*·vo *fa*·re *oo*·na te·le·fo·*na*·ta

I'm lost.
Mi sono perso/a. m/f   mee *so*·no *per*·so/a

Where are the toilets?
Dove sono i gabinetti?   *do*·ve *so*·no ee ga·bee·*ne*·tee

police

Where's the police station?
Dov'è il posto di polizia?   do·*ve* eel *pos*·to dee po·lee·*tsee*·a

I want to report an offence.
Voglio fare una denuncia.   *vo*·lyo *fa*·re *oo*·na de·*noon*·cha

I have insurance.
Ho l'assicurazione.   o la·see·koo·ra·*tsyo*·ne

I've been ...	*Sono stato/a ...* m/f	*so*·no *sta*·to/a ...
assaulted	*aggredito/a* m/f	a·gre·*dee*·to/a
raped	*violentato/a* m/f	vyo·len·*ta*·to/a
robbed	*derubato/a* m/f	roo·*ba*·to/a

I've lost my ...	Ho perso ...	o *per·*so ...
My ... was/were stolen.	Mi hanno rubato ...	mee *a·*no roo·*ba·*to ...
backpack	il mio zaino	eel *mee·*o *dzai·*no
bags	i miei bagagli	ee mee·*ay* ba·*ga·*lyee
credit card	la mia carta di credito	la *mee·*a *kar·*ta dee *kre·*dee·to
handbag	la mia borsa	la *mee·*a *bor·*sa
jewellery	i miei gioielli	ee mee·*ay* jo·*ye·*lee
money	i miei soldi	ee mee·*ay* *sol·*dee
passport	il mio passaporte	eel *mee·*o pa·sa·*por·*te
travellers cheques	i miei assegni di viaggio	ee mee·*ay* a·*se·*nyee dee vee·*a·*jo
wallet	portafoglio	por·ta·*fo·*lyo
I want to contact my ...	Vorrei contattare ...	vo·*ray* kon·ta·*ta·*re ...
consulate	il mio consolato	eel *mee·*o kon·so·*la·*to
embassy	la mia ambasciata	la *mee·*a am·ba·*sha·*ta

health

medical needs

Where's the nearest ...?	Dov'è ... più vicino/a? m/f	do·*ve* ... pyoo vee·*chee·*no/a
dentist	il dentista m	eel den·*tee·*sta
doctor	il medico m	eel *me·*dee·ko
hospital	l'ospedale m	los·pe·*da·*le
(night) pharmacist	la farmacia (di turno) f	la far·ma·*chee·*a (dee *toor·*no)

I need a doctor (who speaks English).
Ho bisogno di un medico (che parli inglese).
o bee·*zo·*nyo dee oon *me·*dee·ko (ke *par·*lee een·*gle·*ze)

Could I see a female doctor?
Posso vedere una dottoressa?
*po·*so ve·*de·*re *oo·*na do·to·*re·*sa

I've run out of my medication.
Ho finito la mia medicina.
o fee·*nee·*to la *mee·*a me·dee·*chee·*na

symptoms, conditions & allergies

| I'm sick. | Mi sento male. | mee sen·to ma·le |
| It hurts here. | Mi fa male qui. | mee fa ma·le kwee |

I have (a) …	Ho …	o …
asthma	asma	as·ma
bronchitis	la bronchite	la bron·kee·te
constipation	la stitichezza	la stee·tee·ke·tsa
cough	la tosse	la to·se
diarrhoea	la diarrea	la dee·a·re·a
fever	la febbre	la fe·bre
headache	mal di testa	mal dee tes·ta
heart condition	un problema cardiaco	oon pro·ble·ma kar·dee·a·ko
nausea	la nausea	la now·ze·a
pain	un dolore	oon do·lo·re
sore throat	mal di gola	mal dee go·la
toothache	mal di denti	mal dee den·tee

I'm allergic to …	Sono allergico/a … m/f	so·no a·ler·jee·ko/a …
antibiotics	agli	a·lyee
	antibiotici	an·tee·bee·o·tee·chee
anti-	agli	a·lyee
inflammatories	antinfiammatori	an·teen·fya·ma·to·ree
aspirin	all'aspirina	a·las·pee·ree·na
bees	alle api	a·le a·pee
codeine	alla codeina	a·la ko·de·ee·na
penicillin	alla penicillina	a·la pe·ne·chee·lee·na

antiseptic	antisettico m	an·tee·se·tee·ko
bandage	fascia f	fa·sha
condoms	preservativi m pl	pre·zer·va·tee·vee
contraceptives	contraccettivi m pl	kon·tra·che·tee·vee
diarrhoea medicine	antidissenterico m	an·tee·dee·sen·te·ree·ko
insect repellent	repellente per	re·pe·len·te per
	gli insetti m	lyee een·se·tee
laxatives	lassativi m pl	la·sa·tee·vee
painkillers	analgesico m	a·nal·je·zee·ko
rehydration salts	sali minerali m pl	sa·lee mee·ne·ra·lee
sleeping tablets	sonniferi m pl	so·nee·fe·ree

english–italian dictionary

Italian nouns in this dictionary, and adjectives affected by gender, have their gender indicated by ⓜ (masculine) or ⓕ (feminine). If it's a plural noun, you'll also see pl. Words are also marked as n (noun), a (adjective), v (verb), sg (singular), pl (plural), inf (informal) and pol (polite) where necessary.

A

accident *incidente* ⓜ een-chee-*den*-te
accommodation *alloggio* ⓜ a-*lo*-jo
adaptor *presa multipla* ⓕ *pre*-sa *mool*-tee-pla
address *indirizzo* ⓜ een-dee-*ree*-tso
after *dopo* do-po
air-conditioned *ad aria condizionata*
    ad a-rya kon-dee-*tsyo*-na-ta
airplane *aereo* ⓜ a-e-re-o
airport *aeroporto* ⓜ a-e-ro-*por*-to
alcohol *alcol* ⓜ *al*-kol
all a *tutto/a* too-to/a
allergy *allergia* ⓕ a-ler-*jee*-a
ambulance *ambulanza* ⓕ am-boo-*lan*-tsa
and e e
ankle *caviglia* ⓕ ka-*vee*-lya
arm *braccio* ⓜ *bra*-cho
ashtray *portacenere* ⓜ por-ta-*che*-ne-re
ATM *Bancomat* ⓜ *ban*-ko-mat

B

baby *bimbo/a* ⓜ/ⓕ *beem*-bo/a
back (body) *schiena* ⓕ *skye*-na
backpack *zaino* ⓜ *dzai*-no
bad *cattivo/a* ⓜ/ⓕ ka-*tee*-vo/a
bag *borsa* ⓕ *bor*-sa
baggage claim *ritiro bagagli* ⓜ ree-*tee*-ro ba-*ga*-lyee
bank *banca* ⓕ *ban*-ka
bar *locale* ⓜ lo-*ka*-le
bathroom *bagno* ⓜ *ba*-nyo
battery *pila* ⓕ *pee*-la
beautiful *bello/a* ⓜ/ⓕ *be*-lo/a
bed *letto* ⓜ *le*-to
beer *birra* ⓕ *bee*-ra
before *prima* *pree*-ma
behind *dietro* *dye*-tro
bicycle *bicicletta* ⓕ bee-chee-*kle*-ta
big *grande* *gran*-de
bill *conto* ⓜ *kon*-to

black *nero/a* ⓜ/ⓕ *ne*-ro/a
blanket *coperta* ⓕ ko-*per*-ta
blood group *gruppo sanguigno* ⓜ *groo*-po san-*gwee*-nyo
blue *azzurro/a* ⓜ/ⓕ a-*dzoo*-ro/a
boat *barca* ⓕ *bar*-ka
book (make a reservation) v *prenotare* pre-no-*ta*-re
bottle *bottiglia* ⓕ bo-*tee*-lya
bottle opener *apribottiglie* ⓜ a-pree-bo-*tee*-lye
boy *ragazzo* ⓜ ra-*ga*-tso
brakes (car) *freno* ⓜ *fre*-no
breakfast (prima) colazione ⓕ (*pree*-ma) ko-la-*tsyo*-ne
broken (faulty) *rotto/a* ⓜ/ⓕ *ro*-to/a
bus *autobus* ⓜ *ow*-to-boos
business *affari* ⓜ pl a-*fa*-ree
buy *comprare* kom-*pra*-re

C

café *bar* ⓜ bar
camera *macchina fotografica* ⓕ
    ma-kee-na fo-to-*gra*-fee-ka
camp site *campeggio* ⓜ kam-*pe*-jo
cancel *cancellare* kan-che-*la*-re
can opener *apriscatole* ⓜ a-pree-*ska*-to-le
car *macchina* ⓕ *ma*-kee-na
cash *soldi* ⓜ pl *sol*-dee
cash (a cheque) v *riscuotere un assegno*
    ree-*skwo*-te-re oon a-se-nyo
cell phone *telefono cellulare* ⓜ te-*le*-fo-no che-loo-*la*-re
centre *centro* ⓜ *chen*-tro
change (money) v *cambiare* kam-*bya*-re
cheap *economico/a* ⓜ/ⓕ e-ko-*no*-mee-ko/a
check (bill) *conto* ⓜ *kon*-to
check-in *registrazione* ⓕ re-jee-stra-*tsyo*-ne
chest *petto* ⓜ *pe*-to
child *bambino/a* ⓜ/ⓕ bam-*bee*-no/a
cigarette *sigaretta* ⓕ see-ga-*re*-ta
city *città* ⓕ chee-*ta*
clean a *pulito/a* ⓜ/ⓕ poo-*lee*-to/a
closed *chiuso/a* ⓜ/ⓕ *kyoo*-zo/a
coffee *caffè* ⓜ ka-*fe*
coins *monete* ⓕ pl mo-*ne*-te

cold a *freddo/a* ⓜ/ⓕ *fre*·do/a
collect call *chiamata a carico del destinatario* ⓕ
  kya·*ma*·ta a ka·ree·ko del des·tee·na·*ta*·ryo
come *venire* ve·*nee*·re
computer *computer* ⓜ kom·*pyoo*·ter
condom *preservativo* ⓜ pre·zer·va·*tee*·vo
contact lenses *lenti a contatto* ⓕ pl *len*·tee a kon·*ta*·to
cook v *cucinare* koo·chee·*na*·re
cost *prezzo* ⓜ *pre*·tso
credit card *carta di credito* ⓕ *kar*·ta dee *kre*·dee·to
cup *tazza* ⓕ *ta*·tsa
currency exchange *cambio valuta* ⓜ *kam*·byo va·*loo*·ta
customs (immigration) *dogana* ⓕ do·*ga*·na

D

dangerous *pericoloso/a* ⓜ/ⓕ pe·ree·ko·*lo*·zo/a
date (time) *data* ⓕ *da*·ta
day *giorno* ⓜ *jor*·no
delay *ritardo* ⓜ ree·*tar*·do
dentist *dentista* ⓜ/ⓕ den·*tee*·sta
depart *partire* par·*tee*·re
diaper *pannolino* ⓜ pa·no·*lee*·no
dictionary *vocabolario* ⓜ vo·ka·bo·*la*·ryo
dinner *cena* ⓕ *che*·na
direct *diretto/a* ⓜ/ⓕ dee·*re*·to/a
dirty *sporco/a* ⓜ/ⓕ *spor*·ko/a
disabled *disabile* dee·za·bee·le
discount *sconto* ⓜ *skon*·to
doctor *medico* ⓜ *me*·dee·ko
double bed *letto matrimoniale* ⓜ *le*·to ma·tree·mo·*nya*·le
double room *camera doppia* ⓕ *ka*·mer·a *do*·pya
drink *bevanda* ⓕ be·*van*·da
drive v *guidare* gwee·*da*·re
drivers licence *patente di guida* ⓕ pa·*ten*·te dee *gwee*·da
drugs (illicit) *droga* ⓕ *dro*·ga
dummy (pacifier) *ciucciotto* ⓜ choo·*cho*·to

E

ear *orecchio* ⓜ o·*re*·kyo
east *est* ⓜ est
eat *mangiare* man·*ja*·re
economy class *classe turistica* ⓕ *kla*·se too·ree·*stee*·ka
electricity *elettricità* ⓕ e·le·tree·chee·*ta*
elevator *ascensore* ⓜ a·shen·*so*·re
email *email* ⓕ e·*mayl*
embassy *ambasciata* ⓕ am·ba·*sha*·ta
emergency *emergenza* ⓕ e·mer·*jen*·tsa
English (language) *inglese* een·*gle*·ze

entrance *entrata* ⓕ en·*tra*·ta
evening *sera* ⓕ *se*·ra
exchange rate *tasso di cambio* ⓜ *ta*·so dee *kam*·byo
exit *uscita* ⓕ *ta*·so dee *kam*·byo
expensive *caro/a* ⓜ/ⓕ *ka*·ro/a
express mail *posta prioritaria* ⓕ *pos*·ta pree·o·ree·*ta*·rya
eye *occhio* ⓜ o·kyo

F

far *lontano/a* ⓜ/ⓕ lon·*ta*·no/a
fast *veloce* ve·*lo*·che
father *padre* ⓜ *pa*·dre
film (camera) *rullino* ⓜ roo·*lee*·no
finger *dito* ⓜ *dee*·to
first-aid kit *valigetta del pronto soccorso* ⓕ
  va·lee·*je*·ta del *pron*·to so·*kor*·so
first class *prima classe* ⓕ *pree*·ma *kla*·se
fish n *pesce* ⓜ *pe*·she
food *cibo* ⓜ *chee*·bo
foot *piede* ⓜ *pye*·de
fork *forchetta* ⓕ for·*ke*·ta
free (of charge) *gratuito/a* ⓜ/ⓕ gra·*too*·ee·to/a
friend *amico/a* ⓜ/ⓕ a·*mee*·ko/a
fruit *frutta* ⓕ *froo*·ta
full *pieno/a* ⓜ/ⓕ *pye*·no/a
funny *divertente* dee·ver·*ten*·te

G

gift *regalo* ⓜ re·*ga*·lo
girl *ragazza* ⓕ ra·*ga*·tsa
glass (drinking) *bicchiere* ⓜ bee·*kye*·re
glasses *occhiali* ⓜ pl o·*kya*·lee
go *andare* an·*da*·re
good *buono/a* ⓜ/ⓕ *bwo*·no/a
green *verde* *ver*·de
guide n *guida* ⓕ *gwee*·da

H

half *mezzo* ⓜ *me*·dzo
hand *mano* ⓕ *ma*·no
handbag *borsetta* ⓕ bor·*se*·ta
happy *felice* ⓜ/ⓕ fe·*lee*·che
have *avere* a·*ve*·re
he *lui* *loo*·ee
head *testa* ⓕ *tes*·ta
heart *cuore* ⓜ *kwo*·re
heat n *caldo* ⓜ *kal*·do

heavy *pesante* pe-*zan*-te
help v *aiutare* a-yoo-*ta*-re
here *qui* kwee
high *alto/a* ⓜ/ⓕ *al*-to/a
highway *autostrada* ow-to-*stra*-da
hike v *fare un'escursione a piedi*
fa-re oon es-koor-*syo*-ne a *pye*-de
holiday *vacanze* ⓕ pl va-*kan*-tse
homosexual n *omosessuale* ⓜ&ⓕ o-mo-se-*swa*-le
hospital *ospedale* ⓜ os-pe-*da*-le
hot *caldo/a* ⓜ/ⓕ *kal*-do/a
hotel *albergo* ⓜ al-*ber*-go
hungry *affamato/a* ⓜ/ⓕ a-fa-*ma*-to
husband *marito* ⓜ ma-*ree*-to

I

I *io* ee-o
identification (card) *carta d'identità* ⓕ
kar-ta dee-den-tee-*ta*
ill *malato/a* ⓜ/ⓕ ma-*la*-to/a
important *importante* eem-por-*tan*-te
included *compreso/a* ⓜ/ⓕ kom-*pre*-zo/a
injury *ferita* ⓕ fe-*ree*-ta
insurance *assicurazione* ⓕ a-see-koo-ra-*tsyo*-ne
Internet *Internet* ⓜ een-ter-net
interpreter *interprete* ⓜ/ⓕ een-*ter*-pre-te
Italy *Italia* ⓕ ee-*ta*-lya
Italian (language) *italiano* ⓜ ee-ta-*lya*-no

J

jewellery *gioielli* ⓜ pl jo-*ye*-lee
job *lavoro* ⓜ la-*vo*-ro

K

key *chiave* ⓕ *kya*-ve
kilogram *chilo* ⓜ *kee*-lo
kitchen *cucina* ⓕ koo-*chee*-na
knife *coltello* ⓜ kol-*te*-lo

L

laundry (place) *lavanderia* ⓕ la-van-de-*ree*-a
lawyer *avvocato/a* ⓜ/ⓕ a-vo-*ka*-to/a
left (direction) *sinistra* see-*nee*-stra
left-luggage office *deposito bagagli* ⓜ
de-*po*-zee-to ba-*ga*-lyee
leg *gamba* ⓕ *gam*-ba

lesbian n *lesbica* ⓕ *lez*-bee-ka
less (di) meno (dee) *me*-no
letter (mail) *lettera* ⓕ *le*-te-ra
lift (elevator) *ascensore* ⓜ a-shen-*so*-re
light *luce* ⓕ *loo*-che
like v *piacere* pya-*che*-re
lock *serratura* ⓕ se-ra-*too*-ra
long *lungo/a* ⓜ/ⓕ *loon*-go/a
lost *perso/a* ⓜ/ⓕ *per*-so/a
lost-property office *ufficio oggetti smarriti* ⓜ
oo-*fee*-cho o-*je*-tee sma-*ree*-tee
love v *amare* a-*ma*-re
luggage *bagaglio* ⓜ ba-*ga*-lyo
lunch *pranzo* ⓜ *pran*-dzo

M

mail *posta* ⓕ *pos*-ta
man *uomo* ⓜ *wo*-mo
map *pianta* ⓕ *pyan*-ta
market *mercato* ⓜ mer-*ka*-to
matches *fiammiferi* ⓜ pl fya-*mee*-fe-ree
meat *carne* ⓕ *kar*-ne
medicine *medicina* ⓕ me-dee-*chee*-na
menu *menu* ⓜ me-*noo*
message *messaggio* ⓜ me-*sa*-jo
milk *latte* ⓕ *la*-te
minute *minuto* ⓜ mee-*noo*-to
mobile phone *telefono cellulare* ⓜ te-*le*-fo-no che-loo-*la*-re
money *denaro* ⓜ de-*na*-ro
month *mese* ⓜ *me*-ze
morning *mattina* ⓕ ma-*tee*-na
mother *madre* ⓕ *ma*-dre
motorcycle *moto* ⓕ *mo*-to
motorway *autostrada* ⓕ ow-to-*stra*-da
mouth *bocca* ⓕ *bo*-ka
music *musica* ⓕ *moo*-zee-ka

N

name *nome* ⓜ *no*-me
napkin *tovagliolo* ⓜ to-va-*lyo*-lo
nappy *pannolino* ⓜ pa-no-*lee*-no
near *vicino (a)* vee-*chee*-no (a)
neck *collo* ⓜ *ko*-lo
new *nuovo/a* ⓜ/ⓕ *nwo*-vo/a
news *notizie* ⓕ pl no-*tee*-tsye
newspaper *giornale* ⓜ jor-*na*-le
night *notte* ⓕ *no*-te
no *no* no

noisy *rumoroso/a* ⓜ/ⓕ roo-mo-*ro*-zo/a

nonsmoking *non fumatore* non foo-ma-*to*-re

north *nord* ⓜ nord

nose *naso* ⓜ *na*-zo

now *adesso* a-*de*-so

number *numero* ⓜ *noo*-me-ro

O

oil (engine) *olio* ⓜ *o*-lyo

old *vecchio/a* ⓜ/ⓕ *ve*-kyo/a

one-way ticket *biglietto di solo andata*
bee-*lye*-to dee so-lo an-*da*-ta

open a *aperto/a* ⓜ/ⓕ a-*per*-to/a

outside *fuori* fwo-ree

P

package *pacchetto* ⓜ pa-*ke*-to

paper *carta* ⓕ *kar*-ta

park (car) v *parcheggiare* par-ke-*ja*-re

passport *passaporto* ⓜ pa-sa-*por*-to

pay *pagare* pa-*ga*-re

pen *penna (a sfera)* ⓕ *pe*-na (a *sfe*-ra)

petrol *benzina* ⓕ ben-*dzee*-na

pharmacy *farmacia* ⓕ far-ma-*chee*-a

phonecard *scheda telefonica* ⓕ *ske*-da te-le-*fo*-nee-ka

photo *foto* ⓕ *fo*-to

plate *piatto* ⓜ *pya*-to

police *polizia* ⓕ po-lee-*tsee*-a

postcard *cartolina* ⓕ kar-to-*lee*-na

post office *ufficio postale* ⓜ oo-*fee*-cho pos-*ta*-le

pregnant *incinta* een-*cheen*-ta

price *prezzo* ⓜ *pre*-tso

Q

quiet *tranquillo/a* ⓜ/ⓕ tran-*kwee*-lo/a

R

rain n *pioggia* ⓜ *pyo*-ja

razor *rasoio* ⓜ ra-*zo*-yo

receipt *ricevuta* ⓕ ree-che-*voo*-ta

red *rosso/a* ⓜ/ⓕ *ro*-so/a

refund *rimborso* ⓜ reem-*bor*-so

registered mail *posta raccomandata* ⓕ
pos-ta ra-ko-man-*da*-ta

rent v *prendere in affitto* pren-de-re een a-*fee*-to

repair v *riparare* ree-pa-*ra*-re

reservation *prenotazione* ⓕ pre-no-ta-*tsyo*-ne

restaurant *ristorante* ⓜ rees-to-*ran*-te

return v *ritornare* ree-tor-*na*-re

return ticket *biglietto di andata e ritorno*
bee-*lye*-to dee an-*da*-ta e ree-*tor*-no

right (direction) *destra* de-stra

road *strada* ⓕ *stra*-da

room *camera* ⓕ *ka*-me-ra

S

safe a *sicuro/a* ⓜ/ⓕ see-*koo*-ro/a

sanitary napkins *assorbenti igienici* ⓜ pl
as-or-*ben*-tee ee-*je*-nee-chee

seat *posto* ⓜ *pos*-to

send *mandare* man-*da*-re

service station *stazione di servizio* ⓕ
sta-*tsyo*-ne dee ser-*vee*-tsyo

sex *sesso* ⓜ *se*-so

shampoo *shampoo* ⓜ *sham*-poo

share (a dorm) *condividere* kon-dee-*vee*-de-re

shaving cream *crema da barba* ⓕ *kre*-ma da *bar*-ba

she *lei* lay

sheet (bed) *lenzuolo* ⓜ len-*tswo*-lo

shirt *camicia* ⓕ ka-*mee*-cha

shoes *scarpe* ⓕ pl *skar*-pe

shop *negozio* ⓜ ne-*go*-tsyo

short *corto/a* ⓜ/ⓕ *kor*-to/a

shower *doccia* ⓕ *do*-cha

single room *camera singola* ⓕ *ka*-me-ra *seen*-go-la

skin *pelle* ⓕ *pe*-le

skirt *gonna* ⓕ *go*-na

sleep v *dormire* dor-*mee*-re

slowly *lentamente* len-ta-*men*-te

small *piccolo/a* ⓜ/ⓕ *pee*-ko-lo/a

smoke (cigarettes) v *fumare* foo-*ma*-re

soap *sapone* ⓜ sa-*po*-ne

some *alcuni/e* ⓜ/ⓕ pl al-*koo*-nee/al-*koo*-ne

soon *fra poco* fra *po*-ko

south *sud* ⓜ sood

souvenir shop *negozio di souvenir* ⓜ
ne-*go*-tsyo dee *soo*-ve-neer

speak *parlare* par-*la*-re

spoon *cucchiaio* ⓜ koo-*kya*-yo

stamp *francobollo* ⓜ fran-ko-*bo*-lo

stand-by ticket *in lista d'attesa* een *lee*-sta da-*te*-za

station (train) *stazione* ⓕ sta-*tsyo*-ne

stomach *stomaco* ⓜ *sto*-ma-ko

stop v *fermare* fer-*ma*-re

stop (bus) *fermata* ⓕ fer-*ma*-ta

street *strada* ① *stra*-da
student *studente/studentessa* ⓜ/①
  stoo-den-te/stoo-den-*te*-sa
sun *sole* ⓜ *so*-le
sunscreen *crema solare* ① *kre*-ma so-*la*-re
swim v *nuotare* nwo-*ta*-re
Switzerland *Svizzera* ① svee-*tse*-ra

T

tampons *assorbenti interni* ⓜ pl
  a-sor-*ben*-tee een-*ter*-nee
taxi *tassì* ⓜ ta-*see*
teaspoon *cucchiaino* ⓜ koo-kya-*ee*-no
teeth *denti* ⓜ pl *den*-tee
telephone *telefono* ⓜ te-*le*-fo-no
television *televisione* ① te-le-vee-*zyo*-ne
temperature (weather) *temperatura* ①
  tem-pe-ra-*too*-ra
tent *tenda* ① *ten*-da
that (one) *quello/a* ⓜ/① *kwe*-lo/a
they *loro* lo-ro
thirsty *assetato/a* ⓜ/① a-se-*ta*-to
this (one) *questo/a* ⓜ/① *kwe*-sto/a
throat *gola* ① *go*-la
ticket *biglietto* ⓜ bee-*lye*-to
time *tempo* ⓜ *tem*-po
tired *stanco/a* ⓜ/① *stan*-ko/a
tissues *fazzolettini di carta* ⓜ pl
  fa-tso-le-*tee*-nee dee *kar*-ta
today *oggi* o-jee
toilet *gabinetto* ⓜ ga-bee-*ne*-to
tomorrow *domani* do-*ma*-nee
tonight *stasera* sta-*se*-ra
toothbrush *spazzolino da denti* ⓜ
  spa-tso-*lee*-no da *den*-tee
toothpaste *dentifricio* ⓜ den-tee-*free*-cho
torch (flashlight) *torcia elettrica* ① *tor*-cha e-*le*-tree-ka
tour *gita* ① *jee*-ta
tourist office *ufficio del turismo* ⓜ
  oo-*fee*-cho del too-*reez*-mo
towel *asciugamano* ⓜ a-shoo-ga-*ma*-no
train *treno* ⓜ *tre*-no
translate *tradurre* tra-*doo*-re
travel agency *agenzia di viaggio* ①
  a-jen-*tsee*-a dee vee-*a*-jo
travellers cheque *assegno di viaggio* ⓜ
  a-se-nyo dee vee-*a*-jo
trousers *pantaloni* ⓜ pl pan-ta-*lo*-nee

twin beds *due letti* doo-e *le*-tee
tyre *gomma* ① *go*-ma

U

underwear *biancheria intima* ⓜ byan-ke-*ree*-a *een*-tee-ma
urgent *urgente* ⓜ/① oor-*jen*-te

V

vacant *libero/a* ⓜ/① *lee*-be-ro/a
vacation *vacanza* ① va-*kan*-tsa
vegetable *verdura* ① ver-*doo*-ra
vegetarian a *vegetariano/a* ⓜ/① ve-je-ta-*rya*-no/a
visa *visto* ⓜ *vee*-sto

W

waiter *cameriere/a* ⓜ/① ka-mer-*ye*-re/a
walk v *camminare* ka-mee-*na*-re
wallet *portafoglio* ⓜ por-ta-*fo*-lyo
warm a *tiepido/a* ⓜ/① *tye*-pee-do/a
wash (something) *lavare* la-*va*-re
watch *orologio* ⓜ o-ro-*lo*-jo
water *acqua* ① *a*-kwa
we *noi* noy
weekend *fine settimana* ⓜ *fee*-ne se-tee-*ma*-na
west *ovest* ⓜ *o*-vest
wheelchair *sedia a rotelle* ① *se*-dya a ro-*te*-le
when *quando* *kwan*-do
where *dove* *do*-ve
white *bianco/a* ⓜ/① *byan*-ko/a
who *chi* kee
why *perché* per-*ke*
wife *moglie* ① *mo*-lye
window *finestra* ① fee-*nes*-tra
wine *vino* ⓜ *vee*-no
with *con* kon
without *senza* *sen*-tsa
woman *donna* ① *do*-na
write *scrivere* *skree*-ve-re

Y

yellow *giallo/a* ⓜ/① *ja*-lo/a
yes *sì* see
yesterday *ieri* *ye*-ree
you sg inf *tu* too
you sg pol *Lei* lay
you pl *voi* voy

Norwegian

norwegian alphabet

A a	B b	C c	D d	E e
a	be	se	de	e
F f	G g	H h	I i	J j
ef	ge	haw	ee	ye
K k	L l	M m	N n	O o
kaw	el	em	en	o
P p	Q q	R r	S s	T t
pe	koo	er	es	te
U u	V v	W w	X x	Y y
oo	ve	*daw*·bel ve	eks	ew
Z z	Æ æ	Ø ø	Å å	
set	ey	eu	aw	

norwegian

NORWEGIAN
norsk

introduction

Norwegian (*norsk* nawrsk), the language from which words such as *fjord*, *reindeer*, *slalom* and *quisling* came into English, has gone a long way since the Vikings roamed the northern seas and the ancient heroic sagas were composed. The ancestor of modern Norwegian ventured as far as Russia, Greenland and even Canada. After centuries of subdued existence in the shadow of Danish, Norwegian ended up in the 21st century as two official languages and many local dialects.

Together with Swedish, Danish, Icelandic and Faroese, Norwegian belongs to the North Germanic (or Scandinavian) group of languages, all of which developed from Old Norse, the language spoken during the Viking era, in the 9th century. The earliest written records of Old Norse, in the form of old runes, can be traced back to around AD 200 and represent the oldest inscriptions in any Germanic language. After the spread of Christianity among the Nordic people in the 12th century, the Roman alphabet gradually came into use. Between the 15th and the 19th century, while Norway was under Denmark's rule, Danish had official status and was used as the written language among the educated urban population.

The 19th century national revival movement resulted in the unique linguistic situation of modern Norway. The two official written forms of Norwegian, actually quite similar and understood by all speakers, are known as *Bokmål* bok·mawl (literally 'book language') and *Nynorsk* new·nawrsk (or 'new Norwegian'). The former developed as the urban-Norwegian variety of Danish, with spelling adapted to reflect Norwegian sounds. The latter is based on the rural dialects spoken by the common people during Danish rule, and draws on the heritage of Old Norwegian. Both varieties are written standards, and are used in written communication only. The spoken language has numerous local dialects. Both written forms are represented in schools, administration and the media. *Bokmål* is predominant in the cities, while *Nynorsk* is more common in the western fjords and the central mountains. It's estimated that out of the 5 million speakers of Norwegian around 85% use *Bokmål* and about 15% use *Nynorsk*.

If the differences in some Norwegian spellings are making you go *berserk* (which, by the way, is a word originating from Old Norse), you should know that as part of Norwegian linguistic policy, many words have two or more officially authorised spellings, and people can choose elements of either written form.

pronunciation

vowel sounds

Length is a distinctive feature of the vowel sounds in Norwegian, as each vowel can be either long or short. Generally, they're long when followed by one consonant and short when followed by two or more consonants. The length of vowels often affects meaning, as in *mat* maat (food) and *matt* mat (faint), or *sur* soor (bad mood) and *surr* sur (confusion).

symbol	english equivalent	norwegian example	transliteration
a	run	*katt*	kat
aa	father	*dag*	daag
ai	aisle	*jeg*	yai
aw	saw	*dato*	*daa·*taw
e	bet	*mett*	met
ee	see	*fin*	feen
eu	nurse	*øre*	*eu·*re
ew	ee pronounced with a flared upper lip	*dyr*	dewr
ey	as in 'bet', but longer	*penger*	peyng·er
i	hit	*litt*	lit
o	pot	*noe*	no·e
oo	zoo	*mulig*	moo·li
ow	cow	*Europa*	ow·roo·pa
oy	toy	*boikott*	boy·kot
u	put	*ku*	ku

consonant sounds

As shown in the table below, Norwegian consonants all have equivalents in English.

symbol	english equivalent	norwegian example	transliteration
b	bed	*bord*	boor
ch	cheat	*kjempe*	*chem*·pe
d	dog	*dere*	*de*·re
f	fat	*flere*	*fle*·re
g	go	*gul*	gool
h	hat	*hus*	hoos
k	kit	*kabel*	*ka*·bel
l	lot	*lys*	lews
m	man	*mange*	*mang*·e
n	not	*Norge*	*nawr*·ge
ng	ring	*ting*	ting
p	pet	*pølse*	*peul*·se
r	red	*rabatt*	ra·*bat*
s	sun	*sol*	sol
sh	shot	*sjø*	sheu
t	top	*topp*	top
v	very	*være*	*ve*·re
y	yes	*jente*	*yen*·te

word stress

Most Norwegian words have stress on the first syllable, and sometimes there's more than one stressed syllable in a word. Words of Latin origin tend to have stress on the last syllable, though. In the pronunciation guides throughout this chapter, the stressed syllables are always in italics.

basics

language difficulties

Do you speak English?
Snakker du engelsk? — sna·ker doo *eyng*·elsk

Do you understand?
Forstår du? — fawr·*stawr* doo

I understand.
Jeg forstår. — yai fawr·*stawr*

I don't understand.
Jeg forstår ikke. — yai fawr·*stawr* i·key

What does (*fint*) mean?
Hva betyr (fint)? — vaa be·*tewr* (feent)

How do you ...? — *Hvordan ...?* — vor·dan ...
  pronounce this — *uttales dette* — ut·*taa*·les de·*tey*
  write (*morsom*) — *skrives (morsom)* — *skree*·ves (*mawr*·som)

Could you please ...? — *Kan du ...?* — kan doo ...
  repeat that — *gjenta det* — *yen*·taa de
  speak more slowly — *snakke langsommere* — *sna*·key *lang*·so·me·re
  write it down — *skrive det* — *skree*·ve de

essentials

Yes.	*Ja.*	yaa
No.	*Nei.*	ney
Please.	*Vær så snill.*	veyr saw snil
Thank you (very much).	*(Tusen) Takk.*	(*too*·sen) tak
You're welcome.	*Ingen årsak.*	*ing*·en *awr*·saak
Excuse me.	*Unnskyld.*	*ewn*·shewl
Sorry.	*Beklager, tilgi meg.*	bey·*klaa*·geyr *til*·yee mai

numbers

0	null	nool	16	seksten	sai·sten
1	en	en	17	sytten	sew·ten
2	to	taw	18	atten	a·ten
3	tre	trey	19	nitten	nee·ten
4	fire	fee·re	20	tjue	shoo·e
5	fem	fem	21	tjueen	shoo·e·en
6	seks	seks	22	tjueto	shoo·e·taw
7	sju	shoo	30	tretti	trey·tee
8	åtte	aw·te	40	førti	feur·tee
9	ni	nee	50	femti	fem·tee
10	ti	tee	60	seksti	seks·tee
11	elleve	el·ve	70	sytti	sew·tee
12	tolv	tawl	80	åtti	aw·tee
13	tretten	trey·ten	90	nitti	nee·tee
14	fjorten	fyaw·ten	100	hundre	hun·dre
15	femten	fem·ten	1000	tusen	tu·sen

time & dates

What time is it?	Hva er klokka?	vaa eyr klaw·ka
It's one o'clock.	Klokka er ett.	klaw·ka eyr et
It's (two) o'clock.	Klokka er (to).	klaw·ka eyr (taw)
Quarter past (one).	Kvart over (ett).	kvaat aw·ver (et)
Half past (one).	Halv (to). (lit: half two)	haal (taw)
Quarter to (eight).	Kvart på (åtte).	kvaat paw (aw·te)
At what time ...?	Når ...?	nawr ...
At ...	Klokka ...	klaw·ka ...
in the morning	om formiddagen	awm fawr·mi·dan
in the afternoon	om ettermiddagen	awm e·ter·mi·dan
in the evening	om kvelden	awm kve·len
Monday	mandag	maan·daa
Tuesday	tirsdag	teers·daa
Wednesday	onsdag	awns·daa
Thursday	torsdag	tawrs·daa
Friday	fredag	frey·daa
Saturday	lørdag	leu·daa
Sunday	søndag	seun·daa

basics – NORWEGIAN

255

January	januar	yaa·nu·*aar*
February	februar	fe·broo·*aar*
March	mars	maars
April	april	aa·*preel*
May	mai	mai
June	juni	*yoo*·nee
July	juli	*yoo*·lee
August	august	ow·*goost*
September	september	sep·*tem*·ber
October	oktober	awk·*taw*·ber
November	november	naw·*veym*·ber
December	desember	de·*seym*·ber

What date is it today?
Hvilken dato er det i dag?   veel·keyn *daa*·taw eyr de ee daag

It's (15 December).
Det er den (femtende desember).   de eyr den (*fem*·te·ne de·*seym*·ber)

| **since (May)** | siden (mai) | *see*·den (mai) |
| **until (June)** | til (juni) | til (*yoo*·nee) |

last ...

night	i natt	ee nat
week	sist uke	sist *oo*·ke
month	sist måned	sist *maw*·ne
year	i fjor	ee fyor

next ...   neste ...   *nes*·te ...

week	uke	*oo*·ke
month	måned	*maw*·ne
year	år	awr

yesterday ...   i går ...   ee gawr ...

morning	morges	*maw*·res
afternoon	ettermiddag	e·*ter*·mee·daa
evening	kveld	kvel

tomorrow ...   i morgen ...   ee *maw*·ren ...

morning	tidlig	*teed*·lee
afternoon	ettermiddag	e·*ter*·mee·daa
evening	kveld	kvel

weather

What's the weather like?
    Hvordan er været?   *vor·dan eyr veyr·re*

It's ...

cloudy	*Det er overskyet.*	de eyr *aw*·ver·shew·et
cold	*Det er kaldt.*	de eyr kalt
hot	*Det er veldig varmt.*	de eyr *vel*·dee varmt
warm	*Det er varmt.*	de eyr varmt
raining	*Det regner.*	de *rai*·ner
snowing	*Det snør.*	de sneur
sunny	*Solen skinner.*	*saw*·len *shi*·ner
windy	*Det blåser.*	de *blaw*·ser
spring	*vår*	vawr
summer	*sommer*	*saw*·mer
autumn	*høst*	heust
winter	*vinter*	*veen*·ter

border crossing

I'm here ...	*Jeg ...*	yai ...
in transit	*skal videre med fly*	skal *vee*·de·re mey flew
on business	*er på forretningsreise*	eyr paw faw·*ret*·neengs·*rai*·se
on holiday	*er på ferie*	eyr paw *fe*·ree·e
I'm here for ...	*Jeg skal være her i ...*	yai skal *vey*·re heyr ee ...
(10) days	*(ti) dager*	(tee) *daa*·ger
(three) weeks	*(tre) uker*	(trey) *oo*·ker
(two) months	*(to) måneder*	(taw) *maw*·ner

I'm going to (Hamar).
    Jeg skal til (Hamar).   yai skal til (*haa*·mar)

I'm staying at the (Grand Hotel).
    Jeg bor på (Grand hotell).   yai boor paw (graan hoo·*tel*)

I have nothing to declare.
    Jeg har ingenting å fortelle.   yai haar *ing*·en·teeng aw fawr·*taw*·le

I have something to declare.
    Jeg har noe å fortelle.   yai haar *naw*·e aw fawr·*taw*·le

That's (not) mine.
    Det er (ikke) mitt.   de eyr (*i*·key) mit

transport

tickets & luggage

Where can I buy a ticket?
Hvor kan jeg kjøpe billett?   vor kan yai *sheu*·pe bee·*let*

Do I need to book a seat?
Er det nødvendig å bestille   eyr de neu·*ven*·dee aw be·*sti*·le
sitteplass?   *see*·te·plas

One ... ticket	*Jeg vil gjerne ha ...*	yai vil *yer*·ne haa ...
(to Bergen), please.	*(til Bergen), takk.*	(til *ber*·gen) tak
one-way	*enveisbillett*	en·*veys*·bee·*let*
return	*returbillett*	re·*toor*·bi·*let*

I'd like to ... my	*Jeg vil gjerne ... min*	yai vil *yer*·ne ... meen
ticket, please.	*billett, takk.*	bee·*let* tak
cancel	*avbestille*	*av*·be·sti·le
change	*endre*	*en*·dre
collect	*hente*	*hen*·te
confirm	*bekrefte*	be·*kref*·te

I'd like a ... seat,	*Jeg vil gjerne ha ...*	yai vil *yer*·ne haa ...
please.	*plass, takk.*	plas tak
nonsmoking	*ikkerøyke*	*i*·key·*roy*·ke
smoking	*røyke*	*roy*·ke

How much is it?
Hvor mye koster det?   vor *mew*·e *kaws*·ter de

Is there air conditioning?
Er det luftkjøling?   eyr de *luft*·sheu·ling

Is there a toilet?
Er det toalett?   eyr de to·aa·*let*

How long does the trip take?
Hvor lenge tar reisen?   vor *leng*·e taar *rai*·sen

Is it a direct route?
Er det en direkterute?   eyr de en dee·*rek*·te·*roo*·te

I'd like a luggage locker.
Jeg vil gjerne ha en   yai vil *yer*·ne haa en
oppbevaringsboks.   awp·be·*vaa*·reengs·bawks

My luggage has been ...	Bagasjen min er ...	ba·*gaa*·shen meen eyr ...
damaged	skadet	ska·det
lost	blitt borte	blit *bawr*·te
stolen	stjålet	styaw·let

getting around

Where does flight (SK50) arrive?
Hvor ankommer flyrute (SK50)? vor an·*kaw*·mer flew·*roo*·te (es·kaw fem·tee)

Where does flight (SK50) depart?
Hvor går flyrute (SK50) fra? vor gawr flew·*roo*·te (es·kaw fem·tee) fra

Where's the ...?	Hvor er ...?	vor eyr ...
arrivals hall	ankomsthallen	an·*kawmst*·ha·len
departures hall	avgangshallen	av·gangs·ha·len
duty-free shop	tollfri butikk	tawl·free boo·tik
gate (12)	utgang (tolv)	oot·gang (tawl)

Is this the ... to (Oslo)?	Er dette ... til (Oslo)?	er de·*tey* ... til (os·law)
boat	båten	baw·ten
bus	bussen	bu·sen
plane	flyet	flew·e
train	toget	taw·ge

What time's the ... bus?	Når går ... buss?	nawr gawr ... bus
first	første	feur·ste
last	siste	si·ste
next	neste	ne·ste

At what time does it arrive/leave?
Når ankommer/går den? nawr an·*kaw*·mer/gawr den

How long will it be delayed?
Hvor mye er det forsinket? vor mew·e eyr de fawr·*sin*·ket

What station/stop is this?
Hvilke stasjon/stopp er dette? veel·key staa·*shawn*/stawp eyr de·*tey*

What's the next station/stop?
Hva er neste stasjon/stopp? vaa eyr nes·te staa·*shawn*/stawp

Does it stop at (Majorstua)?
Stopper denne på (Majorstua)? staw·per *dey*·ne paw (maa·*yoor*·stu·a)

Please tell me when we get to (Oslo).
Kan du si fra når vi kommer til (Oslo)? kan doo see fraa nawr vee *kaw*·mer til (os·law)

How long do we stop here?
Hvor lenge stopper vi her?   vor *leng*·e *staw*·per vee heyr

Is this seat available?
Er denne plassen ledig?   eyr *dey*·ne *pla*·sen le·dee

That's my seat.
Dette er min plass.   de·*tey* eyr meen plas

I'd like a taxi ...	*Jeg vil gjerne ha en drosje ...*	yai vil *yer*·ne haa en *draw*·shey ...
at (9am)	*klokka (ni om morgenen)*	*klaw*·ka (nee awm *mawr*·ge·nen)
now	*nå*	naw
tomorrow	*i morgen*	ee *maw*·ren

Is this taxi available?
Er denne drosjen ledig?   er *dey*·ne *draw*·sheyn le·dee

How much is it to ...?
Hvor mye koster det å kjøre til ...?   vor *mew*·e *kaws*·ter de aw *sheu*·re til ...

Please put the meter on.
Kan du være så snill å skru på taksameteret?   kan doo *vey*·re saw snil aw skroo paw tak·saa·*me*·te·re

Please take me to (this address).
Kan du kjøre meg til (denne adressen)?   kan doo *sheu*·re mai til (*dey*·ne a·*dre*·sen)

Please ...	*Vær så snill å ...*	veyr saw snil aw ...
slow down	*kjør litt saktere*	*sheur* lit *sak*·te·re
stop here	*stoppe her*	*sto*·pe heyr
wait here	*vente her*	*ven*·te heyr

car, motorbike & bicycle hire

I'd like to hire a ...	*Jeg vil gjerne leie en ...*	yai vil *yer*·ne *lai*·e en ...
bicycle	*sykkel*	*sew*·kel
car	*bil*	beel
motorbike	*motorsykkel*	maw·tor·*sew*·kel

with ...	*med ...*	mey ...
a driver	*sjåfør*	shaw·*feur*
air conditioning	*klimaanlegg*	*klee*·ma·an·leg
antifreeze	*frostvæske*	*frawst*·ves·ke
snow chains	*kjettinger*	*shey*·teeng·er

How much for ... hire?	Hvor mye koster det ...?	vor mew·e kaws·ter de ...
hourly	pr. time	per tee·me
daily	pr. dag	per daag
weekly	pr. uke	per oo·ke
air	luft	luft
oil	olje	ol·ye
petrol	bensin	ben·seen
tyres	dekk	dek

I need a mechanic.
Jeg trenger et verksted.   yai treng·er et verk·stey

I've run out of petrol.
Jeg har gått tom for bensin.   yai haar gawt tawm fawr ben·seen

I have a flat tyre.
Jeg har punktert.   yey haar poonk·tert

directions

Where's the ...?	Hvor er ...?	vor eyr ...
bank	banken	ban·ken
city centre	sentrum	sent·rum
hotel	hotellet	hoo·te·ley
market	torget	tawr·gey
police station	politistasjonen	po·lee·tee·sta·shaw·nen
post office	postkontoret	pawst·kawn·taw·rey
public toilet	offentlig toalett	aw·fent·lee to·aa·let
tourist office	turistinformasjon	tu·reest·in·fawr·ma·shawn

Is this the road to (Gol)?
Er dette veien til (Gol)?   eyr de·tey vai·en til (gol)

Can you show me (on the map)?
Kan du vise meg (på kartet)?   kan doo vee·sey mai (paw kar·te)

What's the address?
Hva er adressen?   va eyr aa·dre·seyn

How far is it?
Hvor langt er det?   vor langt eyr de

How do I get there?
Hvordan kommer jeg meg dit?   vor·dan kaw·mer yai mai deet

NORSK – transport

Turn ...	Ta av ...	taa av ...
at the corner	på hjørne	paw *yeur*·ney
at the traffic lights	i lyskrysset	ee *lews*·krew·sey
left/right	til venstre/høyre	til *vens*·trey/*hoy*·rey

It's ...	Det er ...	de eyr ...
behind ...	bak ...	baak ...
far away	langt	laangt
here	her	heyr
in front of ...	foran ...	*faw*·ran ...
left	venstre	*vens*·trey
near to ...	nær ...	neyr ...
next to ...	ved siden av ...	vey *see*·den aav ...
on the corner	på hjørne	paw *yeur*·ney
opposite ...	ovenfor ...	*aw*·ven·fawr ...
right	høyre	*hoy*·rey
straight ahead	rett fram	ret fram
there	der	deyr

by bus	med buss	mey bus
by taxi	med drosje	mey *draw*·shey
by train	med tog	mey tawg
on foot	til fots	til fots

north	nord	noor
south	sør	seur
east	øst	eust
west	vest	vest

signs

Inngang/Utgang	*in*·gang/*oot*·gang	**Entrance/Exit**
Åpen/Stengt	*aw*·pen/stengt	**Open/Closed**
Rom ledig	rom *le*·dee	**Rooms Available**
Fult	fult	**No Vacancies**
Informasjon	in·fawr·ma·*shawn*	**Information**
Politistasjon	po·lee·*tee*·sta·shawn	**Police Station**
Forbudt	fawr·*boot*	**Prohibited**
Toaletter/WC	to·aa·*le*·ter/*ve*·se	**Toilets**
Herrer	*hey*·rer	**Men**
Damer	*da*·mer	**Women**
Varmt/Kaldt	varmt/kalt	**Hot/Cold**

262

accommodation

finding accommodation

Where's a ...?	Hvor finnes det ...?	vor fi·nes de ...
camping ground	en campingplass	en keym·ping·plas
guesthouse	et gjestgiveri	et yest·gi·ve·ree
hotel	et hotell	et hoo·tel
youth hostel	et ungdomsherberge	et ong·dawms·heyr·beyrg

Can you recommend somewhere ...?	Kan du anbefale et ... sted?	kan doo an·be·fa·le et ... stey
cheap	billig	bi·lee
good	godt	gawt
nearby	nærliggende	neyr·li·gen·de

I'd like to book a room, please.
Jeg vil gjerne bestille et rom. yai vil yer·ne be·sti·le et rom

I have a reservation.
Jeg har bestilt. yai har be·stilt

My name's ...
Jeg heter ... yai he·ter ...

Do you have a ... room?	Finnes det et ...?	fi·nes de et ...
single	enkeltrom	eyn·kelt·rom
double	dobbeltrom	daw·belt·rom
twin	tomansrom	taw·mans·rom

How much is it per ...?	Hvor mye koster det pr. ...?	vor mew·e kaws·ter de peyr ...
night	dag	daag
person	person	peyr·son

Can I pay by ...?	Tar du imot ...?	tar doo ee·mot ...
credit card	kredittkort	kre·dit·kawrt
travellers cheque	reisesjekker	rai·se·shey·ker

I'd like to stay for (two) nights.
Jeg har tenkt å bli her i (to) dager.   yai har tenkt aw bli heyr ee (taw) *da*·ger

From (July 2) to (July 6).
Fra (andre juli) til (sjette juli).   fra (*an*·dre *yoo*·lee) til (*shey*·te *yoo*·lee)

Can I see it?
Kan jeg få se det?   kan yai faw se de

Am I allowed to camp here?
Kan jeg slå opp telt her?   kan yai slaw awp telt heyr

Is there a camp site nearby?
Er det en campingplass i nærheten?   eyr de en *kam*·ping·plas ee *neyr*·he·ten

requests & queries

When's breakfast served?
Når serveres frokost?   nawr seyr·*vey*·res *fro*·kost

Where's breakfast served?
Hvor serveres frokost?   vor seyr·*vey*·res *fro*·kost

Please wake me at (seven).
Vær så snill å vekke meg klokka (sju).   veyr saw snil aw *vey*·ke mai *klaw*·ka (shoo)

Could I have my key, please?
Kan jeg få nøkkelen, takk?   kan yai faw *neu*·ke·len tak

Can I get another (blanket)?
Kan jeg få et ekstra (teppe)?   kan yai faw et *eks*·tra (*te*·pe)

This ... isn't clean.	Dette ... er ikke rent.	de·tey ... eyr i·key rent
sheet	lakenet	la·ke·net
towel	håndkledet	hawn·kle

Is there a/an ...?	Er det ...?	eyr de ...
elevator	heis	hais
safe	safe	saif

The room is too ...	Rommet er for ...	ro·me eyr fawr ...
expensive	dyrt	dewrt
noisy	bråkete	braw·ke·te
small	lite	lee·te

The ... doesn't work.	... virker ikke.	... vir·ker i·key
air conditioning	Luftkjøling	luft·sheu·ling
fan	Viften	vif·ten
toilet	Toalettet	to·aa·le·te

checking out

What time is checkout?
Når må jeg sjekke ut?　　　　　　nawr maw yai *shey*·ke oot

Can I leave my luggage here?
Kan jeg la bagasjen stå her?　　　kan yai laa ba·*gaa*·shen staw heyr

Could I have	*Kan jeg få tilbake*	kan yai faw til·*baa*·ke
my ..., please?	*..., takk?*	... tak
deposit	*depositumet mitt*	de·*po*·see·tu·me mit
passport	*passet mitt*	*pa*·se mit
valuables	*verdisakene mine*	ver·*dee*·sa·ke·ne *mee*·ne

communications & banking

the internet

Where's the local Internet café?
Finnes det en Internettkafé her?　　*fi*·nes de en *in*·ter·net·ka·*fe* heyr

How much is it per hour?
Hvor mye koster det pr. time?　　vor *mew*·e *kaws*·ter de peyr *tee*·me

I'd like to ...	*Jeg vil gjerne ...*	yai vil *yer*·ne ...
check my email	*sjekke e-post*	*shey*·ke *e*·pawst
get Internet access	*bruke Internett*	*broo*·ke *in*·ter·net
use a printer	*ta utskrift*	taa *ut*·skrift
use a scanner	*bruke skanner*	*broo*·ke *ska*·ner

mobile/cell phone

I'd like a ...	*Jeg vil gjerne ...*	yai vil *yer*·ne ...
mobile/cell phone	*leie en*	*ley*·e en
for hire	*mobiltelefon*	mo·*beel*·te·le·*fon*
SIM card for your	*ha et norsk*	haa et nawrsk
network	*SIM-kort*	*seem* kawrt

What are the rates?　*Hva koster det?*　va *kaws*·ter de

telephone

What's your phone number?
Hva er ditt telefonnummer?   va eyr dit te·le·*fon*·no·mer

The number is ...
Nummeret er ...   *no*·me·re eyr ...

Where's the nearest public phone?
Hvor er nærmeste telefonkiosk?   vor eyr *neyr*·me·ste te·le·*fon*·shosk

I'd like to buy a phonecard.
Jeg ønsker å kjøpe et telefonkort.   yai *eun*·sker aw *shaw*·pe et te·le·*fon*·kawrt

I want to ...	*Jeg vil ...*	yai vil ...
call (Singapore)	*ringe til (Singapore)*	*ring*·e til (*seeng*·aa·pawr)
make a local call	*ringe et lokalt nummer*	*ring*·e et lo·*kalt* no·mer
reverse the charges	*ringe på*	*ring*·e paw
	noteringsoverføring	no·*te*·rings·aw·ver·*feu*·ring

How much does	*Hvor mye*	vor *mew*·e
... cost?	*koster ...?*	*kaws*·ter ...
a (three)-minute	*en (tre) minutters*	en (*trey*) mee·*nu*·ters
call	*samtale*	*sam*·ta·le
each extra minute	*hvert ekstra minutt*	veyrt *eks*·tra mee·*nut*

It's (15) kroner per (minute).
(Femten) kroner pr. (minutt).   (*fem*·ten) *kraw*·ner peyr (mee·*nut*)

post office

I want to send a ...	*Jeg vil sende ...*	yey vil *se*·ne ...
fax	*en faks*	en faks
letter	*et brev*	et brev
parcel	*en pakke*	en *pa*·ke
postcard	*et postkort*	et *pawst*·kawrt

I want to buy ...	Kan jeg få ...	kan yai faw ...
an envelope	en konvolutt	en kawn·vaw·lut
stamps	frimerker	free·mer·ker

Please send it	Vennligst send	ven·list sen
(to Australia) by ...	(til Australia) med ...	(til ow·stra·lee·a) mey ...
airmail	luftpost	luft·pawst
express mail	ekspresspost	eks·pres·pawst
registered mail	rekommandert post	re·ko·man·deyrt pawst
surface mail	overflatepost	aw·ver·fla·te·pawst

| Is there any mail for me? | Er det post til meg? | eyr de pawst til mai |

bank

Where's a/an ...?	Er det ...?	eyr de ...
ATM	en minibank	en mi·nee·bank
foreign exchange office	valutaveksling	va·lu·ta·vek·sling

I'd like to ...	Jeg vil gjerne ...	yai vil yer·ne ...
Where can I ...?	Hvor kan jeg ...?	vor kan yai ...
arrange a transfer	overføre	aw·ver·feu·re
cash a cheque	heve en sjekk	hey·ve en sheyk
change a travellers cheque	heve en reisesjekk	hey·ve en rai·se·sheyk
change money	veksle penger	vek·sle peyng·er
get a cash advance	få kontantforskudd	faw kon·tant·fawr·skud
withdraw money	ta ut penger	ta oot peyng·er

What's the ...?	Hva ...?	va ...
charge for that	koster det	kaws·ter de
commission	er gebyret	eyr ge·boo·re
exchange rate	er valutakursen	eyr va·lu·ta·kur·sen

It's ...	Det ...	de ...
(12) kroner	koster (tolv) kroner	kaws·ter (tawl) kraw·ner
free	er gratis	eyr gra·tis

What time does the bank open?
Når åpner banken?   nawr awp·ner ban·ken

Has my money arrived yet?
Har pengene mine kommet ennå?   har peng·e·ne mee·ne kaw·met e·naw

sightseeing

getting in

What time does it open/close?
Når åpner/stenger det?
nawr *awp*·ner/*steng*·er de

What's the admission charge?
Hvor mye koster det å komme inn?
vor *mew*·e *kos*·ter de aw *kaw*·me in

Is there a discount for children/students?
Er det barnerabatt/studentrabatt?
eyr de *bar*·ney·ra·bat/stu·*dent*·ra·bat

I'd like a ...	*Jeg vil gjerne ha ...*	yai vil *yer*·ne haa ...
catalogue	*en katalog*	en ka·ta·*lawg*
guide	*en guide*	en gaid
local map	*et lokalkart*	et lo·*kal*·kart

I'd like to see ...
Jeg vil gjerne se ...
yai vil *yer*·ne se ...

What's that?
Hva er det?
va eyr de

Can I take a photo?
Kan jeg ta bilde?
kan yai ta *bil*·dey

tours

When's the next...?	*Når går neste ...?*	nawr gawr *nes*·te ...
day trip	*dagstur*	*dags*·toor
tour	*tur*	toor

Is ... included?	*Er ... inkludert?*	eyr ... ing·kloo·*deyrt*
accommodation	*losji*	lo·*shee*
the admission charge	*inngangsbillett*	*in*·gangs·bee·*let*
food	*mat*	maat
transport	*transport*	trans·*pawrt*

How long is the tour?
Hvor lang tid tar turen?
vor lang tee tar *too*·ren

What time should we be back?
Når vil vi være tilbake?
nawr vil vee *vey*·re til·*baa*·ke

castle	slott	slawt
cathedral	katedral	ka-te-*dral*
church	kirke	*shir*-ke
main square	stortorget	stor-*tawr*-ge
monastery	kloster	*klaws*-ter
monument	monument	maw-noo-*ment*
museum	museum	moo-se-um
old city	gamlebyen	gam-le-*boo*-en
palace	slott	slawt
ruins	ruiner	roo-*ee*-ner
stadium	stadion	*sta*-dee-on
statues	statuer	sta-*too*-er

shopping

enquiries

Where's a ...?	Hvor er det ...?	vor eyr de ...
bank	bank	bank
bookshop	bokhandel	bok-*han*-del
camera shop	fotobutikk	fo-to-boo-*tik*
department store	varemagasin	va-re-ma-ga-*sin*
grocery store	matbutikk	*maat*-boo-tik
market	marked	*mar*-ked
newsagency	kiosk	shosk
supermarket	matbutikk	*maat*-boo-tik

Where can I buy (a padlock)?
Hvor kan jeg kjøpe (en hengelås)? vor kan yai *sheu*-pe (en *heng*-e-laws)

I'm looking for ...
Jeg leter etter ... yai *ley*-ter e-*ter* ...

Can I look at it?
Kan jeg få se på det? — kan yai faw se paw de

Do you have any others?
Har du andre? — har doo *an*·dre

Does it have a guarantee?
Er det med garanti? — eyr de mey ga·ran·*tee*

Can I have it sent overseas?
Kan jeg få det sendt til utlandet? — kan yai faw de sent til *oot*·lan·de

Can I have my ... repaired?
Kan jeg få min ... reparert? — kan yai faw meen ... re·paa·*rert*

It's faulty.
Den er ødelagt. — den eyr *eud*·lagt

I'd like ..., please.	*Jeg vil gjerne ..., takk.*	yai vil *yer*·ne ... tak
a bag	*ha en veske*	haa en *veys*·ke
a refund	*ha refusjon*	haa re·foo·*shawn*
to return this	*returnere dette*	re·toor·*ne*·re *dey*·te

paying

How much is it?
Hvor mye koster det? — vor *mew*·e *kaws*·ter de

Can you write down the price?
Kan du skrive ned prisen? — kan doo *skree*·ve ned *pree*·sen

That's too expensive.
Det er for dyrt. — de eyr fawr dewrt

What's your lowest price?
Hva er din absolutt laveste pris? — va eyr deen ab·saw·*lut* la·ves·te prees

I'll give you (15) kroner.
Jeg gir deg (femten) kroner. — yai geer dey (*fem*·ten) *kraw*·ner

There's a mistake in the bill.
Det er en feil på regningen. — de eyr en fail paw *rai*·ning·en

Do you accept ...?	*Tar du imot ...?*	taar doo ee·*mot* ...
credit cards	*kredittkort*	kre·*dit*·kawrt
debit cards	*debetkort*	*dey*·bet·kawrt
travellers cheques	*reisesjekker*	*rai*·se·*shey*·ker

I'd like ..., please.	Jeg vil gjerne ha igjen ..., takk.	yai vil yer·ne haa ee·yen ... tak
a receipt	kvittering	kvee·te·ring
my change	vekslepenger	vek·sle·peyng·er

clothes & shoes

Can I try it on?
Kan jeg prøve denne? — kan yai praw·ve dey·ne

My size is (42).
Jeg bruker størrelse (førtito). — yai broo·ker steu·rel·se (fawr·tee·taw)

It doesn't fit.
Den passer ikke. — den paa·ser i·key

small	liten	lee·ten
medium	medium	mey·di·um
large	stor	stor

books & music

I'd like a ...	Kan jeg få en ...?	kan yai faw en ...
newspaper (in English)	(engelsk) avis	(eyng·elsk) a·vees
pen	penn	pen

Is there an English-language bookshop?
Finnes det en bokhandel med engelske bøker? — fi·nes de en bok·han·del mey eyng·els·ke beu·ker

I'm looking for something by (Edvard Grieg/Henrik Ibsen).
Jeg ser etter noe av (Edvard Grieg/Henrik Ibsen). — yai seyr e·ter naw·e av (ed·var grig/hen·rik ip·sen)

Can I listen to this?
Kan jeg høre på denne? — kan yai heu·re paw dey·ne

photography

Could you ...?	Kan du ...?	kan doo ...
burn a CD from	brenne en CD	brey·ne en se·de
my memory card	fra minnekortet	fra mi·ne·kawr·te
develop this film	fremkalle	frem·ka·le
load my film	sette i film for meg	sey·te ee film fawr mai

I need a/an ... film	Jeg vil gjerne ha ...	yai vil yer·ne haa ...
for this camera.	film til dette kameraet.	film til dey·te ka·me·raa
APS	APS	aa·pe·es
B&W	svart-hvitt	svart·vit
colour	farge	far·ge
slide	lysbilde	lews·bil·de
(200) speed	(tohundre)	(taw·hun·dre)
	lukkerhastighet	lo·ker·has·tee·het

| When will it be ready? | Når er den ferdig? | nawr eyr den fer·dee |

meeting people

greetings, goodbyes & introductions

Hello.	God dag.	go·daag
Hi.	Hei.	hai
Good night.	God natt.	go·nat
Goodbye.	Ha det.	haa·de
See you later.	Vi sees senere.	vee sees se·ne·re

Mr	herr	heyr
Mrs	fru	froo
Miss	frøken	freu·ken

How are you?
Hvordan har du det?   vor·dan haar doo de

Fine, thanks. And you?
Bra, takk. Og du?   braa tak aw doo

What's your name?
Hva heter du? — vaa *hey*·ter doo

My name is ...
Jeg heter ... — yai *hey*·ter ...

I'm pleased to meet you.
Hyggelig å treffe deg. — *hew*·ge·lee aw *tre*·fe dai

This is my ...	Dette er min ...	dey·te eyr meen ...
boyfriend	kjæreste	shey·re·ste
brother	bror	bror
daughter	datter	da·ter
father	far	faar
friend	venn/venninne m/f	ven/ve·ni·ne
girlfriend	kjæreste	shey·re·ste
husband	mann	man
mother	mor	mawr
partner (intimate)	samboer	sam·bo·er
sister	søster	seus·ter
son	sønn	seun
wife	kone	kaw·ne

Here's my ...	Her er min ...	heyr eyr meen ...
What's your ...?	Hva er din ...?	vaa eyr deen ...
address	adresse	a·dre·se
email address	e-postadresse	ey·post·a·dre·se
fax number	faksnummer	faks·no·mer
phone number	telefonnummer	te·le·fon·no·mer

occupations

What's your occupation? *Hva driver du med?* — vaa *dree*·ver doo mey

I'm a/an ...	Jeg er ...	yai eyr ...
artist	kunstner	koonst·ner
businessperson	forretningsdrivende	faw·ret·nings·dri·ven·de
farmer	bonde	baw·ne
manual worker	kropsarbeider	krawps·ar·bai·der
office worker	kontoransatt	kon·tor·an·sat
scientist	forsker	fawr·sker
student	student	stu·dent
tradesperson	håndtverker	hawnt·ver·ker

background

Where are you from?	*Hvor er du fra?*	vor eyr doo fra
I'm from ...	*Jeg er fra ...*	yai eyr fraa ...
Australia	*Australia*	ow-*stra*-li-aa
Canada	*Canada*	*ka*-na-da
England	*England*	*eyng*-lan
Ireland	*Irland*	*ir*-lan
New Zealand	*Ny Zealand*	new *se*-lan
the USA	*USA*	oo-es-*aa*
Are you married?	*Er du gift?*	eyr doo yft
I'm married.	*Jeg er gift.*	yai eyr yft
I'm single.	*Jeg er enslig.*	yai eyr *en*-slee

age

How old ...?	*Hvor gammel ...?*	vor *ga*-mel er ...
are you	*du*	doo
is your daughter	*din datter*	din *da*-ter
is your son	*din sønn*	din seun
I'm ... years old.		
Jeg er ... år gammel.		yai eyr ... awr *ga*-mel
He/She is ... years old.		
Han/Hun er ... år gammel.		han/hun eyr ... awr *ga*-mel

feelings

I'm (not) ...	*Jeg ... (ikke).*	yai ... (*ee*-key)
Are you ...?	*Er du ...?*	eyr du ...
happy	*lykkelig*	*lu*-ke-lee
hot	*varm*	varm
hungry	*sulten*	*sool*-ten
sad	*nedfor*	*ney*-fawr
thirsty	*tørst*	teurst
tired	*trøtt*	treut
Are you cold?	*Fryser du?*	*fru*-ser doo
I'm (not) cold.	*Jeg fryser (ikke).*	yai *fru*-ser (*i*-key)

entertainment

going out

Where can I find ...?	Hvor er det ...?	vor eyr de ...
clubs	klubber	kloo-ber
gay venues	homseklubber	hom-se-kloo-ber
pubs	barer	ba-rer

I feel like going to a/the...	Jeg vil gjerne gå på ...	yai vil yer-ne gaw paw ...
concert	konsert	kawn-sert
movies	kino	shee-naw
party	fest	fest
restaurant	restaurant	res-tu-rang
theatre	teater	te-aa-ter

interests

Do you like ...?	Liker du ...?	lee-ker doo ...
I (don't) like ...	Jeg liker (ikke) ...	yai lee-ker (i-key) ...
art	kunst	koonst
cooking	matlaging	maat-la-ging
movies	å gå på kino	aw gaw paw shee-naw
nightclubs	nattklubber	nat-kloo-ber
reading	å lese	aw ley-se
shopping	å handle	aw hand-le
sport	sport	spawrt
travelling	å reise	aw rai-se

Do you like to ...?	Liker du å ...?	lee-ker doo aw ...
dance	danse	dan-se
go to concerts	gå på konserter	gaw paw kawn-ser-ter
listen to music	høre på musikk	heu-re paw moo-sik

food & drink

finding a place to eat

Can you recommend a ...?	Kan du anbefale en ...?	kan doo an·be·fa·le en ...
bar	bar	baar
café	kafé	ka·fe
restaurant	restaurant	res·tu·rang

I'd like ..., please.	Jeg vil gjerne ha ..., takk.	yai vil yer·ne ha ... tak
a table for (four)	et bord til (fire)	et bawr til (fee·re)
the nonsmoking section	på ikke-røyke	paw i·key·roy·ke
the smoking section	der man kan røyke	deyr man kan roy·ke

ordering food

breakfast	frokost	fro·kost
lunch	lunsj	loonsh
dinner	middag	mi·da
snack	noe godt	naw·e gawt
today's menu	dagens meny	da·gens me·ni
today's special	dagens rett	da·gens ret

eat	spise	spi·se
drink	drikke	dri·ke

What would you recommend?
Hva vil du anbefale?   va vil doo an·be·fa·le

I'd like (the) ...	Kan jeg få ..., takk.	kan yai faw ... tak
bill	regningen	rai·ning·en
drink list	vinlisten	veen·lis·ten
menu	menyen	me·new·en
that dish	den retten	den re·ten

drinks

(cup of) coffee ...	(en kopp) kaffe ...	(en kawp) kaa·fe ...
(cup of) tea ...	(en kopp) te ...	(en kawp) te ...
with milk	med melk	mey melk
without sugar	med sukker	mey soo·ker
(orange) juice	(appelsin)jus	(a·pel·seen·)joos
soft drink	brus	broos
boiled water	kokt vann	kokt van
mineral water	mineralvann	mi·ne·ral·van
sparkling mineral water	Farris	fa·ris
water	vann	van

in the bar

I'll have ...
Jeg vil ha ... — yai vil haa ...

I'll buy you a drink.
Jeg spanderer en dram på deg. — yai span·de·rer en dram paw dai

What would you like?
Hva vil du ha? — va vil doo ha

Cheers!
Skål! — skawl

brandy	brandy	bran·dee
cocktail	cocktail	kawk·tail
cognac	konjakk	kon·yak
a shot of (whisky)	et glass (whisky)	et glas (vees·ki)
a ... of beer	... øl	... eul
bottle	en flaske	en flas·ke
glass	et glass	et glas
a bottle of ...	en flaske ...	en flas·ke ...
a glass of ...	et glass ...	et glas ...
red wine	rødvin	reu·veen
sparkling wine	musserende vin	mu·sey·ren·de veen
white wine	hvitvin	veet·veen

self-catering

What's the local speciality?
Hva er den lokale spesialiteten?　va eyr den lo-*ka*-le spe-see-a-lee-*te*-ten

What's that?
Hva er det?　va eyr de

How much is (a kilo of cheese)?
Hvor mye koster (et kilo ost)?　vor *mew*-e *kaws*-ter (et *shee*-lo ost)

I'd like ...	*Jeg tar ...*	yey taar ...
(100) grams	*(hundre) gram*	(*hun*-dre) gram
(two) kilos	*(to) kilo*	(taw) *shee*-lo
(three) pieces	*(tre) stykker*	(trey) *stew*-ker
(six) slices	*(seks) skiver*	(seks) *shee*-ver

Less.	*Mindre.*	*min*-dre
Enough.	*Nok.*	nawk
More. (countable)	*Flere.*	*fley*-re
More. (uncountable)	*Mer.*	meyr

special diets & allergies

Is there a vegetarian restaurant near here?
Finnes det en vegetariansk　*fi*-nes dey en ve-ge-ta-ree-*ansk*
restaurant i nærheten?　res-tu-*rang* ee *neyr*-he-ten

Do you have vegetarian food?
Har du vegetariansk mat her?　har doo ve-ge-ta-ree-*ansk* maat heyr

Could you prepare	*Kan du lage*	kan doo *la*-ge
a meal without ...?	*maten uten ...?*	*maa*-ten *oo*-ten ...
butter	*smør*	smeur
eggs	*egg*	eg
meat stock	*kjøttbuljong*	sheut-bul-*yong*

I'm allergic to ...	*Jeg er allergisk mot ...*	yai eyr a-*ler*-gisk mot ...
dairy produce	*melkeprodukt*	*mel*-ke-pro-*dukt*
gluten	*gluten*	*gloo*-ten
MSG	*MSG*	em-es-*ge*
nuts	*nøtter*	*neu*-ter
seafood	*sjømat*	*sheu*-maat

menu decoder

arme riddere	ar·me·*ri*·de·re	*bread dipped in batter, fried & served with jam*
benløse fugler	ben·*leu*·se *fou*·ler	*rolled slices of veal stuffed with minced meat*
blodpudding	*blaw*·pu·ding	*black pudding*
bløtkake	*bleut*·ka·ke	*rich sponge layer cake with whipped cream*
brissel	*bri*·sel	*sweetbread*
dyrestek	*dew*·re·stek	*roast venison*
fårikål	*faw*·ree·kawl	*lamb in cabbage stew*
fenalår n	*fey*·na·lawr	*cured leg of lamb*
fiskeboller	*fis*·ke·bo·ler	*fish dumpling*
fiskegrateng	*fis*·ke·gra·teng	*fish casserole*
fiskekake	*fis*·ke·ka·ke	*fried fish dumpling*
fiskepudding	*fis*·ke·poo·ding	*fish pâté fried in a pan*
flatbrød n	*flat*·breu	*thin wafer of rye or barley*
fleskepannekake	*fles*·ke·pa·ne·*ka*·ke	*thick pancake with bacon, baked in the oven*
fleskepølse	*fles*·ke·peul·se	*pork sandwich spread*
fløtevaffel	*fleu*·te·va·fel	*cream-enriched waffle (served with jam)*
gaffelbiter	*ga*·fel·bee·ter	*salt- & sugar-cured sprat or herring fillets*
gammalost	*ga*·mel·ost	*hard cheese with strong flavour*
geitost	*geyt*·ost	*sweet brown goat cheese*
gravlaks	*grav*·laks	*salt- & sugar-cured salmon with dill (served with mustard sauce)*
gryte(rett)	*grew*·te(·ret)	*casserole*
julekake	*yu*·le·ka·ke	*rich fruit cake*
kalvetunge	*kal*·ve·tung·e	*calf's tongue*
kaviar	ka·vi·*ar*	*smoked cod-roe spread*

koldtbord n	kolt-bawr	cold buffet (fish, meat, cheese & salad)
kjøttkake	sheut-ka-ke	small hamburger steak
kjøttpålegg n	sheut-paw-leg	cold meat cuts
kjøttpudding	sheut-poo-ding	meat loaf
klippfisk	klip-fisk	salted & dried cod
kringle	kring-le	ring-twisted bread with raisins
kålruletter	kawl-ru-le-ter	minced meat in cabbage leaves
lapskaus	laps-kows	thick stew of diced meat, potatoes, onions & other vegetables
lefse	lef-se	traditional thin griddle cake (without eggs)
lutefisk	lu-te-fisk	dried cod, boiled or steamed & served with potatoes, peas & white sauce
medaljong	me-dal-yong	small round fillet
mysost	mews-ost	brown whey cheese
napoleonskake	na-po-le-ons-ka-ke	custard slice
pinnekjøtt	pi-ne-sheut	smoked, salted & steamed mutton ribs
plukkfisk	plok-fisk	poached fish in white sauce
postei	po-stai	meat, liver or fish pâté
pultost	pult-ost	soft fermented cheese with caraway seeds
pyttipanne	pew-tee-pa-ne	leftover meat & potatoes fried with onions
rakefisk	ra-ke-fisk	cured & fermented fish (often trout)
rislapper	ris-la-per	small sweet rice cake
rødgrøt	reu-grawt	fruit pudding with custard
sildesalat	si-le-sa-lat	herring salad
spekesild	spe-ke-sil	salted, cured herring
surkål	soor-kawl	boiled cabbage flavoured with caraway seeds, sugar & vinegar

emergencies

basics

Help!	Hjelp!	yelp
Stop!	Stopp!	stawp
Go away!	Forsvinn!	fawr·svin
Thief!	Tyv!	teev
Fire!	Brann!	bran
Watch out!	Pass!	pas

Call ...!	Ring ...!	ring ...
a doctor	en lege	en le·ge
an ambulance	etter sykebil	e·ter sew·ke·bil
the police	politiet	po·lee·tee·ay

It's an emergency!
Dette er en nødsituasjon! de·tey eyr en neud·si·tu·a·shawn

Could you help me, please?
Kan du være så snill å hjelpe meg? kan doo vey·re saw snil aw yel·pe mai

I have to use the telephone.
Jeg må låne telefonen. yai maw law·ne te·le·fo·nen

I'm lost.
Jeg har gått meg vill. yai har gawt mai vil

Where are the toilets?
Hvor er toalettene? vor eyr to·aa·le·te·ne

police

Where's the police station?
Hvor er politistasjonen? vor eyr po·lee·tee·sta·shaw·nen

I want to report an offence.
Jeg ønsker å rapportere noe ulovlig. yai eun·sker aw ra·pawr·te·re naw·e oo·lov·lee

I have insurance.
Jeg har forsikring. yai har fawr·si·kring

I've been ...	Jeg er blitt ...	yai eyr blit ...
assaulted	overfalt	aw·ver·falt
raped	voldtatt	vol·tat
robbed	rana	ra·na

I've lost my ...	Jeg har mistet ...	yai har *mis*·tet ...
backpack	*ryggsekken min*	*rewg*·se·ken meen
bags	*bagasjen min*	ba·*gaa*·shen meen
credit card	*kredittkortet mitt*	kre·*dit*·kawr·te mit
handbag	*vesken min*	*veys*·ken meen
jewellery	*smykkene mine*	*smew*·ke·ne *mee*·ne
money	*pengene mine*	*peng*·e·ne *mee*·ne
passport	*passet mitt*	*pa*·se mit
travellers cheques	*reisesjekkene mine*	*rai*·se·*shey*·ke·ne *mee*·ne
wallet	*lommeboken min*	*lo*·me·bo·ken meen

I want to contact my ...	Vær så snill å la meg få kontakte ...	veyr saw snil aw la mai faw kon·*tak*·te ...
consulate	*mitt konsulat*	mit kon·su·*lat*
embassy	*min ambassade*	meen am·ba·*sa*·de

health

medical needs

Where's the nearest ...?	Hvor er nærmeste ...?	vor eyr *neyr*·me·ste ...
dentist	*tannlege*	*tan*·le·ge
doctor	*lege*	*le*·ge
hospital	*sykehus*	*sew*·ke·hus
(night) pharmacist	*(nattåpent) apotek*	(*nat*·aw·pent) a·po·*tek*

I need a doctor (who speaks English).
Jeg trenger en lege
(som snakker engelsk).
yai *tren*·ger en *le*·ge
(som *sna*·ker *eyng*·elsk)

Could I see a female doctor?
Kan jeg få snakke med en
kvinnelig lege?
kan yai faw *sna*·ke mey en
kvi·ne·lee *le*·ge

I ran out of my medication.
Jeg har sluppet opp for medisiner.
yai har *slu*·pet awp fawr me·de·*see*·ner

symptoms, conditions & allergies

I'm sick.	*Jeg er syk.*	yai er sewk
It hurts here.	*Det gjør vondt her.*	de yeur vont heyr
I have nausea.	*Jeg er kvalm.*	yai er kvalm

I have (a) ...	*Jeg har ...*	yai har ...
asthma	*astma*	*as*-ma
bronchitis	*bronkitt*	*bron*-kit
constipation	*forstoppelse*	fawr-*staw*-pel-se
cough	*hoste*	*hos*-te
diarrhoea	*diaré*	dee-a-*re*
fever	*feber*	*fe*-ber
headache	*vondt i hodet*	vont ee *ho*-de
heart condition	*hjertefeil*	*yer*-te-fail
pain	*smerte*	*smer*-te
sore throat	*vondt i halsen*	vont ee *hal*-sen
toothache	*tannverk*	*tan*-verk

I'm allergic to ...	*Jeg er allergisk mot ...*	yai eyr a-*ler*-gisk mot ...
antibiotics	*antibiotika*	an-ti-bi-*o*-ti-ka
anti-inflammatories	*betennelsesdempende middel*	be-*te*-nel-ses-*dem*-pen-de *mi*-del
aspirin	*Dispril*	dis-*pril*
bees	*bier*	*bi*-er
codeine	*kodein*	ko-de-*in*
penicillin	*penicillin*	pen-se-*lin*

antiseptic	*desinfeksjonsmiddel*	des-in-fek-*shawns*-mi-del
bandage	*bandasje*	ban-*da*-she
condoms	*kondom* n	kawn-*dom*
contraceptives	*prevensjonsmiddel*	pre-van-*shawns*-mi-del
diarrhoea medicine	*middel mot diaré*	*mi*-del mot dee-a-*re*
insect repellent	*myggspray*	mewg-sprai
laxatives	*avførende middel*	av-*feu*-ren-de *mi*-del
painkillers	*smertestillende*	*smer*-te-*sti*-len-de
rehydration salts	*salt-tabletter*	*salt*-ta-be-le-ter
sleeping tablets	*sovetabletter*	*saw*-ve-*ta*-be-le-ter

english–norwegian dictionary

In this dictionary, words are marked as n (noun), a (adjective), v (verb), sg (singular), pl (plural), inf (informal) and pol (polite) where necessary. Note that Norwegian nouns are either masculine, feminine or neuter. Masculine and feminine forms (known as 'common gender') take the indefinite article en (a) while the neuter forms take the article et (a). Every Norwegian noun needs to be learned with its indefinite article (en or et). Only in Nynorsk is the distinction between masculine and feminine still relevant, so we've only indicated the neuter nouns with ⓝ after the Norwegian word. Note also that the ending 't' is added to adjectives for the neuter form (ie when they accompany indefinite singular nouns). In some cases both forms of the adjective (ie ⓜ & ⓕ form and ⓝ form) are spelled out in full and separated with a slash.

A

accident ulykke oo-lew-ke
accommodation losji lo-shee
adaptor adapter a-dap-ter
address n adresse a-dre-se
after etter e-ter
air-conditioned luftkjøling luft-sheu-ling
airplane fly ⓝ flew
airport flyplass flew-plas
alcohol alkohol al-ko-hol
all alt alt
allergy allergi a-ler-gee
ambulance sykebil sew-ke-bil
and og aw
arm arm arm
ashtray askebeger as-ke-be-ger
ATM minibank mee-ni-bank

B

baby baby bai-bee
back (body) rygg rewg
backpack ryggsekk rewg-sek
bad dårlig dawr-lee
bag bag bag
baggage claim bagasjeskranke ba-ga-she-skran-ke
bank bank bank
bar bar bar
bathroom bad ⓝ baad
battery batteri ⓝ ba-te-ree
beautiful vakker(t) va-ker(t)
bed seng seng
beer øl eul
before før feur
behind bak bak

bicycle sykkel sew-kel
big stor stor
bill regning rai-ning
black svart svart
blanket teppe ⓝ te-pe
blood group blodtype blo-tew-pe
blue blå(tt) blaw(t)
boat båt bawt
book (make a reservation) v bestille be-stee-le
bottle flaske flas-ke
bottle opener flaskeåpner flas-ke-awp-ner
boy gutt goot
brakes (car) bremser brem-ser
breakfast frokost fro-kost
broken (faulty) ødelagt eud-lagt
bus buss bus
business forretning fo-ret-ning
buy kjøpe sheu-pee

C

café kafé ka-fe
camera kamera ⓝ ka-me-ra
camp site campingplass keym-ping-plas
cancel avbestill av-be-stil
can opener boksåpner boks-awp-ner
car bil beel
cash n kontanter kon-tan-ter
cash (a cheque) v veksle (en sjekk) vek-sle (en sheyk)
cell phone mobiltelefon mo-beel-te-le-fon
centre sentrum ⓝ sen-trum
change (money) v veksle (penger) vek-sle (peyng-er)
cheap billig(t) bi-lee
check (bill) sjekk sheyk
check-in n sjekke inn shey-ke in
chest bryst ⓝ brewst

child *barn* Ⓝ barn
cigarette *sigarett* si-ga-*ret*
city *by* bew
clean a *ren(t)* ren(t)
closed *stengt* stengt
coffee *kaffe* ka-fe
coins *mynter* mewn-ter
cold a *kald(t)* kal(t)
collect call *noteringsoverføring*
no-te-rings-aw-ver-*feu*-ring
come *komme* kaw-me
computer *datamaskin* da-ta-ma-sheen
condom *kondom* Ⓝ kon-dom
contact lenses *kontaktlinse* kon-takt-lin-se
cook v *lage mat* la-ge maat
cost n *pris* pris
credit card *kredittkort* Ⓝ kre-dit-kawrt
cup *kopp* en kawp
currency exchange *valutaveksling* va-lu-ta-vek-sling
customs (immigration) *toll* tawl

D

dangerous *farlig(t)* far-lee
date (time) *dato* daa-taw
day *dag* daag
delay n *forsinkelse* for-sin-kel-se
dentist *tannlege* tan-le-ge
depart *avreise* av-rai-se
diaper *bleie* blai-ey
dictionary *ordbok* or-bok
dinner *middag* mi-daa
direct *direkte* di-rek-te
dirty *skitten(t)* shi-ten(t)
disabled *funksjonshemmet* funk-shons-he-met
discount n *rabatt* ra-bat
doctor *lege* le-ge
double bed *dobbelseng* daw-bel-seng
double room *dobbeltrom* Ⓝ daw-belt-rom
drink n *drikke* dri-ke
drive v *kjøre* sheu-re
drivers licence *førerkort* Ⓝ feu-rer-kawrt
drug (illicit) *narkotika* nar-ko-ti-ka
dummy (pacifier) *smokk* smok

E

ear *øre* Ⓝ eu-re
east *øst* eust
eat *spise* spi-se

economy class *økonomiklasse* eu-ko-no-*mi*-kla-se
electricity *elektrisitet* e-lek-tri-si-*tet*
elevator *heis* hais
email *e-post* e-post
embassy *ambassade* am-ba-*sa*-de
emergency *akuttmottak* Ⓝ a-*kut*-mo-tak
English (language) *engelsk* eyng-elsk
entrance *inngang* in-gang
evening *kveld* kvel
exchange rate *vekslingskurs* vek-slings-kurs
exit n *utgang* oot-gang
expensive *dyr(t)* dewr(t)
express mail *ekspresspost* eks-pres-pawst
eye *øye* Ⓝ oy-e

F

far *langt* langt
fast *rask(t)* rask(t)
father *far* far
film (camera) *film* film
finger *finger* fin-ger
first-aid kit *førstehjelpsskrin* Ⓝ feur-ste-yelp-skrin
first class *førsteklasse* feur-ste-kla-se
fish n *fisk* fisk
food *mat* maat
foot *fot* fot
fork *gaffel* ga-fel
free (of charge) *gratis* gra-tis
friend *venn/venninne* Ⓜ/Ⓕ ven/ve-ni-ne
fruit *frukt* frookt
full *full(t)* ful(t)
funny *morsom(t)* mawr-som(t)

G

gift *gave* ga-ve
girl *jente* yen-te
glass (drinking) *glass* Ⓝ glas
glasses *briller* bri-ler
go *gå* gaw
good *god(t)* go(t)
green *grønn(t)* greun(t)
guide n *guide* gaid

H

half n *halv(t)* hal(t)
hand *hånd* hawn
handbag *veske* veys-ke

happy *glad* glaa
have *ha* haa
he *han* han
head *hode* ⓝ ho-de
heart *hjerte* ⓝ yer-te
heat ⓝ *varme* var-me
heavy *tung(t)* tung(t)
help v *hjelp* yelp
here *her* heyr
high *høy(t)* hoy(t)
highway *motorvei* maw-tor-vey
hike v *tur* toor
holiday *ferie* fe-ree-e
homosexual ⓝ *homoseksuell* ho-mo-sek-su-el
hospital *sykehus* ⓝ sew-ke-hoos
hot *het(t)* heyt/het
hotel *hotell* ⓝ hoo-*tel*
hungry *sulten* sul-ten
husband *mann* man

I

I *jeg* yai
identification (card) *legitimasjon* le-gi-ti-ma-*shawn*
ill *syk* sewk
important *viktig* vik-tee
included *inkludert* in-kloo-*deyrt*
injury *skade* ska-de
insurance *forsikring* fawr-*si*-kring
Internet *Internett* in-ter-net
interpreter *translatør* tran-sla-*teur*

J

jewellery *smykke* ⓝ smew-ke
job *jobb* yob

K

key *nøkkel* neu-kel
kilogram *kilo* ⓝ shee-lo
kitchen *kjøkken* ⓝ sheu-ken
knife *kniv* kniv

L

laundry (place) *vaskeri* ⓝ vas-ke-*ree*
lawyer *advokat* ad-voo-*kat*
left (direction) *venstre* ven-strey

left-luggage office *gjenglemt bagasjeskranke*
    yen-glemt ba-*gaa*-she-skran-ke
leg *bein* bain
lesbian n *lesbisk* les-bisk
less *mindre* min-dre
letter (mail) *brev* ⓝ brev
lift (elevator) *heis* hais
light *lys* ⓝ lews
like v *like* li-ke
lock n *lås* laws
long *lang* lang
lost *mistet* mis-tet
lost-property office *bortkommet bagasjeskranke*
    bawrt-kaw-met ba-*gaa*-she-skran-ke
love v *elsker* eyls-ker
luggage *bagasje* ba-*gaa*-she
lunch *lunsj* leunsh

M

mail n *post* pawst
man *mann* man
map *kart* ⓝ kart
market *marked* ⓝ mar-ked
matches *fyrstikker* fewr-sti-ker
meat *kjøtt* sheut
medicine *medisin* me-de-*seen*
menu *meny* me-new
message *beskjed* be-*shey*
milk *melk* melk
minute *minutt* ⓝ mi-*nut*
mobile phone *mobiltelefon* mo-beel-te-le-*fon*
money *penger* peyng-er
month *måned* maw-ne
morning *morgen* maw-ren
mother *mor* mawr
motorcycle *motorsykkel* maw-tor-sew-kel
motorway *motorvei* maw-tor-vey
mouth *munn* mun
music *musikk* mu-*sik*

N

name *navn* ⓝ navn
napkin *tallerken* ta-*ler*-ken
nappy *bleie* blai-ey
near *nær* neyr
new *ny(tt)* new(t)

I

news *nyheter* new·he·ter
newspaper *avis* a·vis
night *natt* nat
no *nei* nai
noisy *bråkete* braw·ke·te
nonsmoking *ikke-røyke* i·key·roy·ke
north *nord* nor
Norway *Norge* nawr·gai
Norwegian (language) *norsk* nawrsk
Norwegian a *norsk* nawrsk
nose *nese* ney·se
now *nå* naw
number *nummer* ⓝ no·mer

O

oil (engine) *olje* ol·ye
old *gammel(t)* ga·mel(t)
one-way ticket *enveisbillett* en·veys·bee·*let*
open v *åpen(t)* aw·pen(t)
outside *utenfor* u·ten·fawr

P

package *pakke* pa·ke
paper *papir* ⓝ pa·peer
park (car) v *parkere* par·key·re
passport *pass* ⓝ pas
pay *betale* be·ta·le
pen *penn* pen
petrol *bensin* ben·seen
pharmacy *apotek* ⓝ a·po·tek
phonecard *telefonkort* ⓝ te·le·fon·kawrt
photo *foto* ⓝ fo·to
plate *tallerken* ta·ler·ken
police *politi* ⓝ po·lee·tee
postcard *postkort* ⓝ pawst·kawrt
post office *postkontor* ⓝ pawst·kawn·tawr
pregnant *gravid* gra·veed
price *pris* pris

Q

quiet *stille* sti·le

R

rain n *regn* rain
razor *barberhøvel* bar·ber·heu·vel

receipt n *kvittering* kvi·te·ring
red *rød(t)* reu(t)
refund n *refusjon* re·foo·shawn
registered mail *rekommandert post*
   re·ko·man·*deyrt* pawst
rent v *leie* lai·e
repair v *reparasjon* re·pa·ra·shawn
reservation *reservasjon* re·ser·va·shawn
restaurant *restaurant* res·tu·rang
return v *retur* re·toor
return ticket *returbillett* re·toor·bi·*let*
right (direction) *høyre* heu·rey
road *vei* vai
room *rom* ⓝ rom

S

safe a *trygg* trewg
sanitary napkin *bind* ⓝ bin
seat *sete* ⓝ se·te
send *sende* sen·de
service station *bensinstasjon* ben·seen·staa·shawn
sex *sex* seks
shampoo *sjampo* sham·po
share (a dorm) *dele* de·le
shaving cream *barberskum* bar·ber·skom
she *hun* hun
sheet (bed) *laken* ⓝ la·ken
shirt *skjorte* shor·te
shoes *sko* sko
shop n *butikk* boo·tik
short *kort* kawrt
shower n *dusj* dush
single room *enkeltrom* ⓝ eyn·kelt·rom
skin *hud* hood
skirt *skjørt* ⓝ sheurt
sleep v *sove* saw·ve
slowly *sakte* sak·te
small *liten/lite* lee·ten/lee·te
smoke (cigarettes) v *røyke* roy·ke
soap *såpe* saw·pe
some *noen* naw·en
soon *snart* snart
south *sør* seur
souvenir shop *suvenirbutikk* su·ve·neer·boo·tik
speak *snakke* sney·ke
spoon *skje* shai
stamp *frimerke* ⓝ free·mer·key

stand-by ticket *reservebillett* re-ser-vey-bee-*let*
station (train) *stasjon* staa-*shawn*
stomach *mage* ma-ge
stop v *stopp* stawp
stop (bus) n *busstopp* bus-stawp
street *gate* ga-te
student *student* stu-*dent*
sun *sol* sol
sunscreen *solfaktor* sol-*fak*-tor
swim v *svømme* sveu-me

T

tampons *tamponger* tam-*pong*-er
taxi *drosje* draw-shey
teaspoon *teskje* te-shey
teeth *tenner* te-ner
telephone n *telefon* te-le-fon
television *TV* te-ve
temperature (weather) *temperatur* tem-pe-ra-*toor*
tent *telt* ⓝ telt
that (one) *den* den
they *de* dey
thirsty *tørst* teurst
this (one) *denne/dette* dey-ne/dey-te
ticket *billett* bee-*let*
time *tid* teed
tired *trøtt* treut
tissues *papirserviett* pa-peer-ser-vee-et
today *i dag* ee dag
toilet *toalett* ⓝ to-aa-*let*
tomorrow *i morgen* ee *maw*-ren
tonight *i kveld* ee kvel
toothbrush *tannbørste* tan-beur-ste
toothpaste *tannkrem* tan-krem
torch (flashlight) *lommelykt* lo-mey-lewkt
tour n *tur* toor
tourist office *turistinformasjon*
   tu-*reest*-in-fawr-ma-*shawn*
towel *håndkle* ⓝ hawn-kle
train *tåg* ⓝ tawg
translate *oversette* aw-ver-se-te
travel agency *reisebyrå* ⓝ *rai*-se-bew-raw
travellers cheque *reisesjekker* rai-se-shey-ker
trousers *bukser* buk-ser
twin beds *to enkeltsenger* taw eyn-kelt-seng-er
tyre *dekk* ⓝ dek

U

underwear *undertøy* un-der-toy
urgent *haster* has-ter

V

vacant *ledig* le-dee
vacation *ferie* fe-ree-e
vegetable n *grønnsak* greun-sak
vegetarian a *vegetariansk* ve-ge-ta-ree-*ansk*
visa *visum* ⓝ vee-sum

W

waiter *kelner* kel-ner
walk v *gå* gaw
wallet *lommebok* lo-mey-bok
warm a *varm(t)* varm(t)
wash (something) *vaske* vas-ke
watch n *se* se
water *vann* van
we *vi* vee
weekend *helg* helg
west *vest* vest
wheelchair *rullestol* ru-le-stol
when *når* nawr
where *hvor* vor
white *hvit* veet
who *hvem* vem
why *hvorfor* vor-fawr
wife *kone* ko-ne
window *vindu* ⓝ vin-du
wine *vin* veen
with *med* mey
without *uten* u-ten
woman *kvinne* kvi-ne
write *skrive* skree-ve

Y

yellow *gul(t)* gool(t)
yes *ja* yaa
yesterday *i går* ee gawr
you sg inf *du* doo
you sg pol *De* dee
you pl *dere* dey-re

Portuguese

portuguese alphabet				
A a aa	*B b* be	*C c* se	*D d* de	*E e* e
F f e·fe	*G g* je	*H h* a·*gaah*	*I i* ee	*J j* *jo*·ta
K k *ka*·pa	*L l* e·le	*M m* e·me	*N n* e·ne	*O o* o
P p pe	*Q q* ke	*R r* e·rre	*S s* e·se	*T t* te
U u oo	*V v* ve	*W w* *da*·blyoo	*X x* sheesh	*Y y* *eeps*·lon
Z z ze				

■ portuguese

PORTUGUÊS

introduction

Portuguese (*português* poor·too·*gesh*), the language which produced words such as *albino*, *brocade* and *molasses*, comes from the Romance language family and is closely related to Spanish, French and Italian. Descended from the colloquial Latin spoken by Roman soldiers, it's now used by over 200 million people worldwide.

Linguists believe that before the Roman invasion of the Iberian Peninsula in 218 BC, the locals of modern-day Portugal spoke a Celtic language. That local language was supplanted by the vernacular form of Latin (sometimes called 'Romance') spoken by the occupying forces under the Romans' 500-year rule of the province of Lusitania (present-day Portugal and Spanish Galicia). During this period, Portuguese also absorbed elements of the languages of invading Germanic tribes. The greatest influence on today's Portuguese, however, was a result of the Moorish invasion of the peninsula in AD 711. Arabic was imposed as the official language of the region until the expulsion of the Moors in 1249, and although Romance was still spoken by the masses, the Moorish language left its mark on the vocabulary. From the 16th century on, there were only minor changes to the language, mostly influences from France and Spain. The earliest written documents were composed in the 12th century, and the Portuguese used in 1572 by Luís de Camões (author of the first great Portuguese classic, *Os Lusíadas*) was already identifiable as the language of José Saramago's Nobel Prize-winning works in the 20th century.

The global distribution of the Portuguese language began during the period know as *Os Descobrimentos* (the Discoveries), the golden era of Portugal's colonial expansion into Africa, Asia and South America. In the 15th and 16th centuries, the peninsular nation was a world power and had enormous economic, cultural and political influence. The empire's reach can be seen today in the number of countries besides Portugal where Portuguese still has the status of an official language – Brazil, Madeira and the Azores in the Atlantic Ocean off Europe, Cape Verde, São Tomé and Príncipe, Guinea-Bissau, Angola and Mozambique (all in Africa), and Macau and East Timor in Asia.

While there are differences between European Portuguese and that spoken elsewhere, you shouldn't have many problems being understood throughout the Portuguese-speaking world. As the Portuguese say, *Quem não arrisca, não petisca* keng nowng a·*rreesh*·ka, nowng pe·*teesh*·ka (If you don't take a risk, you won't eat delicacies).

pronunciation

vowel sounds

The vowel sounds in Portuguese are quite similar to those found in English. Most vowel sounds in Portuguese also have a nasal version with an effect similar to the silent '-ng' ending in English, as in *amanhã* aa·ma·*nyang* (tomorrow), for example. The letter 'n' or 'm' at the end of a syllable or a tilde (~) in written Portuguese indicate that the vowel is nasal.

symbol	english equivalent	portuguese example	transliteration
a	run	*maçã*	ma·*sang*
aa	father	*tomate*	too·*maa*·te
ai	aisle	*pai*	pai
ay	say	*lei*	lay
e	bet	*cedo*	*se*·doo
ee	see	*fino*	*fee*·noo
o	pot	*sobre*	*so*·bre
oh	oh	*couve*	*koh*·ve
oo	book	*gato*	*ga*·too
ow	how	*Austrália*	ow·*shtraa*·lya
oy	toy	*noite*	*noy*·te

word stress

In Portuguese, stress generally falls on the second-to-last syllable of a word, though there are exceptions. If a written vowel has a circumflex (ˆ) or an acute (´) or grave (`) accent marked on it, this cancels the general rule and the stress falls on that syllable. When a word ends in a written *i, im, l, r, u, um* or *z*, or is pronounced with a nasalised vowel, the stress falls on the last syllable. Don't worry too much about it when using phrases from this book though – the stressed syllable is always italicised in our coloured pronunciation guides.

PORTUGUÊS – pronunciation

consonant sounds

Most of the consonant sounds in Portuguese are also found in English, and even *r* (rr) will be familiar to many people (it's similar to the French 'r'). Note that the letter ç ('c' with a cedilla) is pronounced as s rather than k.

symbol	english equivalent	portuguese example	transliteration
b	bed	*beber*	be-*ber*
d	dog	*dedo*	de-*doo*
f	fat	*faca*	*faa*-ka
g	go	*gasolina*	ga-zoo-*lee*-na
k	kit	*cama*	*ka*-ma
l	lot	*lixo*	*lee*-shoo
ly	million	*muralhas*	moo-*raa*-lyash
m	man	*macaco*	ma-*kaa*-koo
n	not	*nada*	*naa*-da
ng	ring (indicates the nasalisation of the preceding vowel)	*ambos*, *uns*, *amanhã*	*ang*-boosh, oo*ngsh*, aa-ma-*nyang*
ny	canyon	*linha*	*lee*-nya
p	pet	*padre*	*paa*-dre
r	like 'tt' in 'butter' said fast	*hora*	o-*ra*
rr	run (throaty)	*relva*	*rrel*-va
s	sun	*criança*	kree-*ang*-sa
sh	shot	*chave*	*shaa*-ve
t	top	*tacho*	*taa*-shoo
v	very	*vago*	*vaa*-goo
w	win	*água*	*aa*-gwa
y	yes	*edifício*	ee-dee-*fee*-syoo
z	zero	*camisa*	ka-*mee*-za
zh	pleasure	*cerveja*	serr-ve-*zha*

basics

language difficulties

Do you speak English?
Fala inglês?   faa·la eeng·glesh

Do you understand?
Entende?   eng·teng·de

I (don't) understand.
(Não) Entendo.   (nowng) eng·teng·doo

What does (*bem-vindo*) mean?
O que quer dizer (bem-vindo)?   oo ke ker dee·zer (beng·veeng·doo)

How do you ...?	*Como é que se ...?*	ko·moo e ke se ...
pronounce this	*pronuncia isto*	proo·noong·see·a esh·too
write (*ajuda*)	*escreve (ajuda)*	shkre·ve (a·zhoo·da)

Could you please ...?	*Podia ..., por favor?*	poo·dee·a ... poor fa·vor
repeat that	*repetir isto*	rre·pe·teer eesh·too
speak more slowly	*falar mais devagar*	fa·laar maish de·va·gaar
write it down	*escrever isso*	shkre·ver ee·soo

essentials

Yes.	*Sim.*	seeng
No.	*Não.*	nowng
Please.	*Por favor.*	poor fa·vor
Thank you	*(Muito)*	*(mweeng·too)*
(very much).	*Obrigado/a.* m/f	o·bree·gaa·doo/a
You're welcome.	*De nada.*	de naa·da
Excuse me.	*Faz favor!*	faash fa·vor
Sorry.	*Desculpe.*	desh·kool·pe

0	*zero*	ze·roo	16	*dezasseis*	de·za·*saysh*
1	*um*	oong	17	*dezassete*	de·za·*se*·te
2	*dois*	doysh	18	*dezoito*	de·*zoy*·too
3	*três*	tresh	19	*dezanove*	de·za·*no*·ve
4	*quatro*	*kwaa*·troo	20	*vinte*	*veeng*·te
5	*cinco*	*seeng*·koo	21	*vinte e um*	*veeng*·te e oong
6	*seis*	saysh	22	*vinte e dois*	*veeng*·te e doysh
7	*sete*	*se*·te	30	*trinta*	*treeng*·ta
8	*oito*	*oy*·too	40	*quarenta*	kwa·*reng*·ta
9	*nove*	*no*·ve	50	*cinquenta*	seeng·*kweng*·ta
10	*dez*	desh	60	*sessenta*	se·*seng*·ta
11	*onze*	*ong*·ze	70	*setenta*	se·*teng*·ta
12	*doze*	*do*·ze	80	*oitenta*	oy·*teng*·ta
13	*treze*	*tre*·ze	90	*noventa*	no·*veng*·ta
14	*catorze*	ka·*tor*·ze	100	*cem*	seng
15	*quinze*	*keeng*·ze	1000	*mil*	meel

time & dates

What time is it?	*Que horas são?*	kee *o*·rash sowng
It's one o'clock.	*É uma hora.*	e *oo*·ma *o*·ra
It's (10) o'clock.	*São (dez) horas.*	sowng (desh) *o*·rash
Quarter past (10).	*(Dez) e quinze.*	(desh) e *keeng*·ze
Half past (10).	*(Dez) e meia.*	(desh) e *may*·a
Quarter to (10).	*Quinze para as (dez).*	*keeng*·ze *pa*·ra ash (desh)
At what time ...?	*A que horas ...?*	a ke *o*·rash ...
At ...	*Às ...*	ash ...
in the morning	*da manhã*	da ma·*nyang*
in the afternoon	*da tarde*	da *taar*·de
in the evening	*da noite*	da *noy*·te
Monday	*segunda-feira*	se·*goong*·da·*fay*·ra
Tuesday	*terça-feira*	*ter*·sa·*fay*·ra
Wednesday	*quarta-feira*	*kwaar*·ta·*fay*·ra
Thursday	*quinta-feira*	*keeng*·ta·*fay*·ra
Friday	*sexta-feira*	*saysh*·ta·*fay*·ra
Saturday	*sábado*	*saa*·ba·doo
Sunday	*domingo*	doo·*meeng*·goo

January	Janeiro	zha·nay·roo
February	Fevereiro	fe·vray·roo
March	Março	maar·soo
April	Abril	a·breel
May	Maio	maa·yoo
June	Junho	zhoo·nyoo
July	Julho	zhoo·lyoo
August	Agosto	a·gosh·too
September	Setembro	se·teng·broo
October	Outubro	oh·too·broo
November	Novembro	no·veng·broo
December	Dezembro	de·zeng·broo

What date is it today?
Qual é a data de hoje?   kwaal e a *daa*·ta de o·zhe

It's (18 October).
Hoje é dia (dezoito de Outubro).   o·zhe e dee·a (de·zoy·too de oh·too·broo)

| since (May) | desde (Maio) | desh·de (maa·yoo) |
| until (June) | até (Junho) | a·te (zhoo·nyoo) |

last ...		
night	a noite passada	a noy·te pa·saa·da
week	a semana passada	a se·ma·na pa·saa·da
month	o mês passado	oo mesh pa·saa·doo
year	o ano passado	oo a·noo pa·saa·doo

next ...		
week	na próxima semana	na pro·see·ma se·ma·na
month	no próximo mês	noo pro·see·moo mesh
year	no próximo ano	noo pro·see·moo a·noo

yesterday/tomorrow ...	ontem/amanhã ...	ong·teng/aa·ma·nyang ...
morning	de manhã	de ma·nyang
afternoon	à tarde	aa taar·de
evening	à noite	aa noy·te

weather

What's the weather like?	Como está o tempo?	ko·moo shtaa oo teng·poo
It's ...	Está ...	shtaa ...
cloudy	enublado	e·noo·blaa·doo
cold	frio	free·oo
hot	muito quente	mweeng·too keng·te
raining	a chover	a shoo·ver
snowing	a nevar	a ne·vaar
sunny	sol	sol
warm	quente	keng·te
windy	ventoso	veng·to·zoo
spring	primavera f	pree·ma·ve·ra
summer	verão m	ve·rowng
autumn	outono m	oh·to·noo
winter	inverno m	eeng·ver·noo

border crossing

I'm here ...	Estou ...	shtoh ...
in transit	em trânsito	eng trang·zee·too
on business	em negócios	eng ne·go·syoosh
on holiday	de férias	de fe·ree·ash
I'm here for ...	Vou ficar por ...	voh fee·kaar poor ...
(10) days	(dez) dias	(desh) dee·ash
(three) weeks	(três) semanas	(tresh) se·ma·nash
(two) months	(dois) meses	(doysh) me·zesh

I'm going to (Elvas).
Vou para (Elvas).   voh pa·ra (el·vash)

I'm staying at the (Hotel Lisbon).
Estou no (Hotel Lisboa).   shtoh noo (o·tel leezh·bo·a)

I have nothing to declare.
Não tenho nada a declarar.   nowng ta·nyoo naa·da a de·kla·raar

I have something to declare.
Tenho algo a declarar.   ta·nyoo al·goo a de·kla·raar

That's (not) mine.
Isto (não) é meu.   eesh·too (nowng) e me·oo

transport

tickets & luggage

Where can I buy a ticket?
Onde é que eu compro o bilhete?   ong·de e ke e·oo kong·proo oo bee·lye·te

Do I need to book a seat?
Preciso de fazer reserva?   pre·see·zoo de fa·zer rre·zer·va

One ... ticket	*Um bilhete de ...*	oong bee·lye·te de ...
(to Braga), please.	*(para Braga), por favor.*	(pra braa·ga) poor fa·vor
one-way	*ida*	ee·da
return	*ida e volta*	ee·da ee vol·ta

I'd like to ...	*Queria ... o bilhete,*	ke·ree·a ... oo bee·lye·te
my ticket, please.	*por favor.*	poor fa·vor
cancel	*cancelar*	kang·se·laar
change	*trocar*	troo·kaar
collect	*cobrar*	koo·braar
confirm	*confirmar*	kong·feer·maar

I'd like a ... seat,	*Queria um lugar ...*	ke·ree·a oong loo·gaar ...
please.	*por favor.*	poor fa·vor
nonsmoking	*de não fumadores*	de nowng foo·ma·do·resh
smoking	*para fumadores*	pra foo·ma·do·resh

How much is it?
Quanto é?   kwang·too e

Is there air conditioning?
Tem ar condicionado?   teng aar kong·dee·syoo·naa·doo

Is there a toilet?
Tem casa de banho?   teng kaa·za de ba·nyoo

How long does the trip take?
Quanto tempo é que   kwang·too teng·poo e ke
leva a viagem?   le·va a vee·aa·zheng

Is it a direct route?
É uma rota directa?   e oo·ma rro·ta dee·re·ta

I'd like a luggage locker.
Queria o depósito de   ke·ree·a oo de·po·zee·too de
bagagens.   ba·gaa·zhengsh

My luggage has been ...	A minha bagagem ...	a *mee*·nya ba·*gaa*·zheng ...
damaged	foi danificada	foy da·nee·fee·*kaa*·da
lost	perdeu-se	per·*de*·oo·se
stolen	foi roubada	foy rroh·*baa*·da

getting around

Where does flight (TP 615) arrive/depart?

De onde pára/parte o voo (TP 615)?	de *ong*·de *paa*·ra/*paar*·te oo *vo*·oo (te pe saysh·*seng*·toosh e *keeng*·ze)

Where's (the) ...?	Onde é ...?	*ong*·de e ...
arrivals hall	a porta de chegada	a *por*·ta de she·*gaa*·da
departures hall	a porta de partida	a *por*·ta de par·*tee*·da
duty-free shop	a loja duty-free	a *lo*·zha doo·*tee*·free
gate (12)	a porta (doze)	a *por*·ta (*do*·ze)

Is this the ... to (Lisbon)?	Este é o ... para (Lisboa)?	*esh*·te e oo ... pra (leezh·*bo*·a)
boat	barco	*baar*·koo
bus	autocarro	ow·to·*kaa*·rroo
plane	avião	a·vee·*owng*
train	comboio	kong·*boy*·oo

What time's the ... bus?	Quando é que sai o ... autocarro?	*kwang*·doo e ke sai oo ... ow·to·*kaa*·rroo
first	primeiro	pree·*may*·roo
last	último	*ool*·tee·moo
next	próximo	*pro*·see·moo

At what time does it arrive/leave?

A que horas chega/sai?	a ke *o*·rash *she*·ga/sai

How long will it be delayed?

Quanto tempo é que vai chegar atrasado?	*kwang*·too *teng*·poo e ke vai she·*gaar* a·tra·*zaa*·doo

What station/stop is this?

Qual estação/paragem é este?	kwaal shta·*sowng*/pa·*raa*·zheng e *esh*·te

What's the next station/stop?

Qual é a próxima estação/ paragem?	kwaal e a *pro*·see·ma shta·*sowng*/ pa·*raa*·zheng

Does it stop at (Amarante)?
Pára em (Amarante)? — paa·ra eng (a·ma·rang·te)

Please tell me when we get to (Évora).
Por favor avise-me quando chegarmos a (Évora). — poor fa·vor a·vee·ze·me kwang·doo she·gaar·moosh a (e·voo·ra)

How long do we stop here?
Quanto tempo vamos ficar parados aqui? — kwang·too teng·poo va·moosh fee·kaar pa·raa·doosh a·kee

Is this seat available?
Este lugar está vago? — esh·te loo·gaar shtaa va·goo

That's my seat.
Este é o meu lugar. — esh·te e oo me·oo loo·gaar

I'd like a taxi ...
Queria chamar um táxi ... — ke·ree·a sha·maar oong taak·see ...

at (9am)	*para as (nove da manhã)*	pra ash (no·ve da ma·nyang)
now	*agora*	a·go·ra
tomorrow	*amanhã*	aa·ma·nyang

Is this taxi available?
Este táxi está livre? — esh·te taak·see shtaa lee·vre

How much is it to ...?
Quanto custa até ao ...? — kwang·too koosh·ta a·te ow ...

Please put the meter on.
Por favor, ligue o taxímetro. — poor fa·vor lee·ge oo taak·see·me·troo

Please take me to (this address).
Leve-me para (este endereço), por favor. — le·ve·me pa·ra (esh·te eng·de·re·soo) poor fa·vor

Please ...
Por favor ... — poor fa·vor ...

slow down	*vá mais devagar*	vaa maish de·va·gaar
stop here	*pare aqui*	paa·re a·kee
wait here	*espere aqui*	shpe·re a·kee

car, motorbike & bicycle hire

I'd like to hire a ...	Queria alugar ...	ke·ree·a a·loo·gaar ...
bicycle	uma bicicleta	oo·ma bee·see·kle·ta
car	um carro	oong kaa·rroo
motorbike	uma mota	oo·ma mo·ta

with ...	com ...	kong ...
a driver	motorista	moo·too·reesh·ta
air conditioning	ar condicionado	aar kong·dee·syoo·naa·doo

How much	Quanto custa para	kwang·too koosh·ta pa·ra
for ... hire?	alugar por ...?	a·loo·gaar poor ...
hourly	hora	o·ra
daily	dia	dee·a
weekly	semana	se·ma·na

air	ar m	aar
oil	óleo m	o·le·oo
petrol	gasolina f	ga·zoo·lee·na
tyres	pneus m pl	pe·ne·oosh

I need a mechanic.
Preciso de um mecânico.   pre·see·zoo de oong me·kaa·nee·koo

I've run out of petrol.
Estou sem gasolina.   shtoh seng ga·zoo·lee·na

I have a flat tyre.
Tenho um furo no pneu.   ta·nyoo oong foo·roo noo pe·ne·oo

directions

Where's the ...?	Onde é ...?	ong·de e ...
bank	o banco	oo bang·koo
city centre	o centro da cidade	oo seng·troo da see·daa·de
hotel	o hotel	oo o·tel
market	o mercado	oo mer·kaa·doo
police station	a esquadra da polícia	a shkwaa·dra da poo·lee·sya
post office	o correio	oo koo·rray·oo
public toilet	a casa de banho	a kaa·za de ba·nyoo
	pública	poo·blee·ka
tourist office	o escritório de	oo shkree·to·ryoo de
	turismo	too·reezh·moo

Is this the road to (Sintra)?
Esta é a estrada para (Sintra)? esh·ta e a *shtraa*·da *pa*·ra (*seeng*·tra)

Can you show me (on the map)?
Pode-me mostrar (no mapa)? po·de·me moosh·*traar* (noo *maa*·pa)

How far is it?
A que distância fica? a ke deesh·*tang*·sya *fee*·ka

How do I get there?
Como é que eu chego lá? ko·moo e ke *e*·oo *she*·goo laa

Turn ...	*Vire ...*	*vee*·re ...
at the corner	*na esquina*	na *shkee*·na
at the traffic lights	*nos semáforos*	noosh se·*maa*·foo·roosh
left	*à esquerda*	aa *shker*·da
right	*à direita*	aa dee·*ray*·ta

It's ...	*É ...*	e ...
behind ...	*atrás de ...*	a·*traash* de ...
far away	*longe*	*long*·zhe
here	*aqui*	a·*kee*
in front of ...	*em frente de ...*	eng *freng*·te de ...
left	*à esquerda*	aa *shker*·da
near (to ...)	*perto (de ...)*	*per*·too (de ...)
next to ...	*ao lado de ...*	ow *laa*·doo de ...
on the corner	*na esquina*	na *shkee*·na
opposite ...	*do lado oposto ...*	doo *laa*·doo oo·*posh*·too ...
right	*à direita*	aa dee·*ray*·ta
straight ahead	*em frente*	eng *freng*·te
there	*lá*	laa

by bus	*de autocarro*	de ow·to·*kaa*·rroo
by taxi	*de táxi*	de *taak*·see
by train	*de comboio*	de kong·*boy*·oo
on foot	*a pé*	a pe

north	*norte*	*nor*·te
south	*sul*	sool
east	*leste*	*lesh*·te
west	*oeste*	o·*esh*·te

signs

Entrada/Saída	eng·traa·da/sa·ee·da	Entrance/Exit
Aberto/Fechado	a·ber·too/fe·shaa·doo	Open/Closed
Há Vaga	aa vaa·ga	Rooms Available
Não Há Vaga	nowng aa vaa·ga	No Vacancies
Informação	eeng·for·ma·sowng	Information
Esquadra da Polícia	shkwaa·dra da poo·lee·sya	Police Station
Proibido	pro·ee·bee·doo	Prohibited
Casa de Banho	kaa·za de ba·nyoo	Toilets
Homens	o·mengsh	Men
Mulheres	moo·lye·resh	Women
Quente/Frio	keng·te/free·oo	Hot/Cold

accommodation

finding accommodation

Where's a ...?
Onde é que há ...?
ong·de e ke aa ...

  camping ground
um parque de campismo
oong paar·ke de kang·peezh·moo

  guesthouse
uma casa de hóspedes
oo·ma kaa·za de osh·pe·desh

  hotel
um hotel
oong o·tel

  youth hostel
uma pousada de juventude
oo·ma poh·zaa·da de zhoo·veng·too·de

Can you recommend somewhere ...?
Pode recomendar algum lugar ...?
po·de rre·koo·meng·daar aal·goong loo·gaar ...

  cheap
barato
ba·raa·too

  good
bom
bong

  nearby
perto daqui
per·too da·kee

I'd like to book a room, please.
Eu queria fazer uma reserva, por favor.
e·oo ke·ree·a fa·zer oo·ma rre·zer·va poor fa·vor

I have a reservation.
Eu tenho uma reserva.
e·oo ta·nyoo oo·ma rre·zer·va

My name's ...
O meu nome é ...
oo me·oo no·me e ...

Do you have a ... room?	Tem um quarto ...?	teng oong *kwaar*·too ...
single	de solteiro	de sol·*tay*·roo
double	de casal	de ka·*zaal*
twin	duplo	*doo*·ploo

How much is it per ...?	Quanto custa por ...?	*kwang*·too *koosh*·ta poor ...
night	noite	*noy*·te
person	pessoa	pe·*so*·a

Can I pay by ...?	Posso pagar com ...?	*po*·soo pa·*gaar* kong ...
credit card	cartão de crédito	kar·*towng* de *kre*·dee·too
travellers cheque	traveller cheque	*tra*·ve·ler shek

I'd like to stay for (three) nights.
Para (três) noites. — *pa*·ra (tresh) *noy*·tesh

From (2 July) to (6 July).
De (dois de julho) até (seis de julho). — de (doysh de *zhoo*·lyoo) a·*te* (saysh de *zhoo*·lyoo)

Can I see it?
Posso ver? — *po*·soo ver

Am I allowed to camp here?
Posso acampar aqui? — *po*·soo a·kang·*paar* a·*kee*

Where can I find a camping ground?
Onde é o parque de campismo? — *ong*·de e oo *par*·ke de kang·*peesh*·moo

requests & queries

When/Where is breakfast served?
Quando/Onde é que servem o pequeno almoço? — *kwang*·doo/*ong*·de e ke *ser*·veng oo pe·*ke*·noo aal·*mo*·soo

Please wake me at (seven).
Por favor acorde-me às (sete). — poor fa·*vor* aa·*kor*·de·me aash (*se*·te)

Could I have my key, please?
Pode-me dar a minha chave, por favor? — *po*·de·me daar a *mee*·nya *shaa*·ve poor fa·*vor*

Can I get another (blanket)?
Pode-me dar mais um (cobertor)? — *po*·de·me daar maish oong (koo·ber·*tor*)

Is there a/an ...?	Tem ...?	teng ...
elevator	elevador	e·le·va·dor
safe	cofre	ko·fre

The room is too ...	É demasiado ...	e de·ma·zee·aa doo ...
expensive	caro	kaa·roo
noisy	barulhento	ba·roo·lyeng·too
small	pequeno	pe·ke·noo

The ... doesn't work.	... não funciona.	... nowng foong·see·o·na
air conditioner	O ar condicionado	oo aar kong·dee·syoo·naa·doo
fan	A ventoínha	a veng·too·ee·na
toilet	A sanita	a sa·nee·ta

This ... isn't clean.	Esta ... está suja.	esh·ta ... shtaa soo·zha
pillow	almofada	aal·moo·faa·da
towel	toalha	twaa·lya

| This sheet isn't clean. | Este lençol está sujo. | esh·te leng·sol shtaa soo·zho |

checking out

What time is checkout?
A que horas é a partida?
a ke o·rash e a par·tee·da

Can I leave my luggage here?
Posso deixar as minhas
malas aqui?
po·soo day·shaar ash mee·nyash
maa·lash a·kee

Could I have	Pode-me devolver	po·de·me de·vol·ver
my ..., please?	..., por favor?	... poor fa·vor
deposit	o depósito	oo de·po·zee·too
passport	o passaporte	oo paa·sa·por·te
valuables	os objectos	oosh o·be·zhe·toosh
	de valor	de va·lor

communications & banking

the internet

Where's the local Internet café?
Onde fica um café da internet — ong·de *fee*·ka oong ka·*fe* da eeng·ter·*net*
nas redondezas? — nash rre·dong·*de*·zash

How much is it per hour?
Quanto custa por hora? — kwang·too *koosh*·ta pooro·ra

I'd like to ...	*Queria ...*	ke·*ree*·a ...
check my email	*ler o meu email*	ler oo *me*·oo ee·*mayl*
get Internet access	*ter acesso à internet*	ter a·se·soo aa eeng·ter·*net*
use a printer	*usar uma*	oo·*zaar* oo·ma
	impressora	eeng·pre·*so*·ra
use a scanner	*usar um*	oo·*zaar* oong
	digitalizador	dee·zhee·ta·lee·za·*dor*

mobile/cell phone

I'd like a ...	*Queria ...*	ke·*ree*·a ...
mobile/cell	*alugar um*	a·loo·*gaar* oong
phone for hire	*telemóvel*	te·le·*mo*·vel
SIM card for	*cartão SIM*	kar·*towng* seeng
your network	*para a sua rede*	*pa*·ra a *soo*·a rre·de

What are the rates? *Qual é o valor cobrado?* — kwaal e oo va·*lor* koo·*braa*·doo

telephone

What's your phone number?
Qual é o seu número de telefone? — kwaal e oo *se*·oo *noo*·me·roo de te·le·*fo*·ne

The number is ...
O número é ... — oo *noo*·me·roo e ...

Where's the nearest public phone?
Onde fica o telefone — ong·de *fee*·ka o te·le·*fo*·ne
público mais perto? — *poo*·blee·koo maish *per*·too

I'd like to buy a phonecard.
Quero comprar um — ke·roo kong·*praar* oong
cartão telefónico. — kar·*towng* te·le·*fo*·nee·koo

I want to ...	Quero ...	ke·roo ...
call (Singapore)	telefonar (para Singapura)	te·le·foo·naar (pa·ra seeng·ga·poo·ra)
make a local call	fazer uma chamada local	fa·zer oo·ma sha·maa·da loo·kaal
reverse the charges	fazer uma chamada a cobrar	fa·zer oo·ma sha·maa·da a koo·braar
How much does ... cost?	Quanto custa ...?	kwang·too koosh·ta ...
a (three)-minute call	uma ligação de (três) minutos	oo·ma lee·ga·sowng de (tresh) mee·noo·toosh
each extra minute	cada minuto extra	kaa·da mee·noo·too aysh·tra

It's (30c) per (30) seconds.
(Trinta cêntimos) por (trinta) segundos.
(treeng·ta seng·tee·moosh) poor (treeng·ta) se·goong·doosh

post office

I want to send a ...	Quero enviar ...	ke·roo eng·vee·aar ...
fax	um fax	oong faks
letter	uma carta	oo·ma kaar·ta
parcel	uma encomenda	oo·ma eng·koo·meng·da
postcard	um postal	oong poosh·taal
I want to buy a/an ...	Quero comprar um ...	ke·roo kong·praar oong ...
envelope	envelope	eng·ve·lo·pe
stamp	selo	se·loo
Please send it (to Australia) by ...	Por favor envie isto (para Australia) por ...	poor fa·vor eng·vee·e eesh·too (pa·ra owsh·traa·lya) poor ...
airmail	via aérea	vee·a a·e·ree·a
express mail	correio azul	koo·rray·oo a·zool
registered mail	registado/a m/f	rre·zheesh·taa·doo/a
surface mail	via terrestre	vee·a te·rresh·tre

Is there any mail for me?
Há alguma correspondência para mim?
aa aal·goo·ma koo·rresh·pong·deng·sya pa·ra meeng

bank

English	Portuguese	Pronunciation
Where's a/an ...?	Onde é que há ...?	ong·de e ke aa ...
ATM	um caixa automático	oong kai·sha ow·too·maa·tee·koo
foreign exchange office	um câmbio	oong kang·byoo
I'd like to ...	Queria ...	ke·ree·a ...
Where can I ...?	Onde é que posso ...?	ong·de e ke po·soo ...
arrange a transfer	fazer uma transferencia	faa·zer oo·ma trans·fe·reng·sya
cash a cheque	trocar um cheque	troo·kaar oong she·ke
change a travellers cheque	trocar traveller cheque	troo·kaar tra·ve·ler shek
change money	trocar dinheiro	troo·kaar dee·nyay·roo
get a cash advance	fazer um levantamento adiantado	fa·zer oong le·vang·ta·meng·too a·dee·ang·taa·doo
withdraw money	levantar dinheiro	le·vang·taar dee·nyay·roo
What's the ...?	Qual é ...?	kwaal e ...
commission	a comissão	a koo·mee·sowng
charge for that	o imposto	oo eeng·posh·too
exchange rate	o câmbio do dia	oo kang·byoo doo dee·a
It's ...	É ...	e ...
(12) euros	(doze) euros	(do·ze) e·oo·roosh
free	gratuito	gra·twee·too

What time does the bank open?
A que horas é que abre o banco?   a ke o·rash e ke aa·bre oo bang·koo

Has my money arrived yet?
O meu dinheiro já chegou?   oo me·oo dee·nyay·roo zhaa she·goh

sightseeing

getting in

What time does it open/close?
A que horas abre/fecha?
a ke o·rash aa·bre/fe·sha

What's the admission charge?
Qual é o preço de entrada?
kwaal e oo pre·soo de eng·traa·da

Is there a discount for children/students?
Tem desconto para crianças/
estudantes?
teng desh·kong·too pa·ra kree·ang·sash/
shtoo·dang·tesh

English	Portuguese	Pronunciation
I'd like a ...	*Queria um ...*	ke·ree·a oong ...
catalogue	*catálogo*	ka·taa·loo·goo
guide	*guia*	gee·a
local map	*mapa local*	maa·pa loo·kaal

English	Portuguese	Pronunciation
I'd like to see ...	*Eu gostava de ver ...*	e·oo goosh·taa·va de ver ...
What's that?	*O que é aquilo?*	oo ke e a·kee·loo
Can I take a photo?	*Posso tirar uma* *fotografia?*	po·soo tee·raar oo·ma foo·too·gra·fee·a

tours

English	Portuguese	Pronunciation
When's the next ...?	*Quando é ...?*	kwang·doo e ...
day trip	*o próximo passeio*	oo pro·see·moo pa·say·oo
tour	*a próxima excursão*	a pro·see·ma shkoor·sowng

English	Portuguese	Pronunciation
Is ... included?	*Inclui ...?*	eeng·kloo·ee ...
accommodation	*hospedagem*	osh·pe·daa·zheng
the admission charge	*preço de entrada*	pre·soo de eng·traa·da
food	*comida*	koo·mee·da
transport	*transporte*	trangsh·por·te

How long is the tour?
Quanto tempo dura
a excursão?
kwang·too teng·poo doo·ra
a shkoor·sowng

What time should we be back?
A que hora é que devemos
estar de volta?
a ke o·ra e ke de·ve·moosh
shtaar de vol·ta

sightseeing

castle	*castelo* m	kash·*te*·loo
cathedral	*catedral* f	ka·te·*draal*
church	*igreja* f	ee·*gre*·zha
main square	*praça principal* f	*praa*·sa preeng·see·*paal*
monastery	*mosteiro* m	moosh·*tay*·roo
monument	*monumento* m	moo·noo·*meng*·too
museum	*museu* m	moo·*ze*·oo
old city	*cidade antiga* f	see·*daa*·de ang·*tee*·ga
palace	*palácio* m	pa·*laa*·syoo
ruins	*ruínas* f pl	rroo·ee·nash
stadium	*estádio* m	*shtaa*·dyoo
statues	*estátuas* f pl	shtaa·too·ash

shopping

enquiries

Where's a ...?	*Onde é ...?*	ong·de e ...
bank	*o banco*	oo *bang*·koo
bookshop	*a livraria*	a lee·vra·*ree*·a
department store	*loja de departamentos*	*lo*·zha de de·par·ta·*meng*·toosh
grocery store	*a mercearia*	a mer·see·a·*ree*·a
market	*o mercado*	oo mer·*kaa*·doo
newsagency	*o quiosque*	oo kee·*osh*·ke
supermarket	*o supermercado*	oo soo·per·mer·*kaa*·doo

Where can I buy (a padlock)?
Onde é que posso comprar   ong·de e ke *po*·soo kong·*praar*
(um cadeado)?   (oong ka·de·*aa*·doo)

I'm looking for ...
Estou à procura de ...   shtoh aa proo·*koo*·ra de ...

Can I look at it?
Posso ver?   *po*·soo ver

Do you have any others?
Tem outros?   teng *oh*·troosh

Does it have a guarantee?
  Tem garantia?   teng ga·rang·*tee*·a

Can I have it sent overseas?
  Podem enviar para o   *po*·deng eng·vee·*aar pa*·ra oo
  estrangeiro?   shtrang·*zhay*·roo

Can I have my ... repaired?
  Vocês consertam ...?   vo·*sesh* kong·*ser*·tang ...

It's faulty.
  Tem defeito.   teng de·*fay*·too

I'd like ..., please.   *Queria ..., por favor.*   ke·*ree*·a ... poor fa·*vor*
  a bag   *um saco*   oong *saa*·koo
  a refund   *ser reembolsado/a* m/f   ser rre·eng·bol·*saa*·doo/a
  to return this   *devolver isto*   de·vol·*ver eesh*·too

paying

How much is it?
  Quanto custa?   *kwang*·too *koosh*·ta

Can you write down the price?
  Pode escrever o preço?   *po*·de shkre·*ver* oo *pre*·soo

That's too expensive.
  Está muito caro.   shtaa *mweeng*·too *kaa*·roo

What's your lowest price?
  Qual é o seu último preço?   kwaal e oo *se*·oo *ool*·tee·moo *pre*·soo

I'll give you (five) euros.
  Dou-lhe (cinco) euros.   *doh*·lye (*seeng*·koo) e·*oo*·roosh

There's a mistake in the bill.
  Há um erro na conta.   aa oong e·rroo na *kong*·ta

Do you accept ...?   *Aceitam ...?*   a·*say*·tang ...
  credit cards   *cartão de crédito*   kar·*towng* de *kre*·dee·too
  debit cards   *multibanco*   mool·tee·*bang*·koo
  travellers cheques   *travellers cheques*   tra·ve·ler *she*·kesh

I'd like ..., please.   *Queria ..., por favor.*   ke·*ree*·a ... poor fa·*vor*
  a receipt   *um recibo*   oong rre·*see*·boo
  my change   *o troco*   oo *tro*·koo

clothes & shoes

Can I try it on?	Posso experimentar?	po·soo shpree·meng·taar
My size is (40).	O meu número é (quarenta).	oo me·oo noo·me·roo e (kwa·reng·ta)
It doesn't fit.	Não serve.	nowng ser·ve
small	pequeno/pequena m/f	pe·ke·noo/pe·ke·na
medium	meio/meia m/f	may·oo/may·a
large	grande m&f	grang·de

books & music

I'd like a ...	Queria comprar ...	ke·ree·a kong·praar ...
newspaper	um jornal	oong zhor·naal
(in English)	(em inglês)	(eng eeng·glesh)
pen	uma caneta	oo·ma ka·ne·ta

Is there an English-language bookshop?
Há uma livraria de língua inglesa?
aa oo·ma lee·vra·ree·a de leeng·gwa eeng·gle·za

I'm looking for something by (Fernando Pessoa).
Estou à procura de qualquer coisa do (Fernando Pessoa).
shtoh aa proo·koo·ra de kwaal·ker koy·za doo (fer·nang·doo pe·so·a)

Can I listen to this?
Posso ouvir?
po·soo oh·veer

photography

I need a/an ... film for this camera.	Preciso de filme ... para esta máquina.	pre·see·zoo de feel·me ... pa·ra esh·ta maa·kee·na
APS	sistema APS	seesh·te·ma aa pe e·se
B&W	a preto e branco	a pre·too e brang·koo
colour	a cores	a ko·resh
slide	de diapositivos	de dee·a·po·zee·tee·voosh
(200) ASA	de (duzentos) ASA	de (doo·zeng·toosh) aa·za
When will it be ready?	Quando fica pronto?	kwang·doo fee·ka prong·too

Can you ...?	Pode ...?	po·de ...
develop this film	revelar este filme	rre·ve·*laar* esh·te feel·me
load my film	carregar o filme	kaa·rre·*gaar* oo feel·me
transfer photos	transferir as	trangsh·fe·*reer* ash
from my camera	fotografias	foo·too·gra·*fee*·ash
to CD	da minha máquina	da *mee*·nya *maa*·kee·na
	para um CD	*pa*·ra oong se·*de*

meeting people

greetings, goodbyes & introductions

Hello/Hi.	Olá.	o·*laa*
Good night.	Boa noite.	bo·a *noy*·te
Goodbye/Bye.	Adeus.	a·*de*·oosh
See you later.	Até logo.	a·*te* lo·goo

Mr	Senhor	se·*nyor*
Mrs	Senhora	se·*nyo*·ra
Ms	Senhorita	se·nyo·*ree*·ta

How are you?	Como está?	ko·moo shtaa
Fine. And you?	Bem. E você?	beng e vo·*se*
What's your name?	Qual é o seu nome?	kwaal e oo se·oo *no*·me
My name is ...	O meu nome é ...	oo me·oo *no*·me e ...
I'm pleased to	Prazer em conhecê-lo/	pra·*zer* eng koo·nye·*se*·lo/
meet you.	conhecê-la. m/f	koo·nye·*se*·la

This is my ...	Este é o meu ... m	esh·te e oo *me*·oo ...
	Esta é a minha ... f	esh·ta e a *mee*·nya ...
brother	irmão	eer·*mowng*
daughter	filha	*fee*·lya
father	pai	pai
friend	amigo/a m/f	a·*mee*·goo/a
husband	marido	ma·*ree*·doo
mother	mãe	maing
partner (intimate)	companheiro/a m/f	kong·pa·*nyay*·roo/a
sister	irmã	eer·*mang*
son	filho	*fee*·lyoo
wife	esposa	*shpo*·za

Here's my ...	Aqui está o meu ...	a·kee shtaa oo me·oo ...
What's your ...?	Qual é o seu ...?	kwaal e oo se·oo ...
address	endereço	eng·de·re·soo
email address	email	ee·mayl
fax number	número de fax	noo·me·roo de faaks
phone number	número de telefone	noo·me·roo de te·le·fo·ne

occupations

What's your occupation?
Qual é a sua profissão?   kwaal e a soo·a proo·fee·sowng

I'm a/an ...	Sou ...	soh ...
artist	artista m&f	ar·teesh·ta
business person	homem/mulher de negócios m/f	o·meng/moo·lyer de ne·go·syoosh
farmer	agricultor m&f	a·gree·kool·tor
manual worker	trabalhador m	tra·ba·lya·dor
	trabalhadora f	tra·ba·lya·do·ra
office worker	empregado/a de escritório m/f	eng·pre·gaa·doo/a de shkree·to·ryoo
scientist	cientista m&f	see·eng·teesh·ta
student	estudante m&f	shtoo·dang·te
tradesperson	comerciante m&f	koo·mer·see·aang·te

background

Where are you from? *De onde é?*   dong·de e

I'm from ...	Eu sou ...	e·oo soh ...
Australia	da Austrália	da owsh·traa·lya
Canada	do Canadá	doo ka·na·daa
England	da Inglaterra	da eeng·gla·te·rra
New Zealand	da Nova Zelândia	da no·va ze·lang·dya
the USA	dos Estados Unidos	doosh shtaa·doosh oo·nee·doosh

Are you married? *É casado/a? m/f*   e ka·zaa·doo/a

I'm ...	Eu sou ...	e·oo soh ...
married	casado/a m/f	ka·zaa·doo/a
single	solteiro/a m/f	sol·tay·roo/a

age

How old ...?	Quantos anos ...?	kwang·toosh a·noosh ...
are you	tem	teng
is your daughter	tem a sua filha	teng a soo·a fee·lya
is your son	tem o seu filho	teng oo se·oo fee·lyoo
I'm ... years old.	Tenho ... anos.	ta·nyoo ... a·noosh
He/She is ... years old.	Ele/Ela tem ... anos.	e·le/e·la teng ... a·noosh

feelings

I'm (not) ...	(Não) Estou ...	(nowng) shtoh ...
Are you ...?	Está ...	shtaa ...
cold	com frio	kong free·oo
happy	feliz	fe·leesh
hot	com calor	kong ka·lor
hungry	com fome	kong fo·me
OK	bem	beng
sad	triste	treesh·te
thirsty	com sede	kong se·de
tired	cansado/a m/f	kang·saa·doo/a

entertainment

going out

Where can I find ...?	Onde é que há ...?	ong·de e ke aa ...
clubs	discotecas	deesh·koo·te·kash
gay/lesbian	lugares de	loo·gaa·resh de
venues	gays/lésbicas	gaysh/lezh·bee·kash
pubs	bares	ba·resh
I feel like	Está-me a	shtaa·me a
going to a ...	apetecer ir a ...	a·pe·te·ser eer a ...
concert	um concerto	oong kong·ser·too
movies	um filme	oong feel·me
party	uma festa	oo·ma fesh·ta
restaurant	um restaurante	oong rresh·tow·rang·te
theatre	uma peça de teatro	oo·ma pe·sa de tee·aa·troo

interests

Do you like ...?	Gosta de ...?	gosh·ta de ...
I (don't) like ...	Eu (não) gosto de ...	e·oo (nowng) gosh·too de ...
art	arte	aar·te
cooking	cozinhar	koo·zee·nyaar
movies	ver filmes	ver feel·mesh
reading	ler	ler
sport	fazer desporto	fa·zer desh·por·too
travelling	viajar	vee·a·zhaar
Do you like to ...?	Costuma ...?	koosh·too·ma ...
dance	ir dançar	eer dang·saar
go to concerts	ir a concertos	eer a kong·ser·toosh
listen to music	ouvir música	oh·veer moo·zee·ka

food & drink

finding a place to eat

Can you	Pode-me	po·de·me
recommend a ...?	recomendar um ...?	rre·koo·meng·daar oong ...
bar	bar	bar
café	café	ka·fe
restaurant	restaurante	rresh·tow·rang·te
I'd like ..., please.	Queria uma ..., por favor.	ke·ree·a oo·ma ... poor fa·vor
a table for (five)	mesa para (cinco)	me·za pa·ra (seeng·koo)
the (non)smoking section	mesa de (não) fumador	me·za de (nowng) foo·ma·dor

ordering food

breakfast	pequeno almoço m	pe·ke·noo aal·mo·soo
lunch	almoço m	aal·mo·soo
dinner	jantar m	zhang·taar
snack	lanche m	lang·she

What would you recommend?
O que é que recomenda?   oo ke e ke rre·koo·meng·da

I'd like (the) ..., please.	Queria ..., por favor.	ke·ree·a ...poor fa·vor
bill	a conta	a kong·ta
drink list	a lista das bebidas	a leesh·ta dash be·bee·dash
menu	um menu	oong me·noo
that dish	aquele prato	a·ke·le praa·too

drinks

(cup of) coffee ...	(chávena de) café ...	(shaa·ve·na de) ka·fe ...
(cup of) tea ...	(chávena de) chá ...	(shaa·ve·na de) shaa ...
with milk	com leite	kong lay·te
without sugar	sem açúcar	seng a·soo·kar
(orange) juice	sumo (de laranja) m	soo·moo (de la·rang·zha)
soft drink	refrigerante m	rre·free·zhe·rang·te
... water	água ...	aa·gwa ...
hot	quente	keng·te
(sparkling) mineral	mineral (com gás)	mee·ne·raal (kong gaash)

in the bar

I'll have ...	Eu queria ...	e·oo ke·ree·a ...
I'll buy you a drink.	Eu pago-lhe uma bebida.	e·oo paa·goo·lye oo·ma be·bee·da
What would you like?	O que é que quer?	oo ke e ke ker
Cheers!	À nossa!	aa no·sa
brandy	brandy f	brang·dee
cocktail	cocktail m	kok·tayl
a shot of (whisky)	um copinho de (uísque)	oong koo·pee·nyoo de (oo·eesh·kee)
a ... of beer	... de cerveja	... de ser·ve·zha
bottle	uma garrafa	oo·ma ga·rraa·fa
glass	um copo	oong ko·poo
a bottle of ... wine	uma garrafa de vinho ...	oo·ma ga·rraa·fa de vee·nyoo ...
a glass of ... wine	um copo de vinho ...	oong ko·poo de vee·nyoo ...
red	tinto	teeng·too
sparkling	espumante	shpoo·mang·te
white	branco	brang·koo

self-catering

What's the local speciality?
Qual é a especialidade local?   kwaal e a shpe·see·a·lee·*daa*·de loo·*kaal*

What's that?
O que é aquilo?   oo ke e a·*kee*·loo

How much is (a kilo of cheese)?
Quanto é (um quilo de queijo)?   *kwang*·too e (oong *kee*·loo de *kay*·zhoo)

I'd like ...	*Eu queria ...*	e·oo ke·*ree*·a ...
(200) grams	*(duzentos) gramas*	(doo·*zeng*·toosh) *graa*·mash
(two) kilos	*(dois) quilos*	(doysh) *kee*·loosh
(three) pieces	*(três) peças*	(tresh) *pe*·sash
(six) slices	*(seis) fatias*	(saysh) fa·*tee*·ash

Less.	*Menos.*	*me*·noosh
Enough.	*Chega.*	*she*·ga
More.	*Mais.*	maish

special diets & allergies

Is there a vegetarian restaurant near here?
Há algum restaurante   aa aal·*goong* rresh·tow·*rang*·te
vegetariano perto daqui?   ve·zhe·ta·ree·*aa*·noo *per*·too da·*kee*

Do you have vegetarian food?
Tem comida vegetariana?   teng koo·*mee*·da ve·zhe·ta·ree·*aa*·na

Could you prepare	*Pode preparar*	*po*·de pre·pa·*raar*
a meal without ...?	*sem ...?*	seng ...
butter	*manteiga*	mang·*tay*·ga
eggs	*ovos*	*o*·voosh
meat stock	*caldo de carne*	*kaal*·doo de *kaar*·ne

I'm allergic to ...	*Eu sou alérgico/a*	e·oo soh a·*ler*·zhee·koo/a
	a ... m/f	a ...
dairy produce	*produtos lácteos*	pro·*doo*·toosh *laak*·tee·oosh
gluten	*glúten*	*gloo*·teng
MSG	*MSG*	e·me·e·se·*zhe*
nuts	*oleaginosas*	o·lee·a·zhee·*no*·zash
seafood	*marisco*	ma·*reesh*·koo

menu decoder

açorda f	a-*sor*-da	bread-based thick soup, flavoured with garlic, coriander & olive oil
alheiras f pl	a-*lyay*-rash	bread, garlic, chilli & meat sausage
arroz árabe m	a-*rrosh aa*-ra-be	rice with raisins, nuts & dried fruit
arroz de bacalhau m	a-*rrosh* de ba-ka-*lyow*	rice with shredded salt cod
assado de peixe m	a-*saa*-doo de *pay*-she	mix of roasted or baked fish
bacalhau no borralho m	ba-ka-*lyow* noo boo-*rraa*-lyoo	salt cod steak wrapped in cabbage leaves & bacon
bacalhau roupa-velha m	ba-ka-*lyow* rroh-pa-*ve*-lya	mixture of cabbage, salt cod & potatoes, sautéed in olive oil & garlic
bifana no pão f	bee-*fa*-na noo powng	thin pork steak sandwich
bitoque m	bee-*to*-ke	steak or fillet with a fried egg on top
bolo de mel m	*bo*-loo de mel	rich molasses & spice cake with candied fruit & almonds
borrachões m pl	boo-rra-*shoyngsh*	fried ring-shaped biscuits flavoured with brandy or white wine & cinnamon
caldeirada f	kaal-day-*raa*-da	soup-like stew, usually with fish
chanfana f	shang-*fa*-na	hearty stew with goat or mutton in heavy red wine sauce
chouriço m	shoh-*ree*-soo	garlicky pork sausage flavoured with red pepper paste
coelho à caçador m	koo-e-*lyoo* aa ka-sa-*dor*	rabbit stewed with wine & tomato
cozido à Portuguesa m	koo-*zee*-doo aa poor-too-*ge*-za	hearty meal with chunks of meats & sausages, vegetables, beans & rice
dobrada f	doo-*braa*-da	tripe with white beans & rice
duchesse f	doo-*shes*	puff pastry filled with whipped cream & topped with fruit

escabeche m	shka-*be*-she	*raw meat or fish pickled in olive oil, vinegar, garlic & bay leaf*
favada à Portuguesa f	fa-*vaa*-da aa poor-too-*ge*-za	*stew of fava beans, sausage & sometimes poached eggs*
feijoada f	fay-*zhwaa*-da	*bean stew with sausages or other meat*
francesinha f	frang-se-*zee*-nya	*ham, sausage & cheese in a tomato-cream sauce, on slices of bread*
gaspacho m	gash-*paa*-shoo	*chilled tomato & garlic bread soup with olive oil, vinegar & oregano*
jesuítas m pl	zhe-zoo-ee-tash	*puff pastry with baked meringue icing*
manjar branco m	mang-*zhaar* brang-koo	*coconut-milk & prunes pudding with syrup poured over the top*
migas f pl	*mee*-gash	*a side dish, usually bread flavoured with olive oil, garlic & spices & fried*
morgados m pl	mor-*gaa*-doosh	*sweetmeats made with almonds & figs*
pastéis de feijão m pl	pash-*taysh* de fay-*zhowng*	*rich lima bean & almond mixture in flaky pastry shells*
pataniscas de bacalhau f pl	pa-ta-*neesh*-kash de ba-ka-*lyow*	*seasoned salt cod fritters*
prato de grão m	*praa*-too de growng	*chickpea stew flavoured with tomato, garlic, bay leaf & cumin*
salada de atum f	sa-*laa*-da de a-*toong*	*salad of tuna, potato, peas, carrots & eggs in an olive oil & vinegar dressing*
salame de chocolate m	sa-*la*-me de shoo-koo-*laa*-te	*dense chocolate fudge roll studded with bits of biscuits, served sliced*
sopa de pedra f	*so*-pa de *pe*-dra	*vegetable soup with red beans, onions, potatoes, pig's ear, bacon & sausages*
tecolameco m	te-koo-la-*me*-koo	*rich orange & almond cake*
tripas à moda do Porto f pl	*tree*-pash aa *mo*-da doo *por*-too	*slow-cooked dried beans, trotters, tripe, chicken, vegetables & sausages*

emergencies

basics

Help!	*Socorro!*	soo·*ko*·rroo
Stop!	*Stop!*	stop
Go away!	*Vá-se embora!*	vaa·se eng·*bo*·ra
Thief!	*Ladrão!*	la·*drowng*
Fire!	*Fogo!*	*fo*·goo
Watch out!	*Cuidado!*	kwee·*daa*·doo

Call ...!	*Chame ...!*	*shaa*·me ...
a doctor	*um médico*	oong *me*·dee·koo
an ambulance	*uma ambulância*	*oo*·ma ang·boo·*lang*·sya
the police	*a polícia*	a poo·*lee*·sya

It's an emergency.
É uma emergência.   e *oo*·ma ee·mer·*zheng*·sya

Could you help me, please?
Pode ajudar, por favor?   *po*·de a·zhoo·*daar* poor fa·*vor*

Can I use the telephone?
Posso usar o seu telefone?   *po*·soo oo·*zaar* oo *se*·oo te·le·*fo*·ne

I'm lost.
Estou perdido/a. m/f   shtoh per·*dee*·doo/a

Where are the toilets?
Onde é a casa de banho?   *ong*·de e a *kaa*·za de *ba*·nyoo

police

Where's the police station?
Onde é a esquadra da polícia?   *ong*·de e a shkwaa·dra da poo·*lee*·sya

I want to report an offence.
Eu quero denunciar um crime.   e·oo *ke*·roo de·noong·see·*aar* oong *kree*·me

I have insurance.
Eu estou coberto/a pelo seguro. m/f   e·oo shtoh koo·*ber*·too/a *pe*·loo se·*goo*·roo

I've been assaulted.	*Eu fui agredido/a.* m/f	e·oo fwee a·gre·*dee*·doo/a
I've been raped.	*Eu fui violado/a.* m/f	e·oo fwee vee·oo·*laa*·doo/a
I've been robbed.	*Eu fui roubado/a.* m/f	e·oo fwee rroh·*baa*·doo/a

I've lost my ...	Eu perdi ...	e·oo per·dee
My ... was/were stolen.	Roubaram ...	rroh·baa·rang ...
backpack	a minha mochila	a meeng·nya moo·shee·la
bags	os meus sacos	oosh me·oosh saa·koosh
credit card	o meu cartão de crédito	oo me·oo kar·towng de kre·dee·too
handbag	a minha bolsa	a mee·nya bol·sa
jewellery	as minhas jóias	ash mee·nyash zhoy·ash
money	o meu dinheiro	oo me·oo dee·nyay·roo
passport	o meu passaporte	oo me·oo paa·sa·por·te
travellers cheques	os meus travellers cheques	oosh me·oosh tra·ve·ler she·kesh
wallet	a minha carteira	a mee·nya kar·tay·ra

I want to contact my ...	Eu quero contactar com ...	e·oo ke·roo kong·tak·taar kong ...
consulate	o meu consulado	oo me·oo kong·soo·laa·doo
embassy	a minha embaixada	a mee·nya eng·bai·shaa·da

health

medical needs

Where's the nearest ...?	Qual é ... mais perto?	kwaal e ... maish per·too
dentist	o dentista	oo deng·teesh·ta
doctor	o médico m	oo me·dee·koo
	a médica f	a me·dee·ka
hospital	o hospital	oo osh·pee·taal
(night) pharmacist	a farmácia (de serviço)	a far·maa·sya (de ser·vee·soo)

I need a doctor (who speaks English).
Eu preciso de um médico — e·oo pre·see·zoo de oong me·dee·koo
(que fale inglês). — (que faa·le eeng·glesh)

Could I see a female doctor?
Posso ser vista por uma médica? — po·soo ser veesh·ta poor oo·ma me·dee·ka

I've run out of my medication.
Os meus medicamentos — oosh me·oosh me·dee·ka·meng·toosh
acabaram. — a·ka·baa·rowng

symptoms, conditions & allergies

| I'm sick. | Estou doente. | shtoh doo·*eng*·te |
| It hurts here. | Dói-me aqui. | doy·me a·*kee* |

I have (a) ...	Eu tenho ...	e·oo ta·nyoo ...
asthma	asma	*ash*·ma
bronchitis	bronquite	brong·*kee*·te
constipation	prisão de ventre	pree·*zowng* de *veng*·tre
cough	tosse	*to*·se
diarrhoea	diarreia	dee·a·*rray*·a
fever	febre	*fe*·bre
headache	dor de cabeça	dor de ka·*be*·sa
heart condition	problemas cardíacos	proo·*ble*·mash kar·*dee*·a·koosh
nausea	náusea	*now*·zee·a
pain	dor	dor
sore throat	dores de garganta	*do*·resh de gar·*gang*·ta
toothache	uma dor de dentes	*oo*·ma dor de *deng*·tesh

I'm allergic to ...	Eu sou alérgico/a	e·oo soh a·*ler*·zhee·koo/a
	a ... m/f	a ...
antibiotics	antibióticos	ang·tee·bee·*o*·tee·koosh
anti-	anti-	ang·tee·
inflammatories	inflamatórios	eeng·fla·ma·*to*·ryoosh
aspirin	aspirina	ash·pee·*ree*·na
bees	abelhas	a·*be*·lyash
codeine	codeína	ko·de·*ee*·na
penicillin	penicilina	pe·nee·see·*lee*·na

antiseptic	antiséptico m	ang·tee·*se*·tee·koo
bandage	ligadura f	lee·ga·*doo*·ra
condoms	preservativos m pl	pre·zer·va·*tee*·voosh
contraceptives	contraceptivos m pl	kong·tra·se·*tee*·voosh
diarrhoea medicine	remédio para	re·*me*·dyo *pa*·ra
	diarreia m	dee·a·*rray*·a
insect repellent	repelente m	rre·pe·*leng*·te
laxatives	laxantes m pl	la·*shang*·tesh
painkillers	comprimidos	kong·pree·*mee*·doosh
	para as dores m pl	*pa*·ra ash *do*·resh
rehydration salts	sais rehidratantes m pl	saish rre·ee·dra·*tang*·tesh
sleeping tablets	pílulas para	*pee*·loo·laash *pa*·ra
	dormir f pl	door·*meer*

english–portuguese dictionary

Portuguese nouns and adjectives in this dictionary have their gender indicated with ⓜ (masculine) and ⓕ (feminine). If it's a plural noun, you'll also see pl. Words are also marked as v (verb), n (noun), a (adjective), pl (plural), sg (singular), inf (informal) and pol (polite) where necessary.

A

A

accident *acidente* ⓜ a-see-*deng*-te
accommodation *hospedagem* ⓕ osh-pe-*daa*-zheng
adaptor *adaptador* ⓜ a-da-pe-ta-*dor*
address *endereço* ⓜ eng-de-*re*-soo
after *depois* de-*poysh*
air conditioned *com ar condicionado* kong aar kong-dee-syoo-*naa*-doo
airplane *avião* ⓜ a-vee-*owng*
airport *aeroporto* ⓜ a-e-ro-*por*-too
alcohol *alcoól* ⓜ al-ko-*ol*
all a *todo/a* ⓜ/ⓕ *to*-doo/a
allergy *alergia* ⓕ a-ler-*zhee*-a
ambulance *ambulância* ⓕ ang-boo-*lang*-sya
and *e* e
ankle *tornozelo* ⓜ toor-noo-ze-loo
arm *braço* ⓜ *braa*-soo
ashtray *cinzeiro* ⓜ seeng-*zay*-roo
ATM *caixa automático* ⓜ *kai*-sha ow-too-*maa*-tee-koo

B

baby *bebé* ⓜ&ⓕ be-*be*
back (body) *costas* ⓕ pl *kosh*-tash
backpack *mochila* ⓕ moo-*shee*-la
bad *mau/má* ⓜ/ⓕ *ma*-oo/maa
bag *saco* ⓜ *saa*-koo
baggage claim *balcão de bagagens* ⓜ bal-*kowng* de ba-*gaa*-zhengsh
bank *banco* ⓜ *bang*-koo
bar *bar* ⓜ baar
bathroom *casa de banho* ⓕ *kaa*-za de ba-*nyoo*
battery *pilha* ⓕ *pee*-lya
beautiful *bonito/a* ⓜ/ⓕ boo-*nee*-too/a
bed *cama* ⓕ *ka*-ma
beer *cerveja* ⓕ ser-*ve*-zha
before *antes* *ang*-tesh
behind *atrás* a-*traash*
bicycle *bicicleta* ⓕ bee-see-*kle*-ta
big *grande* ⓜ&ⓕ *grang*-de

bill *conta* ⓕ *kong*-ta
black *preto/a* ⓜ/ⓕ *pre*-too/a
blanket *cobertor* ⓜ koo-ber-*tor*
blood group *grupo sanguíneo* ⓜ *groo*-poo sang-*gwee*-nee-oo
blue *azul* a-*zool*
boat *barco* ⓜ *baar*-koo
book (make a reservation) v *reservar* rre-zer-*vaar*
bottle *garrafa* ⓕ ga-*rraa*-fa
bottle opener *saca-rolhas* ⓕ *saa*-ka-*rro*-lyash
boy *menino* ⓜ me-*nee*-noo
brake (car) *travão* ⓜ tra-*vowng*
breakfast *pequeno almoço* ⓜ pe-*ke*-noo aal-*mo*-soo
broken (faulty) *defeituoso/a* ⓜ/ⓕ de-fay-too-*o*-zoo/a
bus *autocarro* ⓜ ow-to-*kaa*-roo
business *negócios* ⓜ pl ne-*go*-syoosh
buy *comprar* kong-*praar*

C

café *café* ⓜ ka-*fe*
camera *máquina fotográfica* ⓕ *maa*-kee-na foo-too-*graa*-fee-ka
camp site *parque de campismo* ⓜ *paar*-ke de kang-*peezh*-moo
cancel *cancelar* kang-se-*laar*
can opener *abre latas* ⓕ *aa*-bre *laa*-tash
car *carro* ⓜ *kaa*-rroo
cash *dinheiro* ⓜ dee-*nyay*-roo
cash (a cheque) v *levantar (um cheque)* le-vang-*taar* (oong she-ke)
cell phone *telemóvel* ⓜ te-le-*mo*-vel
centre *centro* ⓜ *seng*-troo
change (money) v *trocar* troo-*kaar*
cheap *barato/a* ba-*raa*-too/a
check (bill) *conta* ⓕ *kong*-ta
check-in *check-in* ⓜ shek-*eeng*
chest *peito* ⓜ *pay*-too
child *criança* ⓜ&ⓕ kree-*ang*-sa
cigarette *cigarro* ⓜ see-*gaa*-rroo
city *cidade* ⓕ see-*daa*-de
clean a *limpo/a* ⓜ/ⓕ *leeng*-poo/a

closed *fechado/a* ⓜ/ⓕ fe-shaa-doo/a
coffee *café* ⓜ ka-*fe*
coins *moedas* ⓕ pl moo-e-dash
cold a *frio/a* ⓜ/ⓕ free-oo/a
collect call *ligação a cobrar* ⓕ lee-ga-*sowng* a koo-braar
come *vir* veer
computer *computador* ⓜ kong-poo-ta-*dor*
condom *preservativo* ⓜ pre-zer-va-*tee*-voo
contact lenses *lentes de contacto* ⓜ pl
    leng-tesh de kong-*taak*-too
cook v *cozinhar* koo-zee-*nyaar*
cost *preço* ⓜ *pre*-soo
credit card *cartão de crédito* ⓜ kar-*towng* de *kre*-dee-too
cup *chávena* ⓕ *shaa*-ve-na
currency exchange *câmbio* ⓜ *kang*-byoo
customs (immigration) *alfândega* ⓕ aal-*fang*-de-ga

D

dangerous *perigoso/a* ⓜ/ⓕ pe-ree-*go*-zoo/a
date (time) *data* ⓕ *daa*-ta
day *dia* ⓜ *dee*-a
delay n *atraso* ⓜ a-*traa*-zoo
dentist *dentista* ⓜ&ⓕ deng-*teesh*-ta
depart *partir* par-*teer*
diaper *fralda* ⓕ *fraal*-da
dictionary *dicionário* ⓜ dee-syoo-*naa*-ryoo
dinner *jantar* ⓜ zhang-*taar*
direct *directo/a* ⓜ/ⓕ dee-*re*-too/a
dirty *sujo/a* ⓜ/ⓕ *soo*-zhoo/a
disabled *deficiente* de-fee-see-*eng*-te
discount *desconto* ⓜ desh-*kong*-too
doctor *médico/a* ⓜ/ⓕ *me*-dee-koo/a
double bed *cama de casal* ⓕ *ka*-ma de ka-*zaal*
double room *quarto de casal* ⓜ *kwaar*-too de ka-*zaal*
drink *bebida* ⓕ be-*bee*-da
drive v *conduzir* kong-doo-*zeer*
drivers licence *carta de condução* ⓕ
    kaar-ta de kong-doo-*sowng*
drugs (illicit) *droga* ⓕ *dro*-ga
dummy (pacifier) *chupeta* ⓕ shoo-*pe*-ta

E

ear *orelha* ⓕ o-*re*-lya
east *leste* *lesh*-te
eat *comer* koo-*mer*
economy class *classe económica* ⓕ
    klaa-se ee-koo-*no*-mee-ka
electricity *electricidade* ⓕ ee-le-tree-see-*daa*-de

elevator *elevador* ⓜ ee-le-va-*dor*
email *email* ⓜ ee-*mayl*
embassy *embaixada* ⓕ eng-bai-*shaa*-da
emergency *emergência* ⓕ ee-mer-*zheng*-sya
English (language) *inglês* ⓜ eeng-*glesh*
entrance *entrada* ⓕ eng-*traa*-da
evening *noite* ⓕ *noy*-te
exchange rate *taxa de câmbio* ⓕ *taa*-sha de *kang*-byoo
exit *saída* ⓕ saa-*ee*-da
expensive *caro/a* ⓜ/ⓕ *kaa*-roo/a
express mail *correio azul* ⓜ koo-*rray*-oo a-*zool*
eye *olho* ⓜ *o*-lyoo

F

far *longe* *long*-zhe
fast *rápido/a* ⓜ/ⓕ *rraa*-pee-doo/a
father *pai* ⓜ pai
film (camera) *filme* ⓜ *feel*-me
finger *dedo* ⓜ *de*-doo
first-aid kit *estojo de primeiros socorros* ⓜ
    shto-zhoo de pree-*may*-roosh so-*ko*-rroosh
first class *primeira classe* ⓕ pree-*may*-ra *klaa*-se
fish *peixe* ⓜ *pay*-she
food *comida* ⓕ koo-*mee*-da
foot *pé* ⓜ pe
fork *garfo* ⓜ *gaar*-foo
free (of charge) ⓐ *grátis graa*-teesh
friend *amigo/a* ⓜ/ⓕ a-*mee*-goo/a
fruit *fruta* ⓕ *froo*-ta
full *cheio/a* ⓜ/ⓕ *shay*-oo/a
funny *engraçado/a* ⓜ/ⓕ eng-gra-*saa*-doo/a

G

gift *presente* ⓜ pre-*zeng*-te
girl *menina* ⓕ me-*nee*-na
glass (drinking) *copo* ⓜ *ko*-poo
glasses *óculos* ⓜ pl *o*-koo-loosh
go *ir* eer
good *bom/boa* ⓜ/ⓕ bong/*bo*-a
green *verde ver*-de
guide n *guia* ⓕ *gee*-a

H

half *metade* ⓕ me-*taa*-de
hand *mão* ⓕ mowng
handbag *mala de mão* ⓕ *maa*-la de mowng
happy *feliz* ⓜ&ⓕ fe-*leesh*

have *ter* ter
he *ele* e·le
head *cabeça* ⓕ ka·be·sa
heart *coração* ⓜ koo·ra·sowng
heat *calor* ⓜ ka·lor
heavy *pesado/a* ⓜ/ⓕ pe·zaa·doo/a
help v *ajudar* a·zhoo·daar
here *aqui* a·kee
high *alto/a* ⓜ/ⓕ aal·too/aa
highway *autoestrada* ⓕ ow·to·shtraa·da
hike v *caminhar* ka·mee·nyaar
holiday *feriado* ⓜ fe·ree·aa·doo
homosexual n&a *homosexual* ⓜ&ⓕ
   o·mo·sek·soo·aal
hospital *hospital* ⓜ osh·pee·taal
hot *quente* keng·te
hotel *hotel* ⓜ o·tel
hungry *faminto/a* ⓜ/ⓕ fa·meeng·too/a
husband *marido* ⓜ ma·ree·doo

I

I *eu* e·oo
identification (card) *bilhete de identidade* ⓜ
   bee·lye·te de ee·deng·tee·daa·de
ill *doente* ⓜ&ⓕ doo·eng·te
important *importante* ⓜ&ⓕ eeng·por·tang·te
included *incluído/a* ⓜ/ⓕ eeng·kloo·ee·doo/a
injury *ferimento* ⓜ fe·ree·meng·too
insurance *seguro* se·goo·roo
Internet *internet* ⓕ eeng·ter·net
interpreter *intérprete* ⓜ&ⓕ eeng·ter·pre·te

J

jewellery *ourivesaria* ⓕ oh·ree·ve·za·ree·a
job *emprego* ⓜ eng·pre·goo

K

key *chave* ⓕ shaa·ve
kilogram *quilograma* ⓜ kee·loo·graa·ma
kitchen *cozinha* ⓕ koo·zee·nya
knife *faca* ⓕ faa·ka

L

laundry (place) *lavandaria* ⓕ la·vang·da·ree·a
lawyer *advogado/a* ⓜ/ⓕ a·de·voo·gaa·doo/a
left (direction) *esquerda* ⓕ shker·da

left-luggage office *perdidos e achados* ⓜ pl
   per·dee·doosh ee aa·shaa·doosh
leg *perna* ⓕ per·na
lesbian n&a *lésbica* ⓕ lezh·bee·ka
less *menos* me·noosh
letter (mail) *carta* ⓕ kaar·ta
lift (elevator) *elevador* ⓜ ee·le·va·dor
light *luz* ⓕ loosh
like v *gostar* goosh·taar
lock *tranca* ⓕ trang·ka
long *longo/a* ⓜ/ⓕ long·goo/a
lost *perdido/a* ⓜ/ⓕ per·dee·doo/a
lost-property office *gabinete de perdidos e achados* ⓜ
   gaa·bee·ne·te de per·dee·doosh ee a·shaa·doosh
love v *amar* a·maar
luggage *bagagem* ⓕ ba·gaa·zheng
lunch *almoço* ⓜ aal·mo·soo

M

mail *correio* ⓜ koo·rray·oo
man *homem* ⓜ o·meng
map *mapa* ⓜ maa·pa
market *mercado* ⓜ mer·kaa·doo
matches *fósforos* ⓜ pl fosh·foo·roosh
meat *carne* ⓕ kaar·ne
medicine *medicamentos* ⓜ pl me·dee·ka·meng·toosh
menu *ementa* ⓕ ee·meng·ta
message *mensagem* ⓕ meng·saa·zheng
milk *leite* ⓜ lay·te
minute *minuto* ⓜ mee·noo·too
mobile phone *telemóvel* ⓜ te·le·mo·vel
money *dinheiro* ⓜ dee·nyay·roo
month *mês* ⓜ mesh
morning *manhã* ⓕ ma·nyang
mother *mãe* ⓕ maing
motorcycle *mota* ⓕ mo·ta
motorway *autoestrada* ⓕ ow·to·shtraa·da
mouth *boca* ⓕ bo·ka
music *música* ⓕ moo·zee·ka

N

name *nome* ⓜ no·me
napkin *guardanapo* ⓜ gwar·da·naa·poo
nappy *fralda* ⓕ fraal·da
near *perto* per·too
neck *pescoço* ⓜ pesh·ko·soo
new *novo/a* ⓜ/ⓕ no·voo/a
news *notícias* ⓕ pl noo·tee·syash

newspaper *jornal* (m) zhor-*naal*
night *noite* (f) *noy*-te
no *não* nowng
noisy *barulhento/a* (m)/(f) ba-roo-*lyeng*-too/a
nonsmoking *não-fumador* nowng-foo-ma-*dor*
north *norte* nor-te
nose *nariz* (m) na-*reesh*
now *agora* a-*go*-ra
number *número* (m) *noo*-me-roo

O

oil (engine) *petróleo* (m) pe-*tro*-lyoo
old *velho/a* (m)/(f) *ve*-lyoo/a
one-way ticket *bilhete de ida* bee-*lye*-te de *ee*-da
open a *aberto/a* (m)/(f) a-*ber*-too/a
outside *fora* fo-ra

P

package *embrulho* (m) eng-*broo*-lyoo
paper *papel* (m) pa-*pel*
park (car) v *estacionar* shta-syoo-*naar*
passport *passaporte* (m) paa-sa-*por*-te
pay *pagar* pa-*gaar*
pen *caneta* (f) ka-*ne*-ta
petrol *gasolina* (f) ga-zoo-*lee*-na
pharmacy *farmácia* (f) far-*maa*-sya
phonecard *cartão telefónico* (m)
  kar-*towng*-te-le-fo-nee-koo
photo *fotografia* (f) foo-too-gra-*fee*-a
plate *prato* (m) *praa*-too
police *polícia* (f) poo-*lee*-sya
Portugal *Portugal* (m) poor-too-*gaal*
Portuguese (language) *português* (m) poor-too-*gesh*
postcard *postal* (m) poosh-*taal*
post office *correio* (m) koo-*rray*-oo
pregnant *grávida* (f) *graa*-vee-da
price *preço* (m) *pre*-soo

Q

quiet *calado/a* (m)/(f) ka-*laa*-doo/a

R

rain *chuva* (f) *shoo*-va
razor *gilete* (f) zhee-*le*-te
receipt *recibo* (m) rre-*see*-boo
red *vermelho/a* (m)/(f) ver-*me*-lyoo/a

refund *reembolso* (m) rre-eng-*bol*-soo
registered mail *correio registado* (m)
  koo-*rray*-oo re-zhee-*shtaa*-doo
rent v *alugar* a-loo-*gaar*
repair v *consertar* konq-ser-*tnar*
reservation *reserva* (f) rre-*zer*-va
restaurant *restaurante* (m) rresh-tow-*rang*-te
return v *voltar* vol-*taar*
return ticket *bilhete de ida e volta* (m)
  bee-*lye*-te de *ee*-da ee *vol*-ta
right (direction) *direita* (f) dee-*ray*-ta
road *estrada* (f) *shtraa*-da
room *quarto* (m) *kwaar*-too

S

safe a *seguro/a* (m)/(f) se-*gon*-roo/a
sanitary napkin *penso higiénico* (m)
  peng-soo ee-zhee-e-nee-koo
seat *assento* (m) a-*seng*-too
send *enviar* eng-vee-*aar*
service station *posto de gasolina* (m)
  posh-too de ga-zoo-*lee*-na
sex *sexo* (m) *sek*-soo
shampoo *champô* (m) shang-*poo*
share (a dorm) *partilhar* par-tee-*lyaar*
shaving cream *creme de barbear* (m)
  kre-me de bar-bee-*aar*
she *ela* e-la
sheet (bed) *lençol* (m) leng-*sol*
shirt *camisa* (f) ka-*mee*-za
shoes *sapatos* (m) pl sa-*paa*-toosh
shop n *loja* (f) *lo*-zha
short *curto/a* (m)/(f) *koor*-too/a
shower n *chuveiro* (m) shoo-*vay*-roo
single room *quarto de solteiro* (m)
  kwaar-too de sol-*tay*-roo
skin *pele* (f) *pe*-le
skirt *saia* (f) *sai*-a
sleep v *dormir* door-*meer*
slowly *vagarosamente* va-ga-ro-za-*meng*-te
small *pequeno/a* (m)/(f) pe-*ke*-noo/a
smoke (cigarettes) v *fumar* foo-*maar*
soap *sabonete* (m) sa-boo-*ne*-te
some *uns/umas* (m)/(f) pl oongsh/*oo*-mash
soon *em breve* eng *bre*-ve
south *sul* sool
souvenir shop *loja de lembranças* (f)
  lo-zha de leng-*brang*-sash
speak *falar* fa-*laar*

spoon *colher* ① koo-*lyer*
stamp *selo* ⓜ se-loo
stand-by ticket *bilhete sem garantia* ⓜ
bee-*lye*-te seng ga-rang-*tee*-a
station (train) *estação* ① shta-*sowng*
stomach *estômago* ⓜ *shto*-ma-goo
stop v *parar* pa-*raar*
stop (bus) *paragem* ① pa-*raa*-zheng
street *rua* ① *rroo*-a
student *estudante* ⓜ&① shtoo-*dang*-te
sun *sol* ⓜ sol
sunscreen *protecção anti-solar* ①
proo-te-*sowng* ang-tee-soo-*laar*
swim v *nadar* na-*daar*

T

tampons *tampões* ⓜ pl tang-*powngsh*
taxi *táxi* ⓜ *taak*-see
teaspoon *colher de chá* ① koo-*lyer* de shaa
teeth *dentes* ⓜ pl *deng*-tesh
telephone *telefone* ① te-le-*fo*-ne
television *televisão* ① te-le-vee-*zowng*
temperature (weather) *temperatura* ①
teng-pe-ra-*too*-ra
tent *tenda* ① *teng*-da
that (one) *aquele/a* ⓜ/① a-*ke*-le/a
they *eles/elas* ⓜ/① *e*-lesh/*e*-lash
thirsty *sedento/a* ⓜ/① se-*deng*-too/a
this (one) *este/a* ⓜ/① *esh*-te/a
throat *garganta* ① gar-*gang*-ta
ticket *bilhete* ⓜ bee-*lye*-te
time *tempo* ⓜ *teng*-poo
tired *cansado/a* ⓜ/① kang-*saa*-doo/a
tissues *lenços de papel* ⓜ pl *leng*-soosh de pa-*pel*
today *hoje* o-zhe
toilet *casa de banho* ① *kaa*-za de *ba*-nyoo
tomorrow *amanhã* aa-ma-*nyang*
tonight *hoje à noite* o-zhe aa *noy*-te
toothbrush *escova de dentes* ① *shko*-va de *deng*-tesh
toothpaste *pasta de dentes* ① *paash*-ta de *deng*-tesh
torch (flashlight) *lanterna eléctrica* ①
lang-*ter*-na e-*le*-tree-ka
tour n *excursão* ① shkoor-*sowng*
tourist office *escritório de turismo* ⓜ
shkree-*to*-ryoo de too-*reezh*-moo
towel *toalha* ① *twaa*-lya
train *comboio* ⓜ kong-*boy*-oo
translate *traduzir* tra-doo-*zeer*

travel agency *agência de viagens* ①
a-*zheng*-sya de vee-*aa*-zhengsh
travellers cheque *travellers cheque* ⓜ *tra*-ve-ler shek
trousers *calças* ① pl *kaal*-sash
twin beds *camas gémeas* ① pl *ka*-mash *zhe*-me-ash
tyre *pneu* ⓜ pe-*ne*-oo

U

underwear *roupa interior* ① *rroh*-pa eeng-te-ree-*or*
urgent *urgente* ⓜ&① oor-*zheng*-te

V

vacant *vago/a* ⓜ/① *vaa*-goo/a
vacation *férias* ① pl *fe*-ree-ash
vegetable *legume* ⓜ le-*goo*-me
vegetarian a *vegetariano/a* ⓜ/① ve-zhe-ta-ree-*a*-noo/a
visa *visto* ⓜ *veesh*-too

W

waiter *criado/a de mesa* ⓜ/① kree-*aa*-doo/a de *me*-za
walk v *caminhar* ka-mee-*nyaar*
wallet *carteira* ① kar-*tay*-ra
warm a *morno/a* ⓜ/① *mor*-noo/a
wash (something) *lavar* la-*vaar*
watch *relógio* ⓜ rre-*lo*-zhyoo
water *água* ① *aa*-gwa
we *nós* nosh
weekend *fim-de-semana* ⓜ feeng-de-se-*ma*-na
west *oeste* o-*esh*-te
wheelchair *cadeira de rodas* ① ka-*day*-ra de *rro*-dash
when *quando* *kwang*-doo
where *onde* *ong*-de
white *branca/a* ⓜ/① *brang*-koo/a
who *quem* keng
why *porquê* poor-*ke*
wife *esposa* ① *shpo*-za
window *janela* ① zha-*ne*-la
wine *vinho* ⓜ *vee*-nyoo
with *com* kong
without *sem* seng
woman *mulher* ① moo-*lyer*
write *escrever* shkre-*ver*

Y

yellow *amarelo/a* ⓜ/① a-ma-*re*-loo/a
yes *sim* seeng
yesterday *ontem* *ong*-teng
you inf sg/pl *tu/vocês* too/vo-*sesh*
you pol sg/pl *você/vós* vo-se/vosh

Spanish

spanish alphabet

A a a	B b be	C c the	Ch ch che	D d de
E e e	F f e·fe	G g khe	H h a·che	I i ee
J j kho·ta	K k ka	L l e·le	LL ll e·lye	M m e·me
N n e·ne	Ñ ñ e·nye	O o o	P p pe	Q q koo
R r e·re	S s e·se	T t te	U u oo	V v oo·ve
W w oo·ve do·vle	X x e·kees	Y y ee·grye·ga	Z z the·ta	

spanish

ESPAÑOL

SPANISH

español

introduction

The lively and picturesque language of Cervantes' *Don Quijote* and Almodóvar's movies, Spanish (*español* es·pa·*nyol*), or Castilian (*castellano* kas·te·*lya*·no), as it's also called in Spain, has over 390 million speakers worldwide. Outside Spain, it's the language of most of Latin America and the West Indies and is also spoken in the Philippines and Guam, in some areas of the African coast and in the US.

Spanish belongs to the Romance group of languages – the descendents of Latin – together with French, Italian, Portuguese and Romanian. It's derived from Vulgar Latin, which Roman soldiers and merchants brought to the Iberian Peninsula during the period of Roman conquest (3rd to 1st century BC). By 19 BC Spain had become totally Romanised and Latin became the language of the peninsula in the four centuries that followed. Thanks to the Arabic invasion in AD 711 and the Arabs' continuing presence in Spain during the next eight centuries, Spanish has also been strongly influenced by Arabic, although mostly in the vocabulary. Today's Castilian is spoken in the north, centre and south of Spain. Completing the colourful linguistic profile of the country, Basque (*euskera* e·oos·ke·ra), Catalan (*catalán* ka ta·*lan*) and Galician (*gallego* ga·*lye*·go) are also official languages in Spain, though Castilian covers by far the largest territory.

Besides the shared vocabulary of Latin origin that English and Spanish have in common, there's also a large corpus of words from the indigenous American languages that have entered English via Spanish. After Columbus' discovery of the New World in 1492, America's indigenous languages had a considerable impact on Spanish, especially in words to do with flora, fauna and topography (such as *tobacco*, *chocolate*, *coyote*, *canyon*, to name only a few).

Even if you're not familiar with the sound of Spanish through, say, the voices of José Carreras or Julio Iglesias, you'll be easily seduced by this melodic language and have fun trying to roll your *rr*'s like the locals. You may have heard the popular legend about one of the Spanish kings having a slight speech impediment which prompted all of Spain to mimick his lisp. Unfortunately, this charming explanation of the lisping 's' is only a myth – it's actually due to the way Spanish evolved from Latin and has nothing to do with lisping monarchs at all. So, when you hear someone say *gracias* gra·thyas, they're no more lisping than when you say 'thank you' in English.

pronunciation

vowel sounds

Vowels are pronounced short and fairly closed. The sound remains level, and each vowel is pronounced as an individual unit. There are, however, a number of cases where two vowel sounds become very closely combined (so-called diphthongs).

symbol	english equivalent	spanish example	transliteration
a	run	*agua*	*a*·gwa
ai	aisle	*bailar*	bai·*lar*
ay	say	*seis*	says
e	bet	*número*	*noo*·me·ro
ee	see	*día*	*dee*·a
o	pot	*ojo*	*o*·kho
oo	zoo	*gusto*	*goo*·sto
ow	how	*autobús*	ow·to·*boos*
oy	toy	*hoy*	oy

word stress

Spanish words have stress, which means you emphasise one syllable of a word over another. Here's a rule of thumb: when a written word ends in *n*, *s* or a vowel, the stress falls on the second-last syllable. Otherwise, the final syllable is stressed. If you see an accent mark over a syllable, it cancels out this rule and you just stress that syllable instead. You needn't worry about this though, as the stressed syllables are always italicised in our pronunciation guides .

consonant sounds

Remember that in Spanish the letter *h* is never pronounced. The Spanish *v* sounds more like a b, said with the lips pressed together. When ending a word, *d* is pronounced soft, like a th, or it's so slight it doesn't get pronounced at all. Finally, try to roll your *r*'s, especially at the start of a word and in words with *rr*.

symbol	english equivalent	spanish example	transliteration
b	bed	*barco*	*bar*-ko
ch	cheat	*chica*	*chee*-ka
d	dog	*dinero*	dee-*ne*-ro
f	fat	*fiesta*	*fye*-sta
g	go	*gato*	*ga*-to
k	kit	*cabeza, queso*	ka-*be*-tha, *ke*-so
kh	loch (harsh and guttural)	*jardín, gente*	khar-*deen*, *khen*-te
l	lot	*lago*	*la*-go
ly	million	*llamada*	lya-*ma*-da
m	man	*mañana*	ma-*nya*-na
n	not	*nuevo*	*nwe*-vo
ny	canyon	*señora*	se-*nyo*-ra
p	pet	*padre*	*pa*-dre
r	like 'tt' in 'butter' said fast	*hora*	*o*-ra
rr	run (but stronger and rolled)	*ritmo, burro*	*rreet*-mo, *boo*-rro
s	sun	*semana*	se-*ma*-na
t	top	*tienda*	*tyen*-da
th	thin	*Barcelona, manzana*	bar-**the**-*lo*-na, man-*tha*-na
v	soft 'b', between 'v' and 'b'	*abrir*	a-*vreer*
w	win	*guardia*	*gwar*-dya
y	yes	*viaje*	*vya*-khe

basics

language difficulties

Do you speak English?
¿Habla inglés?   *ab*·la een·*gles*

Do you understand?
¿Me entiende?   me en·*tyen*·de

I (don't) understand.
(No) Entiendo.   (no) een·*tyen*·do

What does (*cuenta*) mean?
¿Qué significa (cuenta)?   ke seeg·nee·*fee*·ka (*kwen*·ta)

How do you ...?	*¿Cómo se ...?*	*ko*·mo se ...
pronounce this	*pronuncia esta*	pro·*noon*·thya *es*·ta
word	*palabra*	pa·*lab*·ra
write (*ciudad*)	*escribe (ciudad)*	es·*kree*·be (thee·oo·*da*)

Could you	*¿Puede ...,*	*pwe*·de ...
please ...?	*por favor?*	por fa·*vor*
repeat that	*repetir*	rre·pe·*teer*
speak more slowly	*hablar más despacio*	ab·*lar* mas des·*pa*·thyo
write it down	*escribirlo*	es·kree·*beer*·lo

numbers

0	cero	*the*·ro	16	*dieciséis*	dye·thee·*seys*
1	uno	*oo*·no	17	*diecisiete*	dye·thee·*sye*·te
2	dos	dos	18	*dieciocho*	dye·thee·*o*·cho
3	tres	tres	19	*diecinueve*	dye·thee·*nwe*·ve
4	cuatro	*kwa*·tro	20	*veinte*	*veyn*·te
5	cinco	*theen*·ko	21	*veintiuno*	veyn·tee·*oo*·no
6	seis	seys	22	*veintidós*	veyn·tee·*dos*
7	siete	*sye*·te	30	*treinta*	*treyn*·ta
8	ocho	*o*·cho	40	*cuarenta*	kwa·*ren*·ta
9	nueve	*nwe*·ve	50	*cincuenta*	theen·*kwen*·ta
10	diez	dyeth	60	*sesenta*	se·*sen*·ta
11	once	*on*·the	70	*setenta*	se·*ten*·ta
12	doce	*do*·the	80	*ochenta*	o·*chen*·ta
13	trece	*tre*·the	90	*noventa*	no·*ven*·ta
14	catorce	ka·*tor*·the	100	*cien*	thyen
15	quince	*keen*·the	1000	*mil*	mil

time & dates

What time is it?	*¿Qué hora es?*	ke *o*·ra es
It's one o'clock.	*Es la una.*	es la *oo*·na
It's (10) o'clock.	*Son (las diez).*	son (las dyeth)
Quarter past (one).	*Es (la una) y cuarto.*	es (la *oo*·na) ee *kwar*·to
Half past (one).	*Es (la una) y media.*	es (la *oo*·na) ee *me*·dya
Quarter to (one).	*Es (la una) menos cuarto.*	es (la *oo*·na) *me*·nos *kwar*·to
At what time ...?	*¿A qué hora ...?*	a ke *o*·ra ...
At ...	*A las ...*	a las ...
am	*de la mañana*	de la ma·*nya*·na
pm	*de la tarde*	de la *tar*·de
Monday	*lunes*	*loo*·nes
Tuesday	*martes*	*mar*·tes
Wednesday	*miércoles*	*myer*·ko·les
Thursday	*jueves*	*khwe*·ves
Friday	*viernes*	*vyer*·nes
Saturday	*sábado*	*sa*·ba·do
Sunday	*domingo*	do·*meen*·go

January	enero	e·*ne*·ro
February	febrero	fe·*bre*·ro
March	marzo	*mar*·tho
April	abril	a·*breel*
May	mayo	*ma*·yo
June	junio	*khoo*·nyo
July	julio	*khoo*·lyo
August	agosto	a·*gos*·to
September	septiembre	sep·*tyem*·bre
October	octubre	ok·*too*·bre
November	noviembre	no·*vyem*·bre
December	diciembre	dee·*thyem*·bre

What date is it today?
   ¿Qué día es hoy?   ke *dee*·a es oy

It's (18 October).
   Es (el dieciocho de octubre).   es (el dye·thee·o·cho de ok·*too*·bre)

| since (May) | desde (mayo) | *des*·de (*ma*·yo) |
| until (June) | hasta (junio) | *as*·ta (*khoo*·nyo) |

last ...		
night	anoche	a·*no*·che
week	la semana pasada	la se·*ma*·na pa·*sa*·da
month	el mes pasado	el mes pa·*sa*·do
year	el año pasado	el *a*·nyo pa·*sa*·do

next ...	... que viene	... ke *vye*·ne
week	la semana	la se·*ma*·na
month	el mes	el mes
year	el año	el *a*·nyo

yesterday/tomorrow ...	ayer/mañana por la ...	a·*yer*/ma·*nya*·na por la ...
morning	mañana	ma·*nya*·na
afternoon	tarde	*tar*·de
evening	noche	*no*·che

weather

What's the weather like?	¿Qué tiempo hace?	ke *tyem*·po *a*·the

It's ...

cloudy	Está nublado.	es·*ta* noo·*bla*·do
cold	Hace frío.	*a*·the *free*·o
hot	Hace calor.	*a*·the ka·*lor*
raining	Está lloviendo.	es·*ta* lyo·*vyen*·do
snowing	Está nevando.	es·*ta* ne·*van*·do
sunny	Hace sol.	*a*·the sol
warm	Hace calor.	*a*·the ka·*lor*
windy	Hace viento.	*a*·the *vyen*·to

spring	*primavera* f	pree·ma·*ve*·ra
summer	*verano* m	ve·*ra*·no
autumn	*otoño* m	o·*to*·nyo
winter	*invierno* m	een·*vyer*·no

border crossing

I'm here ...	Estoy aquí ...	es·*toy* a·*kee* ...
in transit	en tránsito	en *tran*·see·to
on business	de negocios	de ne·*go*·thyos
on holiday	de vacaciones	de va·ka·*thyo*·nes

I'm here for ...	Estoy aquí por ...	es·*toy* a·*kee* por ...
(10) days	(diez) días	(dyeth) *dee*·as
(three) weeks	(tres) semanas	(tres) se·*ma*·nas
(two) months	(dos) meses	(dos) *me*·ses

I'm going to (Salamanca).
Voy a (Salamanca).   voy a (sa·la·*man*·ka)

I'm staying at the (Flores Hotel).
Me estoy alojando en (hotel Flores).   me es·*toy* a·lo·*khan*·do en (o·*tel flo*·res)

I have nothing to declare.
No tengo nada que declarar.   no *ten*·go *na*·da ke dek·la·*rar*

I have something to declare.
Quisiera declarar algo.   kee·*sye*·ra dek·la·*rar al*·go

That's (not) mine.
Eso (no) es mío.   eso (no) es *mee*·o

transport

tickets & luggage

Where can I buy a ticket?
¿Dónde puedo comprar un billete?   *don*·de *pwe*·do kom·*prar* oon bee·*lye*·te

Do I need to book a seat?
¿Tengo que reservar?   *ten*·go ke rre·ser·*var*

One ... ticket to   *Un billete ... a*   oon bee·*lye*·te ... a
(Barcelona), please.   *(Barcelona), por favor.*   (bar·the·*lo*·na) por fa·*vor*
  one-way   *sencillo*   sen·*thee*·lyo a
  return   *de ida y vuelta*   de ee·da ee *vwel*·ta

I'd like to ...   *Me gustaría ...*   me goos·ta·*ree*·a ...
my ticket.   *mi billete.*   mee bee·*lye*·te
  cancel   *cancelar*   kan·the·*lar*
  change   *cambiar*   kam·*byar*
  confirm   *confirmar*   kon·feer·*mar*

How much is it?
¿Cuánto cuesta?   kwan·to *kwes*·ta

Is there air conditioning?
¿Hay aire acondicionado?   ai *ai*·re a·kon·dee·thyo·*na*·do

Is there a toilet?
¿Hay servicios?   ai ser·*vee*·thyos

How long does the trip take?
¿Cuánto se tarda?   *kwan*·to se *tar*·da

Is it a direct route?
¿Es un viaje directo?   es oon *vya*·khe dee·*rek*·to

I'd like a luggage locker.
Quisiera un casillero de consigna.   kee·*sye*·ra oon ka·see·*lye*·ro de kon·*seeg*·na

My luggage	Mis maletas	mees ma·le·tas
has been ...	han sido ...	an see·do ...
damaged	dañadas	da·nya·das
lost	perdidas	per·dee·das
stolen	robadas	rro·ba·das

getting around

Where does flight (G10) arrive/depart?
¿Dónde llega/sale el vuelo (G10)?   don·de lye·ga/sa·le el vwe·lo (khe dyeth)

Where's the ...?	¿Dónde está...?	don·de es·ta ...
arrivals hall	el hall de partidas	el hol de par·tee·das
departures hall	el hall de llegadas	el hol de lye·ga·das
duty-free shop	la tienda libre de	la tyen·da lee·bre de
	impuestos	eem·pwe·stos
gate (12)	la puerta (doce)	la pwer·ta (do·the)

Is this the ...	¿Es el ... para	es el ... pa·ra
to (Valencia)?	(Valencia)?	(va·len·thya)
boat	barco	bar·ko
bus	autobús	ow·to·boos
plane	avión	a·vyon
train	tren	tren

What time's	¿A qué hora es el	a ke o·ra es el
the ... bus?	... autobús?	... ow·to·boos
first	primer	pree·mer
last	último	ool·tee·mo
next	próximo	prok·see·mo

At what time does it arrive/leave?
¿A qué hora llega/sale?   a ke o·ra lye·ga/sa·le

How long will it be delayed?
¿Cuánto tiempo se retrasará?   kwan·to tyem·po se rre·tra·sa·ra

What station/stop is this?
¿Cuál es esta estación/parada?   kwal es es·ta es·ta·thyon/pa·ra·da

What's the next station/stop?
¿Cuál es la próxima   kwal es la prok·see·ma
estación/parada?   es·ta·thyon/pa·ra·da

Does it stop at (Aranjuez)?
¿Para en (Aranjuez)?   pa·ra en (a·ran·khweth)

Please tell me when we get to (Seville).
¿Puede avisarme   pwe·de a·vee·sar·me
cuando lleguemos a (Sevilla)?   kwan·do lye·ge·mos a (se·vee·lya)

How long do we stop here?
¿Cuánto tiempo vamos a parar aquí?   kwan·to tyem·po va·mos a pa·rar a·kee

Is this seat available?
¿Está libre este asiento?   es·ta lee·bre es·te a·syen·to

That's my seat.
Ése es mi asiento.   e·se es mee a·syen·to

I'd like a taxi ...	*Quisiera un taxi ...*	kee·sye·ra oon tak·see ...
at (9am)	*a (las nueve*	a (las nwe·ve
	de la mañana)	de la ma·nya·na)
now	*ahora*	a·o·ra
tomorrow	*mañana*	ma·nya·na

Is this taxi available?
¿Está libre este taxi?   es·ta lee·bre es·te tak·see

How much is it to ...?
¿Cuánto cuesta ir a ...?   kwan·to kwes·ta eer a ...

Please put the meter on.
Por favor, ponga el taxímetro.   por fa·vor pon·ga el tak·see·me·tro

Please take me to (this address).
Por favor, lléveme a (esta dirección).   por fa·vor lye·ve·me a (es·ta dee·rek·thyon)

Please ...	*Por favor ...*	por fa·vor ...
slow down	*vaya más despacio*	va·ya mas des·pa·thyo
stop here	*pare aquí*	pa·re a·kee
wait here	*espere aquí*	es·pe·re a·kee

car, motorbike & bicycle hire

I'd like to hire a ...	*Quisiera alquilar ...*	kee·sye·ra al·kee·lar ...
bicycle	*una bicicleta*	oo·na bee·thee·kle·ta
car	*un coche*	oon ko·che
motorbike	*una moto*	oo·na mo·to

with ...	con ...	kon ...
a driver	chófer	cho-fer
air conditioning	aire acondicionado	ai-re a-kon-dee-thyo-na-do
antifreeze	anticongelante	an-tee-kon-khe-lan-te
snow chains	cadenas de nieve	ka-de-nas de nye-ve

How much for	¿Cuánto cuesta	kwan-to kwes-ta
... hire?	el alquiler por ...?	el al-kee-ler por ...
hourly	hora	o-ra
daily	día	dee-a
weekly	semana	se-ma-na

air	aire m	ai-re
oil	aceite m	a-they-te
petrol	gasolina f	ga-so-lee-na
tyres	neumáticos f pl	ne-oo-ma-tee-kos

I need a mechanic.
Necesito un mecánico.   ne-the-see-to oon me-ka-nee-ko

I've run out of petrol.
Me he quedado sin gasolina.   me e ke-da-do seen ga-so-lee-na

I have a flat tyre.
Tengo un pinchazo.   ten-go oon peen-cha-tho

directions

Where's the ...?	¿Dónde está/ están ...? sg/pl	don-de es-ta/ es-tan ...
bank	el banco sg	el ban-ko
city centre	el centro de la ciudad sg	el then-tro de la theew-da
hotel	el hotel sg	el o-tel
market	el mercado sg	el mer-ka-do
police station	la comisaría sg	la ko-mee-sa-ree-a
post office	el correos sg	el ko-rre-os
public toilet	los servicios pl	los ser-vee-thyos
tourist office	la oficina de turismo sg	la o-fee-thee-na de too-rees-mo

Is this the road to (Valladolid)?
¿Se va a (Valladolid) por esta carretera? — se va a (va·lya·do·*lee*) por *es*·ta ka·rre·*te*·ra

Can you show me (on the map)?
¿Me lo puede indicar (en el mapa)? — me lo *pwe*·de een·dee·*kar* (en el *ma*·pa)

What's the address?
¿Cuál es la dirección? — *kwal* es la dee·rek·*thyon*

How far is it?
¿A cuánta distancia está? — a *kwan*·ta dees·*tan*·thya es·*ta*

How do I get there?
¿Cómo se llega ahí? — *ko*·mo se *lye*·ga a·*ee*

Turn ...	Doble ...	do·ble ...
at the corner	en la esquina	en la es·*kee*·na
at the traffic lights	en el semáforo	en el se·*ma*·fo·ro
left	a la izquierda	a la eeth·*kyer*·da
right	a la iderecha	a la de·*re*·cha

It's ...	Está ...	es·ta ...
behind ...	detrás de ...	de·*tras* de ...
far away	lejos	*le*·khos
here	aquí	a·*kee*
in front of ...	enfrente de ...	en·*fren*·te de ...
left	por la izquierda	por la eeth·*kyer*·da
near (to ...)	cerca (de ...)	*ther*·ka (de ...)
next to ...	al lado de ...	al *la*·do de ...
opposite ...	frente a ...	*fren*·te a ...
right	por la derecha	por la de·*re*·cha
straight ahead	todo recto	*to*·do *rrek*·to
there	ahí	a·*ee*

by bus	por autobús	por *ow*·to·boos
by taxi	por taxi	por *tak*·see
by train	por tren	por tren
on foot	a pie	a pye

north	norte m	*nor*·te
south	sur m	soor
east	este m	*es*·te
west	oeste m	o·*es*·te

Acceso/Salida	ak-*the*-so/sa-*lee*-da	**Entrance/Exit**
Abierto/Cerrado	a-*byer*-to/the-*rra*-do	**Open/Closed**
Hay Lugar	ai loo-*gar*	**Rooms Available**
No Hay Lugar	no ai loo-*gar*	**No Vacancies**
Información	een-for-ma-*thyon*	**Information**
Comisaría	ko-mee-sa-*ree*-a	**Police Station**
de Policía	de po-lee-*thee*-a	
Prohibido	pro-ee-*bee*-do	**Prohibited**
Servicios	ser-*vee*-thyos	**Toilets**
Caballeros	ka-ba-*lye*-ros	**Men**
Señoras	se-*nyo*-ras	**Women**
Caliente/Frío	ka-*lyen*-te/*free*-o	**Hot/Cold**

accommodation

finding accommodation

Where's a ...?	*¿Dónde hay ...?*	*don*-de ai ...
camping ground	*un terreno de cámping*	oon te-*rre*-no de *kam*-peeng
guesthouse	*una pensión*	*oo*-na pen-*syon*
hotel	*un hotel*	oon o-*tel*
youth hostel	*un albergue juvenil*	oon al-*ber*-ge khoo-ve-*neel*
Can you recommend	*¿Puede recomendar*	*pwe*-de rre-ko-men-*dar*
somewhere ...?	*algún sitio ...?*	al-*goon see*-tio ...
cheap	*barato*	ba-*ra*-to
good	*bueno*	*bwe*-no
nearby	*cercano*	ther-*ka*-no

I'd like to book a room, please.
Quisiera reservar una habitación. kee-*sye*-ra rre-ser-*var oo*-na a-bee-ta-*thyon*

I have a reservation.
He hecho una reserva. e *e*-cho *oo*-na rre-*ser*-va

My name's ...
Me llamo ... me *lya*-mo ...

Do you have a ... room?	¿Tiene una habitación ...?	tye·ne oo·na a·bee·ta·thyon ...
single	individual	een·dee·vee·dwal
double	doble	do·ble
twin	con dos camas	kon dos ka·mas

How much is it per ...?	¿Cuánto cuesta por ...?	kwan·to kwes·ta por ...
night	noche	no·che
person	persona	per·so·na

Can I pay by ...?	¿Puedo pagar con ...?	pwe·do pa·gar con ...
credit card	tarjeta de crédito	tar·khe·ta de kre·dee·to
travellers cheque	cheque de viajero	che·ke de vya·khe·ro

I'd like to stay for (three) nights/weeks.
Quisiera quedarme por (tres) noches/semanas.
kee·sye·ra ke·dar·me por (tres) no·ches/se·ma·nas

From (July 2) to (July 6).
Desde (el dos de julio) hasta (el seis de julio).
des·de (el dos de khoo·lyo) as·ta (el seys de khoo·lyo)

Can I see it?
¿Puedo verla?
pwe·do ver·la

Am I allowed to camp here?
¿Se puede acampar aquí?
se pwe·de a·kam·par a·kee

Is there a camp site nearby?
¿Hay un terreno de cámping cercano?
ai oon te·rre·no de kam·peeng ther·ka·no

requests & queries

When/Where's breakfast served?
¿Cuándo/Dónde se sirve el desayuno?
kwan·do/don·de se seer·ve el de·sa·yoo·no

Please wake me at (seven).
Por favor, despiérteme a (las siete).
por fa·vor des·pyer·te·me a (las sye·te)

Could I have my key, please?
¿Me puede dar la llave, por favor?
me pwe·de dar la lya·ve por fa·vor

Can I get another (blanket)?
¿Puede darme otra (manta)?
pwe·de dar·me ot·ra (man·ta)

Is there a/an ...?	¿Hay ...?	ai ...
elevator	ascensor	as·then·sor
safe	una caja fuerte	oo·na ka·kha fwer·te

The room is too ...	Es demasiado ...	es de·ma·sya·do ...
expensive	cara	ka·ra
noisy	ruidosa	rrwee·do·sa
small	pequeña	pe·ke·nya

The ... doesn't work.	No funciona ...	no foon·thyo·na ...
air conditioning	el aire acondicionado	el ai·re a·kon·dee·thyo·na·do
fan	el ventilador	el ven·tee·la·dor
toilet	el retrete	el rre·tre·te

This ... isn't clean.	Esta ... no está limpia.	es·ta ... no es·ta leem·pya
pillow	almohada	al·mwa·da
sheet	sábana	sa·ba·na
towel	toalla	to·a·lya

checking out

What time is checkout?
¿A qué hora hay que dejar libre la habitación?
a ke o·ra ai ke de·khar lee·bre la a·bee·ta·thyon

Can I leave my luggage here?
¿Puedo dejar las maletas aquí?
pwe·do de·khar las ma·le·tas a·kee

Could I have ..., please?	¿Me puede dar ..., por favor?	me pwe·de dar ... por fa·vor
my deposit	mi depósito	mee de·po·see·to
my passport	mi pasaporte	mee pa·sa·por·te
my valuables	mis objetos de valor	mees ob·khe·tos de va·lor

communications & banking

the internet

Where's the local Internet café?
¿Dónde hay un cibercafé cercano?
don·de ai oon thee·ber·ka·fe ther·ka·no

How much is it per hour?
¿Cuánto cuesta por hora?
kwan·to kwes·ta por o·ra

I'd like to ...	Quisiera ...	kee·sye·ra ...
check my email	revisar mi correo electrónico	rre·vee·sar mee ko·re·o e·lek·tro·nee·ko
get Internet access	usar el Internet	oo·sar el een·ter·net
use a printer	usar una impresora	oo·sar oo·na eem·pre·so·ra
use a scanner	usar un escáner	oo·sar oon es·ka·ner

mobile/cell phone

I'd like a ...	Quisiera ...	kee·sye·ra ...
mobile/cell phone for hire	un móvil para alquilar	oon mo·veel pa·ra al·kee·lar
SIM card for your network	una tarjeta SIM para su red	oo·na tar·khe·ta seem pa·ra soo rred

What are the rates? *¿Cuál es la tarifa?* kwal es la ta·ree·fa

telephone

What's your phone number?
¿Cuál es su/tu número de teléfono? pol/inf
kwal es soo/too noo·me·ro de te·le·fo·no

The number is ...
El número es ...
el noo·me·ro es ...

Where's the nearest public phone?
¿Dónde hay una cabina telefónica?
don·de ai oo·na ka·bee·na te·le·fo·nee·ka

I'd like to buy a phonecard.
Quiero comprar una tarjeta telefónica.
kye·ro kom·prar oo·na tar·khe·ta te·le·fo·nee·ka

I want to ...	Quiero ...	kye·ro ...
call (Singapore)	hacer una llamada (a Singapur)	a·ther oo·na lya·ma·da (a seen·ga·poor)
make a local call	hacer una llamada local	a·ther oo·na lya·ma·da lo·kal
reverse the charges	hacer una llamada a cobro revertido	a·ther oo·na lya·ma·da a ko·bro rre·ver·tee·do

How much does ... cost?	¿Cuánto cuesta ...?	kwan·to kwes·ta ...
a (three)-minute call	una llamada de (tres) minutos	oo·na lya·ma·da de (tres) mee·noo·tos
each extra minute	cada minuto extra	ka·da mee·noo·to ek·stra

It's (one euro) per (minute).
(Un euro) por (un minuto).   (oon e·oo·ro) por (oon mee·noo·to)

post office

I want to send a ...	Quisiera enviar ...	kee·sye·ra en·vee·ar ...
fax	un fax	oon faks
letter	una carta	oo·na kar·ta
parcel	un paquete	oon pa·ke·te
postcard	una postal	oo·na pos·tal

I want to buy ...	Quisiera comprar ...	kee·sye·ra kom·prar ...
an envelope	un sobre	oon so·bre
stamps	sellos	se·lyos

Please send it (to Australia) by ...	Por favor, mándelo (a Australia) por ...	por fa·vor man·de·lo (a ows·tra·lya) por ...
airmail	vía aérea	vee·a a·e·re·a
express mail	correo urgente	ko·rre·o oor·khen·te
registered mail	correo certificado	ko·rre·o ther·tee·fee·ka·do
surface mail	vía terrestre	vee·a te·rres·tre

Is there any mail for me?
¿Hay alguna carta para mí?   ai al·goo·na kar·ta pa·ra mee

communications & banking – SPANISH

347

bank

English	Español	Pronunciation
Where's a/an ...?	*¿Dónde hay ...?*	don·de ai ...
ATM	*un cajero automático*	oon ka·khe·ro ow·to·ma·tee·ko o
foreign exchange office	*una oficina de cambio*	oo·na o·fee·thee·na de kam·byo
I'd like to ...	*Me gustaría ...*	me goos·ta·ree·a ...
cash a cheque	*cambiar un cheque*	kam·byar oon che·ke
change a travellers cheque	*cobrar un cheque de viajero*	ko·brar oon che·ke de vee·a·khe·ro
change money	*cambiar dinero*	kam·byar dee·ne·ro
get a cash advance	*obtener un adelanto*	ob·te·ner oon a·de·lan·to
withdraw money	*sacar dinero*	sa·kar dee·ne·ro
What's the ...?	*¿Cuál es ...?*	kwal es ...
commission	*la comisión*	la ko·mee·syon
exchange rate	*el tipo de cambio*	el tee·po de kam·byo
It's (12) euros.	*Es (doce) euros.*	es (do·the) e·oo·ros
It's free.	*Es gratis.*	es gra·tees

What's the charge for that?
¿Cuánto hay que pagar por eso? — kwan·to ai ke pa·gar por e·so

What time does the bank open?
¿A qué hora abre el banco? — a ke o·ra a·bre el ban·ko

Has my money arrived yet?
¿Ya ha llegado mi dinero? — ya a lye·ga·do mee dee·ne·ro

sightseeing

getting in

What time does it open/close?
¿A qué hora abren/cierran? — a ke o·ra ab·ren/thye·rran

What's the admission charge?
¿Cuánto cuesta la entrada? — kwan·to kwes·ta la en·tra·da

Is there a discount for children/students?
¿Hay descuentos para niños/estudiantes? — ai des·kwen·tos pa·ra nee·nyos/es·too·dyan·tes

I'd like a ...	Quisiera ...	kee-sye-ra ...
catalogue	un catálogo	oon ka-ta-lo-go
guide	una guía	oo-na gee-a
(local) map	un mapa (de la zona)	oon ma-pa (de la tho-na)

I'd like to see ...	Me gustaría ver ...	me goos-ta-ree-a ver ...
What's that?	¿Qué es eso?	ke es e-so
Can I take a photo?	¿Puedo tomar un foto?	pwe-do to-mar un fo-to

tours

When's the next day trip?
¿Cuándo es la próxima
excursión de un día?
kwan-do es la prok-see-ma
eks-koor-syon de oon dee-a

When's the next tour?
¿Cuándo es el próximo recorrido?
kwan-do es ela prok-see-mo rre-ko-rree-do

Is ... included?	¿Incluye ...?	een-kloo-ye ...
accommodation	alojamiento	a-lo-kha-myen-to
the admission charge	entrada	en-tra-da
food	comida	ko-mee-da
transport	transporte	trans-por-te

How long is the tour?
¿Cuánto dura el recorrido?
kwan-to doo-ra el rre-ko-rree-do

What time should we be back?
¿A qué hora tenemos que volver?
a ke o-ra te-ne-mos ke vol-ver

sightseeing

castle	castillo m	kas-tee-lyo
cathedral	catedral f	ka-te-dral
church	iglesia f	ee-gle-sya
main square	plaza mayor f	pla-tha ma-yor
monastery	monasterio m	mo-na-ste-ryo
monument	monumento m	mo-noo-men-to
museum	museo m	moo-se-o
old city	casco antiguo m	kas-ko an-tee-gwo
palace	palacio m	pa-la-thyo
ruins	ruinas f pl	rrwee-nas
stadium	estadio m	es-ta-dyo
statues	estatuas f pl	es-ta-twas

shopping

enquiries

Where's a ...?	¿Dónde está ...?	don·de es·ta ...
bank	el banco	el ban·ko
bookshop	la librería	la lee·bre·ree·a
camera shop	la tienda de	la tyen·da de
	fotografía	fo·to·gra·fee·a
department store	el centro comercial	el then·tro ko·mer·thyal
grocery store	la tienda de	la tyen·da de
	comestibles	ko·mes·tee·bles
market	el mercado	el mer·ka·do
newsagency	el quiosco	el kyos·ko
supermarket	el supermercado	el soo·per·mer·ka·do

Where can I buy (a padlock)?
   ¿Dónde puedo comprar   don·de pwe·do kom·prar
   (un candado)?   (oon kan·da·do)

I'm looking for ...
   Estoy buscando ...   es·toy boos·kan·do ...

Can I look at it?
   ¿Puedo verlo?   pwe·do ver·lo

Do you have any others?
   ¿Tiene otros?   tye·ne o·tros

Does it have a guarantee?
   ¿Tiene garantía?   tye·ne ga·ran·tee·a

Can I have it sent overseas?
   ¿Pueden enviarlo por   pwe·den en·vee·ar·lo por
   correo a otro país?   ko·rre·o a o·tro pa·ees

Can I have my ... repaired?
   ¿Puede reparar mi ... aquí?   pwe·de rre·pa·rar mee ... a·kee

It's faulty.
   Es defectuoso.   es de·fek·too·o·so

I'd like …, please.	Quisiera …, por favor.	kee-*sye*-ra … por fa-*vor*
a bag	una bolsa	*oo*-na *bol*-sa
a refund	que me devuelva	ke me de-*vwel*-va
	el dinero	el dee-*ne*-ro
to return this	devolver esto	de-vol-*ver* es-to

paying

How much is it?
¿Cuánto cuesta esto?   kwan-to *kwes*-ta es-to

Can you write down the price?
¿Puede escribir el precio?   *pwe*-de es-kree-*beer* el *pre*-thyo

That's too expensive.
Es muy caro.   es mooy *ka*-ro

What's your lowest price?
¿Cuál es su precio más bajo?   kwal es soo *pre*-thyo mas *ba*-kho

I'll give you (five) euros.
Te daré (cinco) euros.   te da-*re* (*theen*-ko) e-oo-ros

There's a mistake in the bill.
Hay un error en la cuenta.   ai oon e-*rror* en la *kwen*-ta

Do you accept …?	¿Aceptan …?	a-*thep*-tan …
credit cards	tarjetas de crédito	tar-*khe*-tas de *kre*-dee-to
debit cards	tarjetas de débito	tar-*khe*-tas de *de*-bee-to
travellers cheques	cheques de viajero	*che*-kes de vya-*khe*-ro

I'd like …, please.	Quisiera …, por favor.	kee-*sye*-ra … por fa-*vor*
a receipt	un recibo	oon rre-*thee*-bo
my change	mi cambio	mee *kam*-byo

clothes & shoes

Can I try it on?	¿Me lo puedo probar?	me lo *pwe*-do pro-bar
My size is (40).	Uso la talla (cuarenta).	*oo*-so la *ta*-lya (kwa-*ren*-ta)
It doesn't fit.	No me queda bien.	no me *ke*-da byen
small	pequeño/a m/f	pe-*ke*-nyo/a
medium	mediano/a m/f	me-*dya*-no/a
large	grande m&f	*gran*-de

books & music

I'd like a ...	Quisiera un ...	kee-sye-ra oon ...
newspaper	periódico	pe-ryo-dee-ko
(in English)	(en inglés)	(en een-gles)
pen	bolígrafo	bo-lee-gra-fo

Is there an English-language bookshop?
¿Hay alguna librería en inglés?
ai al-goo-na lee-bre-ree-a en een-gles

I'm looking for something by (Enrique Iglesias).
Estoy buscando algo de (Enrique Iglesias).
es-toy boos-kan-do al-go de (en-ree-ke ee-gle-syas)

Can I listen to this?
¿Puedo escuchar esto aquí?
pwe-do es-koo-char es-to a-kee

photography

Can you ...?	¿Puede usted ...?	pwe-de oos-ted ...
burn a CD from my memory card	copiar un disco compacto de esta tarjeta de memoria	ko-pyar oon dees-ko kom-pak-to de es-ta tar-khe-ta de me-mo-rya
develop this film	revelar este carrete	rre-ve-lar es-te ka-rre-te
load my film	cargar el carrete	kar-gar el ka-rre-te

I need a ... film for this camera.	Necesito película ... para esta cámara.	ne-the-see-to pe-lee-koo-la ... pa-ra es-ta ka-ma-ra
APS	APS	a pe e-se
B&W	en blanco y negro	en blan-ko y ne-gro
colour	en color	en ko-lor
slide	para diapositivas	pa-ra dya-po-see-tee-vas
(200) speed	de sensibilidad (doscientos)	de sen-see-bee-lee-da (dos-thyen-tos)

When will it be ready? *¿Cuándo estará listo?* kwan-do es-ta-ra lees-to

meeting people

greetings, goodbyes & introductions

Hello/Hi.	*Hola.*	*o*·la
Good night.	*Buenas noches.*	*bwe*·nas *no*·ches
Goodbye/Bye.	*Adiós.*	a·*dyos*
See you later.	*Hasta luego.*	*as*·ta *lwe*·go
Mr	*Señor*	se·*nyor*
Mrs	*Señora*	se·*nyo*·ra
Miss	*Señorita*	se·nyo·*ree*·ta
How are you?	*¿Qué tal?*	ke tal
Fine, thanks.	*Bien, gracias.*	byen *gra*·thyas
And you?	*¿Y Usted/tú?* pol/inf	ee oos·*te*/too
What's your name?	*¿Cómo se llama Usted?* pol	*ko*·mo se *lya*·ma oos·*te*
	¿Cómo te llamas? inf	*ko*·mo te *lya*·mas
My name is …	*Me llamo …*	me *lya*·mo …
I'm pleased to meet you.	*Mucho gusto.*	*moo*·cho *goos*·to
This is my …	*Éste/Ésta es mi …* m/f	*es*·te/a es mee …
boyfriend	*novio*	*no*·vyo
brother	*hermano*	er·*ma*·no
daughter	*hija*	*ee*·kho
father	*padre*	*pa*·dre
friend	*amigo/a* m/f	a·*mee*·go/a
girlfriend	*novia*	*no*·vya
husband	*marido*	ma·*ree*·do
mother	*madre*	*ma*·dre
partner (intimate)	*pareja*	pa·*re*·kha
sister	*hermana*	er·*ma*·na
son	*hijo*	*ee*·kho
wife	*esposa*	es·*po*·sa
Here's my …	*Éste/Ésta es mi …* m/f	*es*·te/a es mee …
What's your …?	*¿Cuál es su/tu …?* pol/inf	kwal es soo/too …
address	*dirección* f	dee·rek·*thyon*
email address	*dirección de email* f	dee·rek·*thyon* de *ee*·mayl
fax number	*número de fax* m	*noo*·me·ro de faks
phone number	*número de teléfono* m	*noo*·me·ro de te·*le*·fo·no

occupations

What's your occupation?	¿A qué se dedica Usted? pol	a ke se de·*dee*·ka oos·te
	¿A qué te dedicas? inf	a ke te de·*dee*·kas
I'm a/an ...	Soy un/una ... m/f	soy oon/*oo*·na ...
artist	artista m&f	ar·*tees*·ta
business person	comerciante m&f	ko·mer·*thyan*·te
farmer	agricultor m	a·gree·kool·*tor*
	agricultora f	a·gree·kool·*to*·ra
manual worker	obrero/a m/f	o·*bre*·ro/a
office worker	oficinista m&f	o·fee·thee·*nees*·ta
scientist	científico/a m/f	thyen·*tee*·fee·ko/a
student	estudiante m&f	es·too·*dyan*·te
tradesperson	artesano/a m/f	ar·te·*sa*·no/a

background

Where are you from?	¿De dónde es Usted? pol	de *don*·de es oos·te
	¿De dónde eres? inf	de *don*·de e·res
I'm from ...	Soy de ...	soy de ...
Australia	Australia	ow·*stra*·lya
Canada	Canadá	ka·na·*da*
England	Inglaterra	een·gla·*te*·rra
New Zealand	Nueva Zelanda	*nwe*·va the·*lan*·da
the USA	los Estados Unidos	los es·*ta*·dos oo·nee·dos
Are you married?	¿Estás casado/a? m/f	es·tas ka·*sa*·do/a
I'm married.	Estoy casado/a. m/f	es·*toy* ka·*sa*·do/a
I'm single.	Soy soltero/a. m/f	soy sol·*te*·ro/a

age

How old ...?	¿Cuántos años ...?	*kwan*·tos *a*·nyos ...
are you	tienes inf	*tye*·nes
is your daughter	tiene su hija pol	*tye*·ne soo ee·kha
is your son	tiene su hijo pol	*tye*·ne soo ee·kho
I'm ... years old.	Tengo ... años.	*ten*·go ... *a*·nyos
He/She is ... years old.	Tiene ... años.	*tye*·ne ... *a*·nyos

feelings

I'm (not) ...	(No) Tengo ...	(no) ten·go ...
Are you ...?	¿Tiene Usted ...? pol	tye·ne oos·te ...
	¿Tienes ...? inf	tye·nes ...
cold	frío	free·o
hot	calor	ka·lor
hungry	hambre	am·bre
thirsty	sed	se

I'm (not) ...	(No) Estoy ...	(no) es·toy ...
Are you ...?	¿Está Usted ...? pol	es·ta oos·te ...
	¿Estás ...? inf	es·tas ...
happy	feliz m&f	fe·leeth
OK	bien m&f	byen
sad	triste m&f	trees·te
tired	cansado/a m/f	kan·sa·do/a

entertainment

going out

Where can I find ...?	¿Dónde hay ...?	don·de ai ...
clubs	clubs nocturnos	kloobs nok·toor·nos
gay venues	lugares gay	loo·ga·res gai
pubs	bares	ba·res

I feel like going to a/the ...	Tengo ganas de ir ...	ten·go ga·nas de eer ...
concert	a un concierto	a oon kon·thyer·to
movies	al cine	al thee·ne
party	a una fiesta	a oo·na fyes·ta
restaurant	a un restaurante	a oon rres·tow·ran·te
theatre	al teatro	al te·a·tro

interests

Do you like ...	¿Le/Te gusta ...? pol/inf	le/te *goos*·ta ...
I (don't) like ...	(No) Me gusta ...	(no) me *goos*·ta ...
art	el arte	el *ar*·te
movies	el cine	el *thee*·ne
reading	leer	le·*er*
sport	el deporte	el de·*por*·te
travelling	viajar	vya·*khar*
Do you like to ...?	¿Le/Te gusta ...? pol/inf	le/te *goos*·ta ...
dance	ir a bailar	eer a bai·*lar*
go to concerts	ir a conciertos	eer a kon·*thyer*·tos
listen to music	escuchar música	es·koo·*char* moo·see·ka

food & drink

finding a place to eat

Can you recommend a ...?	¿Puede recomendar un ...?	*pwe*·de rre·ko·men·*dar* oon ...
bar	bar	bar
café	café	ka·*fe*
restaurant	restaurante	rres·tow·*ran*·te
I'd like ..., please.	Quisiera ..., por favor.	kee·*sye*·ra ... por fa·*vor*
a table for (two)	una mesa para (dos)	*oo*·na *me*·sa *pa*·ra (dos)

ordering food

breakfast	desayuno m	de·sa·*yoo*·no
lunch	comida f	ko·*mee*·da
dinner	almuerzo m	al·*mwer*·tho
snack	tentempié m	ten·tem·*pye*

What would you recommend?

¿Qué recomienda?	ke rre·ko·*myen*·da

I'd like (the) ...	Quisiera ..., por favor.	kee-*sye*-ra ... por fa-*vor*
bill	la cuenta	la *kwen*-ta
drink list	la lista de bebidas	la *lees*-ta de be-*bee*-das
menu	el menú	el me-*noo*
that dish	ese plato	e-se *pla*-to

drinks

(cup of) coffee ...	(taza de) café ...	(*ta*-tha de) ka-*fe* ...
(cup of) tea ...	(taza de) té ...	(*ta*-tha de) te ...
with milk	con leche	kon *le*-che
without sugar	sin azúcar	seen a-*thoo*-kar
(orange) juice	zumo de (naranja) m	*zoo*-mo de (na-*ran*-kha)
soft drink	refresco m	rre-*fres*-ko
... water	agua ...	*a*-gwa ...
boiled	hervida	er-*vee*-da
(sparkling) mineral	mineral (con gas)	mee-ne-*ral* (kon gas)

in the bar

I'll have ...	Para mí ...	*pa*-ra mee ...
I'll buy you a drink.	Te invito a una copa. inf	le/te een-*vee*-to a *oo*-na *ko*-pa
What would you like?	¿Qué quieres tomar? inf	ke *kye*-res to-*mar*
Cheers!	¡Salud!	sa-*loo*
brandy	coñac m	ko-*nyak*
cocktail	combinado m	kom-bee-*na*-do
red-wine punch	sangría f	san-*gree*-a
a shot of (whisky)	chupito de (güisqui)	choo-*pee*-to de (*gwees*-kee)
a ... of beer	una ... de cerveza	*oo*-na ... de ther-*ve*-tha
bottle	botella	bo-*te*-lya
glass	caña	*ka*-nya
a bottle/glass of	una botella/copa	*oo*-na bo-*te*-lya/*ko*-pa
... wine	de vino ...	de *vee*-no ...
red	tinto	*teen*-to
sparkling	espumoso	es-poo-*mo*-so
white	blanco	*blan*-ko

self-catering

What's the local speciality?
  ¿Cuál es la especialidad de la zona?   kwal es la es·pe·thya·lee·*da* de la *tho*·na

What's that?
  ¿Qué es eso?   ke es *e*·so

How much is (a kilo of cheese)?
  ¿Cuánto vale (un kilo de queso)?   *kwan*·to *va*·le (oon *kee*·lo de *ke*·so)

I'd like ...	*Póngame ...*	*pon*·ga·me ...
(200) grams	*(doscientos) gramos*	(dos·*thyen*·tos) *gra*·mos
(two) kilos	*(dos) kilos*	(dos) *kee*·los
(three) pieces	*(tres) piezas*	(tres) *pye*·thas
(six) slices	*(seis) lonchas*	(seys) *lon*·chas

Less.	*Menos.*	*me*·nos
Enough.	*Basta.*	*ba*·sta
More.	*Más.*	mas

special diets & allergies

Is there a vegetarian restaurant near here?
  ¿Hay un restaurante   ai oon rres·tow·*ran*·te
  vegetariano por aquí?   ve·khe·ta·*rya*·no por a·*kee*

Do you have vegetarian food?
  ¿Tienen comida vegetariana?   *tye*·nen ko·*mee*·da ve·khe·ta·*rya*·na

Could you prepare a	*¿Me puede preparar*	me *pwe*·de pre·pa·*rar*
meal without ...?	*una comida sin ...?*	*oo*·na ko·*mee*·da seen ...
butter	*mantequilla*	man·te·*kee*·lya
eggs	*huevos*	*we*·vos
meat stock	*caldo de carne*	*kal*·do de *kar*·ne

I'm allergic to ...	*Soy alérgico/a ...* m/f	soy a·*ler*·khee·ko/a ...
dairy produce	*a los productos*	a los pro·*dook*·tos
	lácteos	*lak*·te·os
gluten	*al gluten*	al *gloo*·ten
MSG	*al glutamato*	al gloo·ta·*ma*·to
	monosódico	mo·no·so·dee·ko
nuts	*a las nueces*	a las *nwe*·thes
seafood	*a los mariscos*	a los ma·*rees*·kos

ESPAÑOL – food & drink

menu decoder

aceitunas rellenas f pl	a·they·*too*·nas rre·*lye*·nas	*stuffed olives*
albóndigas f pl	al·*bon*·dee·gas	*meatballs*
almejas f pl	al·*me*·khas	*clams*
arroz con leche m	a·*rroth* kon *le*·che	*rice pudding*
atún m	a·*toon*	*tuna*
bacalao m	ba·ka·*low*	*salted cod*
beicon con queso m	*bey*·kon kon *ke*·so	*cold bacon with cheese*
berberechos m pl	ber·be·*re*·chos	*cockles*
boquerones fritos m pl	bo·ke·*ro*·nes *free*·tos	*fried anchovies*
butifarra f	boo·tee·*fa*·rra	*thick sausage*
calamares m pl	ka·la·*ma*·res	*squid*
camarón m	ka·ma·*ron*	*shrimp • small prawn*
cangrejo m	kan·*gre*·kho	*crab*
caracol m	ka·ra·*kol*	*snail*
cazuela f	ka·*thwe*·la	*casserole*
champiñones m pl	cham·pee·*nyo*·nes	*mushrooms*
charcutería f	char·koo·te·*ree*·a	*cured pork meats*
chorizo m	cho·*ree*·tho	*spicy red or white sausage*
churrasco m	choo·*rras*·ko	*grilled meat in a tangy sauce*
churro m	*choo*·rro	*long, deep-fried doughnut*
cocido m	ko·*thee*·do	*stew of chickpeas, pork & chorizo*
cuajada f	kwa·*kha*·da	*milk junket with honey*
ensaladilla f	en·sa·la·*dee*·lya	*vegetable salad*
escabeche m	es·ka·*be*·che	*pickled or marinated fish*
estofado m	es·to·*fa*·do	*stew*

fideos m pl	fee-*de*-os	*thin pasta noodles with sauce*
flan m	flan	*crème caramel*
gachos m pl	*ga*-chos	*type of porridge*
gazpacho m	gath-*pa*-cho	*cold soup with garlic, tomato & vegetables*
helado m	e-*la*-do	*ice cream*
jamón m	kha-*mon*	*ham*
langosta f	lan-*gos*-ta	*spiny lobster*
langostino m	lan-gos-*tee*-no	*large prawn*
lomo m	*lo*-mo	*pork loin • sausage*
longaniza f	lon-ga-*nee*-tha	*dark pork sausage*
magdalena f	mag-da-*le*-na	*fairy cake (often dunked in coffee)*
mejillones m pl	me-khee-*lyo*-nes	*mussels*
natillas f pl	na-*tee*-lyas	*creamy milk dessert*
ostras f pl	*os*-tras	*oysters*
paella f	pa-e-lya	*rice & seafood dish (sometimes with meat)*
peregrina f	pe-re-*gree*-na	*scallop*
pescaíto frito m	pes-*kai*-to *free*-to	*tiny fried fish*
picadillo m	pee-ka-*dee*-lyo	*minced meat*
pinchitos m pl	peen-*chee*-tos	*Moroccan-style kebabs*
pulpo m	*pool*-po	*octopus*
salchicha f	sal-*chee*-cha	*fresh pork sausage*
sobrasada f	so-bra-*sa*-da	*soft pork sausage*
tortilla española f	tor-*tee*-lya es-pa-*nyo*-la	*potato omelette*
trucha f	*troo*-cha	*trout*
zarzuela f	thar-*thwe*-la	*fish stew*

emergencies

basics

Help!	¡Socorro!	so·ko·ro
Stop!	¡Pare!	pa·re
Go away!	¡Váyase!	va·ya·se
Thief!	¡Ladrón!	lad·ron
Fire!	¡Fuego!	fwe·go
Watch out!	¡Cuidado!	kwee·da·do
Call ...!	¡Llame a ...!	lya·me a ...
a doctor	un médico	oon me·dee·ko
an ambulance	una ambulancia	oo·na am·boo·lan·thya
the police	la policía	la po·lee·thee·a

It's an emergency.
Es una emergencia. es oo·na e·mer·khen·thya

Could you help me, please?
¿Me puede ayudar, por favor? me pwe·de a·yoo·dar por fa·vor

I have to use the telephone.
Necesito usar el teléfono. ne·the·see·to oo·sar el te·le·fo·no

I'm lost.
Estoy perdido/a. m/f es·toy per·dee·do/a

Where are the toilets?
¿Dónde están los servicios? don·de es·tan los ser·vee·thyos

police

Where's the police station?
¿Dónde está la comisaría? don·de es·ta la ko·mee·sa·ree·a

I want to report an offence.
Quiero denunciar un delito. kye·ro de·noon·thyar oon de·lee·to

I have insurance.
Tengo seguro. ten·go se·goo·ro

I've been assaulted.	He sido asaltado/a. m/f	e see·do a·sal·ta·do/a
I've been raped.	He sido violado/a. m/f	e see·do vee·o·la·do/a
I've been robbed.	Me han robado.	me an rro·ba·do

I've lost my ...	He perdido ...	e per·dee·do ...
backpack	mi mochila	mee mo·chee·la
bags	mis maletas	mees ma·le·tas
credit card	mi tarjeta de crédito	mee tar·khe·ta de kre·dee·to
handbag	mi bolso	mee bol·so
jewellery	mis joyas	mees kho·yas
money	mi dinero	mee dee·ne·ro
passport	mi pasaporte	mee pa·sa·por·te
travellers cheques	mis cheques de viajero	mees che·kes de vya·khe·ro
wallet	mi cartera	mee kar·te·ra

I want to contact my ...	Quiero ponerme en contacto con mi ...	kye·ro po·ner·me en kon·tak·to kon mee ...
consulate	consulado	kon·soo·la·do
embassy	embajada	em·ba·kha·da

health

medical needs

Where's the nearest ...?	¿Dónde está el ... más cercano?	don·de es·ta el ... mas ther·ka·no
dentist	dentista	den·tees·ta
doctor	médico	me·dee·ko
hospital	hospital	os·pee·tal

Where's the nearest (night) pharmacist?
¿Dónde está la farmacia
(de guardia) más cercana?
don·de es·ta la far·ma·thya
(de gwar·dya) mas ther·ka·na

I need a doctor (who speaks English).
Necesito un médico
(que hable inglés).
ne·the·see·to oon me·dee·ko
(ke a·ble een·gles)

Could I see a female doctor?
¿Puede examinarme una
médica?
pwe·de ek·sa·mee·nar·me oo·na
me·dee·ka

I've run out of my medication.
Se me terminaron los
medicamentos.
se me ter·mee·na·ron los
me·dee·ka·men·tos

symptoms, conditions & allergies

| I'm sick. | Estoy enfermo/a. m/f | es·toy en·fer·mo/a |
| It hurts here. | Me duele aquí. | me dwe·le a·kee |

I have (a) ...	Tengo...	ten·go ...
asthma	asma	as·ma
bronchitis	bronquitis	bron·kee·tees
constipation	estreñimiento	es·tre·nyee·myen·to
cough	tos	tos
diarrhoea	diarrea	dya·rre·a
fever	fiebre	fye·bre
headache	dolor de cabeza	do·lor de ka·be·tha
heart condition	una condición	oo·na kon·dee·thyon
	cardíaca	kar·dee·a·ka
nausea	náusea	now·se·a
pain	dolor	do·lor
sore throat	dolor de garganta	do·lor de gar·gan·ta
toothache	dolor de muelas	do·lor de mwe·las

I'm allergic to ...	Soy alérgico/a a ... m/f	soy a·ler·khee·ko/a a ...
antibiotics	los antibióticos	los an·tee·byo·tee·kos
anti-	los anti-	los an·tee-
inflammatories	inflamatorios	een·fla·ma·to·ryos
aspirin	la aspirina	la as·pee·ree·na
bees	las abejas	las a·be·khas
codeine	la codeína	la ko·de·ee·na
penicillin	la penicilina	la pe·nee·thee·lee·na

antiseptic	antiséptico m	an·tee·sep·tee·ko
bandage	vendaje m	ven·da·khe
condoms	condones m pl	kon·do·nes
contraceptives	anticonceptivos m pl	an·tee·kon·thep·tee·vos
diarrhoea medicine	medicina para diarrea f	me·dee·thee·na pa·ra dya·rre·a
insect repellent	repelente de insectos m	re·pe·len·te de een·sek·tos
laxatives	laxantes m pl	lak·san·tes
painkillers	analgésicos m pl	a·nal·khe·see·kos
rehydration salts	sales rehidratantes f pl	sa·les re·eed·ra·tan·tes
sleeping tablets	pastillas para dormir f pl	pas·tee·lyas pa·ra dor·meer

health – SPANISH

363

english–spanish dictionary

Spanish nouns in this dictionary, and adjectives affected by gender, have their gender indicated by ⓜ (masculine) or ⓕ (feminine). If it's a plural noun, you'll also see pl. Words are also marked as v (verb), n (noun), a (adjective), pl (plural), sg (singular), inf (informal) and pol (polite) where necessary.

A

accident *accidente* ⓜ ak-thee-*den*-te
accommodation *alojamiento* ⓜ a-lo-kha-*myen*-to
adaptor *adaptador* ⓜ a-dap-ta-*dor*
address *dirección* ⓕ dee-rek-*thyon*
after *después de* des-*pwes* de
air-conditioned *con aire acondicionado*
  kon *ai*-re a-kon-dee-thyo-*na*-do
airplane *avión* ⓜ a-*vyon*
airport *aeropuerto* ⓜ ay-ro-*pwer*-to
alcohol *alcohol* ⓜ al-col
all a *todo/a* to-do/a
allergy *alergia* ⓕ a-ler-khya
ambulance *ambulancia* ⓕ am-boo-*lan*-thya
ankle *tobillo* ⓜ to-*bee*-lyo
and y ee
arm *brazo* ⓜ *bra*-tho
ashtray *cenicero* ⓜ the-nee-*the*-ro
ATM *cajero automático* ka-*khe*-ro ow-to-*ma*-tee-ko

B

baby *bebé* ⓜ be-*be*
back (body) *espalda* ⓕ es-*pal*-da
backpack *mochila* ⓕ mo-*chee*-la
bad *malo/a* ⓜ/ⓕ *ma*-lo/a
bag *bolso* ⓜ *bol*-so
baggage claim *recogida de equipajes* ⓕ
  rre-ko-*khee*-da de e-kee-*pa*-khes
bank *banco* ⓜ *ban*-ko
bar *bar* ⓜ bar
bathroom *baño* ⓜ *ba*-nyo
battery (general) *pila* ⓕ *pee*-la
battery (car) *batería* ⓕ ba-te-*ree*-a
beautiful *hermoso/a* ⓜ/ⓕ er-mo-so/a
bed *cama* ⓕ *ka*-ma
beer *cerveza* ⓕ ther-*ve*-tha
before *antes* *an*-tes
behind *detrás de* de-*tras* de
bicycle *bicicleta* ⓕ bee-thee-*kle*-ta

big *grande* *gran*-de
bill *cuenta* ⓕ *kwen*-ta
black *negro/a* ⓜ/ⓕ *ne*-gro/a
blanket *manta* ⓕ *man*-ta
blood group *grupo sanguíneo* ⓜ *groo*-po san-*gee*-neo
blue *azul* a-*thool*
boat *barco* ⓜ *bar*-ko
book (make a reservation) v *reservar* rre-ser-*var*
bottle *botella* ⓕ bo-*te*-lya
bottle opener *abrebotellas* ⓜ a-bre-bo-*te*-lyas
boy *chico* ⓜ *chee*-ko
brakes (car) *frenos* ⓜ pl *fre*-nos
breakfast *desayuno* ⓜ des-a-*yoo*-no
broken (faulty) *roto/a* ⓜ/ⓕ *ro*-to/a
bus *autobús* ⓜ ow-to-*boos*
business *negocios* ⓜ pl ne-*go*-thyos
buy *comprar* kom-*prar*

C

café *café* ⓜ ka-*fe*
camera *cámara (fotográfica)* ⓕ
  ka-ma-ra (fo-to-*gra*-fee-ka)
camp site *cámping* ⓜ *kam*-peen
cancel *cancelar* kan-the-*lar*
can opener *abrelatas* ⓜ a-bre-*la*-tas
car *coche* ⓜ *ko*-che
cash *dinero en efectivo* ⓜ dee-*ne*-ro en e-fek-*tee*-vo
cash (a cheque) v *cambiar (un cheque)*
  kam-*byar* (oon *che*-ke)
cell phone *teléfono móvil* ⓜ te-*le*-fo-no *mo*-veel
centre *centro* ⓜ *then*-tro
change (money) v *cambiar* kam-*byar*
cheap *barato/a* ⓜ/ⓕ ba-*ra*-to/a
check (bill) *cuenta* ⓕ *kwen*-ta
check-in *facturación de equipajes* ⓕ
  fak-too-ra-*thyon* de e-kee-*pa*-khes
chest *pecho* ⓜ *pe*-cho
child *niño/a* ⓜ/ⓕ *nee*-nyo/a
cigarette *cigarrillo* ⓜ thee-ga-*ree*-lyo
city *ciudad* ⓕ theew-*da*
clean a *limpio/a* ⓜ/ⓕ *leem*-pyo/a

closed *cerrado/a* ⓜ/ⓕ the-*rra*-do/a
coffee *café* ⓜ ka-*fe*
coins *monedas* ⓕ pl mo-*ne*-das
cold a *frío/a* ⓜ/ⓕ *free*-o/a
collect call *llamada a cobro revertido* ⓕ
   lya-*ma*-da a *ko*-bro re-ver-*tee*-do
come *venir* ve-*neer*
computer *ordenador* ⓜ or-de-na-*dor*
condom *condones* ⓜ pl kon-*do*-nes
contact lenses *lentes de contacto* ⓜ pl
   len-tes de kon-*tak*-to
cook v *cocinar* ko-thee-*nar*
cost *precio* ⓜ *pre*-thyo
credit card *tarjeta de crédito* ⓕ
   tar-*khe*-ta de *kre*-dee-to
cup *taza* ⓕ *ta*-tha
currency exchange *cambio de dinero* ⓜ
   kam-byo de dee-*ne*-ro
customs (immigration) *aduana* ⓕ a-*dwa*-na

D

dangerous *peligroso/a* ⓜ/ⓕ pe-lee-*gro*-so/a
date (time) *fecha* ⓕ *fe*-cha
day *día* ⓜ *dee*-a
delay *demora* ⓕ de-*mo*-ra
dentist *dentista* ⓜ/ⓕ den-*tees*-ta
depart *salir de* sa-*leer* de
diaper *pañal* ⓜ pa-*nyal*
dictionary *diccionario* ⓜ deek-thyo-*na*-ryo
dinner *cena* ⓕ *the*-na
direct *directo/a* ⓜ/ⓕ dee-*rek*-to/a
dirty *sucio/a* ⓜ/ⓕ *soo*-thyo/a
disabled *minusválido/a* ⓜ/ⓕ mee-noos-*va*-lee-do/a
discount *descuento* ⓜ des-*kwen*-to
doctor *doctor/doctora* ⓜ/ⓕ dok-*tor*/dok-*to*-ra
double bed *cama de matrimonio* ⓕ
   ka-ma de ma-tree-*mo*-nyo
double room *habitación doble* ⓕ a-bee-ta-*thyon do*-ble
drink *bebida* ⓕ be-*bee*-da
drive v *conducir* kon-doo-*theer*
drivers licence *carnet de conducir* ⓜ
   kar-*ne* de kon-doo-*theer*
drugs (illicit) *droga* ⓕ *dro*-ga
dummy (pacifier) *chupete* ⓜ choo-*pe*-te

E

ear *oreja* ⓕ o-*re*-kha
east *este* *es*-te
eat *comer* ko-*mer*

economy class *clase turística* ⓕ *kla*-se too-*rees*-tee-ka
electricity *electricidad* ⓕ e-lek-tree-thee-*da*
elevator *ascensor* ⓜ as-then-*sor*
email *correo electrónico* ⓜ ko-*rre*-o e-lek-*tro*-nee-ko
embassy *embajada* ⓕ em-ba-*kha*-da
emergency *emergencia* ⓕ e-mer-*khen*-thya
English (language) *inglés* ⓜ een-*gles*
entrance *entrada* ⓕ en-*tra*-da
evening *noche* ⓕ *no*-che
exchange rate *tipo de cambio* ⓕ *tee*-po de *kam*-byo
exit *salida* ⓕ sa-*lee*-da
expensive *caro/a* ⓜ/ⓕ *ka*-ro/a
express mail *correo urgente* ⓜ ko-*rre*-o oor-*khen*-te
eye *ojo* ⓜ *o*-kho

F

far *lejos* le-khos
fast *rápido/a* ⓜ/ⓕ *rra*-pee-do/a
father *padre* ⓜ *pa*-dre
film (camera) *carrete* ⓜ ka-*rre*-te
finger *dedo* ⓜ *de*-do
first-aid kit *maletín de primeros auxilios* ⓜ
   ma-le-*teen* de pree-*me*-ros ow-ksee-lyos
first class *de primera clase* de pree-*me*-ra *kla*-se
fish *pez* ⓜ peth
food *comida* ⓕ ko-*mee*-da
foot *pie* ⓜ pye
fork *tenedor* ⓜ te-ne-*dor*
free (of charge) *gratis* *gra*-tees
friend *amigo/a* ⓜ/ⓕ a-*mee*-go/a
fruit *fruta* ⓕ *froo*-ta
full *lleno/a* ⓜ/ⓕ *lye*-no/a
funny *gracioso/a* ⓜ/ⓕ gra-*thyo*-so/a

G

gift *regalo* ⓜ rre-*ga*-lo
girl *chica* ⓕ *chee*-ka
glass (drinking) *vaso* ⓜ *va*-so
glasses *gafas* ⓕ pl *ga*-fas
go *ir* eer
good *bueno/a* ⓜ/ⓕ *bwe*-no/a
green *verde* *ver*-de
guide n *guía* ⓜ/ⓕ *gee*-a

H

half *mitad* ⓕ mee-*tad*
hand *mano* ⓕ *ma*-no
handbag *bolso* ⓜ *bol*-so

happy *feliz* fe-*leeth*
have *tener* te-*ner*
he *él* el
head *cabeza* ① ka-*be*-tha
heart *corazón* ⓜ ko-ra-*thon*
heat *calor* ⓜ ka-*lor*
heavy *pesado/a* ⓜ/① pe-*sa*-do/a
help v *ayudar* a-yoo-*dar*
here *aquí* a-*kee*
high *alto/a* ⓜ/① *al*-to/a
highway *autovía* ① ow-to-*vee*-a
hike v *ir de excursión* eer de eks-koor-*syon*
holiday *vacaciones* ① pl va-ka-*thyo*-nes
homosexual *homosexual* ⓜ/① o-mo-se-*kswal*
hospital *hospital* ⓜ os-pee-*tal*
hot *caliente* ka-*lyen*-te
hotel *hotel* ⓜ o-*tel*
hungry *hambriento/a* ⓜ/① am-bree-*en*-to/a
husband *marido* ⓜ ma-*ree*-do

I

I *yo* yo
identification (card) *carnet de identidad* ⓜ
 kar-*net* de ee-den-tee-*da*
ill *enfermo/a* ⓜ/① en-*fer*-mo/a
important *importante* eem-por-*tan*-te
included *incluido* een-kloo-*ee*-do
injury *herida* ① e-*ree*-da
insurance *seguro* ⓜ se-*goo*-ro
Internet *Internet* ⓜ een-ter-*net*
interpreter *intérprete* ⓜ/① een-*ter*-pre-te

J

jewellery *joyas* ① pl *kho*-yas
job *trabajo* ⓜ tra-*ba*-kho

K

key *llave* ① *lya*-ve
kilogram *kilogramo* ⓜ kee-lo-*gra*-mo
kitchen *cocina* ① ko-*thee*-na
knife *cuchillo* ⓜ koo-*chee*-lyo

L

laundry (place) *lavadero* ⓜ la-va-*de*-ro
lawyer *abogado/a* ⓜ/① a-bo-*ga*-do/a
left (direction) *izquierda* ① eeth-*kyer*-da

left-luggage office *consigna* ① kon-*seeg*-na
leg *pierna* ① *pyer*-na
lesbian *lesbiana* ① les-bee-*a*-na
less *menos* *me*-nos
letter (mail) *carta* ① *kar*-ta
lift (elevator) *ascensor* ⓜ as-then-*sor*
light *luz* ① looth
like v *gustar* goos-*tar*
lock *cerradura* ① the-rra-*doo*-ra
long *largo/a* ⓜ/① *lar*-go/a
lost *perdido/a* ⓜ/① per-*dee*-do/a
lost-property office *oficina de objetos perdidos* ①
 o-fee-*thee*-na de ob-*khe*-tos per-*dee*-dos
love v *querer* ke-*rer*
luggage *equipaje* ⓜ e-kee-*pa*-khe
lunch *almuerzo* ⓜ al-*mwer*-tho

M

mail *correo* ⓜ ko-*rre*-o
man *hombre* ⓜ *om*-bre
map *mapa* ⓜ *ma*-pa
market *mercado* ⓜ mer-*ka*-do
matches *cerillas* ① pl the-*ree*-lyas
meat *carne* ① *kar*-ne
medicine *medicina* ① me-dee-*thee*-na
menu *menú* ⓜ me-*noo*
message *mensaje* ⓜ men-*sa*-khe
milk *leche* ① *le*-che
minute *minuto* ⓜ mee-*noo*-to
mobile phone *teléfono móvil* ⓜ te-*le*-fo-no *mo*-veel
money *dinero* ⓜ dee-*ne*-ro
month *mes* ⓜ mes
morning *mañana* ① ma-*nya*-na
mother *madre* ① *ma*-dre
motorcycle *motocicleta* ① mo-to-thee-*kle*-ta
motorway *autovía* ① ow-to-*vee*-a
mouth *boca* ① *bo*-ka
music *música* ① *moo*-see-ka

N

name *nombre* ⓜ *nom*-bre
napkin *servilleta* ① ser-vee-*lye*-ta
nappy *pañal* ⓜ pa-*nyal*
near *cerca* *ther*-ka
neck *cuello* ⓜ *kwe*-lyo
new *nuevo/a* ⓜ/① *nwe*-vo/a
news *noticias* ① pl no-*tee*-thyas
newspaper *periódico* ⓜ pe-*ryo*-dee-ko

night *noche* ① *no-*che
no *no* no
noisy *ruidoso/a* ⓜ/① rrwee-*do-*so/a
nonsmoking *no fumadores* no foo-ma-*do-*res
north *norte* ⓜ *nor-*te
nose *nariz* ① na-*reeth*
now *ahora* a-o-ra
number *número* ⓜ *noo-*me-ro

O

oil (engine) *aceite* ⓜ a-*they-*te
old *viejo/a* ⓜ/① *vye-*kho/a
one-way ticket *billete sencillo* ⓜ bee-*lye-*te sen-*thee-*lyo
open a *abierto/a* ⓜ/① a-*byer-*to/a
outside *exterior* ⓜ eks-te-*ryor*

P

package *paquete* ⓜ pa-*ke-*te
paper *papel* ⓜ pa-*pel*
park (car) ∨ *estacionar* es-ta-thyo-*nar*
passport *pasaporte* ⓜ pa-sa-*por-*te
pay *pagar* pa-*gar*
pen *bolígrafo* ⓜ bo-*lee-*gra-fo
petrol *gasolina* ① ga-so-*lee-*na
pharmacy *farmacia* ① far-*ma-*thya
phonecard *tarjeta de teléfono* ①
   tar-*khe-*ta de te-*le-*fo-no
photo *foto* ① *fo-*tn
plate *plato* ⓜ *pla-*to
police *policía* ① po-lee-*thee-*a
postcard *postal* ① pos-*tal*
post office *correos* ⓜ ko-*rre-*os
pregnant *embarazada* ① em-ba-ra-*tha-*da
price *precio* ⓜ *pre-*thyo

Q

quiet *tranquilo/a* ⓜ/① tran-*kee-*lo/a

R

rain *lluvia* ① *lyoo-*vya
razor *afeitadora* ① a-fey-ta-*do-*ra
receipt *recibo* ⓜ rre-*thee-*bo
red *rojo/a* ⓜ/① *rro-*kho/a
refund *reembolso* ⓜ rre-em-*bol-*so
registered mail *correo certificado* ⓜ
   ko-*rre-*o ther-tee-fee-*ka-*do

rent ∨ *alquilar* al-kee-*lar*
repair ∨ *reparar* rre-pa-*rar*
reservation *reserva* ① rre-*ser-*va
restaurant *restaurante* ⓜ rres-tow-*ran-*te
return ∨ *volver* vol-*ver*
return ticket *billete de ida y vuelta* ⓜ
   bee-*lye-*te de ee-da ee *vwel-*ta
right (direction) *derecha* de-*re-*cha
road *carretera* ① ka-rre-*te-*ra
room *habitación* ① a-bee-ta-*thyon*

S

safe a *seguro/a* ⓜ/① se-*goo-*ro/a
sanitary napkin *compresas* ① pl kom-*pre-*sas
seat *asiento* ⓜ a-*syen-*to
send *enviar* en-vee-*ar*
service station *gasolinera* ① ga-so-lee-*ne-*ra
sex *sexo* ⓜ *se-*kso
shampoo *champú* ⓜ cham-*poo*
share (a dorm) *compartir* kom-par-*teer*
shaving cream *espuma de afeitar* ①
   es-*poo-*ma de a-fey-*tar*
she *ella* ① *e-*lya
sheet (bed) *sábana* ① *sa-*ba-na
shirt *camisa* ① ka-*mee-*sa
shoes *zapatos* ⓜ pl tha-*pa-*tos
shop *tienda* ① *tyen-*da
short *corto/a* ⓜ/① *kor-*to/a
shower *ducha* ① *doo-*cha
single room *habitación individual* ①
   a-bee-ta-*thyon* een-dee-vee-*dwal*
skin *piel* ① pyel
skirt *falda* ① *fal-*da
sleep ∨ *dormir* dor-*meer*
slowly *despacio* des-*pa-*thyo
small *pequeño/a* ⓜ/① pe-*ke-*nyo/a
smoke (cigarettes) ∨ *fumar* foo-*mar*
soap *jabón* ⓜ kha-*bon*
some *alguno/a* ⓜ/① al-*goo-*no/a
soon *pronto* *pron-*to
south *sur* ⓜ soor
souvenir shop *tienda de recuerdos* ①
   *tyen-*da de re-*kwer-*dos
Spain *España* ① es-*pa-*nya
Spanish (language) *español/castellano* ⓜ
   es-pa-*nyol/*kas-te-*lya-*no
speak *hablar* a-*blar*
spoon *cuchara* ① koo-*cha-*ra
stamp *sello* ⓜ *se-*lyo

stand-by ticket *billete de lista de espera* ⓜ bee-*lye*-te de *lees*-ta de es-*pe*-ra

station (train) *estación* ① es-ta-*thyon*

stomach *estómago* ⓜ es-*to*-ma-go

stop v *parar* pa-*rar*

stop (bus) *parada* ① pa-*ra*-da

street *calle* ① *ka*-lye

student *estudiante* ⓜ/① es-too-*dyan*-te

sun *sol* ⓜ sol

sunscreen *crema solar* ① *kre*-ma so-*lar*

swim v *nadar* na-*dar*

T

tampons *tampones* ⓜ pl tam-*po*-nes

taxi *taxi* ⓜ *tak*-see

teaspoon *cucharita* ① koo-cha-*ree*-ta

teeth *dientes* ⓜ pl *dyen*-tes

telephone *teléfono* ⓜ te-*le*-fo-no

television *televisión* ① te-le-vee-*syon*

temperature (weather) *temperatura* ① tem-pe-ra-*too*-ra

tent *tienda (de campaña)* ① *tyen*-da (de kam-*pa*-nya)

that (one) *ése/a* ⓜ/① *e*-se/a

they *ellos/ellas* ⓜ/① *e*-lyos/e-lyas

thirsty *sediento/a* ⓜ/① se-dee-*en*-to/a

this (one) *éste/a* ⓜ/① *es*-te/a

throat *garganta* ① gar-*gan*-ta

ticket *billete* ⓜ bee-*lye*-te

time *tiempo* ⓜ *tyem*-po

tired *cansado/a* ⓜ/① kan-*sa*-do/a

tissues *pañuelos de papel* ⓜ pl pa-*nywe*-los de pa-*pel*

today *hoy* oy

toilet *servicio* ⓜ ser-*vee*-thyo

tomorrow *mañana* ma-*nya*-na

tonight *esta noche* es-ta *no*-che

toothbrush *cepillo de dientes* ⓜ the-*pee*-lyo de *dyen*-tes

toothpaste *pasta dentífrica* ① *pas*-ta den-*tee*-free-ka

torch (flashlight) *linterna* ① leen-*ter*-na

tour *excursión* ① eks-koor-*syon*

tourist office *oficina de turismo* ① o-fee-*thee*-na de too-*rees*-mo

towel *toalla* ① to-*a*-lya

train *tren* ⓜ tren

translate *traducir* tra-doo-*theer*

travel agency *agencia de viajes* ① a-*khen*-thya de *vya*-khes

travellers cheque *cheque de viajero* ⓜ *che*-ke de vya-*khe*-ro

trousers *pantalones* ⓜ pl pan-ta-*lo*-nes

twin beds *dos camas* ① pl dos *ka*-mas

tyre *neumático* ⓜ ne-oo-*ma*-tee-ko

U

underwear *ropa interior* ① *rro*-pa een-te-*ryor*

urgent *urgente* oor-*khen*-te

V

vacant *vacante* va-*kan*-te

vacation *vacaciones* ① pl va-ka-*thyo*-nes

vegetable *verdura* ① ver-*doo*-ra

vegetarian a *vegetariano/a* ⓜ/① ve-khe-ta-*rya*-no/a

visa *visado* ⓜ vee-*sa*-do

W

waiter *camarero/a* ⓜ/① ka-ma-*re*-ro/a

walk v *caminar* ka-mee-*nar*

wallet *cartera* ① kar-*te*-ra

warm a *templado/a* ⓜ/① tem-*pla*-do/a

wash (something) *lavar* la-*var*

watch *reloj de pulsera* ⓜ rre-*lokh* de pool-*se*-ra

water *agua* ① *a*-gwa

we *nosotros/nosotras* ⓜ/① no-*so*-tros/ no-*so*-tras

weekend *fin de semana* ⓜ feen de se-*ma*-na

west *oeste* ⓜ o-*es*-te

wheelchair *silla de ruedas* ① *see*-lya de *rrwe*-das

when *cuando* kwan-do

where *donde* *don*-de

white *blanco/a* ⓜ/① *blan*-ko/a

who *quien* kyen

why *por qué* por ke

wife *esposa* ① es-*po*-sa

window *ventana* ① ven-*ta*-na

wine *vino* ⓜ *vee*-no

with *con* kon

without *sin* seen

woman *mujer* ① moo-*kher*

write *escribir* es-kree-*beer*

Y

yellow *amarillo/a* a-ma-*ree*-lyo/a

yes *sí* see

yesterday *ayer* a-*yer*

you sg inf/pol *tú/Usted* too/oos-te

you pl *vosotros/vosotras* ⓜ/① vo-*so*-tros/vo-*so*-tras

Swedish

swedish alphabet

A a aa	*B b* bey	*C c* sey	*D d* dey	*E e* ey
F f ef	*G g* gey	*H h* hoh	*I i* ee	*J j* yoy
K k koh	*L l* el	*M m* em	*N n* en	*O o* oh
P p pey	*Q q* ku	*R r* er	*S s* es	*T t* tey
U u u	*V v* vey	*W w* do-belt vey	*X x* eks	*Y y* ew
Z z set	*Å å* aw	*Ä ä* e	*Ö ö* eu	

■ swedish

SVENSKA

SWEDISH

svenska

introduction

The Swedish language (*svenska sven·ska*) gave us *ombudsman* and *smorgasbord*, which just confirms the image of the Swedes as a nation that's good at making the most of life in more ways than one. As a member of the Germanic language family, Swedish shares common roots with English and German. German, in particular, has influenced Swedish in the form of numerous loanwords. However, the closest relatives of Swedish are, of course, the other Scandinavian languages, Danish and Norwegian – all of them descendants of Old Norse, which started branching out from the 9th century and the Viking age.

The oldest inscriptions in Old Norse, dating from the same period, used the runic alphabet and were written on stone or wood. The missionaries who introduced Christianity in the 12th century brought the Roman alphabet (and the custom of writing on parchment) to the emerging Scandinavian languages, but some modification was necessary to represent the specific vowel sounds, so additional letters were eventually developed. The turning point in the evolution of Swedish coincided with the achievement of independence from Danish rule in 1526, when the first translation of the New Testament appeared. The modern literary language was shaped after the first Swedish translation of the whole Bible, known as *Gustav Vasas Bibel* as it was published under the patronage of King Gustav Vasa in 1541.

The standard language or *Rikssvenska* reek·sven·ska (lit: kingdom-Swedish) is based on the central dialects from the area around Stockholm. Some of the rural dialects that are spoken across the country are quite diverse – for example, *Skånska skawn·ska*, spoken in the southern province of Skåne, has flatter vowel sounds (and sounds a lot more like Danish), whereas *Dalmål daal·mawl*, spoken in the central region of Dalarna, has a very up-and-down sound.

Interestingly, Swedish doesn't have official status in Sweden itself, but it does in neighbouring Finland. This is easily explained though – Swedish is the national language of Sweden, spoken by the majority of residents (around 8.5 million), and it simply wasn't felt necessary to enforce its use by law. Finland, on the other hand, was part of Sweden from the mid-14th century until 1809, and Swedish was the language of administration. Today, it shares official status with Finnish and is a mandatory subject in schools, but it's the first language for only about 300,000 people or 6% of Finland's population. PS: any traveller to Sweden should know that the Swedish Chef from the Muppets doesn't really speak Swedish at all.

pronunciation

vowel sounds

Swedish vowel sounds can be either short or long – generally the stressed vowels are long, except when they are followed by double consonants, in which case they are short. The vowels in unstressed syllables are also short.

symbol	english equivalent	swedish example	transliteration
a	run	*glass*	glas
aa	father	*glas*	glaas
ai	aisle	*kaj*	kai
aw	saw	*gå*	gaw
e	bet	*vän*	ven
air	hair	*gärna*	*yair*·na
ee	see	*hit*	heet
eu	nurse	*söt*	seut
ew	ee pronounced with rounded lips	*nytt*	newt
ey	as in 'bet', but longer	*heta*	*hey*·ta
i	hit	*hitta*	*hi*·ta
o	pot	*kopp*	kop
oh	oh	*bott*	boht
oo	zoo	*kul*	kool
u	put	*buss*	bus

consonant sounds

Most Swedish consonants sounds are similar to their English counterparts. One exception is the fh sound (a breathy sound pronounced with rounded lips, like saying 'f' and 'w' at the same time), but with a little practice, you'll soon get it right.

symbol	english equivalent	swedish example	transliteration
b	bed	*bil*	beel
ch	cheat	*tjur*	choor
d	dog	*dyr*	dewr
f	fat	*filt*	filt
fh	f pronounced with rounded lips	*sjuk*	fhook
g	go	*gård*	gawrd
h	hat	*hård*	hawrd
k	kit	*kung*	kung
l	lot	*land*	land
m	man	*man*	man
n	not	*nej*	ney
ng	ring	*sång*	sawng
p	pet	*penna*	pe·na
r	red	*rosa*	roh·sa
s	sun	*sol*	sohl
sh	shot	*första*	feush·ta
t	top	*tröja*	tror·ya
v	very	*vit*	veet
y	yes	*jag*	yaag

word stress

In Swedish, stress usually falls on the first syllable in a word, but sometimes it falls on two syllables. It's important to get the stress right, as it can change the meaning of words (eg *anden an·*den 'duck' versus *anden an·den* 'spirit'). Words borrowed from other languages are often stressed on the last syllable (eg *bibliotek bib·li·o·tek* 'library'). In this chapter, the stressed syllables are always in italics.

basics

language difficulties

Do you speak English?
Talar du engelska?   taa·lar doo *eng*·el·ska

Do you understand?
Förstår du?   feur·*shtawr* doo

I (don't) understand.
Jag förstår (inte).   yaa feur·*shtawr* (*in*·te)

What does (snus) mean?
Vad betyder (snus)?   vaad be·*tew*·der (snoos)

How do you ...?	*Hur ...?*	hoor ...
pronounce this	*uttalar man detta*	*ut*·taa·lar man *de*·ta
write (spårvagn)	*skrivar man*	*skree*·var man
	(spårvagn)	*(spawr*·vangn)

Could you please ...?	*Kan du vara snäll och ...?*	*kan* doo vaa·ra snel o ...
repeat that	*upprepa det*	*up*·rey·pa det
speak more	*tala lite*	*taa*·la *lee*·te
slowly	*långsammare*	*lawng*·sa·ma·re
write it down	*skriva ner det*	*skree*·va *neyr* de

essentials

Yes.	*Ja.*	yaa
No.	*Nej.*	ney
Please.	*Tack.*	tak
Thank you (very much).	*Tack (så mycket).*	tak (saw *mew*·ke)
You're welcome.	*Varsågod.*	var·sha·*gohd*
Excuse me.	*Ursäkta mig.*	oor·*shek*·ta mey
Sorry.	*Förlåt.*	feur·*lawt*

numbers

0	noll	nol	16	sexton	seks·ton	
1	ett	et	17	sjutton	fhu·ton	
2	två	tvaw	18	arton	ar·ton	
3	tre	trey	19	nitton	ni·ton	
4	fyra	few·ra	20	tjugo	shoo·go	
5	fem	fem	21	tjugoett	shoo·go·et	
6	sex	seks	22	tjugotvå	shoo·go·tvaw	
7	sju	fhoo	30	trettio	tre·tee	
8	åtta	o·ta	40	fyrtio	fewr·tee	
9	nio	nee·oh	50	femtio	fem·tee	
10	tio	tee·oh	60	sextio	seks·tee	
11	elva	el·va	70	sjuttio	fhu·tee	
12	tolv	tolv	80	åttio	o·tee	
13	tretton	tre·ton	90	nittio	ni·tee	
14	fjorton	fyor·ton	100	ett hundra	et hun·dra	
15	femton	fem·ton	1000	ett tusen	et too·sen	

time & dates

What time is it?	Hur mycket är klockan?	hur mew·ke air klo·kan
It's one o'clock.	Klockan är en.	klo·kan air eyn
It's (two) o'clock.	Klockan är (två).	klo·kan air (tvaw)
Quarter past (one).	Kvart över (en).	kvart eu·ver (eyn)
Half past (one).	Halv (två). (lit: half two)	halv (tvaw)
Quarter to (nine).	Kvart i (nio).	kvart ee (nee·oh)
At what time ...?	Hur dags ...?	hur daks ...
At (10) o'clock.	Klockan (tio).	klo·kan (tee·oh)
am	förmiddagen (f m)	feur·mi·daa·gen
pm	eftermiddagen (e m)	ef·ter·mi·daa·gen
Monday	måndag	mawn·daa
Tuesday	tisdag	tees·taa
Wednesday	onsdag	ohns·daa
Thursday	torsdag	torsh·daa
Friday	fredag	frey·daa
Saturday	lördag	leur·daa
Sunday	söndag	seun·daa

January	januari	ya·nu·aa·ree
February	februari	fe·bru·aa·ree
March	mars	mars
April	april	a·preel
May	maj	mai
June	juni	yoo·nee
July	juli	yoo·lee
August	augusti	aw·gus·tee
September	september	sep·tem·ber
October	oktober	ok·toh·ber
November	november	noh·vem·ber
December	december	dey·sem·ber

What date is it today?
Vilket datum är det idag?   vil·ket daa·tum air de ee·daag

It's (15 December).
Det är (femtonde December).   de air (fem·ton·de dey·sem·ber)

| since (May) | sedan (maj) | seyn (mai) |
| until (June) | till (juni) | til (yoo·nee) |

last ...
night	igår kväll	ee·gawr kvel
week	förra veckan	feu·ra ve·kan
month	förra månaden	feu·ra maw·na·den
year	förra året	feu·ra aw·ret

next ...
week	nästa ...	nes·ta ...
week	vecka	ve·ka
month	månad	maw·nad
year	år	awr

yesterday ...
	igår ...	ee·gawr ...
morning	morse	mor·she
afternoon	eftermiddag	ef·ter·mi·daag
evening	kväll	kvel

tomorrow ...
	imorgon ...	ee·mor·ron ...
morning	bitti	bi·ti
afternoon	eftermiddag	ef·ter·mi·daag
evening	kväll	kvel

weather

What's the weather like?	*Hur är vädret?*	hur air *vey*·dret

It's...

cold	*Det är kallt.*	de air kalt
cloudy	*Det är molnigt.*	de air *mol*·nit
hot	*Det är het.*	de air heyt
raining	*Det regnar.*	de *reng*·nar
snowing	*Det snöar.*	de *sneu*·ar
sunny	*Solen skiner.*	*soh*·len *fhee*·ner
warm	*Det är varmt.*	de air varmt
windy	*Det blåser.*	de *blaw*·ser

spring	*vår*	vawr
summer	*sommar*	*so*·mar
autumn	*höst*	heust
winter	*vinter*	*vin*·ter

border crossing

I'm here ...	*Jag är ...*	yaa air ...
in transit	*i transit*	i *tran*·sit
on business	*på affärsresa*	paw a·*fairsh*·rey·sa
on holiday	*på semester*	paw se·*mes*·ter

I'm here for ...	*Jag stannar här ...*	yaa *sta*·nar hair ...
(10) days	*(tio) dagar*	(*tee*·oh) *daa*·gar
(three) weeks	*(tre) veckor*	(trey) *ve*·kor
(two) months	*(två) månader*	(tvaw) *maw*·na·der

I'm going to (Trelleborg).
Jag resar till (Trelleborg). — yaa *rey*·sa til (tre·le·*bory*)

I'm staying at the (Grand Hotel).
Jag bor på (Grand Hotell). — yaa bor paw (grand hoh·*tel*)

I have nothing to declare.
Jag har ingenting att förtulla. — yaa har *ing*·en·ting at feur·*tu*·la

I have something to declare.
Jag har något att förtulla. — yaa har *naw*·got at feur·*tu*·la

That's (not) mine.
Det är (inte) min. — de air (*in*·te) min

tickets & luggage

Where can I buy a ticket?
Var kan jag köpa en biljett?   var kan yaa *sheu*·pa eyn bil·*yet*

Do I need to book a seat?
Måste man boka?   maw·ste man *boh*·ka

One ... ticket (to Stockholm), please.	*Jag skulle vilja ha en ... (till Stockholm).*	yaa *sku*·le *vil*·ya haa eyn ... (til *stok*·holm)
one-way	*enkelbiljett*	*en*·kel·bil·*yet*
return	*returbiljett*	re·*toor*·bil·*yet*

I'd like to ... my ticket, please.	*Jag vill gärna ... min biljett.*	yaa vil *yair*·na ... min bil·*yet*
cancel	*upphäva*	*up*·hey·va
change	*ändra*	*en*·dra
collect	*hämta*	*hem*·ta
confirm	*bekräfta*	be·*kref*·ta

I'd like a ... seat, please.	*Jag vill gärna ha en ... plads.*	yaa vil *yair*·na haa eyn ... plads
nonsmoking	*icke-rökande*	*i*·ke·reu·kan·de
smoking	*rökande*	*reu*·kan·de

How much is it?
Hur mycket kostar det?   hoor *mew*·ke *kos*·tar de

Is there air conditioning?
Finns det luft-konditionering?   fins de *luft*·kon·di·fho·*ney*·ring

Is there a toilet?
Finns det en toalett?   fins de eyn toh·aa·*let*

How long does the trip take?
Hur länge undgår resan?   hoor *leng*·e *und*·gawr *rey*·san

Is it a direct route?
Är det en direktförbindelse?   air de eyn dee·*rekt*·feur·bin·del·se

I'd like a luggage locker.
Jag vill gärna få ett låsbara skåp till mit bagage.   yaa vil *yair*·na faw et *laws*·ba·ra skawp til mit ba·*gaash*

My luggage has been ...	Mit bagage är blivit ...	mit ba·*gaash* air *blee*·vit ...
damaged	skadat	*skaa*·dat
lost	förlorat	feur·*loh*·rat
stolen	stulit	*stoo*·lit

getting around

Where does flight (SK403) arrive/depart?
Var ankommer/avgår flyg (SK403)?
var *an*·ko·mar/*aav*·gawr flewg (es koh *few*·ra nol trey)

Where's (the) ...?	Var finns ...?	var fins ...
arrivals hall	ankomsthallen	*an*·komst·ha·len
departures hall	avgångshallen	*aav*·gawngs·ha·len
duty-free shop	en duty-free affär	eyn *dyoo*·tee·*free* a·*fair*
gate (12)	gate (tolv)	gayt (tolv)

Is this the ... to (Stockholm)?	Är den här ... till (Stockholm)?	air den hair ... til (*stok*·holm)
boat	båten	*baw*·ten
bus	bussen	*bu*·sen

Is this the ... to (Stockholm)?	Är det här ... till (Stockholm)?	air de hair ... til (*stok*·holm)
plane	planet	*plaa*·net
train	tåget	*taw*·get

What time's the ... bus?	När går ...?	nair gawr ...
first	första bussen	*feursh*·ta *bu*·sen
last	sista bussen	*sis*·ta *bu*·sen
next	nästa buss	*nes*·ta bus

At what time does it arrive/leave?
Hur dags anländer/avgår den?
hoor daks an·len·der/*aav*·gawr deyn

How long will it be delayed?
Hur mycket är det försenat?
hoor *mew*·ket air dey feur·*shey*·nat

What station/stop is this?
Vilken station/hållplats är denna?
vil·ken sta·*fhohn*/*hawl*·plats air *dey*·na

What's the next station/stop?
Vilken är nästa station/hållplats?
vil·ken air *nes*·ta sta·*fhohn*/*hawl*·plats

Does it stop at (Lund)?
Stannar den på (Lund)? — sta·nar deyn paw (lund)

Please tell me when we get to (Linköping).
Kan du säga till när vi kommer — kan doo say·ya til nair vee ko·mer
till (Linköping)? — til (lin·sheu·ping)

How long do we stop here?
Hur länge stannar vi här? — hoor leng·e sta·nar vee hair

Is this seat available?
Är denna plads ledig? — air dey·na plats ley·dig

That's my seat.
Det är min plads. — de air min plats

I'd like a taxi ... *Jag vill gärna få* — yaa vil yair·na faw
 en taxi ... — eyn tak·see ...
 at (9am) *klockan (nio* — klo·kan (nee·oh
 på morgonen) — paw mo·ro·nen)
 now *nu* — noo
 tomorrow *imorgon* — ee·mo·ron

Is this taxi available?
Är denna taxi ledig? — air dey·na tak·see ley·di

How much is it to ...?
Vad kostar det till ...? — vaad kos·tar de til ...

Please put the meter on.
Kan du kör på taxametern? — kan doo sheur paw tak·sa·mey·tern

Please take me to (this address).
Kan du köra mig till (denna address)? — kan doo sheu·ra mey til (dey·na a·dres)

Please ... *Kan du ...?* — kan doo ...
 slow down *sakta ner* — sak·ta neyr
 stop here *stanna här* — sta·na hair
 wait here *vänta här* — ven·ta hair

car, motorbike & bicycle hire

I'd like to hire a ... *Jag vill hyra en ...* — yaa vil hew·ra eyn ...
 bicycle *cykel* — sew·kel
 car *bil* — beel
 motorbike *motorcykel* — moh·tor·sew·kel

with ...	med ...	meyd ...
a driver	chauffőr	fho·*feur*
air conditioning	luft-konditionering	luft·kon·di·fho·*ney*·ring
antifreeze	kylarvätska	*shew*·lar·vet·ska
snow chains	snökedja	*sneu*·she·dya

How much for ... hire?	Hur mycket kostar det ...?	hoor *mew*·ke *kos*·tar de ...
hourly	per timma	peyr *ti*·ma
daily	per dag	peyr *daag*
weekly	per vecka	peyr *ve*·ka

air	luft	luft
oil	olja	*ol*·ya
petrol	bensin	ben·*seen*
tyres	däck n	dek

I need a mechanic.
Jag behöver en mekaniker.   yaa be·*heu*·ver eyn me·*kaa*·ni·ker

I've run out of petrol.
Jag har ingen bensin kvar.   yaa har *ing*·en ben·*seen* kvar

I have a flat tyre.
Jag har fått punktering.   yaa har fawt punk·*tey*·ring

directions

Where's the ...?	Var ligger ...?	var li·ger ...
bank	banken	*ban*·ken
city centre	centrum	*sen*·trum
hotel	hotellet	hoh·*te*·let
market	salutorget	saa·loo·*tor*·yet
police station	polisen	poh·*lee*·sen
post office	posten	*pos*·ten
public toilet	en offentlig toalett	eyn o·*feynt*·lig toh·aa·*let*
tourist office	turistinformationen	too·*rist*·in·for·ma·*fhoh*·nen

Is this the road to (Göteborg)?
Går den här vägen till (Göteborg)? gawr den hair *vey*·gen til (yeu·te·*bory*)

Can you show me (on the map)?
Kan du visa mig (på kartan)? kan doo *vee*·sa mey (paw *kar*·tan)

What's the address?
Vilken adress är det? *vil*·ken a·*dres* air de

How far is it?
Hur långt är det? hoor *lawngt* air de

How do I get there?
Hur kommer man dit? hoor *ko*·mar man *deet*

Turn ...	*Sväng ...*	sveng ...
at the corner	*vid hörnet*	veed *heur*·net
at the traffic lights	*vid trafikljuset*	veed tra·*feek*·yoo·set
left/right	*till vänster/höger*	til *ven*·ster/*heu*·ger

It's ...	*Det är ...*	de air ...
behind ...	*bakom ...*	*baa*·kom ...
far away	*långt*	lawngt
here	*här*	hair
in front of ...	*framför ...*	*fram*·feur ...
left	*till vänster*	til *ven*·ster
near (to ...)	*nära (på ...)*	*nair*·ra (paw ...)
next to ...	*bredvid ...*	breyd·*veed* ...
on the corner	*vid hörnet*	veed *heur*·net
opposite ...	*mitt emot ...*	mit ey·*moht* ...
right	*till höger*	til *heu*·ger
straight ahead	*rakt fram*	raakt fram
there	*där*	dair

by boat	*med båt*	me *bawt*
by bus	*med buss*	me *bus*
by taxi	*med taxi*	me *tak*·see
by train	*med tåg*	me *tawg*
on foot	*till fods*	til fohts

north	*nord*	nord
south	*syd*	sewd
east	*öst*	eust
west	*väst*	vest

Ingång/Utgång	*in*-gawng/*oot*-gawng	**Entrance/Exit**
Öppet/Stängt	*eu*-pet/stengt	**Open/Closed**
Lediga Rum	*ley*-di-ga *rum*	**Rooms Available**
Fullt/Inga Lediga Rum	fult/*ing*-a *ley*-di-ga *rum*	**No Vacancies**
Information	in-fur-ma-*fhohn*	**Information**
Polisstation	poh-*lees*-sta-*fhohn*	**Police Station**
Förbjudet	feur-*byoo*-det	**Prohibited**
Toaletter	toh-aa-*le*-ter	**Toilets**
Herrar	*her*-ar	**Men**
Damer	*daa*-mer	**Women**
Varm/Kall	varm/kal	**Hot/Cold**

accommodation

finding accommodation

Where's a ...?	*Var finns det ...?*	var fins de ...
camping ground	*en campingplats*	eyn *kam*-ping-*plats*
guesthouse	*ett gästhus*	et *yest*-hoos
hotel	*ett hotell*	et hoh-*tel*
youth hostel	*ett vandrarhem*	et *van*-drar-hem
Can you recommend	*Kan ni rekommendera*	kan nee re-ko-men-*dey*-ra
somewhere ...?	*något ...?*	*naw*-got ...
cheap	*billigt*	*bi*-lit
good	*bra*	braa
nearby	*i närheten*	ee *nair*-hey-ten

I'd like to book a room, please.
Jag skulle vilja boka ett rum.   yaa *sku*-le *vil*-ya *boh*-ka et rum

I have a reservation.
Jag har bokat.   yaa har *boh*-kat

My name's ...
Jag heter ...   yaa *hey*-ter ...

Do you have a ... room?	*Har ni ...?*	har nee ...
single	*ett enkeltrum*	et *en*-kelt-rum
double	*ett dubbeltrum*	et *du*-belt-rum
twin	*ett rum med två sängar*	et rum me tvaw *seng*-ar

How much is it per ...?	*Hur mycket kostar det per ...?*	hoor *mew*-ket *kos*-tar de peyr ...
night	*natt*	nat
person	*person*	*peyr*-shohn

Can I pay by ...?	*Tar ni ...?*	taar nee ...
credit card	*kreditkort*	kre-*deet*-kort
travellers cheque	*resecheckar*	*rey*-se-*she*-kar

I'd like to stay for (two) nights.
Jag tänker stanna (två) dagar.   yaa *ten*-kar *sta*-na (tvaw) *daa*-gar

From (July 2) to (July 6).
Från (annan Juli) till (sjätte Juli).   frawn (*a*-nen *yoo*-lee) til (*fhe*-te *yoo*-lee)

Can I see it?
Kan jag få se rummet?   kan yaa *faw* se *ru*-met

Am I allowed to camp here?
Får jag campa här?   fawr yaa *kam*-pa hair

Is there a campsite nearby?
Finns det någon campingplats i närheten?   fins de nawn *kam*-ping-*plats* ee *nair*-hey-ten

requests & queries

When/Where is breakfast served?
När/Var serveras frukost?   nair/var ser-*vey*-ras *froo*-kost

Please wake me at (seven).
Kan ni väcka mig klockan (sju).   kan nee *ve*-ka mey *klo*-kan (fhoo)

Could I have my key, please?
Jag vill gärna ha min nyckel.   yaa vil *yair*-na haa min *new*-kel

Can I get another (blanket)?
Kan jag få en (filt) till?   kan yaa fawr eyn (filt) *till*

Is there an elevator/a safe?
Finns det en hiss/förvaringsbox?   fins de eyn his/feur-*vaa*-rings-boks

The room is too ...	Rummet är för ...	ru·met air feur ...
expensive	dyrt	dewrt
noisy	bullrigt	bul·rit
small	litet	lee·tet

The ... doesn't work.	... funkar inte.	... fun·kar in·te
air conditioning	Luftkonditioneringen	luft·kon·di·fho·ney·ring·en
fan	Flakten	flek·ten
toilet	Toaletten	toh·aa·le·ten

This ... isn't clean.	Denna ... är inte ren.	dey·na ... air in·te reyn
pillow	kudde	ku·de
sheet	lakan	laa·kan
towel	handduk	han·duk

checking out

What time is checkout?
Hur dags måste mun checka ut?   hoor daks *maw*·ste man *she*·ka ut

Can I leave my luggage here?
Kan jag lämna min bagage här?   kan yaa *lem*·na min ba·*gaash* hair

Could I have my ..., please?	Kan jag få ...?	kan yaa fawr ...
deposit	min depositionsavgift	min de·poh·si·fhohns·aav·yift
passport	mitt pass	mit pas
valuables	mina värdesaker	mee·na vair·de·saa·ker

communications & banking

the internet

Where's the local Internet café?
Var finns det lokala Internet kaféet?   var fins de loh·*kaa*·la *in*·ter·net ka·*fey*·et

How much is it per hour?
Hur mycket kostar det per timma?   hoor *mew*·ke *kos*·tar de par *ti*·ma

I'd like to ...	Jag skulle vilja ...	yaa sku·le vil·ya ...
check my email	kolla min e-post	ko·la min ey·post
get Internet	koppla upp mig	kop·la up mey
access	till Internetet	til in·ter·ne·tet
use a printer	använda en printer	an·ven·da eyn prin·ter
use a scanner	använda en scanner	an·ven·da eyn ska·ner

mobile/cell phone

I'd like a ...	Jag skulle vilja ha ...	yaa sku·le vil·ya haa ...
mobile/cell phone	en mobil telefon	eyn moh·beel te·le·fohn
for hire	till hyra	til hew·ra
SIM card for your	ett sim-kort till detta	et sim·kort til de·ta
network	nätverk	neyt·verk

What are the rates?	Vad är prisarna?	vaad air pree·sar·na

telephone

What's your phone number?
Vad är ditt telefonnummer?   vaad air dit te·le·fohn·nu·mer

The number is ...
Numret är ...   num·ret air ...

Where's the nearest public phone?
Var ligger närmaste publiktelefon?   var li·ger nair·ma·ste pub·leek·te·le·fohn

I'd like to buy a phonecard.
Jag skulle vilja ha ett telefonkort.   yaa sku·le vil·ya haa et te·le·fohn·kort

I want to ...	Jag skulle vilja ...	yaa sku·le vil·ya ...
call (Singapore)	ringa till (Singapore)	ring·a til (sing·a·poor)
make a local call	ringa lokalt	ring·a loh·kaalt
reverse the charges	göra ett ba-samtal	yeu·ra et be·aa·sam·taal

How much does ... cost?	Hur mycket kostar ...?	hoor mew·ke kos·tar ...
a (three)-minute	ett (tre)minuter-	et (trey·)mi·noo·te·
call	samtal	sham·taal
each extra minute	varje extra minut	var·ye eks·tra mi·noot

It's (three) kronor per minute.
(Tre) kronor per minut.   (tre) kroh·nor par mi·noot

post office

I want to send a ...	Jag skulle vilja skicka ett ...	yaa *sku*·le *vil*·ya *fhi*·ka et ...
fax	fax	faks
letter	brev	breyv
parcel	paket	pa·*keyt*
postcard	vykort	*vew*·kort
I want to buy ...	Jag skulle vilja ha ...	yaa *sku*·le *vil*·ya haa ...
an envelope	kuvert	koo·*ver*
stamps	frimärken	*free*·mair·ken
Please send it (to Australia) by ...	Var snäll och skicka den (till Australien) ...	var snel o *fhi*·ka deyn (til o·*straa*·lyen) ...
airmail	med flygpost	me *flewg*·post
express mail	express	eks·*pres*
registered mail	som rekommenderat brev	som re·ko·men·*dey*·rat breyv
surface mail	som ytpost	som *ewt*·post
Is there any mail for me?	Finns det post til mig?	fins de post til mey

bank

Where's a/an ...?	Var finns det en ...?	var fins de eyn ...
ATM	bankomat	ban·koh·*maat*
foreign exchange office	utländsk valuta	*oot*·lensk va·*loo*·ta
I'd like to ...	Jag skulle vilja ...	yaa *sku*·le *vil*·ya ...
arrange a transfer	överföra pengar	*eu*·ver·fer·ra *peng*·ar
cash a cheque	lösa in en check	*leu*·sa in eyn shek
change a travellers cheque	växla resecheckar	*veks*·la *rey*·se·she·kar
change money	växla pengar	*veks*·la *peng*·ar
get a cash advance	ta ut kontant på mitt bankkort	taa oot kon·*tant* paw mit *bank*·kort
withdraw money	dra ut pengar	draa oot *peng*·ar
What's the ...?	Vad är ...?	vaad air ...
charge for that	belastningen för det	be·*last*·ning·en feur de
exchange rate	växelkursen	*vek*·sel·koor·shen

It's ...	Det är ...	de air ...
(25) kronor	(tjugofem) kronor	(shoo·go·fem) kroh·nor
free	gratis	graa·tis

What time does the bank open?
Hur dags öppnar banken? — hoor daks *eup*·nar *ban*·ken

Has my money arrived yet?
Är mina pengar kommit än? — air *mee*·na *peng*·ar *ko*·mit en

sightseeing

getting in

What time does it open/close?
Hur dags öppnar/stänger de? — hoor daks *eup*·nar/*steng*·ar dom

What's the admission charge?
Hur mycket kostar det i inträde? — hoor *mew*·ke *kos*·tar de i *in*·trey·de

Is there a discount for children/students?
Finns det barnrabatt/studentrabatt? — fins de *barn*·ra·bat/*stoo*·dent·ra·bat

I'd like a ...	Jag skulle vilja ha en ...	yaa *sku*·le *vil*·ya haa eyn ...
catalogue	katalog	ka·ta·*lohg*
guide	resehandbok	*rey*·se·hand·bohk
local map	lokal karta	loh·*kaal* kar·ta

I'd like to see ...	Jag skulle vilja se ...	yaa *sku*·le *vil*·ya se ...
What's that?	Vad är det?	vaad air *de*
Can I take a photo?	Får jag fotografera?	fawr yaa foh·toh·gra·*fey*·ra

tours

When's the next ...?	När avgår nästa ...?	nair *aav*·gawr *nes*·ta ...
day trip	dagsturen	*daks*·too·ren
tour	turen	*too*·ren

Is ... included?	Inkluderas ...	in·kloo·*dey*·ras ...
accommodation	logi	lo·*shee*
the admission charge	inträden	*in*·trey·den
food	mat	maat
transport	transport	tran·*sport*

How long is the tour?
Hur länge undgår turen?   hoor *leng*·e *oon*·gawr *too*·ren

What time should we be back?
Hur dags kommer vi tillbaka?   hoor *daks* ko·mar vee til·*baa*·ka

sightseeing		
castle	*slott* n	slot
cathedral	*domkyrka*	*dom*·shewr·ka
church	*kyrka*	*shewr*·ka
main square	*stortorget* n	*stor*·tor·yet
monastery	*kloster* n	*klos*·ter
monument	*monument* n	mo·noo·*ment*
museum	*museum/museet* n	moo·*sey*·oom/moo·*sey*·et
old city	*gamla stan*	*gam*·la *staan*
palace	*palats*	pa·*lats*
ruins	*ruiner*	roo·*ee*·ner
stadium	*idrottsplats*	*i*·drots·plats
statues	*statyer*	sta·*tew*·er

shopping

enquiries

Where's a ...?	*Var finns det ...?*	var finns de ...
bank	*en bank*	eyn bank
bookshop	*en bokhandel*	eyn *bohk*·han·del
camera shop	*en fotoaffär*	eyn *fo*·toh·a·fair
department store	*ett varuhus*	et *va*·roo·hus
grocery store	*en livsmedelsaffär*	eyn *leevs*·mey·dels·a·fair
market	*en torghandel*	eyn *tory*·han·del
newsagency	*en pressbyrå*	eyn *pres*·bew·raw
supermarket	*ett snabbköp*	et *snab*·sheup

Where can I buy a (padlock)?
    Var kan jag köpa ett (hänglås)?   var kan yaa *sheu*·pa et (*heng*·laws)

I'm looking for ...
    Jag letar efter ...   yaa *ley*·tar *ef*·ter ...

Can I look at it?
    Får jag se den?   fawr yaa *se* deyn

Do you have any others?
    Har ni några andra?   har nee *naw*·ra *an*·dra

Does it have a guarantee?
    Har den garanti?   har deyn ga·ran·*tee*

Can I have it sent overseas?
    Kan jag få den skickat utomlands?   kan yaa fawr deyn *fhi*·kat *oo*·tom·lants

Can I have (my backpack) repaired?
    Kan jag får (min ryggsäck) reparerad?   kan yaa fawr (min *rewg*·sek) re·pa·*rey*·rad

It's faulty.
    Den är felaktig.   deyn air *fey*·lak·ti

I'd like ..., please.   *Jag vill gärna ...*   yaa vil *yair*·na ...
    a bag   *ha en kasse*   ha eyn *ka*·se
    a refund   *få en återbäring*   faw eyn *aw*·ter·bai·ring
    to return this   *återlämna denna*   *aw*·ter·lem·na *dey*·na

paying

How much is it?
    Hur mycket kostar det?   hoor *mew*·ke *kos*·tar de

Can you write down the price?
    Kan du skriva ner priset?   kan du *skree*·va neyr *pree*·set

That's too expensive.
    Det är för dyrt.   de air feur *dewrt*

What's your lowest price?
    Vad är dit lägste pris?   vaad air dit *leyg*·ste prees

I'll give you (50) kronor.
    Jag ger dig (femtio) kronor.   yaa yer dey (*fem*·ti) *kroh*·nor

There's a mistake in the bill.
    Det är ett fel på räkningen.   de air et *fel* paw *reyk*·ning·en

Do you accept ...?	*Tar ni ...?*	tar nee ...
credit cards	*kreditkort*	kre-*deet*-kort
debit cards	*betalkort*	be-*taal*-kort
travellers cheques	*resecheckar*	*rey*-se-she-kar

I'd like ..., please.	*Jag vill gärna hu ...*	yaa vil *yair*-na ha ...
a receipt	*ett kvitto*	et *kvi*-to
my change	*min växel*	min *vek*-sel

clothes & shoes

Can I try it on?	*Får jag pröva den?*	fawr yaa *preu*-va deyn
My size is (40).	*Min storlek är (fyrtio).*	min *stor*-leyk air (*fewr*-tee)
It doesn't fit.	*Den passar inte.*	deyn *pa*-sar *in*-te

small	*liten*	*lee*-ten
medium	*medelstor*	*mey*-del-stor
large	*stor*	stor

books & music

I'd like a ...	*Jag skulle vilja ha en ...*	yaa *sku*-le *vil*-ya haa eyn ...
newspaper (in English)	*(engelsk) tidning*	(*eng*-elsk) *teed*-ning
pen	*penna*	*pe*-na

Is there an English-language bookshop?
Finns det an bokhandel   fins de eyn *bohk*-han-del
med böcker på engelska?   me *beu*-ker paw *eng*-el-ska

I'm looking for something by (Henning Mankell).
Jag letar efter något av   yaa *ley*-tar *ef*-ter nawt aav
(Henning Mankell).   (*he*-ning *man*-kel)

Can I listen to this?
Kan jag få höra denna?   kan yaa faw *heu*-ra *dey*-na

photography

Could you ...?	Kan du ...?	kan doo ...
burn a CD from	*bränna en CD från*	bre·na eyn se·de frawn
my memory card	*min memory kort*	min me·mo·ree kort
develop this film	*framkalla denna filmen*	fram·ka·la dey·na fil·men
load my film	*ladda film i min kamera*	la·da film i min kaa·me·ra

I need a ... film	*Jag skulle vilja ha en ...*	yaa sku·le vil·ya haa eyn ...
for this camera.	*till den här kameran.*	til deyn hair kaa·me·ra
APS	*APS-film*	aa·pe·es·film
B&W	*svart-vit film*	svart·vit film
colour	*färg film*	fairg film
slide	*dia-film*	dee·a·film
(200) speed	*(tvåhundra)-film*	(tvaw·hund·ra)·film

When will it be ready?	*När är den klar?*	nair air deyn klaar

meeting people

greetings, goodbyes & introductions

Hello.	*Hej.*	hey
Hi.	*Hejså.*	hey·saw
Good night.	*Godnatt.*	goh·nat
Goodbye.	*Adjö./Hej då.*	aa·yeu/hey daw
See you later.	*Vi ses senare.*	vee seys sey·na·re

Mr	*herr*	her
Mrs	*fru*	froo
Miss	*fröken*	freu·ken

How are you?	*Hur står det till?*	hoor stawr de til
Fine, thanks. And you?	*Bra, tack. Och dig?*	braa tak o dey
What's your name?	*Vad heter du?*	vaad hey·ter doo
My name is ...	*Jag heter ...*	yaa hey·ter ...
I'm pleased to meet you.	*Trevligt att träffas.*	treyv·lit at tre·fas

This is my ...	Detta är min ...	de·ta air min ...
boyfriend	pojkvän	poyk·ven
brother	bror	bror
daughter	dotter	do·ter
father	far	far
friend	vän/väninna m/f	ven/ve·ni·na
girlfriend	flickvän	flik·ven
husband	man	man
mother	mor	mor
partner (intimate)	partner	part·ner
sister	syster	sews·ter
son	son	sohn
wife	fru	froo

Here's my ...	Här är min ...	hair air min ...
What's your ...?	Vad är din ...?	vaad air din ...
address	adress	a·dres
email address	e-post adress	ey·post a·dres

Here's my ...	Här är mitt ...	hair air mit ...
What's your ...?	Vad är ditt ...?	vaad air dit ...
fax number	fax-nummer	faks·nu·mer
phone number	telefonnummer	te·le·fohn·nu·mer

occupations

What's your occupation?	Vad har du för yrke?	vaad har doo feur ewr·ke

I'm a/an ...	Jag är ...	yaa air ...
artist	konstnär	konst·nair
business person	affärsman	a·fairsh·man
office worker	kontorist	kon·to·rist
scientist	naturvetare	na·toor·vey·ta·re
tradesperson	detaljhandlare	de·taly·hand·la·re

background

Where are you from?	Varifrån kommer du?	var·ee·frawn ko·mer doo
I'm from ...	Jag kommer från ...	yaa ko·mer frawn ...
Australia	*Australien*	o·straa·lyen
Canada	*Kanada*	ka·na·da
England	*England*	eng·land
New Zealand	*Nya Zealand*	new·a sey·land
the USA	*USA*	oo·es·aa

Are you married?	Är du gift?	air doo yift
I'm married.	Jag är gift.	yaa air yift
I'm single.	Jag är ogift.	yaa air oh·yift

age

How old ...?	Hur gammal ...?	hoor ga·mal ...
are you	*är du*	air doo
is your daughter	*är din dotter*	air din do·ter
is your son	*är din son*	air din sohn

I'm ... years old.		
Jag är ... år gammal.		yaa air ... awr ga·mal
He/She is ... years old.		
Han/Hon är ... år gammal.		han/hon air ... awr ga·mal

feelings

I'm (not) ...	Jag är (inte) ...	yaa air (in·te) ...
Are you ...?	Är du ...?	air doo ...
happy	*glad*	glaad
hot	*varm*	varm
hungry	*hungrig*	hung·greeg
sad	*ledsen*	le·sen
thirsty	*törstig*	teur·shteeg
tired	*trött*	treut

Are you cold?	Fryser du?	frew·ser doo
I'm (not) cold.	Jag fryser (inte).	yaa frew·ser (in·te)
Are you OK?	Mår du bra?	mawr doo braa
I'm (not) OK.	Jag mår (inte) bra.	yaa mawr (in·te) braa

entertainment

going out

Where can I find ...?	*Var finns ...?*	var fins ...
clubs	*klubbarna*	klu·bar·na
gay venues	*gayklubbarna*	gay·klu·bar·na
pubs	*pubbarna*	pu·bar·na
I feel like going to a/the ...	*Jag vil gärna gå på ...*	yaa vil yair·na gaw paw ...
concert	*konsert*	kon·seyr
movies	*bio*	bee·oh
party	*fest*	fest
restaurant	*restaurang*	res·taw·rang
theatre	*teater*	tee·ay·ter

interests

Do you like ...?	*Tycker du om ...?*	tew·ker doo om ...
I (don't) like ...	*Jag tycker (inte) om ...*	yaa tew·ker (in·te) om ...
art	*konst*	konst
cooking	*att laga mat*	at laa·ga maat
movies	*film*	film
nightclubs	*natklubbar*	nat·klu·bar
reading	*att läsa*	at ley·sa
shopping	*att shoppa*	at sho·pa
sport	*sport*	sport
travelling	*att resa*	at rey·sa
Do you like to ...?	*Tycker du om att ...?*	tew·ker doo om at ...
dance	*dansa*	dan·sa
go to concerts	*gå på konsert*	gaw paw kon·seyr
listen to music	*lyssna på musik*	lews·na paw moo·seek

food & drink

finding a place to eat

Can you	Kan du	kan doo
recommend a ...?	anbefalla en ...?	an·be·fa·la eyn ...
bar	bar	bar
café	kafé	ka·fey
restaurant	restaurang	res·taw·rang
I'd like ..., please.	..., tack.	... tak
a table for (four)	Ett bord för (fyra)	et bord feur (few·ra)
the nonsmoking section	Rökfria avdelningen	reuk·free·a aav·del·ning·en
the smoking section	Rökavdelningen	reuk·aav·del·ning·en

ordering food

breakfast	frukost	froo·kost
lunch	lunch	lunsh
dinner	middag	mi·daa
snack	mellanmål n	me·lan·mawl
today's special	dagens rätt	daa·gens ret

What would you recommend?

    Vad skulle ni anbefalla?   vaad *sku·le* nee *an·be·fa·la*

I'd like (the) ...	Jag skulle vilja ha ...	yaa *sku·le vil·ya* haa ...
bill	räkningen	reyk·ning·en
drink list	drickslistan	driks·lis·tan
menu	menyn	me·newn
that dish	den maträtt	deyn maat·ret

drinks

(cup of) coffee ...	(en kopp) kaffe ...	(eyn kop) ka·fe ...
(cup of) tea ...	(en kopp) te ...	(eyn kop) tey ...
with milk	med mjölk	me myeulk
without sugar	utan socker	oo·taan so·ker
(orange) juice	(apelsin)juice	(a·pel·seen·)djoos
soft drink	läsk	lesk
boiled water	kokt vatten n	kohkt va·ten
mineral water	mineralvatten n	mi·ne·raal·va·ten
water	vatten n	va·ten

in the bar

I'll have ...
Jag vill ha ... — yaa vil haa ...

I'll buy you a drink.
Jag köper dig en drink. — yaa sheu·per dey eyn drink

What would you like?
Vad vill du ha? — vaad vil doo haa

Cheers!
Skål! — skawl

brandy	brandy	bran·dee
cocktail	cocktail	kok·tayl
cognac	cognac	kon·yak
a shot of (whisky)	2 cl (whiskey)	tvaw sen·ti·ley·ter (vis·kee)
a ... of beer	... öl	... eul
bottle	en flaska	eyn flas·ka
glass	ett glass	et glaas
a bottle of ...	en flaska ...	eyn flas·ka ...
a glass of ...	ett glas ...	et glaas ...
red wine	rödvin	reud·veen
sparkling wine	mousserande vin	moo·sey·ran·de veen
white wine	vitt vin	vit veen

self-catering

What's the local speciality?
Vad är den lokala specialiteten? vaad air deyn loh·*kaa*·la spe·si·a·li·*tey*·ten

What's that?
Vad är det? vaad air de

How much is (a kilo of cheese)?
Hur mycket kostar (en kilo ost)? hoor *mew*·ke *kos*·tar (eyn *shee*·loh ohst)

I'd like ...	*Jag vil ha ...*	yaa vil ha ...
(100) grams	*(hundra) gram*	(*hun*·dra) gram
(two) kilos	*(två) kilo*	(tvaw) *shee*·loh
(three) pieces	*(tre) styck*	(trey) stewk
(six) slices	*(sex) skivor*	(seks) *fhee*·vor

Less.	*Mindre.*	*min*·dre
Enough.	*Det räcker.*	de *re*·ker
More.	*Mera.*	*mey*·ra

special diets & allergies

Is there a vegetarian restaurant near here?
Finns det en vegetarisk fins de eyn ve·ge·*taa*·risk
restaurang i närheten? res·taw·*rang* ee *nair*·hey·ten

Do you have vegetarian food?
Har ni vegetarisk mat? har nee ve·ge·*taa*·risk maat

Could you prepare	*Kan ni laga*	kan nee *laa*·ga
a meal without ...?	*en maträtt utan ...?*	eyn *maat*·ret *oo*·tan ...
butter	*smör*	smeur
eggs	*ägg*	eg
meat stock	*köttspad*	*sheut*·spaad

I'm allergic to ...	*Jag är allergisk mot ...*	yaa air al·*leyr*·gisk moht ...
dairy produce	*mejeriprodukter*	me·ye·*ree*·pro·*dook*·ter
gluten	*gluten*	*gloo*·ten
MSG	*MSG*	em·es·*gee*
nuts	*nötter*	*neu*·ter
seafood	*fisk och skaldjur*	fisk o *skaal*·yoor

menu decoder

ärtsoppa	*airt·so·pa*	*yellow pea soup with pork*
biff á la Lindström	*bif a la lind·streum*	*patties of minced meat & beetroot, served with a fried egg*
blodpudding med lingon	*blohd·pu·ding me ling·on*	*black pudding with lingonberry jam*
böckling	*beuk·ling*	*smoked herring*
falukorv	*faa·lu·korv*	*lean sausage cut in thick slices & fried*
glass	*glas*	*ice cream*
gravad lax	*graa·vad laks*	*cured salmon*
grönsakssoppa	*greun·saaks·so·pa*	*vegetable soup*
gryta	*grew·ta*	*casserole*
havskräftor	*haavs·kref·tor*	*prawns*
hönssoppa	*heuns·so·pa*	*chicken soup*
inlagd sill	*in·lagt sil*	*pickled herring*
isterband n	*is·ter·band*	*sausage of pork, beef & barley grains*
Janssons frestelse	*yan·sons fres·tel·se*	*potato, onion & anchovy, oven-baked with lots of cream*
kåldolmar	*kawl·dol·mar*	*stuffed cabbage leaves*
kalops	*ka·lops*	*meat casserole with onions & allspice*
kålsoppa med frikadeller	*kawl·so·pa me fri·ka·de·ler*	*cabbage soup with boiled meatballs (usually pork)*
kanelbulle	*ka·neyl·bu·le*	*sweet roll with cinnamon & cardamom*
kavring	*kaav·ring*	*dark sweetened rye bread*
knäckebröd n	*kne·ke·breud*	*crispbread, usually rye*
köttbullar	*sheut·bu·lar*	*meatballs*
köttsoppa	*sheut·so·pa*	*beef broth with meat & vegetables*

lövbiff	*leuv*·bif	*very thinly sliced beef*
mazarin	ma·za·*reen*	*pastry with almond paste filling*
nässelsoppa	ne·sel·*so*·pa	*nettle soup with a hard-boiled egg*
nyponsoppa	*new*·pon·*so*·pa	*rosehip soup, eaten with cream*
ostkaka	*ost*·kaa·ka	*cheese cake*
pannbiff med lök	*pan*·bif me *leuk*	*minced beef patties with fried onion*
prinsesstårta	prin·ses·*tawr*·ta	*layered sponge cake with jam, cream & custard filling, covered with marzipan*
pyttipanna	*pew*·ti·*pa*·na	*diced meat, boiled potatoes & onion, fried & served with beetroot & a fried egg*
rågbröd n	*rawg*·breud	*rye bread*
raggmunkar	*rag*·mun·kar	*pancakes made from grated potatoes*
räkor	*rey*·kor	*shrimps*
råstekt potatis	*raw*·stekt poh·*taa*·tis	*potato slices fried in oil*
renskav n	*reyn*·skaav	*thinly sliced reindeer meat*
ris á la malta n	*rees* a la *mal*·ta	*rice with whipped cream & orange*
schwartzwaldstårta	*shvarts*·valds·*tawr*·ta	*meringue, cream & chocolate cake*
skalpotatis	*skaal*·poh·*taa*·tis	*potatoes boiled in their jackets*
småländsk ostkaka	*smaw*·lands *awst*·kaa·ka	*baked curd cake with almonds*
sockerkaka	*so*·ker·kaa·ka	*sponge cake flavoured with lemon*
sotare	*soh*·ta·re	*lightly salted & grilled herring*
sötlimpa	*seut*·lim·pa	*sweetened brown loaf*
stuvad potatis	*stoo*·vad poh·*taa*·tis	*potatoes in white sauce*
svampsoppa	*svamp*·*so*·pa	*mushroom soup*
tunnbröd n	*tun*·breud	*very thin crisp or soft barley bread*
viltgryta	vilt·*grew*·ta	*game casserole*
vörtbröd n	*vert*·breud	*rye bread flavoured with wort (a herb)*

emergencies

basics

Help!	Hjälp!	yelp
Stop!	Stanna!	sta·na
Go away!	Försvinn!	feur·shvin
Thief!	Ta fast tjuven!	ta fast shoo·ven
Fire!	Elden är lös!	el·den air leus
Watch out!	Se upp!	se up

Call ...!	Ring ...!	ring ...
a doctor	efter en doktor	ef·ter en dok·tor
an ambulance	efter en ambulans	ef·ter en am·boo·lans
the police	polisen	poh·lee·sen

It's an emergency!
Det är ett nödsituation!   de air et neud·si·too·a·fhohn

Could you help me, please?
Kan du hjälpa mig?   kan doo yel·pa mai

I have to use the telephone.
Jag måste använda telefonen.   yaa maws·te an·ven·da te·le·foh·nen

I'm lost.
Jag har gått vilse.   yaa har got vil·se

Where are the toilets?
Var är toaletten?   var air toh·aa·le·ten

police

Where's the police station?
Var är polisstationen?   var air poh·lees·sta·fhoh·nen

I want to report an offence.
Jag vill anmäla ett brott.   yaa vil an·mey·la et brot

I have insurance.
Jag har försäkring.   yaa har feur·shey·kring

I've been assaulted.
Jag är blivit utsatt för övervåld.   yaa air blee·vit ut·sat feur eu·ver·vawld

I've been ...	Jag har blivit ...	yaa har *blee*·vit ...
raped	*våldtagen*	*vol*·taa·gen
robbed	*rånad*	*raw*·nad

I've lost my ...	Jag har förlorat ...	yaa har feur·*loh*·rat ...
backpack	*min ryggsäck*	min *rewk*·sek
bags	*mina väskor*	*mee*·na *ves*·kor
credit card	*min kreditkort*	min kre·*deet*·kort
handbag	*min handväska*	min *hand*·ves·ka
jewellery	*mina smycken*	*mee*·na *smew*·ken
money	*mina pengar*	*mee*·na *peng*·ar
passport	*mitt pass*	mit pas
travellers cheques	*mina resecheckar*	*mee*·na *rey*·se·she·kar
wallet	*min plånbok*	min *plawn*·bohk

I want to contact my ...	Jag vill kontakta ...	yaa vil kon·*tak*·ta ...
consulate	*mitt konsulat*	mit kon·soo·*laat*
embassy	*min ambassad*	min am·ba·sa·*saad*

health

medical needs

Where's the nearest ...?	Var är närmaste ...?	var air *nair*·ma·ste ...
dentist	*tandläkaren*	*tand*·ley·ka·ren
doctor	*doktorn*	*dok*·torn
hospital	*sjukhuset*	*fhook*·hu·set
(night) pharmacist	*(natt)apoteket*	*(nat*·)a·poh·*te*·ket

I need a doctor (who speaks English).
Jag behöver en läkare   yaa be·*heu*·ver eyn *ley*·ka·re
(som talar engelska).   (som *taa*·lar *eng*·el·ska)

Could I see a female doctor?
Kan jag få träffa en kvinnlig läkare?   kan yaa faw *tre*·fa eyn *kvin*·li *ley*·ka·re

I've run out of my medication.
Jag har ingen medikament kvar.   yaa har *ing*·en me·di·ka·*ment* kvar

symptoms, conditions & allergies

I'm sick.	Jag är sjuk.	yaa air fhook
It hurts here.	Det gör ont här.	de yeur ont hair
I have nausea.	Jag mår illa.	yaa mawr i·la

I have (a) ...	Jag har ...	yaa haa ...
asthma	astma	ast·maa
bronchitis	bronkit	bron·keet
constipation	förstoppning	feur·shtop·ning
cough	en hosta	eyn hoh·sta
diarrhoea	diarré	dee·a·rey
fever	feber	fey·ber
headache	huvudvärk	hoo·vud·vairk
heart condition	en hjärttillstånd	eyn yairt·til·stawnd
pain	ont	ont
sore throat	ont i halsen	ont ee hal·sen
toothache	tandvärk	tand·verk

I'm allergic to ...	Jag är allergisk mot ...	yaa air a·leyr·gisk moht ...
antibiotics	antibiotika	an·tee·bee·oh·ti·ka
anti-inflammatories	anti-inflammatoriska medel	an·tee·in·fla·ma·toh·ri·ska mey·del
aspirin	magnecyl	mag·ne·sewl
bees	bin	been
codeine	kodein	koh·deen
penicillin	penicillin	pe·ne·si·leen

antiseptic	antiseptiskt medel n	an·tee·sep·tiskt mey·del
bandage	förband n	feur·band
condoms	kondomer	kon·doh·mer
diarrhoea medicine	medel mot diarré n	mey·del moht dee·a·rey
insect repellent	insektsmedel n	in·sekts·mey·del
laxatives	laxermedel n	lak·ser·mey·del
painkillers	smärtstillande medel n	smairt·sti·lan·de mey·del
rehydration salts	vätskeersätt·ningsmedel n	vet·ske·er·set·nings·mey·del
sleeping tablets	sovmedel n	sohv·mey·del

health – SWEDISH

403

english–swedish dictionary

In this dictionary, words are marked as n (noun), a (adjective), v (verb), sg (singular), pl (plural), inf (informal) and pol (polite) where necessary. Note that Swedish nouns are either masculine, feminine or neuter. Masculine and feminine forms (known as 'common gender') take the indefinite article *en* (a) while the neuter forms take the article *ett* (a). Every Swedish noun needs to be learned with its indefinite article (*en* or *ett*). We've only indicated the neuter nouns with ⓝ after the Swedish word. Note also that the ending 't' is added to adjectives for the neuter form (ie when they accompany indefinite singular nouns). In some cases both forms of the adjective (ie ⓜ & ⓕ form and ⓝ form) are spelled out in full and separated with a slash.

A

accident *olycka* oh-lew-ka
accommodation *husrum* ⓝ hus-rum
adaptor *adapter* a-dap-ter
address n *adress* a-dres
after *efter* ef-ter
air-conditioned *luftkonditionerad/luftkonditionerat* luft-kon-di-fho-ney-rad/luft-kon-di-fho-ney-rat
airplane *flygplan* ⓝ flewg-plaan
airport *flygplats* flewg-plats
alcohol *alkohol* al-ko-hohl
all *alla* a-la
all (everything) n *allt* alt
allergy *allergi* a-ler-gee
ambulance *ambulans* am-bu-lans
and *och* ok
ankle *vrist* wrist
arm *arm* arm
ashtray *askfat* ⓝ ask-faat
ATM *bankomat* bang-koh-maat

B

baby *baby* bey-bee
back (body) *rygg* rewg
backpack *ryggsäck* rewg-sek
bad *dårlig(t)* dawr-lig/dawr-lit
bag *väska* ves-ka
baggage claim *bagageavhämtning* ba-gaash-aav-hemt-ning
bank *bank* bank
bar *bar* baar
bathroom *badrum* ⓝ baad-rum
battery *batteri* ⓝ ba-te-ree
beautiful *vacker(t)* va-ker(t)
bed *säng* seng

beer *öl* ⓝ eul
before *framför* fram-feur
behind *bakom* baa-kom
bicycle *cykel* sew-kel
big *stor(t)* stawr(t)
bill *räkning* reyk-ning
black *svart* svart
blanket *filt* filt
blood group *blodgrupp* blohd-grup
blue *blå(tt)* blaw/blot
boat *båt* bawt
book (make a reservation) v *boka* boh-ka
bottle *flaska* flas-ka
bottle opener *flasköppnare* flask-eup-na-re
boy *pojke* poy-ke
brakes (car) *bromsar* brom-sar
breakfast *frukost* froo-kost
broken (faulty) *sönder* seun-der
bus *buss* bus
(do) business *handla* hand-la
buy *köpa* sheu-pa

C

café *kafé* ⓝ ka-fey
camera *kamera* kaa-me-ra
camp site *campingplats* kam-ping-plats
cancel *upphäva* up-hey-va
can opener *burköppnare* burk-eup-na-re
car *bil* beel
cash n *kontant* kon-tant
cash (a cheque) v *lösa in (en check)* leu-sa in (eyn shek)
cell phone *mobiltelefon* moh-beel-te-le-fohn
centre *center* ⓝ sen-ter
change (money) v *växla (pengar)* veyk-sla (peng-ar)
cheap *billig(t)* bi-lig/bi-lit
check (bill) *räkning* reyk-ning

check-in *incheckning* in-chek-ning
chest *bröst* ⓝ breust
child *barn* ⓝ barn
cigarette *cigarett* si-ga-ret
city *storstad* stawr-staad
clean a *ren(t)* reyn(t)
closed *stängd/stängt* stengd/stengt
coffee *kaffe* ⓝ ka-fe
coins *mynt* ⓝ mewnt
cold a *kylig(t)* shew-lig/shew-lit
collect call *ba-samtal* ⓝ be-aa-sam-taal
come *komma* ko-ma
computer *dator* daa-tor
condom *kondom* kon-dohm
contact lenses *kontaklinser* kon-takt-lin-ser
cook v *laga mat* laa-ga maat
cost n *kostnad* kost-nad
credit card *kreditkort* ⓝ kre-deet-kort
cup *kopp* kop
currency exchange *växel* veyk-sel
customs (immigration) *tullen* tu-len

D

dangerous *farlig(t)* far-lig/far-lit
date (time) *datum* ⓝ daa-tum
day *dag* daag
delay *dröjsmål* ⓝ dreuys-mawl
dentist *tandläkare* tand-ley-ka-re
depart *avresa* aav-rey-sa
diaper *blöja* bleu-ya
dictionary *ordbok* ord-bohk
dinner *middag* mi-daag
direct *direkt* dee-rekt
dirty *smutsig(t)* smut-sig/smut-sit
disabled *handikappad* han-dee-ka-pad
discount n *rabatt* ra-bat
doctor *läkare* ley-ka-re
double bed *dubbelsäng* du-bel-seng
double room *dubbelt rum* ⓝ du-belt rum
drink n *dricka* dri-ka
drive v *köra* sheu-ra
drivers licence *körkort* ⓝ sheur-kort
drug (illicit) *narkotika* nar-koh-ti-ka
dummy (pacifier) *napp* nap

E

ear *öra* eu-ra
east *öst* eust

eat *äta* ey-ta
economy class *ekonomiklass* e-ko-noh-mee-klas
electricity *elektricitet* ey-lek-tri-si-teyt
elevator *hiss* his
email *e-post* ey-post
embassy *ambassad* am-ba-saad
emergency *nödsituation* ⓝ neud-si-too-a-fhohn
English (language) *engelska* eng-el-ska
entrance *ingång* in-gawng
evening *kväll* kvel
exchange rate *växelkurs* veyk-sel-kursh
exit n *utgång* oot-gawng
expensive *dyr(t)* dewr(t)
express mail *expresspost* eks-pres-post
eye *öga* ⓝ eu-ga

F

far *långt* lawngt
fast *snabb(t)* snab(t)
father *far* faar
film (camera) *film* film
finger *finger* ⓝ fing-er
first-aid kit *förbandslåda* feur-bants-law-da
first class *första klass* feu-shta klas
fish n *fisk* fisk
food *mat* maat
foot *fot* foht
fork *gaffel* ga-fel
free (of charge) *gratis* graa-tis
friend *vän/vänninna* ⓜ/ⓕ ven/ve-ni-na
fruit *frukt* frukt
full *fylld/fyllt* fewld/fewlt
funny *rolig(t)* roh-lig/roh-lit

G

gift *gåva* gaw-va
girl *flicka* fli-ka
glass (drinking) *glas* ⓝ glaas
glasses *glasögon* ⓝ glaa-seu-gon
go *åka* aw-ka
good *bra* braa
green *grön(t)* greun(t)
guide n *guide* gaid

H

half n *halv* halv
hand *hand* hand

handbag *handväska* hand-vey-ska
happy *glad* glaad
have *ha* haa
he *han* han
head *huvud* ⓝ hoo-vud
heart *hjärta* yair-ta
heat ⓝ *hetta* he-ta
heavy *tung(t)* tung(t)
help ⓥ *hjälp* yelp
here *här* hair
high *hög(t)* heug(t)
highway *huvudväg* hoo-vud-veyg
hike ⓥ *fotvandra* foht-van-dra
holiday *semester* se-mes-ter
homosexual ⓝ&ⓐ *homosexuell* hoh-moh-sek-soo-el
hospital *sjukhus* ⓝ fhook-hoos
hot *varm(t)* varm(t)
hotel *hotell* ⓝ hoh-tel
hungry *hungrig(t)* hung-grig/hung-grit
husband *man* man

I

I *jag* yaag
identification (card) *identitetskort* ⓝ ee-den-ti-teyts-kort
ill *sjuk(t)* fhook(t)
important *viktig(t)* vik-tig/vik-tit
included *inklusiv* in-kloo-seev
injury *skada* skaa-da
insurance *försäkring* feu-shey-kring
Internet *Internet* ⓝ in-ter-net
interpreter *tolk* tolk

J

jewellery *smycke* ⓝ smew-ke
job *arbete* ⓝ aar-bey-te

K

key *nyckel* new-kel
kilogram *kilo(gram)* ⓝ shee-loh(-gram)
kitchen *kök* ⓝ sheuk
knife *kniv* kneev

L

laundry (place) *tvättstuga* tvet-stoo-ga
lawyer *advokat* ad-voh-kaat

left (direction) *vänster* ven-ster
left-luggage office *resgodsinlämning* reys-gohds-in-lem-ning
leg *ben* ⓝ beyn
lesbian ⓐ *lesbisk* lez-bisk
less *mindre* min-dre
letter (mail) *brev* ⓝ breyv
lift (elevator) *hiss* his
light *ljus* ⓝ yoos
like ⓥ *tycka om* tew-ka om
lock ⓝ *lås* laws
long *lång(t)* lawng(t)
(be) lost (of a person) *vilse* vil-se
(be) lost (of property) *borta* bor-ta
lost-property office *hittegodsexpedition* hi-te-gohds-eks-pe-di-fhohn
love ⓥ *älska* el-ska
luggage *bagage* ⓝ ba-gaash
lunch *lunch* lunsh

M

mail ⓝ *post* post
man *man* man
map *karta* kar-ta
market *marknad/torg* ⓝ mark-naad/tory
matches *tändstickor* ten-sti-kor
meat *kött* ⓝ sheut
medicine *medicin* me-di-seen
menu *meny/matsedel* me-new/maat-sey-del
message *bud* ⓝ bood
milk *mjölk* myeulk
minute *minut* mi-noot
mobile phone *mobiltelefon* moh-beel-te-le-fohn
money *pengar* peng-ar
month *månad* maw-nad
morning *morgon* mor-gon
mother *mor* mawr
motorcycle *motorcykel* moh-tor-sew-kel
motorway *motorväg* moh-tor-veyg
mouth *mun* mun
music *musik* moo-seek

N

name *namn* ⓝ namn
napkin *servett* seyr-vet
nappy *blöja* bleu-ya
near *nära* nair-a

neck *hals* hals
new *ny(tt)* new(t)
news *nyheter* new-hey-ter
newspaper *tidning* teed-ning
night *natt* nat
no *nej* ney
noisy *bullrig(t)* bul-rig/bul-rit
nonsmoking *icke-rökande* i-ke-reu-kan-de
north *nord* nord
nose *näsa* ney-sa
now *nu* noo
number *nummer* ⓝ nu-mer

O

oil (engine) *olja* ol-ya
old *gammal(t)* ga-mal(t)
one-way ticket *enkelbiljett* en-kel-bil-yet
open a *öppen/öppet* eu-pen/eu-pet
outside *utanför* oo-tan-feur

P

package *paket* ⓝ pa-keyt
paper *papper* ⓝ pa-per
park (car) v *parkera* par-key-ra
passport *pass* ⓝ pas
pay *betala* be-taa-la
pen *penna* pe-na
petrol *bensin* ben-seen
pharmacy *apotek* ⓝ a-poh-teyk
phonecard *telefonkort* ⓝ tel-le-fohn-kort
photo *foto* ⓝ foh-toh
plate *tallrik* tal-reek
police *polis* poh-lees
postcard *postkort* ⓝ post-kort
post office *posten* pos-ten
pregnant *gravid* gra-veed
price *pris* prees

Q

quiet *stilla* stil-la

R

rain n *regn* rengn
razor *rakhyvel* raak-hew-vel
receipt *kvitto* ⓝ kvi-toh

red *röd/rött* reud/reut
refund n *återbäring* aw-ter-bair-ing
registered mail *värdeförsändelse*
    vair-de-feu-shen-del-se
rent v *hyra* hew-ra
repair v *reparera* re-pa-rey-ra
reservation *beställning* be-stel-ning
restaurant *restaurang* res-taw-rang
return v *återvända* aw-ter-ven-da
return ticket *returbiljett* rey-toor-bil-yet
right (direction) *höger* heu-ger
road *väg* veyg
room *rum* ⓝ rum

S

safe a *trygg(t)* trewg(t)
sanitary napkin *dambinda* daam-bin-da
seat *sittplats* sit-plats
send *skicka* fhi-ka
service station *bensinstation* ben-seen-sta-fhohn
sex *samlag* ⓝ sam-laag
shampoo *schampo* ⓝ fham-poo
share (a dorm) *dela* dey-la
shaving cream *rakkräm* raak-kreym
she *hon* hoon
sheet (bed) *lakan* ⓝ laa-kan
shirt *skjorta* fhor-ta
shoes *skor* skor
shop n *affär* a-fair
short *kort* kort
shower n *dusch* doosh
single room *enkelt rum* ⓝ en-kelt rum
skin *hud* hood
skirt *kjol* shohl
sleep v *sova* soh-va
slowly *sakta* sak-ta
small *liten/litet* lee-ten/lee-tet
smoke (cigarettes) v *röka* reu-ka
soap *tvål* tvawl
some *någon/något* naw-gon/naw-got
soon *snart* snart
south *syd* sewd
souvenir shop *souvenir affär* su-ve-neer a-fair
speak *tala* taa-la
spoon *sked* fheyd
stamp *frimärke* ⓝ free-mair-ke
stand-by ticket *standbybiljett* stand-bai-bil-yet
station (train) *(järnvägs)station* (yairn-veyks-)sta-fhohn

stomach *mage maa*-ge
stop v *stanna/hålla sta*-na/*haw*-la
stop (bus) n *(buss)hållplats (bus-)hawl*-plats
street *gata gaa*-ta
student *studerande stoo-dey-ran-*de
sun *sol* sohl
sunscreen *solkräm sohl*-kreym
Sweden *Sverige sve*-rya
Swedish (language) *svenska sven*-ska
Swedish a *svensk(t)* svensk(t)
swim v *simma si*-ma

T

tampons *tampong tam-pong*
taxi *taxi tak*-see
teaspoon *tesked tey*-fheyd
teeth *tänder te*-ner
telephone n *telefon te-le-fohn*
television *TV tey*-vey
temperature (weather) *temperatur tem-pe-ra-toor*
tent *tält* telt
that (one) *den* ⓜ & ⓕ/*det* ⓝ deyn/dey
they *dem* dom
thirsty *törstig(t) teush*-tig/*teush*-tit
this (one) *den här* ⓜ & ⓕ/*det här* ⓝ *den* hair/dey hair
throat *strupe stroo*-pe
ticket *biljett bil*-yet
time *tid* teed
tired *trött* treut
tissues *näsdukar neys*-doo-kar
today *i dag* i daag
toilet *toalett* toh-aa-*let*
tomorrow *imorgon* ee-*mor*-ron
tonight *i kväll* ee kvel
toothbrush *tandbörste tand*-beu-shte
toothpaste *tandkräm tand*-kreym
torch (flashlight) *ficklampa fik*-lam-pa
tour n *tur* toor
tourist office *turistbyrå* too-rist-*bew*-raw
towel *badduk baad*-dook
train *tåg* ⓝ tawg
translate *översätta* eu-ve-se-ta
travel agency *resebyrå* rey-se-*bew*-raw
travellers cheque *resecheck* rey-se-shek
trousers *byxor bewk*-sor
twin beds *två sängar* tvaw seng-ar
tyre *däck* ⓝ dek

U

underwear *underkläder un*-der-kley-der
urgent *angelägen/angeläget*
   an-ye-ley-gen/*an*-ye-ley-get

V

vacant *ledig(t) ley*-dig/ley-dit
vacation *semester* se-*mes*-ter
vegetable n *grönsak greun*-saak
vegetarian a *vegetarian* ve-ge-taa-ree-*aan*
visa *visum* ⓝ *vee*-sum

W

waiter *servitör* ser-vi-*teur*
Waiter! *Vaktmästern!* vakt-mes-tern
walk v *gå* gaw
wallet *plånbok plawn*-bohk
warm a *varm(t)* varm(t)
wash (something) *tvätta tve*-ta
watch n *klocka klo*-ka
water *vatten* ⓝ *va*-ten
we *vi* vee
weekend *helg* hely
west *väst* vest
wheelchair *rullstol rul*-stohl
when *när* nair
where *var* var
white *vit(t)* veet/vit
who *vem* vem
why *varför* var-feur
wife *fru* froo
window *fönster feun*-ster
wine *vin* ⓝ veen
with *med* meyd
without *utan oo*-taan
woman *kvinna kvi*-na
write *skriva skree*-va

Y

yellow *gul(t)* gul(t)
yes *ja* yaa
yesterday *igår* i-*gawr*
you sg inf *du* doo
you sg pol & pl *ni* nee

Turkish

alphabet

A a a	*B b* be	*C c* je	*Ç ç* che	*D d* de
E e e	*F f* fe	*G g* ge	*Ğ ğ* yu·*moo*·shak ge	*H h* he
I ı uh	*İ i* ee	*J j* zhe	*K k* ke	*L l* le
M m me	*N n* ne	*O o* o	*Ö ö* er	*P p* pe
R r re	*S s* se	*Ş ş* she	*T t* te	*U u* oo
Ü ü ew	*V v* ve	*Y y* ye	*Z z* ze	

■ turkish

TÜRKÇE

TURKISH

türkçe

introduction

Turkish (*Türkçe tewrk·che*) – the language which traces its roots as far back as 3500 BC, has travelled through Central Asia, Persia, North Africa and Europe and been written in both Arabic and Latin script – has left us words like *yogurt*, *horde*, *sequin* and *bridge* (the game) along the way. But how did it transform itself from a nomad's tongue spoken in Mongolia into the language of modern Turkey, with a prestigious interlude as the diplomatic language of the Ottoman Empire?

The first evidence of the Turkish language, which is a member of the Ural-Altaic language family, was found on stone monuments from the 8th century BC, in what's now Outer Mongolia. In the 11th century, the Seljuq clan invaded Asia Minor (Anatolia) and imposed their language on the peoples they ruled. Over time, Arabic and Persian vocabulary was adopted to express artistic and philosophical concepts and Arabic script began to be used. By the 14th century, another clan – the Ottomans – was busy establishing the empire that was to control Eurasia for centuries. In their wake, they left the Turkish language. There were then two levels of Turkish – ornate Ottoman Turkish, with flowery Persian phrases and Arabic honorifics (words showing respect), used for diplomacy, business and art, and the language of the common Turks, which still used 'native' Turkish vocabulary and structures.

When the Ottoman Empire fell in 1922, the military hero, amateur linguist and historian Kemal Atatürk came to power and led the new Republic of Turkey. With the backing of a strong language reform movement, he devised a phonetic Latin script that reflected Turkish sounds more accurately than Arabic script. On 1 November 1928, the new writing system was unveiled: within two months, it was illegal to write Turkish in the old script. In 1932 Atatürk created the *Türk Dil Kurumu* (Turkish Language Society) and gave it the brief of simplifying the Turkish language to its 'pure' form of centuries before. The vocabulary and structure was completely overhauled. As a consequence, Turkish has changed so drastically that even Atatürk's own speeches are barely comprehensible to today's speakers of *öztürkçe* ('pure Turkish').

With 70 million speakers worldwide, Turkish is the official language of Turkey and the Turkish Republic of Northern Cyprus (recognised as a nation only by the Turkish government). Elsewhere, the language is also called *Osmanlı os·man·luh*, and is spoken by large populations in Germany, Bulgaria, Macedonia, Greece and the '-stans' of Central Asia. So start practising and you might soon be complimented with *Ağzına sağlık!* a·zuh·na sa·luhk (lit: health to your mouth) – 'Well said!'

pronunciation

vowel sounds

Most Turkish vowel sounds can be found in English, although in Turkish they're generally shorter and slightly harsher. When you see a double vowel, such as *saat* sa·*at* (hour), you need to pronounce both vowels.

symbol	english equivalent	turkish example	transliteration
a	run	*abide*	a·bee·*de*
ai	aisle	*hayvan*	hai·*van*
ay	say	*ney*	nay
e	bet	*ekmek*	ek·*mek*
ee	see	*ile*	ee·le
eu	nurse	*özel*	eu·*zel*
ew	ee pronounced with rounded lips	*üye*	ew·ye
o	pot	*oda*	o·*da*
oo	zoo	*uçak*	oo·*chak*
uh	ago	*ıslak*	uhs·*lak*

word stress

In Turkish, the stress generally falls on the last syllable of the word. Most two-syllable placenames, however, are stressed on the first syllable (eg *Kıbrıs* kuhb·ruhs), and in three-syllable placenames the stress is usually on the second syllable (eg *İstanbul* ees·*tan*·bool). Another common exception occurs when a verb has a form of the negative marker *me* (*me* me, *ma* ma, *mı* muh, *mi* mee, *mu* moo, or *mü* mew) added to it. In those cases, the stress goes onto the syllable before the marker – eg *gelmiyorlar* gel·mee·yor·lar (they're not coming). You don't need to worry too much about this, as the stressed syllable is always in italics in our coloured pronunciation guides.

consonant sounds

Most Turkish consonants sound the same as in English, so they're straightforward to pronounce. The exception is the Turkish r, which is always rolled. Note also that ğ is a silent letter which extends the vowel before it – it acts like the 'gh' combination in 'weigh', and is never pronounced.

symbol	english equivalent	turkish example	transliteration
b	bed	*bira*	*bee·*ra
ch	cheat	*çanta*	chan·*ta*
d	dog	*deniz*	de·*neez*
f	fat	*fabrika*	fab·ree·*ka*
g	go	*gar*	gar
h	hat	*hala*	ha·*la*
j	joke	*cadde*	jad·*de*
k	kit	*kadın*	ka·*duhn*
l	lot	*lider*	lee·*der*
m	man	*maç*	mach
n	not	*nefis*	ne·*fees*
p	pet	*paket*	pa·*ket*
r	red (rolled)	*rehber*	reh·*ber*
s	sun	*saat*	sa·*at*
sh	shot	*şarkı*	shar·*kuh*
t	top	*tas*	tas
v	van (but softer, between 'v' and 'w')	*vadi*	va·*dee*
y	yes	*yarım*	ya·*ruhm*
z	zero	*zarf*	zarf
zh	pleasure	*jambon*	zham·*bon*

basics

language difficulties

Do you speak English?
İngilizce konuşuyor musunuz?   een·gee·*leez*·je ko·noo·*shoo*·yor moo·soo·*nooz*

Do you understand?
Anlıyor musun?   an·*luh*·yor moo·*soon*

I understand.
Anlıyorum.   an·*luh*·yo·room

I don't understand.
Anlamıyorum.   an·*la*·muh·yo·room

What does (*kitap*) mean?
(Kitap) ne demektir?   (kee·*tap*) ne de·*mek*·teer

How do you pronounce this?
Bunu nasıl telaffuz edersiniz?   boo·*noo* na·suhl te·laf·*fooz* e·*der*·see·neez

How do you write (*yabancı*)?
(Yabancı) kelimesini   (ya·ban·*juh*) ke·lee·me·see·*nee*
nasıl yazarsınız?   *na*·suhl ya·*zar*·suh·nuhz

Could you please ...?	*Lütfen ...?*	*lewt*·fen ...
repeat that	*tekrarlar mısınız*	tek·*rar*·lar muh·suh·*nuhz*
speak more	*daha yavaş*	da·*ha* ya·*vash*
slowly	*konuşur musunuz*	ko·noo·*shoor* moo·soo·*nooz*
write it down	*yazar mısınız*	ya·*zar* muh·suh·*nuhz*

essentials

Yes.	*Evet.*	e·*vet*
No.	*Hayır.*	*ha*·yuhr
Please.	*Lütfen.*	*lewt*·fen
Thank you	*(Çok) Teşekkür*	(chok) te·shek·*kewr*
(very much). pol	*ederim.*	e·*de*·reem
Thanks. inf	*Teşekkürler.*	te·shek·kewr·*ler*
You're welcome.	*Birşey değil.*	beer·*shay* de·*eel*
Excuse me.	*Bakar mısınız?*	ba·*kar* muh·suh·*nuhz*
Sorry.	*Özür dilerim.*	eu·*zewr* dee·*le*·reem

numbers

0	sıfır	suh-*fuhr*	16	onaltı	on-al-*tuh*
1	bir	beer	17	onyedi	on-ye-*dee*
2	iki	ee-*kee*	18	onsekiz	on-se-*keez*
3	üç	ewch	19	ondokuz	on-do-*kooz*
4	dört	deurt	20	yirmi	yeer-*mee*
5	beş	besh	21	yirmibir	yeer-mee-*beer*
6	altı	al-*tuh*	22	yirmiiki	yeer-mee-ee-*kee*
7	yedi	ye-*dee*	30	otuz	o-*tooz*
8	sekiz	se-*keez*	40	kırk	kuhrk
9	dokuz	do-*kooz*	50	elli	el-*lee*
10	on	on	60	altmış	alt-*muhsh*
11	onbir	on-*beer*	70	yetmiş	yet-*meesh*
12	oniki	on-ee-*kee*	80	seksen	sek-*sen*
13	onüç	on-*ewch*	90	doksan	dok-*san*
14	ondört	on-*deurt*	100	yüz	yewz
15	onbeş	on-*besh*	1000	bin	been

time & dates

What time is it?	Saat kaç?	sa-*at* kach
It's one o'clock.	Saat bir.	sa-*at* beer
It's (10) o'clock.	Saat (on).	sa-*at* (on)
Quarter past (10).	(Onu) çeyrek geçiyor.	(o-*noo*) chay-*rek* ge-*chee*-yor
Half past (10).	(On) buçuk.	(on) boo-*chook*
Quarter to (11).	(Onbire) çeyrek var.	(on-bee-*re*) chay-*rek* var
At what time ...?	Saat kaçta ...?	sa-*at* kach-*ta* ...
At ...	Saat ...	sa-*at* ...
am (morning)	sabah	sa-*bah*
pm (afternoon)	öğleden sonra	er-le-*den* son-ra
pm (evening)	gece	ge-*je*
Monday	Pazartesi	pa-*zar*-te-see
Tuesday	Salı	sa-*luh*
Wednesday	Çarşamba	char-sham-*ba*
Thursday	Perşembe	per-shem-*be*
Friday	Cuma	joo-*ma*
Saturday	Cumartesi	joo-*mar*-te-see
Sunday	Pazar	pa-*zar*

basics – TURKISH

415

January	*Ocak*	o·*jak*
February	*Şubat*	shoo·*bat*
March	*Mart*	mart
April	*Nisan*	nee·*san*
May	*Mayıs*	ma·*yuhs*
June	*Haziran*	ha·zee·*ran*
July	*Temmuz*	tem·*mooz*
August	*Ağustos*	a·oos·*tos*
September	*Eylül*	ay·*lewl*
October	*Ekim*	e·*keem*
November	*Kasım*	ka·*suhm*
December	*Aralık*	a·ra·*luhk*

What date is it today?
   Bugün ayın kaçı?   boo·*gewn* a·*yuhn* ka·chuh

It's (18 October).
   (Onsekiz Ekim).   (on·se·*keez* e·*keem*)

since (May)	*(Mayıs'tan) beri*	(ma·yuhs·*tan*) be·*ree*
until (June)	*(Haziran'a) kadar*	(ha·zee·ra·*na*) ka·*dar*
yesterday	*dün*	dewn
today	*bugün*	boo·*gewn*
tonight	*bu gece*	boo ge·*je*
tomorrow	*yarın*	ya·*ruhn*
last/next ...	*geçen/gelecek ...*	ge·*chen*/ge·le·*jek* ...
night	*gece*	ge·*je*
week	*hafta*	haf·*ta*
month	*ay*	ai
year	*yıl*	yuhl
yesterday/tomorrow ...	*dün/yarın ...*	dewn/ya·*ruhn* ...
morning	*sabah*	sa·*bah*
afternoon	*öğleden sonra*	eu·le·*den* son·ra
evening	*akşam*	ak·*sham*

weather

What's the weather like?	*Hava nasıl?*	ha·*va* na·suhl
It's ...	*Hava ...*	ha·*va* ...
cloudy	*bulutlu*	boo·loot·*loo*
cold	*soğuk*	so·*ook*
hot	*sıcak*	suh·*jak*
raining	*yağmurlu*	ya·moor·*loo*
snowing	*kar yağışlı*	kar ya·uhsh·*luh*
sunny	*güneşli*	gew·nesh·*lee*
warm	*ılık*	uh·*luhk*
windy	*rüzgarlı*	rewz·gar·*luh*
spring	*ilkbahar*	eelk·ba·har
summer	*yaz*	yaz
autumn	*sonbahar*	son·ba·har
winter	*kış*	kuhsh

border crossing

I'm here ...	*Ben ...*	ben ...
in transit	*transit yolcuyum*	tran·*seet* yol·*joo*·yoom
on business	*iş gezisindeyim*	eesh ge·zee·seen·*de*·yeem
on holiday	*tatildeyim*	ta·teel·*de*·yeem
I'm here for ...	*Ben ... buradayım.*	ben ... boo·ra·*da*·yuhm
(10) days	*(on) günlüğüne*	(on) gewn·lew·ew·*ne*
(three) weeks	*(üç) haftalığına*	(ewch) haf·ta·luh·uh·*na*
(two) months	*(iki) aylığına*	(ee·*kee*) ai·luh·uh·*na*

I'm going to (Sarıyer).
(Sarıyer'e) gidiyorum.   (sa·*ruh*·ye·re) gee·dee·*yo*·room

I'm staying at the (Divan).
(Divan'da) kalıyorum.   (*dee*·van·da) ka·luh·*yo*·room

I have nothing to declare.
Beyan edecek hiçbir şeyim yok.   be·*yan* e·de·*jek* heech·beer she·*yeem* yok

I have something to declare.
Beyan edecek bir şeyim var.   be·*yan* e·de·*jek* beer she·*yeem* var

That's (not) mine.
Bu benim (değil).   boo be·*neem* (de·*eel*)

transport

tickets & luggage

Where can I buy a ticket?
Nereden bilet alabilirim?   ne·re·den bee·*let* a·*la*·bee·lee·reem

Do I need to book a seat?
Yer ayırtmam gerekli mi?   yer a·yuhrt·mam ge·rek·*lee* mee

One ... ticket to (Bostancı), please.	*(Bostancı'ya) ... lütfen.*	*(bos·tan·juh·ya) ... lewt·fen*
one-way	*bir gidiş bileti*	beer gee·*deesh* bee·le·tee
return	*gidiş-dönüş bir bilet*	gee·deesh·deu·*newsh* beer bee·*let*

I'd like to ... my ticket, please.	*Biletimi ... istiyorum.*	bee·le·tee·*mee* ... ees·*tee*·yo·room
cancel	*iptal ettirmek*	eep·*tal* et·teer·*mek*
change	*değiştirmek*	de·eesh·teer·*mek*
collect	*almak*	al·*mak*
confirm	*onaylatmak*	o·nai·lat·*mak*

I'd like a ... seat, please.	*... bir yer istiyorum.*	... beer yer ees·*tee*·yo·room
nonsmoking	*Sigara içilmeyen kısımda*	see·*ga*·ra ee·*cheel*·me·yen kuh·suhm·*da*
smoking	*Sigara içilen kısımda*	see·*ga*·ra ee·*chee*·len kuh·suhm·*da*

How much is it?
Şu ne kadar?   shoo ne ka·*dar*

Is there air conditioning?
Klima var mı?   *klee*·ma var muh

Is there a toilet?
Tuvalet var mı?   too·va·*let* var muh

How long does the trip take?
Yolculuk ne kadar sürer?   yol·joo·*look* ne ka·*dar* sew·rer

Is it a direct route?
Direk güzergah mı?   dee·*rek* gew·zer·*gah* muh

Where's the luggage locker?
Emanet dolabı nerede?   e·ma·*net* do·la·buh ne·re·de

My luggage has been ...	Bagajım ...	ba·ga·zhuhm ...
damaged	zarar gördü	za·rar geu·dew
lost	kayboldu	kai·bol·doo
stolen	çalındı	cha·luhn·duh

getting around

Where does flight (TK0060) arrive?
(TK0060) sefer (te·ka suh·fuhr suh·fuhr alt·muhsh)
sayılı uçak nereye iniyor? se·fer sa·yuh·luh oo·chak ne·re·ye ee·nee·yor

Where does flight (TK0060) depart?
(TK0060) sefer (te·ka suh·fuhr suh·fuhr alt·muhsh)
sayılı uçak nereden kalkıyor? se·fer sa·yuh·luh oo·chak ne·re·den kal·kuh·yor

Where's (the) ...?	... nerede?	... ne·re·de
arrivals hall	Gelen yolcu bölümü	ge·len yol·joo beu·lew·mew
departures hall	Giden yolcu bölümü	gee·den yol·joo beu·lew·mew
duty-free shop	Gümrüksüz	gewm·rewk·sewz
	satış mağazası	sa·tuhsh ma·a·za·suh
gate (12)	(Oniki) numaralı	(on·ee·kee) noo·ma·ra·luh
	kapı	ka·puh

Is this the ... to (Sirkeci)?	(Sirkeci'ye) giden ... bu mu?	(seer·ke·jee·ye) gee·den ... boo moo
boat	vapur	va·poor
bus	otobüs	o·to·bews
plane	uçak	oo·chak
train	tren	tren

What time's the ... bus?	... otobüs ne zaman?	... o·to·bews ne za·man
first	İlk	eelk
last	Son	son
next	Sonraki	son·ra·kee

At what time does it arrive/leave?
Ne zaman varır/kalkacak? ne za·man va·ruhr/kal·ka·jak

How long will it be delayed?
Ne kadar gecikecek? ne ka·dar ge·jee·ke·jek

What station/stop is this?
Bu hangi istasyon/durak?
boo *han*-gee ees-tas-*yon*/doo-*rak*

What's the next station/stop?
Sonraki istasyon/durak hangisi?
son-ra-*kee* ees-tas-*yon*/doo-*rak* han-gee-see

Does it stop at (Kadıköy)?
(Kadıköy'de) durur mu?
(ka-*duh*-kay-de) doo-*roor* moo

Please tell me when we get to (Beşiktaş).
(Beşiktaş'a) vardığımızda
lütfen bana söyleyin.
(be-*sheek*-ta-sha) var-duh-uh-muhz-*da*
lewt-fen ba-*na* say-*le*-yeen

How long do we stop here?
Burada ne kadar duracağız?
boo-ra-*da* ne ka-*dar* doo-ra-ja-uhz

Is this seat available?
Bu koltuk boş mu?
boo kol-*took* bosh moo

That's my seat.
Burası benim yerim.
boo-ra-*suh* be-*neem* ye-*reem*

I'd like a taxi ...
... bir taksi istiyorum.
... beer tak-see ees-tee-yo-room

  at (9am)
  (Sabah dokuzda)
  (sa-*bah* do-kooz-*da*)

  now
  Hemen
  he-men

  tomorrow
  Yarın
  ya-ruhn

Is this taxi available?
Bu taksi boş mu?
boo tak-*see* bosh moo

How much is it to ...?
... ne kadar?
... ne ka-*dar*

Please put the meter on.
Lütfen taksimetreyi
çalıştırın.
lewt-fen tak-*see*-met-re-yee
cha-luhsh-*tuh*-ruhn

Please take me to (this address).
Lütfen beni (bu adrese) götürün.
lewt-fen be-*nee* (boo ad-re-se) geu-*tew*-rewn

Please ...
Lütfen ...
lewt-fen ...

  slow down
  yavaşlayın
  ya-vash-*la*-yuhn

  stop here
  burada durun
  boo-ra-*da* doo-roon

  wait here
  burada bekleyin
  boo-ra-*da* bek-*le*-yeen

car, motorbike & bicycle hire

I'd like to hire a ...	Bir ... kiralamak istiyorum.	beer ... kee·ra·la·mak ees·tee·yo·room
bicycle	bisiklet	bee·seek·let
car	araba	a·ra·ba
motorbike	motosiklet	mo·to·seek·let

with ...		
a driver	şoförlü	sho·feur·lew
air conditioning	klimalı	klee·ma·luh

How much for ... hire?	... kirası ne kadar?	... kee·ra·suh ne ka·dar
hourly	Saatlık	sa·at·luhk
daily	Günlük	gewn·lewk
weekly	Haftalık	haf·ta·luhk

air	hava	ha·va
oil	yağ	ya
petrol	benzin	ben·zeen
tyres	lastikler	las·teek·ler

I need a mechanic.
Tamirciye ihtiyacım var.   ta·meer·jee·ye eeh·tee·ya·juhm var

I've run out of petrol.
Benzinim bitti.   ben·zee·neem beet·tee

I have a flat tyre.
Lastiğim patladı.   las·tee·eem pat·la·duh

directions

Where's the ...?	... nerede?	... ne·re·de
bank	Banka	ban·ka
city centre	Şehir merkezi	she·heer mer·ke·zee
hotel	Otel	o·tel
market	Pazar yeri	pa·zar ye·ree
police station	Polis karakolu	po·lees ka·ra·ko·loo
post office	Postane	pos·ta·ne
public toilet	Umumi tuvalet	oo·moo·mee too·va·let
tourist office	Turizm bürosu	too·reezm bew·ro·soo

Is this the road to (Taksim)?
(Taksim'e) giden yol bu mu? — (tak·see·me) gee·den yol boo moo

Can you show me (on the map)?
Bana (haritada) — ba·na (ha·ree·ta·da)
gösterebilir misiniz? — geus·te·re·bee·leer mee·seen·neez

What's the address?
Adresi nedir? — ad·re·see ne·deer

How far is it?
Ne kadar uzakta? — ne ka·dar oo·zak·ta

How do I get there?
Oraya nasıl gidebilirim? — o·ra·ya na·suhl gee·de·bee·lee·reem

Turn ...	... dön.	... deun
at the corner	Köşeden	keu·she·den
at the traffic lights	Trafik	tra·feek
	ışıklarından	uh·shuhk·la·ruhn·dan
left/right	Sola/Sağa	so·la/sa·a

It's ...		
behind ...	... arkasında.	... ar·ka·suhn·da
far away	Uzak.	oo·zak
here	Burada.	boo·ra·da
in front of ...	... önünde.	... eu·newn·de
left	Solda.	sol·da
near ...	... yakınında.	... ya·kuh·nuhn·da
next to ...	... yanında.	... ya·nuhn·da
on the corner	Köşede.	keu·she·de
opposite ...	... karşısında.	... kar·shuh·suhn·da
right	Sağda.	sa·da
straight ahead	Tam karşıda.	tam kar·shuh·da
there	Şurada.	shoo·ra·da

by bus	otobüslü	o·to·bews·lew
by taxi	taksili	tak·see·lee
by train	trenli	tren·lee
on foot	yürüyerek	yew·rew·ye·rek

north	kuzey	koo·zay
south	güney	gew·nay
east	doğu	do·oo
west	batı	ba·tuh

signs

Giriş/Çıkış	gee-reesh/chuh-kuhsh	Entrance/Exit
Açık/Kapalı	a-chuhk/ka-pa-luh	Open/Closed
Boş Oda	bosh o-da	Rooms Available
Boş Yer Yok	bosh yer yok	No Vacancies
Danışma	da-nuhsh-ma	Information
Polis Karakolu	po-lees ka-ra-ko-loo	Police Station
Yasak	ya-sak	Prohibited
Tuvaletler	too-va-let-ler	Toilets
Erkek	er-kek	Men
Kadın	ka-duhn	Women
Sıcak/Soğuk	suh-jak/so-ook	Hot/Cold

accommodation

finding accommodation

Where's a ...?	Buralarda nerede ... var?	boo-ra-lar-da ne-re-de ... var
camping ground	kamp yeri	kamp ye-ree
guesthouse	misafirhane	mee-sa-feer-ha-ne
hotel	otel	o-tel
youth hostel	gençlik hosteli	gench-leek hos-te-lee

Can you recommend somewhere ...?	... bir yer tavsiye edebilir misiniz?	... beer yer tav-see-ye e-de-bee-leer mee-see-neez
cheap	Ucuz	oo-jooz
good	İyi	ee-yee
nearby	Yakın	ya-kuhn

I'd like to book a room, please.
Bir oda ayırtmak   beer o-da a-yuhrt-mak
istiyorum lütfen.   ees-tee-yo-room lewt-fen

I have a reservation.
Rezervasyonum var.   re-zer-vas-yo-noom var

My name's ...
Benim ismim ...   be-neem ees-meem ...

Do you have a ... room?	... odanız var mı?	... o·da·nuhz var muh
single	Tek kişilik	tek kee·shee·leek
double	İki kişilik	ee·kee kee·shee·leek
twin	Çift yataklı	cheeft ya·tak·luh

How much is it per ...?	... ne kadar?	... ne ka·dar
night	Geceliği	ge·je·lee·ee
person	Kişi başına	kee·shee ba·shuh·na

Can I pay by ...?	... ile ödeyebilir miyim?	... ee·le eu·de·ye·bee·leer mee·yeem
credit card	Kredi kartı	kre·dee kar·tuh
travellers cheque	Seyahat çeki	se·ya·hat che·kee

I'd like to stay for (three) nights.
Kalmak istiyorum (üç) geceliğine.　　kal·mak ees·tee·yo·room (ewch) ge·je·lee·ee·ne

From (2 July) to (6 July).
(İki Temmuz'dan)　　(ee·kee tem·mooz·dan)
(altı Temmuz'a) kadar.　　(al·tuh tem·moo·za) ka·dar

Can I see it?
Görebilir miyim.　　geu·re·bee·leer mee·yeem

Am I allowed to camp here?
Burada kamp yapabilir miyim?　　boo·ra·da kamp ya·pa·bee·leer mee·yeem

Where can I find a camping ground?
Kamp alanı nerede?　　kamp a·la·nuh ne·re·de

requests & queries

When/Where is breakfast served?
Kahvaltı ne zaman/　　kah·val·tuh ne za·man/
nerede veriliyor?　　ne·re·de ve·ree·lee·yor

Please wake me at (seven).
Lütfen beni (yedide) kaldırın.　　lewt·fen be·nee (ye·dee·de) kal·duh·ruhn

Could I have my key, please?
Anahtarımı alabilir miyim?　　a·nah·ta·ruh·muh a·la·bee·leer mee·yeem

Can I get another (blanket)?
Başka bir (battaniye)　　bash·ka beer (bat·ta·nee·ye)
alabilir miyim?　　a·la·bee·leer mee·yeem

Is there an elevator/a safe?
Asansör/Kasanız var mı?　　a·san·seur/ka·sa·nuhz var muh

The room is too ...	Çok ...	chok ...
expensive	pahalı	pa·ha·luh
noisy	gürültülü	gew·rewl·tew·lew
small	küçük	kew·chewk

The ... doesn't work.	... çalışmıyor.	... cha·luhsh·muh·yor
air conditioning	Klima	klee·ma
fan	Fan	fan
toilet	Tuvalet	too·va·let

This ... isn't clean.	Bu ... temiz değil.	boo ... te·meez de·eel
pillow	yastık	yas·tuhk
sheet	çarşaf	char·shaf
towel	havlu	hav·loo

checking out

What time is checkout?
Çıkış ne zaman?   chuh·kuhsh ne za·man

Can I leave my luggage here?
Eşyalarımı burada   esh·ya·la·ruh·muh boo·ra·da
bırakabilir miyim?   buh·ra·ka·bee·leer mee·yeem

Could I have	... alabilir	... a·la·bee·leer
my ..., please?	miyim lütfen?	mee·yeem lewt·fen
deposit	Depozitomu	de·po·zee·to·moo
passport	Pasaportumu	pa·sa·por·too·moo
valuables	Değerli eşyalarımı	de·er·lee esh·ya·la·ruh·muh

communications & banking

the internet

Where's the local Internet café?
En yakın internet kafe nerede?   en ya·kuhn een·ter·net ka·fe ne·re·de

How much is it per hour?
Saati ne kadar?   sa·a·tee ne ka·dar

I'd like to ...	... istiyorum.	... ees·tee·yo·room
check my email	E-postama bakmak	e·pos·ta·ma bak·mak
get Internet access	İnternete girmek	een·ter·ne·te geer·mek
use a printer	Printeri kullanmak	preen·te·ree kool·lan·mak
use a scanner	Tarayıcıyı	ta·ra·yuh·juh·yuh

mobile/cell phone

I'd like a ...	... istiyorum.	... ees·tee·yo·room
mobile/cell phone for hire	Cep telefonu kiralamak	jep te·le·fo·noo kee·ra·la·mak
SIM card for your network	Buradaki şebeke için SİM kart	boo·ra·da·kee she·be·ke ee·cheen seem kart

What are the rates? *Ücret tarifesi nedir?* ewj·ret ta·ree·fe·see ne·deer

telephone

What's your phone number?
Telefon numaranız nedir?   te·le·fon noo·ma·ra·nuhz ne·deer

The number is ...
Telefon numarası ...   te·le·fon noo·ma·ra·suh ...

Where's the nearest public phone?
En yakın telefon   en ya·kuhn te·le·fon
kulübesi nerede?   koo·lew·be·see ne·re·de

I'd like to buy a phonecard.
Telefon kartı almak istiyorum.   te·le·fon kar·tuh al·mak ees·tee·yo·room

I want to ...	... istiyorum.	... ees·tee·yo·room
call (Singapore)	(Singapur'u) aramak	(seen·ga·poo·roo) a·ra·mak
make a local call	Yerel bir görüşme yapmak	ye·rel beer geu·rewsh·me yap·mak
reverse the charges	Ödemeli görüşme yapmak	eu·de·me·lee ger·rewsh·me yap·mak

How much does ... cost?	... ne kadar eder?	... ne ka·dar e·der
a (three)-minute call	(Üç) dakikalık konuşma	(ewch) da·kee·ka·luhk ko·noosh·ma
each extra minute	Her ekstra dakika	her eks·tra da·kee·ka

It's (10) *yeni kuruş* per minute.
Bir dakikası (on) yeni kuruş.   beer da·kee·ka·suh (on) ye·nee koo·roosh

post office

I want to send a ...	Bir ... göndermek istiyorum.	beer ... geun·der·mek ees·tee·yo·room
fax	faks	faks
letter	mektup	mek·toop
parcel	paket	pa·ket
postcard	kartpostal	kart·pos·tal

I want to buy a/an ...	... satın almak istiyorum.	... sa·tuhn al·mak ees·tee·yo·room
envelope	Zarf	zarf
stamp	Pul	pool

Please send it (to Australia) by ...	Lütfen ... (Avustralya'ya) gönderin.	lewt·fen ... (a·voos·tral·ya·ya) geun·de·reen
airmail	hava yoluyla	ha·va yo·looy·la
express mail	ekspres posta	eks·pres pos·ta
registered mail	taahhütlü posta	ta·ah·hewt·lew pos·ta
surface mail	deniz yoluyla	de·neez yo·looy·la

| Is there any mail for me? | Bana posta var mı? | ba·na pos·ta var muh |

bank

Where's a/an ...?	... nerede var?	... ne·re·de var
ATM	Bankamatik	ban·ka·ma·teek
foreign exchange office	Döviz bürosu	deu·veez bew·ro·soo

I'd like to …	… istiyorum.	… ees-tee-yo-room
cash a cheque	Çek bozdurmak	chek boz-door-mak
change a travellers cheque	Seyahat çeki bozdurmak	se-ya-hat che-kee boz-door-mak
change money	Para bozdurmak	pa-ra boz-door-mak
get a cash advance	Avans çekmek	a-vans chek-mek
withdraw money	Para çekmek	pa-ra chek-mek

What's the …?	… nedir?	… ne-deer
charge for that	Ücreti	ewj-re-tee
commission	Komisyon	ko-mees-yon
exchange rate	Döviz kuru	deu-veez koo-roo

It's …		
(12) euros	(Oniki) euro.	(on-ee-kee) yoo-ro
(25) lira	(Yirmibeş) lira.	(yeer-mee-besh) lee-ra
free	Ücretsiz.	ewj-ret-seez

What time does the bank open?
Banka ne zaman açılıyor? — ban-ka ne za-man a-chuh-luh-yor

Has my money arrived yet?
Param geldi mi? — pa-ram gel-dee mee

sightseeing

getting in

What time does it open/close?
Saat kaçta açılır/kapanır? — sa-at kach-ta a-chuh-luhr/ka-pa-nuhr

What's the admission charge?
Giriş ücreti nedir? — gee-reesh ewj-re-tee ne-deer

Is there a discount for children/students?
Çocuk/Öğrenci indirimi var mı? — cho-jook/eu-ren-jee een-dee-ree-mee var muh

I'd like a …	… istiyorum.	… ees-tee-yo-room
catalogue	Katalog	ka-ta-log
guide	Rehber	reh-ber
local map	Yerel Harita	ye-rel ha-ree-ta

I'd like to see ...	... görmek istiyorum.	... geur·mek ees·tee·yo·room
What's that?	Bu nedir?	boo ne·deer
Can I take a photo?	Bir fotoğrafınızı	beer fo·to·ra·fuh·nuh·zuh
	çekebilir miyim?	che·ke·bee·leer mee·yeem

tours

When's the next ...?	Sonraki ... ne zaman?	son·ra·kee ... ne za·man
day trip	gündüz turu	gewn·dewz too·roo
tour	tur	toor
Is ... included?	... dahil mi?	... da·heel mee
accommodation	Kalacak yer	ka·la·jak yer
the admission charge	Giriş	gee·reesh
food	Yemek	ye·mek
transport	Ulaşım	oo·la·shuhm

How long is the tour?
Tur ne kadar sürer? toor ne ka·dar sew·rer

What time should we be back?
Saat kaçta dönmeliyiz? sa·at kach·ta deun·me·lee·yeez

sightseeing

castle	kale	ka·le
church	kilise	kee·lee·se
main square	meydan	may·dan
monument	anıt	a·nuht
mosque	cami	ja·mee
museum	müze	mew·ze
old city	eski şehir	es·kee she·heer
palace	saray	sa·rai
ruins	harabeler	ha·ra·be·ler
stadium	stadyum	stad·yoom
statue	heykel	hay·kel
Turkish bath	hamam	ha·mam

shopping

enquiries

Where's a ...?	... nerede?	... ne·re·de
bank	Banka	ban·ka
bookshop	Kitapçı	kee·tap·chuh
camera shop	Fotoğrafçı	fo·to·raf·chuh
department store	Büyük mağaza	bew·yewk ma·a·za
grocery store	Bakkal	bak·kal
market	Pazar yeri	pa·zar ye·ree
newsagency	Gazete bayii	ga·ze·te ba·yee·ee
supermarket	Süpermarket	sew·per·mar·ket

Where can I buy (a padlock)?
Nereden (asma kilit)   ne·re·den (as·ma kee·leet)
alabilirim?   a·la·bee·lee·reem

I'm looking for ...
... istiyorum.   ... ees·tee·yo·room

Can I look at it?
Bakabilir miyim?   ba·ka·bee·leer mee·yeem

Do you have any others?
Başka var mı?   bash·ka var muh

Does it have a guarantee?
Garantisi var mı?   ga·ran·tee·see var muh

Can I have it sent overseas?
Yurt dışına gönderebilir   yoort duh·shuh·na geun·de·re·bee·leer
misiniz?   mee·see·neez

Can I have my ... repaired?
... burada tamir ettirebilir   ... boo·ra·da ta·meer et·tee·re·bee·leer
miyim?   mee·yeem

It's faulty.
Arızalı.   a·ruh·za·luh

I'd like ..., please.	... istiyorum lütfen.	... ees·tee·yo·room lewt·fen
a bag	Çanta	chan·ta
a refund	Para iadesi	pa·ra ee·a·de·see
to return this	Bunu iade etmek	boo·noo ee·a·de et·mek

paying

How much is it?
Ne kadar? nc ka-*dar*

Can you write down the price?
Fiyatı yazabilir misiniz? fee-ya-*tuh* ya-*za*-bee-leer mee-see-*neez*

That's too expensive.
Bu çok pahalı. boo chok pa-ha-*luh*

Is that your lowest price?
Son fiyatınız bu mu? son fee-ya-tuh-*nuhz* boo moo

I'll give you (30) lira.
(Otuz) lira veririm. (o-*tooz*) lee-*ra* ve-*ree*-reem

There's a mistake in the bill.
Hesapta bir yanlışlık var. he-sap-*ta* beer yan-luhsh-*luhk* var

Do you accept ...?	*... kabul ediyor musunuz?*	... ka-*bool* e-*dee*-yor moo-soo-*nooz*
credit cards	*Kredi kartı*	kre-dee kar-*tuh*
debit cards	*Banka kartı*	ban-ka kar-*tuh*
travellers cheques	*Seyahat çeki*	se-ya-*hat* che-kee
I'd like ..., please.	*... istiyorum lütfen.*	... ees-*tee*-yo-room *lewt*-fen
a receipt	*Makbuz*	mak-*booz*
my change	*Paramın üstünü*	pa-ra-*muhn* ews-tew-*new*

clothes & shoes

Can I try it on?	*Deneyebilir miyim?*	de-ne-*ye*-bee-leer mee-*yeem*
My size is (42).	*(Kırkiki) beden giyiyorum.*	(kuhrk-ee-*kee*) be-*den* gee-*yee*-yo-room
It doesn't fit.	*Olmuyor.*	ol-*moo*-yor
small	*küçük*	kew-*chewk*
medium	*orta*	or-ta
large	*büyük*	bew-*yewk*

books & music

I'd like a ...   ... istiyorum.   ... ees·*tee*·yo·room

newspaper	(İngilizce)	(een·gee·*leez*·je)
(in English)	bir gazete	beer ga·*ze*·te
pen	Tükenmez kalem	tew·ken·*mez* ka·*lem*

Is there an English-language bookshop?
İngilizce yayın satan   een·gee·*leez*·je ya·*yuhn* sa·*tan*
bir dükkan var mı?   beer dewk·*kan* var muh

I'm looking for something by (Yaşar Kemal).
(Yaşar Kemal'in) albümlerine   (ya·*shar* ke·mal·*een*) al·bewm·le·ree·*ne*
bakmak istiyorum.   bak·*mak* ees·*tee*·yo·room

Can I listen to this?
Bunu dinleyebilir miyim?   boo·*noo* deen·le·*ye*·bee·leer mee·*yeem*

photography

Can you ...?   ... misiniz?   ... mee·see·*neez*

develop this film	Bu filmi basabilir	boo feel·*mee* ba·*sa*·bee·leer
load my film	Filmi makineye	feel·*mee* ma·kee·ne·*ye*
	takabilir	ta·*ka*·bee·leer
transfer photos	Kameramdaki	ka·me·ram·da·*kee*
from my	fotoğrafları	fo·to·raf·la·*ruh*
camera to CD	CD'ye aktarabilir	see·dee·ye ak·ta·*ra*·bee·leer

I need a/an ... film	Bu kamera için ...	boo ka·me·*ra* ee·*cheen* ...
for this camera.	film istiyorum.	feelm ees·*tee*·yo·room
APS	APS	a·pe·*se*
B&W	siyah-beyaz	see·*yah*·be·yaz
colour	renkli	renk·*lee*
slide	slayt	slayt
(200) speed	(ikiyüz) hızlı	(ee·*kee*·yewz) huhz·*luh*

When will it be ready?   Ne zaman hazır olur?   ne za·*man* ha·zuhr o·*loor*

meeting people

greetings, goodbyes & introductions

Hello.	*Merhaba.*	mer·ha·ba
Hi.	*Selam.*	se·*lam*
Good night.	*İyi geceler.*	ee·*yee* ge·je·*ler*
Goodbye.	*Hoşçakal.* inf	hosh·*cha*·kal
(by person leaving)	*Hoşçakalın.* pol	hosh·*cha*·ka·luhn
Goodbye.	*Güle güle.*	gew·*le* gew·*le*
(by person staying)		
See you later.	*Sonra görüşürüz.*	*son*·ra ger·rew·*shew*·rewz
Mr	*Bay*	bai
Mrs/Miss	*Bayan*	ba·*yan*
How are you?	*Nasılsın?* inf	*na*·suhl·suhn
	Nasılsınız? pol	*na*·suhl·suh·nuhz
Fine. And you?	*İyiyim. Ya sen/siz?* inf/pol	ee·*yee*·yeem ya sen/seez
What's your name?	*Adınız ne?* inf	a·duh·*nuhz* ne
	Adınız nedir? pol	a·duh·*nuhz* ne·deer
My name is ...	*Benim adım ...*	be·neem a·*duhm* ...
I'm pleased to	*Tanıştığımıza*	ta·nuhsh·tuh·uh·muh·*za*
meet you.	*sevindim.*	se·veen·*deem*
This is my ...	*Bu benim ...*	boo be·*neem* ...
brother	*kardeşim*	kar·de·*sheem*
daughter	*kızım*	kuh·*zuhm*
father	*babayım*	ba·ba·*yuhm*
friend	*arkadaşım*	ar·ka·da·*shuhm*
husband	*kocam*	ko·*jam*
mother	*anneyim*	an·ne·*yeem*
partner (intimate)	*partnerim*	part·ne·*reem*
sister	*kız kardeşim*	kuhz kar·de·*sheem*
son	*oğlum*	o·*loom*
wife	*karım*	ka·*ruhm*
Here's my ...	*İşte benim ...*	eesh·*te* be·*neem* ...
(email) address	*(e-posta) adresim*	(e·pos·ta) ad·re·*seem*
fax number	*faks numaram*	faks noo·ma·*ram*
phone number	*telefon numaram*	te·le·*fon* noo·ma·*ram*

meeting people – TURKISH

What's your ...?	Sizin ... nedir?	see·zeen ... ne·deer
(email) address	(e-posta) adresiniz	(e·pos·ta) ad·re·see·neez
fax number	faks numaranız	faks noo·ma·ra·nuhz
phone number	telefon numaranız	te·le·fon noo·ma·ra·nuhz

occupations

What's your occupation?	Mesleğiniz nedir? pol	mes·le·ee·neez ne·deer
	Mesleğin nedir? inf	mes·le·een ne·deer
I'm a/an ...	Ben ...	ben ...
artist	sanatçıyım m&f	sa·nat·chuh·yuhm
business person	iş adamıyım m	ish a·da·muh·yuhm
	kadınıyım f	ka·duh·nuh·yuhm
farmer	çiftçiyim m&f	cheeft·chee·yeem
manual worker	işçiyim m&f	eesh·chee·yeem
office worker	memurum m&f	me·moo·room
scientist	bilim adamıyım m&f	bee·leem a·da·muh·yuhm

background

Where are you from?	Nerelisiniz? pol	ne·re·le·see·neez
	Nerelisin? inf	ne·re·lee·seen
I'm from ...	Ben ...	ben ...
Australia	Avustralya'lıyım	a·voos·tral·ya·luh·yuhm
Canada	Kanada'lıyım	ka·na·da·luh·yuhm
England	İngiltere'liyim	een·geel·te·re·lee·yeem
the USA	Amerika'lıyım	a·me·ree·ka·luh·yuhm
Are you married?	Evli misiniz?	ev·lee mee·see·neez
I'm married/single.	Ben evliyim/bekarım.	ben ev·lee·yeem/be·ka·ruhm

age

How old ...?	Kaç ...?	kach ...
are you	yaşındasın inf	ya·shuhn·da·suhn
is your son	yaşında oğlunuz	ya·shuhn·da o·loo·nooz
is your daughter	yaşında kızınız	ya·shuhn·da kuh·zuh·nuhz
I'm ... years old.	Ben ... yaşındayım.	ben ... ya·shuhn·da·yuhm
He/She is ... years old.	O ... yaşında.	o ... ya·shuhn·da

feelings

I'm/I'm not ...

cold	Üşüdüm./	ew·shew·*dewm*/
	Üşümedim.	ew·*shew*·me·deem
happy	Mutluyum./	moot·*loo*·yoom/
	Mutlu değilim.	moot·*loo* de·*ee*·leem
hot	Sıcakladım./	suh·jak·la·*duhm*/
	Sıcaklamadım.	suh·jak·*la*·ma·duhm
hungry	Açım./Aç değilim.	*a*·chuhm/ach de·*ee*·leem
sad	Üzgünüm./	ewz·gew·*newm*/
	Üzgün değilim.	ewz·*gewn* de·*ee*·leem
thirsty	Susadım./Susamadım.	soo·sa·*duhm*/soo·*sa*·ma·duhm
tired	Yorgunum./	yor·goo·noom/
	Yorgun değilim.	yor·*goon* de·*ee*·leem

Are you ...?

cold	Üşüdün mü?	ew·shew·*dewn* mew
happy	Mutlu musun?	moot·*loo* moo·*soon*
hot	Sıcakladın mı?	suh·jak·la·*duhn* muh
hungry	Aç mısın?	ach muh·*suhn*
sad	Üzgün musun?	ewz·*gewn* moo·*soon*
thirsty	Susadın mı?	soo·sa·*duhn* muh
tired	Yorgun musun?	yor·*goon* moo·*soon*

entertainment

going out

Where can I find ...?	Buranın ... nerede?	boo·ra·*nuhn* ... *ne*·re·de
clubs	kulüpleri	koo·lewp·le·*ree*
gay venues	gey kulüpleri	gay koo·lewp·le·*ree*
pubs	birahaneleri	bee·ra·ha·ne·le·*ree*
I feel like going to a/the ...	... gitmek istiyor.	... geet·*mek* ees·*tee*·yor
concert	Konsere	kon·se·*re*
movies	Sinemaya	see·ne·ma·*ya*
party	Partiye	par·tee·*ye*
restaurant	Restorana	res·to·ra·*na*
theatre	Oyuna	o·yoo·*na*

interests

Do you like ...?	... sever misin?	... se·*ver* mee·*seen*
I like ...	... seviyorum.	... se·*vee*·yo·room
I don't like ...	... sevmiyorum.	... *sev*·mee·yo·room
art	Sanat	sa·*nat*
movies	Sinemaya gitmeyi	see·ne·ma·*ya* geet·me·*yee*
reading	Okumayı	o·koo·ma·*yuh*
sport	Sporu	spo·*roo*
travelling	Seyahat etmeyi	se·ya·*hat* et·me·*yee*
Do you ...?	... misin/misiniz? inf/pol	... mee·*seen*/mee·see·*neez*
dance	Dans eder	dans e·*der*
go to concerts	Konserlere gider	kon·ser·le·*re* gee·*der*
listen to music	Müzik dinler	mew·*zeek* deen·*ler*

food & drink

finding a place to eat

Can you recommend a ...?	İyi bir ... tavsiye edebilir misiniz?	ee·*yee* beer ... tav·see·*ye* e·*de*·bee·leer mee·see·*neez*
bar	bar	bar
café	kafe	ka·*fe*
restaurant	restoran	res·to·*ran*
I'd like ..., please.	... istiyorum.	... ees·*tee*·yo·room
a table for (five)	(Beş) kişilik bir masa	(besh) kee·shee·*leek* beer ma·*sa*
the nonsmoking section	Sigara içilmeyen bir yer	see·*ga*·ra ee·*cheel*·me·yen beer yer
the smoking section	Sigara içilen bir yer	see·*ga*·ra ee·chee·*len* beer yer

ordering food

breakfast	kahvaltı	kah·val·*tuh*
lunch	öğle yemeği	eu·*le* ye·me·ee
dinner	akşam yemeği	ak·*sham* ye·me·ee
snack	hafif yemek	ha·*feef* ye·mek

What would you recommend?
Ne tavsiye edersiniz?   ne tav·see·ye e·*der*·see·neez

I'd like (a/the)...	... istiyorum.	... ees·*tee*·yo·room
bill	*Hesabı*	he·sa·*buh*
drink list	*İçecek listesini*	ee·che·jek lees·te·see·*nee*
menu	*Menüyü*	me·new·*yew*
that dish	*Şu yemeği*	shoo ye·me·*ee*

drinks

(cup of) coffee ...	*(fincan) kahve ...*	(feen·*jan*) kah·*ve* ...
(cup of) tea ...	*(fincan) çay ...*	(feen·*jan*) chai ...
with milk	*sütlü*	sewt·*lew*
without sugar	*şekersiz*	she·ker·*seez*
(orange) juice	*(portakal) suyu*	(por·ta·*kal*) soo·*yoo*
soft drink	*alkolsüz içecek*	al·kol·*sewz* ee·che·*jek*
sparkling mineral water	*maden sodası*	ma·*den* so·da·*suh*
still mineral water	*maden suyu*	ma·*den* soo·*yoo*
(hot) water	*(sıcak) su*	(suh·*jak*) soo

in the bar

I'll have ...	... alayım.	... a·la·*yuhm*
I'll buy you a drink.	*Sana içecek alayım.*	sa·*na* ee·che·*jek* a·la·*yuhm*
What would you like?	*Ne alırsınız?*	ne a·*luhr*·suh·nuhz
Cheers!	*Şerefe!*	she·re·*fe*
brandy	*brendi*	*bren*·dee
cocktail	*kokteyl*	kok·*tayl*
cognac	*konyak*	kon·*yak*
a shot of (whisky)	*bir tek (viski)*	beer tek (*vees*·kee)
a bottle/glass of beer	*bir şişe/bardak bira*	beer shee·*she*/bar·*dak* bee·ra
a bottle/glass	*bir şişe/bardak*	beer shee·*she*/bar·*dak*
of ... wine	... şarap	... sha·*rap*
red	*kırmızı*	kuhr·muh·*zuh*
sparkling	*köpüklü*	keu·pewk·*lew*
white	*beyaz*	be·*yaz*

self-catering

What's the local speciality?
  Bu yöreye has yiyecekler neler?   boo yeu·re·*ye* has yee·ye·jek·*ler* ne·ler

What's that?
  Bu nedir?   boo ne·deer

How much (is a kilo of cheese)?
  (Bir kilo peynir) Ne kadar?   (beer kee·*lo* pay·*neer*) ne ka·*dar*

I'd like ...	... istiyorum.	... ees·tee·yo·room
(200) grams	(İkiyüz) gram	(ee·*kee*·yewz) gram
(two) kilos	(İki) kilo	(ee·*kee*) kee·*lo*
(three) pieces	(Üç) parça	(ewch) par·*cha*
(six) slices	(Altı) dilim	(al·*tuh*) dee·*leem*

Less.	Daha az.	da·*ha* az
Enough.	Yeterli.	ye·ter·*lee*
More.	Daha fazla.	da·*ha* faz·*la*

special diets & allergies

Where's a vegetarian restaurant?
  Buralarda vejeteryan restoran   boo·ra·lar·*da* ve·zhe·ter·*yan* res·to·*ran*
  var mı?   var muh

Do you have vegetarian food?
  Vejeteryan yiyecekleriniz   ve·zhe·ter·*yan* yee·ye·jek·le·ree·*neez*
  var mı?   var muh

Is it cooked with ...?	İçinde ... var mı?	ee·cheen·*de* ... var muh
butter	tereyağ	te·*re*·ya
eggs	yumurta	yoo·moor·*ta*
meat stock	et suyu	et soo·*yoo*

I'm allergic to ...	... alerjim var.	... a·ler·*zheem* var
dairy produce	Süt ürünlerine	sewt ew·rewn·le·ree·*ne*
gluten	Glutene	gloo·te·*ne*
MSG	Mono sodyum	mo·*no* sod·*yoom*
	glutamata	gloo·ta·ma·*ta*
nuts	Çerezlere	che·rez·le·*re*
seafood	Deniz ürünlerine	de·*neez* ew·rewn·le·ree·*ne*

menu decoder

asma yaprağında sardalya	as·*ma* yap·ra·uhn·*da* sar·*dal*·ya	*sardines in vine leaves*
baklava	bak·la·*va*	*pastry stuffed with pistachio & walnuts*
biber dolması	bee·*ber* dol·ma·*suh*	*stuffed capsicum*
börek	beu·*rek*	*sweet or savoury dishes with a thin crispy pastry*
bumbar	boom·*bar*	*sausage made of rice & meat stuffed in a large sheep or lamb gut*
cacık	ja·*juhk*	*yogurt, mint & cucumber mix*
cevizli bat	je·veez·*lee* bat	*salad of bulgur, lentils, tomato paste & walnuts*
çevirme	che·veer·*me*	*eggplant, chicken, rice & pistachio dish*
çoban salatası	cho·*ban* sa·la·ta·*suh*	*tomato, cucumber & capsicum salad*
çökertme	cheu·kert·*me*	*steak on potatoes with yogurt*
dolma	dol·*ma*	*vine or cabbage leaves stuffed with rice*
erik aşı	e·*reek* a·*shuh*	*plum dish with prunes, rice & sugar*
gökkuşağı salatası	*geuk*·koo·sha·uh sa·la·ta·*suh*	*salad of macaroni, capsicum, mushrooms, pickles & salami*
gül tatlısı	gewl tat·luh·*suh*	*fried pastry in lemon sherbet*
halim aşı	ha·*leem* a·*shuh*	*soup of chickpeas, meaty bones, wheat & tomato*
hamsi tava	ham·*see* ta·*va*	*fried, corn-breaded anchovies with onion & lemon*
höşmerim	heush·me·*reem*	*walnut & pistachio pudding*
humus	hoo·*moos*	*mashed chickpeas with sesame oil, lemon & spices*
imam bayıldı	ee·*mam* ba·yuhl·duh	*eggplant, tomato & onion dish*

menu decoder – TÜRKÇE

439

kadayıf	ka-da-*yuhf*	dessert of dough soaked in syrup with a layer of sour cream
kapuska	ka-poos-*ka*	cold dish of onion, tomato paste & cabbage
karaş	ka-*rash*	berry, grape & nut pudding
kebab/kebap	ke-*bab*/ke-*bap*	skewered meat & vegetables cooked on an open fire
keşkül	kesh-*kewl*	almond, coconut & milk pudding
köfte	keuf-*te*	mincemeat or bulgur balls
kulak çorbası	koo-*lak* chor-ba-*suh*	meat dumplings boiled in stock
lokum	lo-*koom*	Turkish delight
musakka	moo-sak-*ka*	vegetable & meat pie
pastırma	pas-tuhr-*ma*	pressed beef preserved in spices
paşa pilavı	pa-*sha* pee-la-*vuh*	potato, egg & capsicum salad
patlıcan karnıyarık	pat-luh-*jan* kar-*nuh*-ya-ruhk	eggplant stuffed with minced meat
pirpirim çorbası	peer-pee-reem chor-ba-*suh*	chickpea, bean & lentil soup
pişmaniye	peesh-*ma*-nee-ye	dessert of sugar, flour & soapwort
revani	re-*va*-nee	semolina, vanilla & cream cake
soğuk çorba	so-*ook* chor-ba	cold soup of yogurt, rice & capsicum
sucuk	soo-*jook*	spicy sausage
susamlı şeker	soo-sam-*luh* she-*ker*	sugar-coated peanuts & almonds
sütlaç	sewt-*lach*	rice pudding
şiş kebab	sheesh ke-*bab*	meat skewered on an open fire
tarhana	tar-ha-*na*	yogurt, onion, flour & chilli mix
topik	to-*peek*	chickpeas, pistachios, flour & currants topped with sesame sauce
tulumba tatlısı	too-*loom*-ba tat-luh-*suh*	fluted fritters served in sweet syrup
yuvarlama	yoo-var-la-*ma*	chickpea & mince dumpling soup

emergencies

basics

Help!	İmdat!	eem-dat
Stop!	Dur!	door
Go away!	Git burdan!	geet boor-dan
Thief!	Hırsız var!	huhr-suhz var
Fire!	Yangın var!	yan-guhn var
Watch out!	Dikkat et!	deek-kat et
Call ...!	... çağırın!	... cha-uh-ruhn
a doctor	Doktor	dok-tor
an ambulance	Ambulans	am-boo-lans
the police	Polis	po-lees

It's an emergency!
Bu acil bir durum.   boo a-jeel beer doo-room

Could you help me, please?
Yardım edebilir misiniz   yar-duhm e-de-bee-leer mee-see-neez
lütfen?   lewt-fen

Can I use your phone?
Telefonunuzu kullanabilir   te-le-fe-noo-noo-zoo kool-la-na-bee-leer
miyim?   mee-yeem

I'm lost.
Kayboldum.   kai-bol-doom

Where are the toilets?
Tuvaletler nerede?   too-va-let-ler ne-re-de

police

Where's the police station?
Polis karakolu nerede?   po-lees ka-ra-ko-loo ne-re-de

I want to report an offence.
Şikayette bulunmak   shee-ka-yet-te boo-loon-mak
istiyorum.   ees-tee-yo-room

I have insurance.
Sigortam var.   see-gor-tam var

I've been ...	Ben ...	ben ...
assaulted	saldırıya uğradım	sal·duh·ruh·ya oo·ra·duhm
raped	tecavüze uğradım	te·ja·vew·ze oo·ra·duhm
robbed	soyuldum	so·yool·doom

I've lost my ...	... kayıp.	... ka·yuhp
My ... was/were stolen.	... çalındı.	... cha·luhn·duh
backpack	Sırt çantası	suhrt chan·ta·suh
bags	Çantalar	chan·ta·lar
credit card	Kredi kartı	kre·dee kar·tuh
handbag	El çantası	el chan·ta·suh
jewellery	Mücevherler	mew·jev·her·ler
money	Para	pa·ra
passport	Pasaport	pa·sa·port
travellers cheques	Seyahat çekleri	se·ya·hat chek·le·ree
wallet	Cüzdan	jewz·dan

I want to contact	... görüşmek	... geu·rewsh·mek
my ...	istiyorum.	ees·tee·yo·room
consulate	Konsoloslukla	kon·so·los·look·la
embassy	Elçilikle	el·chee·leek·le

health

medical needs

Where's the nearest ...?	En yakın ... nerede?	en ya·kuhn ... ne·re·de
dentist	dişçi	deesh·chee
doctor	doktor	dok·tor
hospital	hastane	has·ta·ne
(night) pharmacist	(nöbetçi) eczane	(neu·bet·chee) ej·za·ne

I need a doctor (who speaks English).
(İngilizce konuşan) (een·gee·leez·je ko·noo·shan)
Bir doktora ihtiyacım var. beer dok·to·ra eeh·tee·ya·juhm var

Could I see a female doctor?
Bayan doktora ba·yan dok·to·ra
görünebilir miyim? geu·rew·ne·bee·leer mee·yeem

I've run out of my medication.
İlacım bitti. ee·la·juhm beet·tee

symptoms, conditions & allergies

I'm sick.	Hastayım.	has·ta·yuhm
It hurts here.	Burası ağrıyor.	boo·ra·suh a·ruh·yor
I have a toothache.	Dişim ağrıyor.	dee·sheem a·ruh·yor
I have (a) ...	Bende ... var.	ben·de ... var

asthma	astım	as·tuhm
bronchitis	bronşit	bron·sheet
constipation	kabızlık	ka·buhz·luhk
cough	öksürük	euk·sew·rewk
diarrhoea	ishal	ees·hal
fever	ateş	a·tesh
headache	baş ağrısı	bash a·ruh·suh
heart condition	kalp rahatsızlığı	kalp ra·hat·suhz·luh·uh
nausea	bulantı	boo·lan·tuh
pain	ağrı	a·ruh
sore throat	boğaz ağrısı	bo·az a·ruh·suh

I'm allergic to ...	... alerjim var.	... a·ler·zheem var
antibiotics	Antibiyotiklere	an·tee·bee·yo·teek·le·re
anti-inflammatories	Anti-emflamatuarlara	an·tee·em·fla·ma·too·ar·la·ra
aspirin	Aspirine	as·pee·ree·ne
bees	Arılara	a·ruh·la·ra
codeine	Kodeine	ko·de·ee·ne
penicillin	Penisiline	pe·nee·see·lee·ne

antiseptic	antiseptik	an·tee·sep·teek
bandage	bandaj	ban·dazh
condoms	prezervatifler	pre·zer·va·teef·ler
contraceptives	doğum kontrol hapı	do·oom kon·trol ha·puh
diarrhoea medicine	ishal ilacı	ees·hal ee·la·juh
insect repellent	sinek kovucu	see·nek ko·voo·joo
laxatives	müsil ilacı	mew·seel ee·la·juh
painkillers	ağrı kesici	a·ruh ke·see·jee
rehydration salts	rehidrasyon tuzları	re·heed·ras·yon tooz·la·ruh
sleeping tablets	uyku hapı	ooy·koo ha·puh

english–turkish dictionary

Words in this dictionary are marked as a (adjective), n (noun), v (verb), sg (singular), pl (plural), inf (informal) and pol (polite) where necessary.

A

accident *kaza* ka-*za*
accommodation *kalacak yer* ka-la-*jak* yer
adaptor *adaptör* a-dap-*teur*
address n *adres* ad-*res*
after *sonra* son-*ra*
air conditioning *klima* klee-ma
airplane *uçak* oo-*chak*
airport *havaalanı* ha-*va*-a-la-nuh
alcohol *alkol* al-kol
all *hepsi* hep-see
allergy *alerji* a-ler-*zhee*
ambulance *ambulans* am-boo-*lans*
and *ve* ve
ankle *ayak bileği* a-yak bee-le-ee
arm *kol* kol
ashtray *kül tablası* kewl tab-la-*suh*
ATM *bankamatik* ban-ka-ma-*teek*

B

baby *bebek* be-*bek*
back (body) *sırt* suhrt
backpack *sırt çantası* suhrt chan-ta-*suh*
bad *kötü* keu-*tew*
bag *çanta* chan-ta
baggage claim *bagaj konveyörü* ba-*gazh* kon-ve-yeu-*rew*
bank *banka* ban-ka
bar *bar* bar
bathroom *banyo* ban-yo
battery *pil* peel
beautiful *güzel* gew-*zel*
bed *yatak* ya-tak
beer *bira* bee-ra
before *önce* eun-je
behind *arkasında* ar-ka-suhn-*da*
bicycle *bisiklet* bee-seek-*let*
big *büyük* bew-*yewk*
bill *hesap* he-*sap*
black *siyah* see-*yah*
blanket *battaniye* bat-*ta*-nee-ye

blood group *kan gurubu* kan goo-roo-*boo*
blue *mavi* ma-vee
boat *vapur* va-*poor*
book (make a reservation) v *yer ayırtmak* yer a-yuhrt-*mak*
bottle *şişe* shee-*she*
bottle opener *şişe açacağı* shee-she a-cha-ja-*uh*
boy *oğlan* o-*lan*
brakes (car) *fren* fren
breakfast *kahvaltı* kah-val-*tuh*
broken (faulty) *bozuk* bo-*zook*
bus *otobüs* o-to-*bews*
business *iş* eesh
buy *satın almak* sa-*tuhn* al-mak

C

café *kafe* ka-fe
camera *kamera* ka-me-ra
camp site *kamp yeri* kamp ye-*ree*
cancel *iptal etmek* eep-*tal* et-mek
can opener *konserve açacağı* kon-ser-ve a-cha-ja-*uh*
car *araba* a-ra-ba
cash n *nakit* na-*keet*
cash (a cheque) v *(çek) bozdurmak* (chek) boz-door-*mak*
cell phone *cep telefonu* jep te-le-fo-*noo*
centre n *merkez* mer-*kez*
change (money) v *bozdurmak* boz-door-*mak*
cheap *ucuz* oo-*jooz*
check (bill) *fatura* fa-too-*ra*
check-in n *giriş* gee-*reesh*
chest *göğüs* geu-*ews*
child *çocuk* cho-*jook*
cigarette *sigara* see-*ga*-ra
city *şehir* she-heer
clean a *temiz* te-*meez*
closed *kapalı* ka-pa-*luh*
coffee *kahve* kah-ve
coins *madeni para* ma-de-nee pa-ra
cold a *soğuk* so-*ook*
collect call *ödemeli telefon* eu-de-me-*lee* te-le-fon
come *gelmek* gel-mek

computer *bilgisayar* beel-gee-sa-*yar*
condom *prezervatif* pre-zer-va-*teef*
contact lenses *kontak lens* kon-*tak* lens
cook v *pişirmek* pee-sheer-*mck*
cost n *fiyat* fee-*yat*
credit card *kredi kartı* kre-dee kar-*tuh*
cup *fincan* feen-*jan*
currency exchange *döviz kuru* deu-*veez* koo-*roo*
customs (immigration) *gümrük* gewm-*rewk*

D

dangerous *tehlikeli* teh-lee-ke-*lee*
date (time) *tarih* ta-*reeh*
day *gün* gewn
delay n *gecikme* ge-jeek-*me*
dentist *dişçi* deesh-*chee*
depart *ayrılmak* ai-ruhl-*mak*
diaper *bebek bezi* be-bek be-*zee*
dictionary *sözlük* seuz-*lewk*
dinner *akşam yemeği* ak-sham ye-me-*ee*
direct *direk* dee-*rek*
dirty *kirli* keer-*lee*
disabled *özürlü* eu-zewr-*lew*
discount n *indirim* een-dee-*reem*
doctor *doktor* dok-*tor*
double bed *iki kişilik yatak* ee-*kee* kee-shee-*leek* ya-*tak*
double room *iki kişilik oda* ee-*kee* kee-shee-*leek* o-*da*
drink n *içecek* ee-che-*jek*
drive v *sürmek* sewr-*mek*
drivers licence *ehliyet* eh-lee-*yet*
drugs (illicit) *uyuşturucu* oo-yoosh-too-roo-*joo*
dummy (pacifier) *emzik* em-*zeek*

E

ear *kulak* koo-*lak*
east *doğu* do-*oo*
eat *yemek* ye-*mek*
economy class *ekonomi sınıfı* e-ko-no-*mee* suh-nuh-*fuh*
electricity *elektrik* e-lek-*treek*
elevator *asansör* a-san-*seur*
email *e-posta* e-pos-ta
embassy *elçilik* el-chee-*leek*
emergency *acil durum* a-jeel doo-*room*
English (language) *İngilizce* een-gee-*leez*-je
entrance *giriş* gee-*reesh*
evening *akşam* ak-*sham*
exchange rate *döviz kuru* deu-*veez* koo-*roo*
exit n *çıkış* chuh-*kuhsh*

expensive *pahalı* pa-ha-*luh*
express mail *ekspres posta* eks-*pres* pos-*ta*
eye *göz* geuz

F

far *uzak* oo-*zak*
fast *hızlı* huhz-*luh*
father *baba* ba-*ba*
film (camera) *film* feelm
finger *parmak* par-*mak*
first-aid kit *ilk yardım çantası* eelk yar-*duhm* chan-ta-*suh*
first class *birinci sınıf* bee-reen-*jee* suh-*nuhf*
fish n *balık* ba-*luhk*
food *yiyecek* yee-ye-*jek*
foot *ayak* a-*yuk*
fork *çatal* cha-*tal*
free (of charge) *ücretsiz* ewj-ret-*seez*
friend *arkadaş* ar-ka-*dash*
fruit *meyve* may-*ve*
full *dolu* do-*loo*
funny *komik* ko-*meek*

G

gift *hediye* he-dee-*ye*
girl *kız* kuhz
glass (drinking) *bardak* bar-*dak*
glasses *gözlük* geuz-*lewk*
go *gitmek* geet-*mek*
good *iyi* ee-*yee*
green *yeşil* ye-*sheel*
guide n *rehber* reh-*ber*

H

half n *yarım* ya-*ruhm*
hand *el* el
handbag *el çantası* el chan-ta-*suh*
happy *mutlu* moot-*loo*
have *sahip olmak* sa-*heep* ol-*mak*
he *o* o
head *baş* bash
heart *kalp* kalp
heat n *ısı* uh-*suh*
heavy *ağır* a-*uhr*
help v *yardım etmek* yar-*duhm* et-*mek*
here *burada* boo-ra-*da*
high *yüksek* yewk-*sek*

highway *otoyol* o-to-yol
hike v *uzun yürüyüşe çıkmak*
  oo-zoon yew-rew-yew-she chuhk-mak
holiday *tatil* ta-teel
homosexual *homoseksüel* ho-mo-sek-sew-el
hospital *hastane* has-ta-ne
hot *sıcak* suh-jak
hotel *otel* o-tel
hungry *aç* ach
husband *koca* ko-ja

I

I *ben* ben
identification (card) *kimlik kartı* keem-leek kar-tuh
ill *hasta* has-ta
important *önemli* eu-nem-lee
included *dahil* da-heel
injury *yara* ya-ra
insurance *sigorta* see-gor-ta
Internet *internet* een-ter-net
interpreter *tercüman* ter-jew-man

J

jewellery *mücevherler* mew-jev-her-ler
job *meslek* mes-lek

K

key *anahtar* a-nah-tar
kilogram *kilogram* kee-log-ram
kitchen *mutfak* moot-fak
knife *bıçak* buh-chak

L

laundry (place) *çamaşırlık* cha-ma-shuhr-luhk
lawyer *avukat* a-voo-kat
left (direction) *sol* sol
left-luggage office *emanet bürosu* e-ma-net bew-ro-soo
leg *bacak* ba-jak
lesbian *lezbiyen* lez-bee-yen
less *daha az* da-ha az
letter (mail) *mektup* mek-toop
lift (elevator) *asansör* a-san-seur
light n *ışık* uh-shuhk
like v *sevmek* sev-mek
lock n *kilit* kee-leet
long *uzun* oo-zoon

lost *kayıp* ka-yuhp
lost-property office *kayıp eşya bürosu*
  ka-yuhp esh-ya bew-ro-soo
love v *aşık olmak* a-shuhk ol-mak
luggage *bagaj* ba-gazh
lunch *öğle yemeği* eu-le ye-me-ee

M

mail n *mektup* mek-toop
man *adam* a-dam
map *harita* ha-ree-ta
market *pazar* pa-zar
matches *kibrit* keeb-reet
meat *et* et
medicine *ilaç* ee-lach
menu *yemek listesi* ye-mek lees-te-see
message *mesaj* me-sazh
milk *süt* sewt
minute *dakika* da-kee-ka
mobile phone *cep telefonu* jep te-le-fo-noo
money *para* pa-ra
month *ay* ai
morning *sabah* sa-bah
mother *anne* an-ne
motorcycle *motosiklet* mo-to-seek-let
motorway *paralı yol* pa-ra-luh yol
mouth *ağız* a-uhz
music *müzik* mew-zeek

N

name *ad* ad
napkin *peçete* pe-che-te
nappy *bebek bezi* be-bek be-zee
near *yakında* ya-kuhn-da
neck *boyun* bo-yoon
new *yeni* ye-nee
news *haberler* ha-ber-ler
newspaper *gazete* ga-ze-te
night *gece* ge-je
no *hayır* ha-yuhr
noisy *gürültülü* gew-rewl-tew-lew
nonsmoking *sigara içilmeyen* see-ga-ra ee-cheel-me-yen
north *kuzey* koo-zay
nose *burun* boo-roon
now *şimdi* sheem-dee
number *sayı* sa-yuh

O

oil (engine) *jağ* ya
old (object/person) *eski/yaşlı* cs *kee/yash-lıh*
one-way ticket *gidiş bilet* gee-*deesh* bee-*let*
open a *açık* a-*chuhk*
outside *dışarıda* duh-sha-ruh-*da*

P

package *ambalaj* am-ba-*lazh*
paper *kağıt* ka-*uht*
park (car) v *park etmek* park et-*mek*
passport *pasaport* pa-sa-*port*
pay *ödemek* eu-*de*-mek
pen *tükenmez kalem* tew-ken-*mez* ka-*lem*
petrol *benzin* ben-*zeen*
pharmacy *eczane* ej-*za*-ne
phonecard *telefon kartı* te-le-*fon* kar-*tuh*
photo *fotoğraf* fo-to-*raf*
plate *tabak* ta-*bak*
police *polis* po-*lees*
postcard *kartpostal* kart-pos-*tal*
post office *postane* pos-*ta*-ne
pregnant *hamile* ha-*mee*-le
price *fiyat* fee-*yat*

Q

quiet *sakin* sa-*keen*

R

rain n *yağmur* ya-*moor*
razor *traş makinesi* trash ma-kee-ne-*see*
receipt n *makbuz* mak-*booz*
red *kırmızı* kuhr-muh-*zuh*
refund n *para iadesi* pa-*ra* ee-a-de-*see*
registered mail *taahhütlü posta* ta-ah-hewt-*lew* pos-*ta*
rent v *kiralamak* kee-ra-la-*mak*
repair v *tamir etmek* ta-*meer* et-*mek*
reservation *rezervasyon* re-zer-vas-*yon*
restaurant *restoran* res-to-*ran*
return v *geri dönmek* ge-*ree* deun-*mek*
return ticket *gidiş-dönüş bilet* gee-*deesh*-deu-*newsh* bee-*let*
right (direction) *doğru yön* do-*roo* yeun

road *yol* yol
room *oda* o-*da*

S

safe a *emniyetli* em-nee-*yet*-lee
sanitary napkin *hijyenik kadın bağı* heezh-ye-*neek* ka-*duhn* ba-*uh*
seat *yer* yer
send *göndermek* geun-der-*mek*
service station *benzin istasyonu* ben-*zeen* ees-tas-yo-*noo*
sex *seks* seks
shampoo *şampuan* sham-poo-*an*
share (a dorm) *paylaşmak* pai-lash-*mak*
shaving cream *traş kremi* tuh-*rash* kre-*mee*
she *o* o
sheet (bed) *çarşaf* char-*shaf*
shirt *gömlek* geum-*lek*
shoes *ayakkabılar* a-yak-ka-buh-*lar*
shop n *dükkan* dewk-*kan*
short *kısa* kuh-*sa*
shower n *duş* doosh
single room *tek kişilik oda* tek kee-shee-*leek* o-*da*
skin *cilt* jeelt
skirt *etek* e-*tek*
sleep v *uyumak* oo-yoo-*mak*
slowly *yavaşça* ya-vash-*cha*
small *küçük* kew-*chewk*
smoke (cigarettes) v *sigara içmek* see-*ga*-ra eech-*mek*
soap *sabun* sa-*boon*
some *biraz* bee-*raz*
soon *yakında* ya-kuhn-*da*
south *güney* gew-*nay*
souvenir shop *hediyelik eşya dükkanı* he-dee-ye-*leek* esh-*ya* dewk-ka-*nuh*
speak *konuşmak* ko-noosh-*mak*
spoon *kaşık* ka-*shuhk*
stamp *pul* pool
stand-by ticket *açık bilet* a-*chuhk* bee-*let*
station (train) *istasyon* ees-tas-*yon*
stomach *mide* mee-*de*
stop v *durmak* door-*mak*
stop (bus) n *durağı* doo-ra-*uh*
street *sokak* so-*kak*
student *öğrenci* eu-ren-*jee*
sun *güneş* gew-*nesh*

sunscreen *güneşten koruma kremi* gew-nesh-ten ko-roo-ma kre-mee

swim V *yüzmek* yewz-mek

T

tampons *tamponlar* tam-pon-lar

taxi *taksi* tak-see

teaspoon *çay kaşığı* chai ka-shuh-uh

teeth *dişler* deesh-ler

telephone n *telefon* te-le-fon

television *televizyon* te-le-veez-yon

temperature (weather) *derece* de-re-je

tent *çadır* cha-duhr

that (one) *şunu/onu* shoo-noo/o-noo

they *onlar* on-lar

thirsty *susamış* soo-sa-muhsh

this (one) *bunu* boo-noo

throat *boğaz* bo-az

ticket *bilet* bee-let

time *zaman* za-man

tired *yorgun* yor-goon

tissues *kağıt mendil* ka-uht men-deel

today *bugün* boo-gewn

toilet *tuvalet* too-va-let

tomorrow *yarın* ya-ruhn

tonight *bu gece* boo ge-je

toothbrush *diş fırçası* deesh fuhr-cha-suh

toothpaste *diş macunu* deesh ma-joo-noo

torch (flashlight) *el feneri* el fe-ne-ree

tour n *tur* toor

tourist office *turizm bürosu* too-reezm bew-ro-soo

towel *havlu* hav-loo

train *tren* tren

translate *çevirmek* che-veer-mek

travel agency *seyahat acentesi* seya-hat a-jen-te-see

travellers cheque *seyahat çeki* se-ya-hat che-kee

trousers *pantolon* pan-to-lon

Turkey *Türkiye* tewr-kee-ye

Turkish (language) *Türkçe* tewrk-che

Turkish Republic of Northern Cyprus (TRNC)

Kuzey Kıbrıs Türk Cumhuriyeti (KKTC) koo-zay kuhb-ruhs tewrk joom-hoo-ree-ye-tee *(ka-ka-te-je)*

twin beds *çift yatak* cheeft ya-tak

tyre *lastik* las-teek

U

underwear *iç çamaşırı* eech cha-ma-shuh-ruh

urgent *acil* a-jeel

V

vacant *boş* bosh

vacation *tatil* ta-teel

vegetable n *sebze* seb-ze

vegetarian a *vejeteryan* ve-zhe-ter-yan

visa *vize* vee-ze

W

waiter *garson* gar-son

walk V *yürümek* yew-rew-mek

wallet *cüzdan* jewz-dan

warm a *ılık* uh-luhk

wash (something) *yıkamak* yuh-ka-mak

watch n *saat* sa-at

water *su* soo

we *biz* beez

weekend *hafta sonu* haf-ta so-noo

west *batı* ba-tuh

wheelchair *tekerlekli sandalye* te-ker-lek-lee san-dal-ye

when *ne zaman* ne za-man

where *nerede* ne-re-de

white *beyaz* be-yaz

who *kim* keem

why *neden* ne-den

wife *karı* ka-ruh

window *pencere* pen-je-re

wine *şarap* sha-rap

with *ile* ee-le

without *-sız/-siz/-suz/-süz* -suhz/-seez/-sooz/-sewz

woman *kadın* ka-duhn

write *yazı yazmak* ya-zuh yaz-mak

Y

yellow *sarı* sa-ruh

yes *evet* e-vet

yesterday *dün* dewn

you sg inf *sen* sen

you sg pol & pl *siz* seez

C	Dan	Dut	Fre	Ger	Gre	Ital	Nor	Por	Spa	Swe	Tur
calendar	16	56	96	136	176	216	256	296	336	376	416
camera	32	72	112	152	192	232	272	312	352	392	432
camping	23, 24	64, 65	103, 104	143, 144	183, 184	223, 224	263, 264	303, 304	343, 344	383, 384	423, 424
car	20	61	100	141	180	220	260	301	340	380	421
cell phone	26	66	106	146	186	225	265	306	346	386	426
checking out	25	66	105	145	185	225	265	305	345	385	425
children (discounts)	28	69	108	148	188	228	268	309	348	388	428
clothes	31	72	111	151	191	231	271	312	351	391	431
communications	26	66	105	145	185	225	265	306	346	385	425
compass points	22	63	102	142	182	222	262	302	342	382	422
complaints	20, 25, 30, 31	65, 71	100, 104, 110	140, 145, 150, 151	180, 184, 190, 191	220, 224, 230	260, 264, 270	300, 305, 311	340, 345, 350, 351	380, 385, 390	420, 425, 430, 431
conditions (health)	43	83	123	163	203	243	283	323	363	403	443
consonant sounds	12	53	93	133	173	212	253	293	332	372	413
contact details	34	74	113	153	193	233	273	314	353	393	433
cost	28, 31	68, 71	107, 110	148, 151	188, 191	227, 230	267, 270	308, 311	348, 351	387, 390	428, 431
credit card	24, 31, 42	64, 71, 82	103, 111, 122	144, 151, 162	183, 191, 202	223, 230, 242	263, 270, 282	304, 311, 322	344, 351, 362	384, 391, 402	424, 431, 442
customs (immigration)	17	57	97	137	177	217	257	297	337	377	417

D	Dan	Dut	Fre	Ger	Gre	Ital	Nor	Por	Spa	Swe	Tur
dates (calendar)	16	56	96	136	176	216	256	296	336	376	416
days of the week	15	55	95	135	175	215	255	295	335	375	415
dentist	42	82	122	162	202	242	282	322	362	402	442
dialects	11	51	91		171	211	251	291	331	371	411
dictionary	44	84	124	164	204	244	284	324	364	404	444
directions	21	62	101	141	181	221	261	301	341	381	421
discounts	28	69	108	148	188	228	268	309	348	388	428
doctor	41, 42	81, 82	121, 122	161, 162	201, 202	241, 242	281, 282	321, 322	361, 362	401, 402	441, 442
duty-free	19	59	99	139	179	219	259	299	339	379	419

E	Dan	Dut	Fre	Ger	Gre	Ital	Nor	Por	Spa	Swe	Tur
eating out	36	76	116	156	196	236	276	316	356	396	436
email	26, 34	66, 74	105, 113	146, 153	185	225, 233	265, 273	306, 314	346, 353	386, 393	426, 433
embassy	42	82	122	162	202	242	282	322	362	402	442
emergencies	41	81	121	161	201	241	281	321	361	401	441

INDEX

451

	Dan	Dut	Fre	Ger	Gre	Ital	Nor	Por	Spa	Swe	Tur
post office	27	67	107	147	187	226	266	307	347	387	427
problems (car & motorbike)	21	62	101	141	181	221	261	301	341	381	421
pronunciation	12	52	92	132	172	212	252	292	332	372	412

Q

	Dan	Dut	Fre	Ger	Gre	Ital	Nor	Por	Spa	Swe	Tur
quantities	38	78	118	158	198	238	278	318	358	398	438
queries (hotel)	24	65	104	144	184	224	264	304	344	384	424
queries (shopping)	30	70	109	150	190	229	269	310	350	389	430
queries (transport)	18	58	98	138	178	218	258	298	338	378	418

R

	Dan	Dut	Fre	Ger	Gre	Ital	Nor	Por	Spa	Swe	Tur
reading	32, 36	72, 76	111, 115	152, 156	192, 195	231, 235	271, 275	312, 316	352, 356	391, 395	432, 436
receipts	31	71	111	151	191	231	271	311	351	391	431
refunds	30	71	110	151	190	230	270	311	351	390	430
repairs	30	71	110	150	190	230	270	311	350	390	430
requests (hotel)	24	65	104	144	184	224	264	304	344	384	424
requests (restaurant)	37	77	116	157		236	276	317	357	396	437
reservations	18, 23, 36	58, 60, 64, 76	98, 100, 103, 116	138, 140, 143, 156	178, 180, 183, 196	218, 220, 223, 236	258, 260, 263, 276	298, 300, 303, 316	338, 340, 343, 356	378, 380, 383, 396	418, 420, 423, 436
restaurant	35, 36	75, 76	115, 116	155, 156	195, 196	235, 236	275, 276	315, 316	355, 356	395, 396	435, 436
room (hotel)	24	64	103	143	183, 184	223, 224	263	303	343, 345	383, 385	423, 425

S

	Dan	Dut	Fre	Ger	Gre	Ital	Nor	Por	Spa	Swe	Tur
seasons	17	57	97	137	177	217	257	297	337	377	417
seating	18, 20	58, 60	98, 100	138, 140	178, 180	218, 220	258, 260	298, 300	338, 340	378, 380	418, 420
self-catering	38	78	118	158	198	238	278	318	358	398	438
shoes	31	72	111	151	191	231	271	312	351	391	431
shopping	30	70	109	150	190	229	269	310	350	389	430
sightseeing	28	69	108	148	188	228	268	309	348	388	428
signs	23	63	102	143	182	222	262	303	343	383	423
sizes (clothes & shoes)	31	72	111	151	191	231	271	312	351	391	431
smoking	18, 36	76	98, 116	138	178, 196	218, 236	258, 276	298, 316	—	378, 396	418, 436
speakers of the language	11	51	91	131	171	211	251	291	331	371	411
special diets	38	78	118	158	198	238	278	318	358	398	438
sport	36	76	115	156	196	235	275	316	356	395	436
symptoms (health)	43	83	123	163	203	243	283	323	363	403	443

festivals in western europe

On the last weekend of June, **Denmark** hosts one of Europe's biggest rock music festivals – the Roskilde Festival. The Copenhagen Jazz Festival, with 10 days of music in early July, presents a wide range of Danish and international jazz, blues and fusion music.

The Amsterdam Fantastic Film Festival, held in April, is a feast of fantasy, horror and science fiction movies. On the *Nationale Molendag* (National Mill Day) in May, nearly every working windmill in the **Netherlands** opens its doors to visitors.

The Cannes Film Festival in May is the world's most glitzy cinema event and a feast for the paparazzi. Another spectacle is the *Tour de France*, the famous bicycle race through **France** and the neighbouring countries, which ends in Paris in July.

The Berlin Love Parade in June is the largest techno party in the world. Hordes of tourists come to **Germany** for the famous beer festival in Munich, the *Oktoberfest* – one of Europe's biggest and most drunken parties, from late September to early October.

The Hellenic Festival in Athens, the major summer arts festival in **Greece**, features international music, dance and theatre. Το φεστιβάλ κρασιού (the wine festival) is held in early September in Dafni, west of Athens, to celebrate the grape harvest.

The San Remo Music Festival in March has been running in **Italy** since 1951 and was the inspiration for the Eurovision Song Contest. The Italian Gran Prix, organised in September at Monza, is one of the oldest circuits in Formula One.

Påske (Easter) is the occasion for the Sami people (Lapps) of **Norway** to organise colourful celebrations with reindeer races and chanting concerts in April. *Jonsok* (Midsummer's Eve) is celebrated with bonfires and dancing on the beach around 23 June.

Festas das Cruzes (Festival of the Crosses), held in May in Barcelos, **Portugal**, is known for processions, folk music and regional handicrafts. In June, Santarém hosts the *Feira Nacional da Agricultura* (National Agricultural Fair) with bullfighting and folk music.

In June, Pamplona combines the *San Fermín* festivities with macho posturing and running bulls, drawing TV crews from all over the world to **Spain**. *Semana Santa* (Holy Week) in April brings parades of holy images and huge crowds, notably in Seville.

On 30 April or *Valborgsmässoafton* (Walpurgis Night), **Sweden** celebrates the coming of spring with choral songs and huge bonfires. The Stockholm Water Festival in August is a major event with all sorts of activities including sport, music and fireworks.

Şeker Bayramı (Sweets Festival) is a three-day festival in **Turkey** at the end of the Muslim lunar month of Ramadan. *Kurban Bayramı* (Sacrifice Festival), two months after Ramadan, lasts for four days during which people make animal sacrifices.